1,000,000 Books

are available to read at

Forgotten Books

www.ForgottenBooks.com

Read online
Download PDF
Purchase in print

ISBN 978-0-282-38650-4
PIBN 10849954

This book is a reproduction of an important historical work. Forgotten Books uses state-of-the-art technology to digitally reconstruct the work, preserving the original format whilst repairing imperfections present in the aged copy. In rare cases, an imperfection in the original, such as a blemish or missing page, may be replicated in our edition. We do, however, repair the vast majority of imperfections successfully; any imperfections that remain are intentionally left to preserve the state of such historical works.

Forgotten Books is a registered trademark of FB &c Ltd.
Copyright © 2018 FB &c Ltd.
FB &c Ltd, Dalton House, 60 Windsor Avenue, London, SW19 2RR.
Company number 08720141. Registered in England and Wales.

For support please visit www.forgottenbooks.com

1 MONTH OF FREE READING

at
www.ForgottenBooks.com

By purchasing this book you are eligible for one month membership to ForgottenBooks.com, giving you unlimited access to our entire collection of over 1,000,000 titles via our web site and mobile apps.

To claim your free month visit:
www.forgottenbooks.com/free849954

* Offer is valid for 45 days from date of purchase. Terms and conditions apply.

English
Français
Deutsche
Italiano
Español
Português

www.forgottenbooks.com

Mythology Photography **Fiction** Fishing Christianity **Art** Cooking Essays Buddhism Freemasonry Medicine **Biology** Music **Ancient Egypt** Evolution Carpentry Physics Dance Geology **Mathematics** Fitness Shakespeare **Folklore** Yoga Marketing **Confidence** Immortality Biographies Poetry **Psychology** Witchcraft Electronics Chemistry History **Law** Accounting **Philosophy** Anthropology Alchemy Drama Quantum Mechanics Atheism Sexual Health **Ancient History Entrepreneurship** Languages Sport Paleontology Needlework Islam **Metaphysics** Investment Archaeology Parenting Statistics Criminology **Motivational**

DUKES O

KARA

GARDN

DUKES & POETS IN FERRARA

A STUDY IN THE POETRY, RELIGION AND
POLITICS OF THE FIFTEENTH AND
EARLY SIXTEENTH CENTURIES

By
EDMUND G. GARDNER, M.A.

Author of "*Dante's Ten Heavens,*"
"*The Story of Florence,*" "*Desiderio,*" *etc.*

LONDON
ARCHIBALD CONSTABLE & CO. LTD
1904

BUTLER & TANNER,
THE SELWOOD PRINTING WORKS,
FROME, AND LONDON.

TO
PROFESSOR
JAMES SMITH REID
THIS BOOK IS
AFFECTIONATELY AND GRATEFULLY
DEDICATED

PREFACE

> Chi pensa a' tiranni se vola il Boiardo
>   Nel cielo de' sogni stellato ?
> Se squilla a battaglia, pensoso e gagliardo,
>   Il buon cavaliere Torquato ?

But the wealth of material at my disposal, published and nnpublished, has proved far too great to be dealt with adequately in one volume, or indeed in a single work.

The two greatest personalities in the story of Ferrara are undoubtedly the second Duke, Ercole I d'Este, and the supreme poet after Dante of the Italian nation, Lodovico Ariosto. The former may be said to have created modern Ferrara, the latter raised it to a world-wide importance n the history of European literature. Ferrarese history falls naturally into two very clearly divided portions, the point of division being not the death of the great Duke Ercole and the accession of the formidable Alfonso I, but the close of the year 1508—the year that witnessed the conclusion of the League of Cambrai. After that year, Ferrarese art, literature and politics take a new turn. The works of Lodovico Ariosto soon after that date begin to be expressed in a different form, and seem impregnated with a new spirit. Between his earlier writings, in verse and prose, and his later poetry, is all the difference between the early and the full Renaissance; and in the carnival of the following year, 1509, with his second prose comedy, the *Suppositi*, he crowned and completed the work for the renovation of the Italian Drama, which his late sovereign Ercole had begun and promoted by his influence and patronage. We see a similar thing in Ferrarese painting. The earlier school still survived in the person of Lorenzo Costa, but Dosso Dossi and Benvenuto Tisi had hardly begun to make themselves known, and practically all their extant

PREFACE

work, all at least that is really significant, was still to come. These first years of Alfonso's reign witnessed the dispersal, by death or otherwise, of the peculiar literary society that had gathered round his father and predecessor, and had given its tone to his Court.

In this present volume, then, I deal with the political and literary history of Ferrara from the epoch immediately preceding the times of Borso and Ercole down to the dispersal of what we may call the Herculean circle in the years 1508-1509; that is, with Leonello d'Este and Borso the first Duke, with the whole reign of Ercole I, with Savonarola and Boiardo and their contemporaries, and with the opening years of Alfonso's reign. I need hardly offer apology or explanation for lingering in some detail over Ercole's relations with Savonarola and other mystical spirits, men and women, of the same Dominican Order. As I read the character of this (to me at least) the most interesting figure among the sovereigns of the early Renaissance, a sincere but somewhat ineffectual mysticism is the leading motive in Ercole's life. There were many Italian princes of the fifteenth and sixteenth centuries who, in their general foreign and domestic policy, followed a line of conduct analogous to his; there was not one, so far as my knowledge extends, who strove so diligently to establish relations with the unseen world.

Although the youth and early manhood of Ferrara's supreme poet fall under the epoch here considered, I have dealt with him merely cursorily. In a second volume, which is already well in hand, but which will be in the form of an entirely independent work, I treat in full of the Life and Work of Ariosto—the King of Court Poets, as I venture to call him. This will naturally include the adventurous and

PREFACE

romantic reign of Alfonso I. I also intend, in a smaller book, to deal separately with the painters of the Ferrarese School. I hope ultimately to complete the history of Ferrara with a volume dealing with Ercole II and Alfonso II; the Protestant Duchess Renata; Torquato Tasso; the enforced surrender of the Duchy to Pope Clement VIII, and the expulsion of the last Duke, Cesare d' Este.

English readers are already familiar with the earlier portion of the reign of Ercole I, in so far as his children are concerned, in the charming pages of Mrs. Ady (Julia Cartwright). To her *Beatrice d' Este* I am happy to acknowledge myself indebted, and I have, as far as possible, avoided going over the same ground. I regret that, but for the present in Italy, I did not become acquainted with her more recent *Isabella d' Este* in time to consult it for the present volume, and do not, therefore, know whether she has been able to add anything to the rich store of material already gathered by Professors Luzio and Renier.

Among modern Italian writers, I must in the first place specially acknowledge my debt to the late Antonio Cappelli, whose publications are of inestimable value to the student of Ferrarese history at every turn. The researches of Alessandro Luzio and Rodolfo Renier have thrown a flood of light upon the inner life of the Italian Renaissance, especially in all that concerns the Houses of Este and Gonzaga, and I trust that in my pages I have made full acknowledgment of what I have derived from their essays and studies, to which no student can be sufficiently grateful. I have made much use of the labours of that band of Italian scholars, led by Naborre Campanini, who raised so excellent a literary monument to Boiardo on the occasion of the fifth centenary of his birth; of the various publications of Count Luigi

x

PREFACE

Alberto Gandini, Angelo Solerti, Adolfo Venturi, and Umberto Dallari ; of Dr. Ludwig Pastor's monumental history of the Popes. More recently still, the work of a younger Italian scholar, Giulio Bertoni, *La Biblioteca Estense e la Coltura Ferrarese ai tempi del Duca Ercole I*, has proved of very great service to me ; not only for what it contains (though that is of much value), but also for its copious references and indications to manuscripts and other sources of information, it is hardly too much to say that Dr. Bertoni's book will prove an indispensable guide to all students who would obtain an independent knowledge of the literary atmosphere of fifteenth century Ferrara.

In leaving this, my first serious contribution to the study of Italian history, it is a pleasant duty to express again my gratitude to the noble books of Professor Villari on Savonarola and Machiavelli, from which so many of us have drawn our first knowledge of that fascinating, many-sided epoch in the world's civilization which is called the Renaissance in Italy.

Except where otherwise stated, my quotations are made directly from the documents in the Archives of Modena and the Vatican. At the risk of incurring the charge of being pedantic, I have indicated, somewhat scrupulously and precisely, when the documents are quoted from the published work of Italian scholars—especially as there seems a growing impression in Italy that of late a somewhat lax standard has sometimes been prevalent among us in England in this respect. I have gone on the principle of always translating Latin or Italian quotations when inserted in the text, but not necessarily when merely quoted in the notes. In an Appendix, I have made a small selection of the rich material in the way of un-

PREFACE

published documents available, partly as specimens and partly for a fuller elucidation of the text; as a rule, with two or three exceptions, I have not published the text of a document in the Appendix which has already been translated in the body of the work. I have modernized the punctuation and accentuation, and expanded the contractions, but otherwise (with the exception of the substitution of *v* for *u*) my transcripts are textual. It has not been a part of my plan to supply a full critical apparatus of documents, which would be out of place in a work intended for the general reader as well as for the professed student of the Renaissance.

My grateful thanks are due to the Cavaliere Giovanni Ognibene and the officials of the Archivio di Stato in Modena, for their ever-ready assistance and invariable courtesy shown me during my researches; to the authorities at the Archivio Segreto of the Vatican; and to Dr. Giulio Bertoni, for some valuable suggestions and for having called my attention to several documents of importance which would otherwise have escaped my notice.

E. G. G.

MODENA, *July* 2, 1903.

CONTENTS

	PAGE
BIBLIOGRAPHY	1

CHAPTER I
UNDER THE WHITE EAGLE OF ESTE 9

CHAPTER II
PRINCES AND HUMANISTS 26

CHAPTER III
THE DUKE OF MODENA 67

CHAPTER IV
THE TRIUMPH OF DUKE BORSO 95

CHAPTER V
UNDER THE SCEPTRE OF ALCIDES 122

CHAPTER VI
THE WAR OF FERRARA 165

CHAPTER VII
IN THE LULL BEFORE THE STORM 212

CHAPTER VIII
MATTEO MARIA BOIARDO 253

CONTENTS

CHAPTER IX
THE DUKE AND THE FRIAR 295

CHAPTER X
IN THE CLOSE OF THE QUATTROCENTO 340

CHAPTER XI
THE COMING OF MADONNA LUCREZIA 382

CHAPTER XII
THE LAST YEARS OF DUKE ERCOLE 424

CHAPTER XIII
THE POETS OF THE HERCULEAN CIRCLE . . . 468

CHAPTER XIV
THE END OF THE HERCULEAN AGE 493

APPENDIX I
UNEDITED POEMS OF THE BORSIAN EPOCH . . . 527

APPENDIX II
A SELECTION OF UNPUBLISHED DOCUMENTS . . . 538

Genealogical Tables of the Houses of Este, Gonzaga, Sforza, Pio and Pico.

INDEX 565

ILLUSTRATIONS

	Facing page
ERCOLE I D'ESTE, SECOND DUKE OF FERRARA. By Dosso Dossi . . . . . . *Frontispiece*	
LEONELLO D'ESTE. By Giovanni Oriolo	49
THE TRIUMPH OF MINERVA (detail). By Francesco del Cossa	90
DUKE BORSO AND HIS COMPANIONS. By Francesco del Cossa	112
A COURT JESTER OF FERRARA. By Dosso Dossi . .	160
THE TRIUMPH OF VENUS (detail). By Francesco del Cossa	282
GIROLAMO SAVONAROLA (in the Character of St. Peter Martyr). By Fra Bartolommeo	320
POPE ALEXANDER VI. By Pintoricchio	359
ST. CATHERINE OF ALEXANDRIA (supposed portrait of Lucrezia Borgia). By Pintoricchio	400
TWO FERRARESE LADIES. Detail from a fresco. By Ercole Grandi	464
ALFONSO I D'ESTE, THIRD DUKE OF FERRARA. After Titian. By Dosso Dossi	496

BIBLIOGRAPHY

I. Unpublished Sources.

A.

ARCHIVIO SEGRETO DELLA SANTA SEDE (referred to in the text as "Archivio Vaticano ").

REALE ARCHIVIO DI STATO IN MODENA (referred to as " Archivio di Modena "): *Cancelleria Ducale, Carteggio dei Principi ; Carteggio degli Ambasciatori ; Minutario Cronologico.*

B.

Croniche facte et scripte per me Ugo Caleffino *notario Ferrarese, figlio del quondam Sr. Recordato cittadino di Ferrara, comenzando dal anno, mese e dì chel ill*ᵐᵒ· *Sr. Messer Hercole mio Patrone e Signore entra Duca della Città de Ferrara* (referred to in the text as Ugo Caleffini, *Croniche del Duca Ercole*). Copied by Giulio Mosti in February, 159?. British Museum. Additional MS. 22, 324.

Storia della Città di Ferrara dal suo principio sino all' anno 1471. A seventeenth century copy of an older MS., apparently originally by Ugo Caleffini. Biblioteca Nazionale di Firenze. Cod. xxv, 8, 539.

Silva Cronicarum Bernardini Zambotti *Iuris Civilis Doctoris Ferrariensis, sed incepta dum esset scolaris anno MCCCCLXXV.* It runs from 1475 to 1504. Biblioteca Civica di Ferrara. Cod. 470.

Cronica Estense di Fra Paolo da Lignago *de' Frati Carmelitani di S. Polo di Ferrara.* R. Archivio di Stato in Modena.

Minutario di Brevi di Sisto IV. From August 25, 1481, to August 24, 1482. Biblioteca Nazionale di Firenze. Cod. II, iii, 256.

Francisci Ariosti Peregrini Iurisconsulti, *De fortunati felicisque illustrissimi Ducis Borsii in Urbem Romam ingressus Dieta, ad illustrissimum et magnanimum divum Herculem Marchionem Estensem Libellus.* Biblioteca Chigiana (Rome). Cod. I, vii, 261.

Francisci Ariosti Peregrini Iurisconsulti, *De novi intra ducalem regiam ferrariensem delubri, in gloriosissime Virginis Domini Iesu*

BIBLIOGRAPHY

Christi Salvatoris Nostri Matris honorem et reverentiam dicati, origine, situ ac veneratione et admirabilis simulacri translatione, Libellus. Biblioteca Estense (Modena). Cod. a, W. 4, 4.
(Both these two MSS. are also in Italian.)

Filippo Nuvolone, *Sonetti e canzone morale e de amore.* British Museum. Additional MS. 22,335.

II. Printed Works and Editions Cited.

Agnelli, Giuseppe. *Ferrara e Pomposa.* Bergamo, 1902 (No. 2 of the series "Italia Artistica").

Alberti, Leon Battista. *Opere volgari.* Edited by A. Bonucci. 5 vols. Florence, 1843-1849.

Alberti, Leon Battista. *Opera inedita et pauca separatim impressa.* Edited by G. M. Mancini. Florence, 1890.

Alvisi, E. *Cesare Borgia, Duca di Romagna.* Imola, 1878.

D'Ancona, Alessandro. *Origini del Teatro Italiano.* 2nd edition. 2 vols. Turin, 1891.

Antolini, C. *Il Dominio Estense in Ferrara: L'Acquisto.* Ferrara, 1896.

Antonelli, G. *Indice dei manoscritti della Civica Biblioteca di Ferrara.* Ferrara, 1884.

Antonelli, G. *Saggio di una bibliografia storica ferrarese.* Ferrara, 1851.

D'Arco, C. *Notizie di Isabella Estense Gonzaga.* (Archivio Storico Italiano. Series I. Appendix, vol. 2). Florence, 1845.

Ariosto, Lodovico. *Lettere, con prefazione storico-critica, documenti e note, per cura di* Antonio Cappelli. 3rd edition. Milan, 1887.

Ariosto, Lodovico. *Opere minori in verso e in prosa.* Edited by F. L. Polidori. 2 vols. Florence, 1894.

Ariosto, Lodovico. *Orlando Furioso.* Edited by G. Casella. Florence, 1877.

Armstrong, E. *Lorenzo de' Medici and Florence in the Fifteenth Century.* London, 1896.

Balan, P. *Storia d' Italia.* Vols. iv-vi. 2nd edition. Modena, 1895, 1896.

Barotti, L. *Serie de' Vescovi et Arcivescovi di Ferrara.* Ferrara, 1781.

Baruffaldi, G. *La Vita di Lodovico Ariosto.* Ferrara, 1807.

Bello, Francesco. *Libro d'Arme e d'Amore nomato Mambriano, composto per* Francisco Cieco *da Ferrara.* Ferrara, 1509.

Bembo, Pietro. *Opere.* Vol. viii. Milan, 1810.

Bertoni, Giulio. *La Biblioteca Estense e la Coltura Ferrarese ai tempi del Duca Ercole I.* Turin, 1903.

BIBLIOGRAPHY

Bianchi, Jacopino de', detto de' Lancellotti. *Cronaca Modenese.* (*Monumenti di Storia Patria delle Provincie Modenesi. Serie delle Cronache.* Tom. I.) Parma, 1862.

Boiardo, Matteo Maria. *Orlando Innamorato.* Edited by E. Costero. Milan, 1890. [See also under Panizzi.]

Boiardo, Matteo Maria. *Le poesie volgari e latine, riscontrate sui manoscritti e su le prime stampe da* Angelo Solerti. Bologna, 1894.

Boiardo, Matteo Maria. *Lettere edite ed inedite.* Edited by N. Campanini. [See below].

Studi su Matteo Maria Boiardo, edited by N. Campanini. Bologna, 1894. A series of essays by G. Ferrari, N. Campanini, P. Rajna, A. Luzio, P. Giorgi, A. Campani, R. Renier, C. Tincani, C. Antolini, G. Mazzoni, to which are added Boiardo's letters edited by Campanini.

Borsa, Mario. *Pier Candido Decembri e l'Umanesimo in Lombardia.* Milan, 1893.

Borsetti, F. G. *Historia Almi Ferrariae Gymnasii.* Ferrara, 1735.

Burckhardt, J. *The Civilization of the Renaissance in Italy.* English translation of the 3rd German Edition by S. G. C. Middlemore. London, 1890.

Caleffini, Ugo. *Cronica de la ill$^{ma.}$ et ex$^{ma.}$ Casa da Este.* See Cappelli, and cf. "Unpublished Sources."

Campanini, N. See Boiardo.

Campori, G. *Notizie per la Vita di Lodovico Ariosto.* Florence, 1896.

Cappelli, Adriano. *La Biblioteca Estense nella prima metà del secolo XV.* (Giornale Storico della Letteratura Italiana, vol. 14). Turin, 1886.

Cappelli, Antonio. *Lettere di Lorenzo de' Medici con notizie tratte dai carteggi diplomatici degli Oratori Estensi a Firenze.* (Atti e memorie delle RR. Deputazioni di Storia Patria per le Provincie Modenesi e Parmensi. Series I, vol. 1). Modena, 1866.

Cappelli, Antonio. *Notizie di Ugo Caleffini con la sua cronaca in rima di Casa d' Este.* (Ibid. vol. 2). Modena, 1867.

Cappelli, Antonio. *La Congiura dei Pio contra Borso d'Este.* (Ibid. vol. 3). Modena, 1868.

Cappelli, Antonio. *Fra Girolamo Savonarola e notizie intorno al suo tempo.* (Ibid. vol. 4). Modena, 1869.

Cappelli, Antonio. *Niccolò di Leonello d'Este.* (Ibid. vol. 5). Modena, 1870.

Cappelli, Antonio. See also Ariosto and Pistofilo.

Capponi, G. *Storia della Repubblica di Firenze.* Vols. 2 and 3. Florence, 1879, etc.

Carducci, Giosuè. *Alla Città di Ferrara: Ode.* Bologna, 1899. (Reprinted in *Rime e Ritmi.*)

BIBLIOGRAPHY

Carducci, Giosuè. *Delle Poesie Latine edite e inedite di Ludovico Ariosto.* 2nd edition. Bologna, 1876.

Cartwright, Julia (Mrs. Henry Ady). *Beatrice d' Este: Duchess of Milan,* 1475–1497. A Study of the Renaissance. London, 1899.

Cittadella, L.N. *Il Castello di Ferrara.* Ferrara, 1875.

Cittadella, L. N. *Notizie relative a Ferrara per la maggior parte inedite.* Ferrara, 1864.

Comines, Philippe de. *The History of Comines, englished by* Thomas Danett anno 1596. Edited by C. Whibley. (The Tudor Translations.) 2 vols. London, 1897.

Conti, Sigismondo dei, da Foligno. *Historiarum sui Temporis.* 2 vols. Rome, 1883.

Corio, B. *Storia di Milano.* Vols. 2 and 3. Edited by A. Butti and C. Ferrario. Milan, 1856, 1857.

Correggio, Niccolò da. *Opere intitulate la Psyche et la Aurora, stampate novamente e ben corrette.* Venice, 1507.

Corvisieri, C. *Il Trionfo Romano di Eleonora d' Aragona.* (Archivio della Società Romana di Storia Patria, vols. 1 and 10). Rome, 1878, 1887.

Dallari, U. *Carteggio tra i Bentivoglio e gli Estensi dal* 1401 *al* 1542 *esistente nell' Archivio di Stato in Modena.* Bologna, 1902.

Decembrio, Angelo. *Politiae Litterariae Angeli Decembrii Mediolanensis, oratoris clarissimi, ad summum Pontificem Pium II, libri septem.* Augsburg, 1540.

Delaito, Jacopo de'. *Annales Estenses* (1393–1409). Muratori, *Rerum Italicarum Scriptores,* vol. 18.

Desjardins, A. *Negociations diplomatiques de la France avec la Toscane.* Vols. 1 and 2. Paris, 1859, 1861.

Diario Ferrarese, dall' anno 1409 fino al 1502, di autori incerti. Muratori, *Rerum Italicarum Scriptores,* vol. 24.

Dispacci al Senato Veneto di Francesco Foscari *e di altri oratori presso l'imperatore Massimiliano I nel* 1496. (Archivio Storico Italiano. Series I, vol. 7.) Florence, 1850.

Foucard, C. *Proposta fatta dalla Corte Estense ad Alfonso I, Re di Napoli* (1445). (Archivio Storico per le Provincie Napolitane. Anno IV). Naples, 1879.

Frizzi, A. *Memorie per la storia di Ferrara raccolte da* Antonio Frizzi *con giunte e note di* C. Laderchi. 2nd edition. Vols. 1–4. Ferrara, 1847, 1848.

Gandini, L. A. *Saggio degli usi e delle costumanze della Corte di Ferrara al tempo di Niccolò III.* (Atti e memorie della R. Deputazione di Storia Patria per Romagna. Series III, vol. 9.) Bologna, 1898.

BIBLIOGRAPHY

Gandini, L. A. *Sulla venuta in Ferrara della Beata Suor Lucia da Narni. Sue lettere ed altri documenti inediti.* Modena, 1901.

Gandini, L. A. *Episodio Storico inedito intorno Lucrezia Borgia nell' imminenza delle sue nozze con Alfonso d' Este.* Bologna, 1902.

Gaspary, A. *Storia della Letteratura Italiana. Volume secondo tradotto dal tedesco da* Vittorio Rossi. Two parts. Turin, 1900, 1901.

Gherardi, A. *Nuovi documenti e studi intorno a Girolamo Savonarola.* Florence, 1887.

Giovanni, Fra. *Annales.* See Johannes.

Giraldi, G. B. *Commentario delle cose di Ferrara et de' principi da Este ; aggiuntovi la vita di Alfonso da Este desunta dal* Giovio. Venice, 1597.

Giraldi, G. B. *Li Hecatommithi ovvero Cento Novelle.* Venice, 1574.

Dispacci di Antonio Giustinian, *Ambasciatore Veneto in Roma, dal 1502 al 1505.* Edited by P. Villari. 3 vols. Florence, 1876.

Gregorovius, F. *Lucrezia Borgia secondo documenti e carteggi dal tempo.* Translated by R. Mariano. Florence, 1883.

Gruyer, G. *L' art ferrarais à l' époque des princes d' Este.* 2 vols. Paris, 1897.

Guicciardini, F. *Storia d' Italia.* Edited by G. Rosini. 5 vols. Turin, 1874, 1875.

Janus Pannonius. *Silva Panegyrica ad Guarinum Veronensem praeceptorem suum* (Jani Pannonii Poëmata. Utrecht, 1784).

Johannes Ferrariensis. *Excerpta ex Annalium Libris illustris Familiae Marchionum Estensium,* 1409-1454. Muratori, *Rerum Italicarum Scriptores,* vol. 20.

Litta, Pompeo. *Le Famiglie celebri italiane.* Milan, 1819, etc.

Lungo, I. Del. *Dante ne' Tempi di Dante ; ritratti e studi.* Bologna, 1888.

Lungo, I. Del. *Florentia : uomini e cose del Quattrocento.* Florence, 1897.

Luzio, A. *I precettori di Isabella d' Este.* Ancona, 1878.

Luzio, A. and Renier, R. *Commedie classiche in Ferrara nel 1499.* (Giornale Storico della Letteratura Italiana, vol. 11). Turin, 1888.

Luzio, A. and Renier, R. *Delle Relazioni di Isabella d' Este Gonzaga con Lodovico e Beatrice Sforza.* (Archivio Storico Lombardo, vol. 17.) Milan, 1890.

Luzio, A. and Renier, R. *Francesco Gonzaga alla Battaglia di Fornovo, secondo i documenti Mantovani.* (Archivio Storico Italiano. Series V, vol. 6). Florence, 1890.

BIBLIOGRAPHY

Luzio, A. and Renier, R. *Mantova e Urbino : Isabella d' Este ed Elisabetta Gonzaga nelle relazioni famigliari e nelle vicende politiche.* Turin, 1893.

Luzio, A. and Renier, R. *Niccolò da Correggio.* (Giornale Storico della Letteratura Italiana. Vols. 21 and 22.) Turin, 1893.

Luzio, A. and Renier, R. *La Coltura e le Relazioni Letterarie di Isabella d' Este Gonzaga.* (Ibid., vols. 33-40.) Turin, 1899-1902.

Machiavelli, N. *Opere.* 8 volumes. Florence, 1813.

Malipiero, Domenico. *Annali Veneti,* 1457-1500. (Archivio Storico Italiano. Series I, vol. 7). Florence, 1843.

Mancini, G. M. *Vita di Leon Battista Alberti.* Florence, 1882.

Muratori, L. A. *Delle Antichità Estensi ed Italiane.* 2 vols. Modena, 1717-1740.

Niccolò da Ferrara, Frate. *Il Libro del Polistore.* Muratori, *Rerum Italicarum Scriptores,* vol. 24.

Novati, F. *Donato degli Albanzani alla Corte Estense.* (Archivio Storico Italiano. Series V, vol. 6.) Florence, 1890.

Olivi, L. *Delle Nozze di Ercole I con Eleonora d'Aragona.* (Memorie della R. Accademia di Scienze, Lettere ed Arti in Modena. Series II, vol. 5.) Modena, 1887.

Panizzi, A. *Orlando Innamorato del Boiardo, with an essay on the romantic narrative poetry of the Italians.* London, 1830.

Pastor, Ludwig. *Geschichte der Päpste im Zeitalter der Renaissance.* 2nd edition. Freiburg im Breisgau. 1891-1895. 3 vols.

Pélissier, L. G. *La Politique du Marquis de Mantoue, pendant la lutte de Louis XII et de Ludovic Sforza* (1498-1500). (Annales de la Faculté des Lettres de Bordeaux, année 1892. No. 1). Paris, 1892.

✗ Pez, B. and Hueber, P. *Thesaurus Anecdotorum Novissimus.* Vol. 6. Augsburg, 1723.

Piccolomini, Enea Silvio (Pius II). *De Viris Illustribus.* (Bibliothek des Literarischen Vereins in Stuttgart, vol. 1). Stuttgart, 1843.

Piccolomini, Enea Silvio (Pius II). *Opera quae extant omnia.* Basle, 1551.

Piccolomini, Enea Silvio (Pius II). *Commentarii Rerum Memorabilium, quae temporibus suis contigerunt.* Rome, 1584.

Piccolomini, Enea Silvio (Pius II). *Historia Rerum Friderici Tertii Imperatoris.* Strassburg, 1685.

Pigna, G. B. *Historia de' Principi d' Este.* Ferrara, 1570.

Pistofilo, Bonaventura. *Vita di Alfonso I d' Este, Duca di Ferrara, etc.* Edited by Antonio Cappelli. (Atti e memorie delle RR. Deputazioni di Storia Patria per le Provincie Modenesi e Parmensi. Series I, vol. 3.) Modena, 1868.

BIBLIOGRAPHY

Pistoia, Il (Antonio Cammelli). *I sonetti del Pistoia giusta l'Apografo Trivulziano, a cura di* Rodolfo Renier. Turin, 1888.

Piva, E. *La Guerra di Ferrara del 1482.* Padua, 1893, 1894.

Rajna, P. *Le Fonti dell' Orlando Furioso.* 2nd edition. Florence, 1900.

Renier, R. See under Luzio and Pistoia.

Rime scelte dei Poeti Ferraresi antichi e moderni [edited by G. Barnfaldi]. Ferrara, 1713.

Romanin, S. *Storia documentata di Venezia.* Vols. 3–5. Venice, 1853–61.

Rosmini, C. de'. *Vita e disciplina di Guarino Veronese e de' suoi discepoli.* 3 vols. Brescia, 1805, 1806.

Rosmini, C. de'. *Dell' istoria intorno alle militari imprese e alla vita di G. J. Trivulzio.* 2 vols. Milan, 1815.

Rossi, V. *Il Quattrocento.* Milan, 1900.

Rua, G. *Novelle del Mambriano.* Turin, 1888.

Sabbadini, R. *Vita documentata di Giovanni Aurispa.* Noto, 1892.

Sanudo, Marino. *Commentarii della Guerra di Ferrara tra li Veneziani ed il Duca Ercole d' Este nel 1482.* Ed. L. Manin. Venice, 1829.

Sanudo, Marino. *La Spedizione di Carlo VIII in Italia.* Ed. R. Fulin. Venice, 1852.

Sanudo, Marino. *I Diarii*, 1496–1533. Edited by Fulin, Barozzi, Stefani, and Berchet. Venice, 1879–1902.

Sanudo, Marino. *Le Vite dei Duchi di Venezia.* Muratori, Rerum Italicarum Scriptores, vol. 22. A new edition by Giovanni Monticolo is in course of publication. Città di Castello, 1900, etc.

Sardi, Gasparo. *Historie Ferraresi.* Ferrara, 1556.

Schivenoglia, A. *Cronaca di Mantova dal 1445 al 1484.* Edited by C. D'Arco. In G. Müller, *Raccolta di Cronisti e Storici Lombardi inediti*, vol. 2. Milan, 1856.

Schmarsow, A. *Melozzo da Forlì.* Berlin and Stuttgart, 1886.

Secco-Suardo, G. *Lo Studio di Ferrara a tutto il secolo XV.* (Atti e memorie della Deputazione Ferrarese di Storia Patria, vol. 6.) Ferrara, 1894.

Segarizzi, A. *Della vita e delle opere di Michele Savonarola.* Padua, 1900.

Sitta, P. *Saggio sulle istituzioni finanziarie del ducato Estense nei secoli XV e XVI.* (Atti e memorie della Deputazione Ferrarese di Storia Patria. Vol. 3.) Ferrara, 1891.

Solerti, A. *Ferrara e la Corte Estense nella seconda metà del secolo decimosesto.* 2nd edition with Map of Ferrara in 1597 by F. Borgatti. Città di Castello, 1900.

BIBLIOGRAPHY

Solerti, A. *Ugo e Parisina: Storia e leggenda secondo nuovi documenti.* (Nuova Antologia, Series iii. vols. 45 and 46). Rome, 1893.
Solerti, A. See also under Boiardo.
Strozzii poetae pater et filius. Edited by Aldus Manutius. Venice, 1513.
Strozzi, Lorenzo. *Le vite degli uomini illustri della Casa Strozzi.* (Ed. P. Stromboli.) Florence, 1892.
Tebaldeo, Antonio. *Soneti e capitoli de Messer Antonio Thebaldeo.* Edited by Jacopo Tebaldi. Modena, 1500.
Theiner, A. *Codex Diplomaticus Dominii Temporalis Sanctae Sedis.* Vol. 3. Rome, 1862.
Tiraboschi, G. *Storia della Letteratura Italiana.* Milan, 1824, etc.
Trinchera, F. *Codice Aragonese, o sia lettere regie, ordinamenti ed altri atti governativi de' Sovrani Aragonesi in Napoli.* 2 vols. Naples, 1866, 1870.
Vasari, G. *Le Vite de' più eccellenti pittori, etc.* Vol. 1.: Gentile da Fabriano ed il Pisanello. Critical edition by A. Venturi. Florence, 1898.
Venturi, A. *L'Arte Ferrarese nel periodo di Borso d' Este.* (Rivista Storica Italiana, II. 4). Turin, 1885.
Venturi, A. *L'Arte Ferrarese nel periodo di Ercole I d' Este.* (Atti e memorie della R. Deputazione di Storia Patria per Romagna. Series iii, vols. 6 and 7.) Bologna, 1888, 1889.
Venturi, G. B. (the elder). *Storia di Scandiano.* Modena, 1822.
Venturi, G. B. (the younger). *Relazioni dei Governatori di Reggio al Duca Ercole I di Ferrara.* (Atti e memorie delle RR. Deputazioni di Storia Patria per le Provincie Modenesi e Parmensi. Series iii, vol. 2.) Modena, 1884.
Villari, P. *La Storia di Girolamo Savonarola e de' suoi tempi.* 2nd edition. Florence, 1887, 1888.
Villari, P. *Niccolò Machiavelli e i suoi tempi.* 2nd edition. Milan, 1895, 1896.
Voigt, G. *Il Risorgimento dell' Antichità Classica, ovvero il primo secolo dell' Umanesimo.* Translated by D. Valbusa, with additions, etc., by G. Zippel. 3 vols. Florence, 1886, 1887.
Yriarte, C. *César Borgia.* 2 vols. Paris, 1889.

[And other works, published and unpublished, registered in the text and notes.]

Chapter I

UNDER THE WHITE EAGLE OF ESTE

FERRARA has been styled the "first really modern city in Europe." To-day it lies magnificent in its desolation. Although the Ferrarese, throughout the struggles that have made Italy one, gave ample proof of their patriotism, the pulse of the new Italian nation beats but feebly in this city that was once among the most characteristic products of the Renaissance. Gabriele d'Annunzio has hymned its "deserta bellezza," and every sympathetic student of modern Italian letters must know the striking poem, *Alla Città di Ferrara*, that Carducci has written upon the contrast of its past glories with its present decay. In the fifteenth and sixteenth centuries, Ferrara was one of the most ardent centres of Italian life and culture, the seat of a refined and brilliant Court, for a while even the jealous rival of Florence, the capital of a potent State that ranked only below the five great powers of the peninsula, and that, in its epoch of greatest extension, stretched right across Italy almost from sea to sea.[1] Florence had given to all

---

[1] "Mira la nobil terra,
   Quasi gran fascia che l'Italia fenda
   E fra due mar si stenda."

Tasso, *Canzone nel viaggio de la illustrissima signora Duchessa di Ferrara per lo Stato* (in September, 1584).

DUKES AND POETS IN FERRARA

the world the supreme poet of the Middle Ages, Dante Alighieri, though she sent him forth to die in exile at Ravenna, with whom she must now share his fame. Although the sovereign singer of the Italian Renaissance, Lodovico Ariosto, was actually born at Reggio, yet Ferrara may, in part at least, justly claim him as her own, and has fairly earned the proud title that Carducci gives her—" Madre de l'itale muse seconda."

The chief glory of Ferrara is still the Castello Vecchio, the great palace castle of the princes of the House of Este. Hardly elsewhere in Italy, save at Urbino, shall we find so magnificent a monument of the very spirit of the age of the Italian Despots, in contrast with such democratic palaces of the Republics as the Palazzo della Signoria at Florence or the Palazzo Pubblico at Siena. Everywhere from the walls its four huge red towers are seen through bowers of green trees, bathed in the first fires of sunrise, transfigured in the glow of an Emilian sunset, or at night looming up dark and threatening against the stars. Wander where we may through the streets of Ferrara—and there are few cities more pleasant to linger in for weeks together, enjoying at every turn some relic of the golden past—we feel its pervading presence. And everywhere throughout the city we touch the memories of the illustrious House that reared the goodly fabric of an ideal Renaissance State, though more than three centuries have passed since the White Eagle of Este was hurled down from the battlements and the last Duke of Ferrara, with set features and eyes fixed upon a letter in his hand, drove out of the gate of his city. The one great poet of the Italian Renaissance having been born a Ferrarese subject, it was inevitable that he should be a Court poet.

UNDER THE WHITE EAGLE OF ESTE

"The laudable discretion of the Marquis of Este," wrote Dante, "and his munificence prepared for all, make him to be beloved."[1] It is probable that these words were written in irony, for elsewhere the Divine Poet never touches, be it ever so lightly, any member of the great Guelf house that, save for two brief intervals, reigned in Ferrara from the beginning of the thirteenth to the end of the sixteenth century, without leaving a lasting scar of infamy upon the name. The fair-haired Obizzo II, fourth Estensian lord of Ferrara, who added Modena and Reggio to his dominions, is plunged with Ezzelino—that ghastliest of mediaeval tyrants, from whom Obizzo's own grandfather, the magnanimous and heroic Azzo Novello, had delivered Italy—into the river of boiling blood, where the fierce Centaurs hunt the damned souls of tyrants and murderers; his pander, the Bolognese Venedico Caccianimici, cowers beneath the lash of the horned demons in the "Evil Pits" of the seducers of women; Obizzo's son and successor, the Marchese Azzo VIII, is branded as a parricide, while one of his victims haunts the shores of the Mountain of Purgation amongst the other dim ghosts of those that fell by the sword.[2] It is more probable that Dante never lingered in Ferrara, and indeed, during the greater part of his wanderings, the princes of the House of Este—Rinaldo and Obizzo III and other nephews of Azzo—were themselves despoiled of their States and in exile, while the vicars of King Robert of Naples and the legates of the Popes of Avignon held their

[1] *De Vulgari Eloquentia*, ii. 6.
[2] *Inferno*, xii. 109-112, xviii. 55-57; *Purgatorio*, v. 77. For the subject of Dante's treatment of the House of Este, see I. Del Lungo, *Dante ne' Tempi di Dante*, pp. 379-434, and T. Sandonnini, *Dante e gli Estensi*, in the *Atti e Memorie delle RR. Deputazioni di Storia Patria per le Provincie Modenesi e Parmensi*, series iv. vol. 4.

capital, and hanged or beheaded Ghibellines and Estensians alike.

Throughout Ferrarese history, we shall find two counteracting forces playing upon Ferrara: Rome and Venice contending for predominance. Although the Popes recognized the Estensi as their vicars *in temporalibus*, they claimed Ferrara as part of the legacy of the Countess Matilda to the Holy See, and at a later epoch made prolonged efforts, crowned at last with success, to bring back the State to their direct dominion. The Republic of Venice, as early as the beginning of the twelfth century, had established a colony in the city for commercial purposes, with special treaty rights. It had joined with the Pope in overthrowing the last of the Salinguerra and restoring Azzo Novello to power in 1240, because these rights had not been respected by Salinguerra and his Ghibellines when they held the place in the name of the Emperor Frederick II. But now that the Venetians were beginning to turn their attention to making acquisitions on the Italian mainland, Ferrara appeared to them a tempting and possible prize.

Wearied out with fruitless efforts to recover by force of arms the cities of Modena and Reggio, which had revolted in 1306, the Marchese Azzo VIII died on the last day of January, 1308, in the castle of Este, whither he had gone for the sake of the baths of the Paduan district. He left no legitimate children. Before leaving Ferrara, in consequence of the feud between him and his brothers Aldobrandino and Francesco, he had made a will leaving the government to his infant grandchild Folco, the legitimate son of his bastard Fresco, and appointed the latter regent; but it was said that, in Este, he had been reconciled to his brothers, had revoked his will and appointed them his heirs.

UNDER THE WHITE EAGLE OF ESTE

A disastrous contest for the possession of Ferrara followed, between Fresco on the one hand, who was in actual possession, and the Marchese Francesco, with his nephews Rinaldo and Obizzo, on the other. The Republic of Venice was ready to take a hand in the game; while Azzo lay on his death-bed, the Doge Gradenigo had sent three Venetian nobles to Ferrara, under the pretext of condoling with the Marquis in his illness and offering their assistance, if need should arise, to investigate the state of things and the disposition of the people, and, in case of his death, to take measures for " the good state of Ferrara," in accordance with Venetian interests.[1] Fresco appealed to Venice, and Venice supported his claim. But Pope Clement V, as suzerain, adopted the cause of the Marchese Francesco, with the real intention of reducing Ferrara to the direct domination of the Holy See. His Legate, the Cardinal Arnufio or Arnaldo Pelagrua, assembled a large army in Ravenna, under the orders of Lamberto da Polenta (the brother of Dante's Francesca), and was joined by the Marchese Francesco himself. On the arrival of the ecclesiastical army, by land and river, beneath the walls of Ferrara, Fresco fled into the fortress of Castel Tedaldo, which protected the city from the south, and then, finding himself unable to resist the superior forces of Francesco and the Legate, made over all Folco's claims on Ferrara to the Venetians, and surrendered the castle to their fleet which had swept up the Po. Seeing the standard of San Marco floating from the battlements of the Castello, the Ferrarese opened their gates to the papal troops—under the impression that they were about to welcome the Marchese Francesco as their rightful sovereign.

[1] Romanin, *Storia documentata di Venezia*, iii. p. 12.

DUKES AND POETS IN FERRARA

"The aforesaid Legate," writes the Benedictine abbot, Fra Niccolò da Ferrara, "with all his army entered into Ferrara with the will of all the people, who all cried out with one voice: '*Viva il Marchese Francesco.*' The latter, who was in everything strenuous and daring, here seemed somewhat timorous. And he began to say to the people : 'O my dearest brothers, cry no more '*Viva il Marchese d'Este*'; but say, '*Viva la Santa Chiesa Romana!*' And in such wise, against the will of the people and of all his friends, the said Marchese Francesco gave the lordship to the aforesaid Messere Arnufio, the Legate, and made him dismount in his own ancient palace, believing without doubt that, in return for so great courtesy and for so great humanity, that Legate would freely give back to him the said lordship, as he had promised. But he did not yet know well these ecclesiastical pastors; for the said Legate kept the lordship, and the Marchese Francesco remained deceived."[1]

A tremendous struggle by land and water followed, for the possession of Ferrara, between Venice and Avignon. The Venetians held the fortress, the papal forces the city, and great cruelties were perpetrated on either side; until, in the latter part of August, 1309, the Marchese Francesco gained a decisive victory on the Po over the Venetian fleet, while the ecclesiastical troops stormed the Castello, and put the whole Venetian garrison to the sword. Venice was forced to make peace in 1311, and recovered her trading rights and privileges; but practically nothing of their dominion was left to the Estensi.

The Pope made over Ferrara to the government Robert of Naples, whose vicars and chamberlains

[1] *Libro del Polistore*, col. 716.

UNDER THE WHITE EAGLE OF ESTE

with Catalan and Gascon mercenaries in the name of the Church and King. The brutal murder of the Marchese Francesco by these Catalans in 1312, the cruel and treacherous execution of the Ferrarese refugees, whom the Bishop of Feltre had betrayed to the royal vicar in 1314 (the tragedy eternalized in certain grim lines of the *Divina Commedia*),[1] are typical of their rule. But in July, 1317, the Ferrarese rose in the mass and recalled the Estensi. The Catalan or Gascon garrison in Castel Tedaldo was slaughtered to a man. Excommunication and interdict followed as a matter of course, and a prolonged struggle with the Pope and his legates, especially the infamous Beltrando dal Poggetto, until the Estensi were formally reconciled to the Church, and in 1332 Pope John XXII finally invested the brothers Rinaldo, Obizzo III, and Niccolò I, with the Vicariate of Ferrara.

With the restoration of the House of Este, followed thus by the recognition of the princes as Vicars of the Church in Ferrara and the general reintegration of their dominions,[2] a

[1] *Paradiso*, ix. 52-60; cf. *Libro del Polistore*, col. 727.
[2] At this epoch the principal places in the Estensian lordship were Ferrara itself and the surrounding country, Argenta, Comacchio, Castel del Finale, Adria, Ariano, Rovigo, Lendinara, and all the Polesine di Rovigo. Modena was recovered in 1336. Este, that fascinating little town at the foot of the Euganean Hills, from which the Lords of Ferrara continued to take the title of Marquis, had been captured by the Paduans in 1213, when they forced the Marchese Azzo VII to become a Paduan citizen. In 1220 the Emperor Frederick II compelled the Paduans to restore it, and to rebuild the palace or castle (Document in Muratori, *Delle Antichità Estensi*, i. p. 415), but it was soon lost again, and, though frequently held out by the Dukes of Milan or the Popes as a bait to lure the Estensi into a war with Venice, it was never permanently recovered. It was burned down in 1317 by Can Grande della Scala, and the present castle is the remains of one that was built by Ubertino da Carrara. In 1331 the Pope compelled the Estensi to drop the title

DUKES AND POETS IN FERRARA

brighter epoch opens. Their discretion and munificence—to adopt in earnest what on Dante's lips had sounded as bitter sarcasm—induced Italians of every State to visit their Court, and even to become their subjects. Among the first to do this were the Ariosti from Bologna, who were destined to give Ferrara and the House of Este their greatest glory. A beautiful Bolognese woman, Lippa di Jacopo Ariosti, had become passionately attached to the Marchese Obizzo in his exile, and on his restoration to Ferrara she followed him and became his mistress. *La bella Lippa da Bologna,* as Messer Lodovico was to call her,[1] bore her princely lover a goodly series of sons, three of whom—Aldobrandino, Niccolò II and Alberto—ascended the throne of the Estensi as vicars of the Church in Ferrara and vicars of the Empire in Modena. Obizzo married her on her deathbed, and she was buried with great state as lawful Marchesana in the church of San Francesco, the Pantheon of the reigning House.[2] Lippa's two brothers Bonifazio and Francesco, and her cousin Niccolò Ariosti, followed her to Ferrara. The two former rose to high honours in the Court, and were among the principal advisers of Obizzo's successors; Niccolò Ariosti founded the third Ferrarese branch of his family, from which the great poet was to be born.

of Marquis of Ancona, which they had used since the beginning of the thirteenth century.

[1] *Orlando Furioso*, xiii. 73.

[2] "On the 27th day of November (1347) died the noble and magnificent lady, Madonna Lippa degli Ariosti of Bologna, wife of the magnificent and illustrious Lord of Ferrara, Marchese Obizzo, whom he espoused in the last infirmity of her death, with the knowledge and licence of the Holy Father, Messere Pope Clement VI. By the which magnificent lady the aforesaid Marchese Obizzo generated eleven children, to wit, seven male and four female. She was buried at the Place of the Friars Minor at Ferrara with most great and magnificent honour" (*Libro del Polistore*, col. 801).

UNDER THE WHITE EAGLE OF ESTE

The first great representative of the New Learning to enter the gates of Ferrara was Francesco Petrarca himself, who found a cordial welcome at the Court of Niccolò II in 1370, and was intimate with his younger brother Ugo.[1] A few years later Benvenuto da Imola, Petrarca's friend and Boccaccio's pupil, made amends for Dante's bitter scorn of the House of Este by dedicating to this same Marquis that famous commentary which an English scholar has given to the public in our own days, and which is still perhaps the best, as it is certainly the most entertaining book ever written upon the *Divina Commedia*.[2] Afterwards, at the Marchese's request, Benvenuto composed for him his *Libellus Augustalis*, a summary of the lives of the Emperors from Julius to Wenceslaus. It was to gratify this same Marquis that Fra Niccolò, "Master of Sacred Theology and Abbot of Santa Maria da Gavello," wrote in the vernacular a species of universal history from the origin of the world down to the year 1367—the *Libro del Polistore*, already quoted.[3] The successor of Niccolò II, the Marchese Alberto, summoned the learned Donato degli Albanzani of Pratovecchio, who (like Benvenuto da Imola) had known Petrarca and Boccaccio, to undertake the education of his heir. A little later, there came from Florence a branch of the Strozzi, flying from popular violence and Medicean guile.

---

[1] *Epist. Rerum Senilium*, xi. 13 and xiii. 1.
[2] *Benvenuti de Rambaldis, Comentum super Dantis Aldigherii Comoediam*, edited by Lacaita and W. Warren Vernon. Florence, 1887.
[3] The latter portions, dealing with the events of the Monk's own days, were published by Muratori, *Rerum Italicarum Scriptores*, vol. xxiv. Alessandro Mortara (*Catalogo dei Manoscritti Italiani nella Biblioteca Bodleiana*, coll. 27, 28) has shown that Muratori and Tiraboschi are in error in ascribing this work to the Dominican, Fra Bartolommeo da Ferrara.

DUKES AND POETS IN FERRARA

Nanni Strozzi, gallant soldier and accomplished courtier—the son of that Carlo Strozzi who, as one of the leaders of the Parte Guelfa, had been expelled from Florence after the Tumult of the Ciompi—settled at Ferrara towards the close of the fourteenth century. He married the daughter of one of the noblest Ferrarese houses, Costanza de' Costabili, served the Estensi for thirty years, and died fighting under their banner in a war against Milan in 1427. We shall find the children and grandchildren of Nanni Strozzi playing no small part in the subsequent history of the Ferrarese Court.

And in the following century, as the Renaissance dawned, others came to make Ferrara a second home; from Padua, the Savonarola; from Sicily and Verona, the humanists Giovanni Aurispa and Guarino, "la diva Grecia rivelando."[1]

Besides the great House of Gonzaga of Mantua, to which they were bound by ties of common interest and frequent intermarriage, there gathered round the sovereigns of Este a group of lesser princes, also connected by numerous marriages with Ferrara and with petty Courts resembling theirs upon a smaller scale. Such were the Counts of Correggio, the Pico of Mirandola, the Pio of Carpi, and the Boiardi, citizens of Reggio, feudal lords first of Rubiera and then of Scandiano.

Thus was gradually constituted the peculiar society of the Court of Este, which during the fifteenth and sixteenth centuries shone with such a blaze of artistic light that it still, to some extent, dazzles our moral eyesight, and which, if it can hardly be said to have inspired, is at least reflected in the work of the two great romantic poets and the one great epic poet of the Renaissance in Italy.

---

[1] Cf. Carducci, *Alla Città di Ferrara* (in *Rime e Ritmi*).

UNDER THE WHITE EAGLE OF ESTE

But, before turning to these princes of the Quattrocento and Cinquecento, a few general remarks must be made upon the State and government of Ferrara.

There was a darker side to this cultured Court life of the Ferrarese capital. The beginning of each reign was marked by palace conspiracies and followed by sanguinary executions. The papal investiture of the vicariate of Ferrara frequently included several members of the family; brother succeeded brother, and bastardy was held no obstacle. There were nephews, therefore, sons born to brothers in lawful wedlock, who saw themselves supplanted by their uncles, and the palaces thronged with discontented bastards of Este, who saw in these young princes a chance of bettering their own position. Sometimes these legitimate scions of the House fled from Ferrara to other States, and attempted to maintain their claim with foreign aid. At other times the unfortunate nephew stood his ground, and was led into a conspiracy against his successful kinsman. In these cases no mercy was ever shown. When Alberto, legitimated son of Obizzo III and Lippa Ariosti, succeeded his elder brother Niccolò II in 1388, there was a nephew Obizzo—the lawful issue of another brother Aldobrandino by his wife, Beatrice da Camino. This prince, who had a large following in the city, took occasion of his uncle's absence from Ferrara shortly after his accession to plot against his life. On Alberto's return, the plot was discovered. Obizzo and his mother were beheaded at night in the dungeons of the newly erected Castello Vecchio, and then, with the most rigid regard for form and ceremony, solemnly buried with full honours in the church of the Friars Minor. Their confederates—including Giovanni d'Este, a bastard brother of Alberto's own, and his wife—were publicly

DUKES AND POETS IN FERRARA

tortured to death in the streets and squares of Ferrara, and a noble lady, Costanza dei Quintavalli, was burned alive.[1]

"The feeling of the Ferrarese towards the ruling House," writes Burckhardt, "was a strange compound of silent dread, of the truly Italian sense of well-calculated interest, and of the loyalty of the modern subject." In theory the people, represented by the Judge of the Sages, confirmed each succession by solemnly consigning the sword and sceptre to the new Prince, and before the high altar of the Duomo received his solemn oath of maintaining justice; in reality the government was an absolute despotism, though usually of a benevolent type. There was less even of the appearance of communal liberty in Ferrara than in almost any other State of northern or central Italy. No popular councils appear even to have been summoned during the two centuries with which we are concerned. The administration of the city was in the hands of a small council, the College of the Twelve Sages, which was presided over by the Judge of the Sages, who was appointed by the sovereign and held office at his pleasure. The Sages held office for a year, and occasionally, in affairs of great importance, some six or more additional members, *aggiunti*, were added to their council—all nominated by the sovereign. A recent writer on Ferrara in the fifteenth century observes that this Council of the Sages in reality is nothing more than "a body of

---

[1] Details of these horrors in Frizzi, iii. p. 377. For similar atrocities, on a smaller scale, on the accession of Alberto's elder brother Aldobrandino in 1352, when Francesco di Bertoldo d'Este (grandson of the Marchese Francesco, whom the Catalans murdered in 1312) attempted to obtain the lordship, see *Libro del Polistore*, coll. 827, 828. This Francesco's son Azzo in his turn conspired against the son of Alberto, Niccolò III. Even more dramatic examples will be found at the beginning of the reigns of Ercole I and Alfonso I.

UNDER THE WHITE EAGLE OF ESTE

magistrates of the Marquis, delegated to direct all the communal business at the expense of the Commune."[1] The Judge and the Sages were paid at the expense of the Commune, and every decision of the College that did not please the Excellence of the Marquis or Duke was at once overruled. The direction of the financial administration of the State was entrusted to the *Fattori Generali*. These officials were usually Ferrarese nobles, chosen by the sovereign to hold office during his pleasure. They were two in number in the fifteenth and early sixteenth centuries (three later in the days of Alfonso II), one mainly to superintend the financial affairs of the capital, the other of the dependent cities and towns. These *fattori* appear usually to have appointed the minor officers and lesser functionaries. They not infrequently bought their posts, and in many cases were corrupt and extortionate in the extreme. It was the policy of the princes to throw all the blame and odium upon these officers; in 1385 there had been a popular rising in which Niccolò II and Alberto had been forced to surrender the most unpopular of their ministers, Tommaso da Tortona, to be torn to pieces by the infuriated crowd. It was after this event that the great Castle of San Michele, now known as the Castello Vecchio, was erected; though the Estensi continued to hold their Court in the Corte Vecchia, what is now the Palazzo del Municipio, which had been begun by Azzo Novello in 1242, after the great siege of Ferrara which had left his family firmly planted on the throne. Nevertheless, the financial system did not work worse than in the other cities of Italy; it was sufficiently good to allow, according to a recent writer, large sums to be gathered up in

[1] G. Secco Suardo, *Lo Studio di Ferrara a tutto il secolo xv.*, P. 150.

the coffers of the State without putting too great a burden upon the resources of the citizens.[1]

In spite of the series of horrible tragedies that stained the palaces of the ruling House, notwithstanding the secret and mysterious murders into which no court of justice dared to pry, there was no State in Italy where the sovereigns were more beloved or more loyally served by their subjects. In case of war, the Estensi could arm their people and trust in their loyalty no less than in the trained skill of their hired mercenaries. Though the Ferrarese hated one Judge of the Sages worse than the devil and cut more than one Fattore to pieces, they did not lay their extortions to the charge of the sovereign. In the last days of the Estensian rule, under the second Alfonso in 1578, the Venetian ambassador wrote that the lower classes, *la gente minuta*, seldom attempted to smuggle or evade the customs; "wherefore, since each pays what he should, the revenues are large, and they will become even greater by reason of the reclaiming of the country near the seashore."[2]

The sovereigns were loud in professions of solicitude for their subjects' welfare, were desirous for them to be richer than those of any other Italian State, encouraged trade and generously supported education. Like the Medici in Florence, it was the policy of the Lords of Ferrara to dazzle their subjects with pageantry, perhaps less from artistic motives than from a desire to impress upon them the splendour and the glory of their illustrious House.

In the other cities of his dominions, the sovereign took

---

[1] Pietro Sitta, *Saggio sulle istituzioni finanziarie del ducato estense nei secoli xv. e xvi.*, p. 97. This can only apply to certain epochs of singular prosperity in the State.

[2] Quoted by Sitta, *loc. cit.*

UNDER THE WHITE EAGLE OF ESTE

cognizance of the most minute details of the conduct of his subjects; his representatives were obliged to furnish him with full reports, sometimes daily, of what went on. Mere peasants, as well as nobles, were forced to travel from the remoter districts of the Duchy to Ferrara, to answer the Prince in person, or to appeal to him from the decisions of his captains or commissaries.[1] The whole life and being of the State was made dependent upon the will and person of the sovereign.

Ostensibly, religion was practised to a high degree. Two princesses of the Estensi had been raised to the altars as saints, and their shrines were highly revered by the people.[2] One, indeed, was known to cry aloud from her tomb, when any special danger threatened the city or its rulers. The princes had been instrumental in the return of the Popes from Avignon, and in the building up of the fabric of the Temporal Power that had followed. They were professedly devoted to the service of their papal suzerains, and frequently received the gift of the Golden Rose in return. They were lavish in donations to the Church; new convents and monasteries arose on every side; the rites and ceremonies of Catholicism were a part of the functions of the State, and were carried out with the utmost pomp. The members of the ruling House followed the Blessed Sacrament

---

[1] This was more notably the case in the reigns of Ercole I and Alfonso I. Striking instances will be found in Boiardo's reports to the former as ducal captain in Reggio, and in Ariosto's letters, when governor of the Garfagnana, to the latter.

[2] The Beata Beatrice I, daughter of Azzo VI (the first Estensian ruler of Ferrara), and the Beata Beatrice II, a daughter of Azzo Novello. But the distinction of sanctity was claimed for many other princes and princesses more or less connected with the Estensi, of whom we may still see a later apotheosis in the curious church of Sant' Agostino at Modena.

DUKES AND POETS IN FERRARA

in procession through the city on the feast of the ⟨...⟩he
Domini, and blasphemy was a penal offence. A ⟨...⟩
chapel was reared to the Blessed Virgin in the court ⟨...⟩
ducal palace, with a much venerated picture of ⟨...⟩
worked countless miracles. The princes were as ⟨...⟩
hunting out nuns conspicuous for their piety to a⟨...⟩
Ferrarese convents, as zealous in welcoming spiritual ⟨...⟩
with a reputation for heroic sanctity, as they ⟨...⟩
procuring men of fine stature and strength to ⟨...⟩
balestrieri or crossbowmen, or in obtaining rare ⟨...⟩
animals for their menagerie. At the same ti⟨...⟩
of them appear to have attempted to rival Solo⟨...⟩
the numbers of their concubines, and their illeg⟨...⟩
children still baffle the computation of historians. ⟨...⟩
lasciva was a recognized part of the Court expense⟨...⟩
until the death of Duke Borso in 1471, it was q⟨...⟩
exception for the reigning sovereign to have been ⟨...⟩
wedlock.

From the beginning of their rule in Ferrara, a ⟨...⟩
poetry had shone round the Court of the Estens⟨...⟩
troubadours of Provence, the singers in the *langue* ⟨...⟩
the thirteenth century, had found generous and co⟨...⟩
patrons and protectors in Azzo VI and Azzo N⟨...⟩
Aimeric de Peguilhan had sung the praises of Beatrice ⟨and⟩
Giovanna, the daughter of the one and the first wife of the
other; the beauty of Costanza d'Este—daughter of Azzo
Novello and wife of that Omberto Aldobrandeschi with
whom Dante held converse in the first terrace of the Mountain of Purgation—was raised to the skies by Ralmenz
Bistors of Arles. An Italian trovatore, Ferrarino, had
frequented the Court of Obizzo II and Azzo VII⟨...⟩
compiled the famous anthology of Provençal son⟨...⟩

UNDER THE WHITE EAGLE OF ESTE

preserved in the Biblioteca Estense at Modena.[1] But Ferrara produced no real poet in the fourteenth century, no lyrist of the *dolce stil nuovo*, no singer of the philosophy of love to match even the lesser lights among the Tuscans and the Bolognese. Antonio dei Beccari, the *quasi poeta* (as Franco Sacchetti calls him) of Ferrara in the Trecento, adored the memory of Dante and carried on a correspondence in sonnets with Petrarca, upon the false report of whose death he composed a well-known canzone; but he stands practically alone, and wisely claims only a very modest place for himself.[2] Half a century of humanism and classical culture—call it pedantry, if you will—was needed for the lyrics and the poetical romance of Boiardo, the latter itself but a prelude to the epics of Ariosto and Tasso.

---

[1] For the literature of this subject, the *Coltura Francese Estense*, which does not come within the scope of the present volume, see G. Bertoni, *La Biblioteca Estense e la Coltura Ferrarese*, etc., pp. 4, 81-84.

[2] At the end of the canzone *Io ho già letto il pianto de' Troiani*, Antonio describes himself as:

"Anton de i Beccar, quel da Ferrara,
Che poco fa, ma volentieri impara."

Petrarca (*Epist. Rer. Senilium*, iii. 7) speaks of him as "that friend of ours of no ignoble genius, but distracted in too many things," and addressed two sonnets to him. He died in 1370. In the previous century an Anselmo da Ferrara, by whom is a sonnet in the *Rime scelte dei Poeti Ferraresi* (p. 1), had corresponded with Fra Guittone d'Arezzo.

Chapter II

PRINCES AND HUMANISTS

AT the beginning of the fifteenth century—while, at Florence, Lorenzo Ghiberti was casting his bronze doors for the Baptistery and Cosimo de' Medici was preparing to overthrow the Republic—Ferrara was ruled by the third Marchese Niccolò da Este, nominally as Vicar of the Church and feudatory of the Pope, practically as absolute sovereign. Niccolò was the twelfth Marquis of the House of Este who thus held the Ferrarese lordship. Like several of the most famous princes of his family, he was not born in wedlock, but was the legitimated son by Isotta Albaresani, a Ferrarese lady, of the Marchese Alberto—that devout and bloodstained Alberto whose somewhat mean statue in pilgrim's dress still frowns on the façade of the holding the Golden Rose that had been bestowed up by Pope Boniface IX.[1] Succeeding his father in 139 a boy of ten years old, Niccolò had been subject to a of regency until 1402, and in the meanwhile there h

[1] The Bull of Boniface IX, confirming the concession vicariate of the city of Ferrara and its county and district t Marquis of Este and his sons *ad vitam*, under the annua (*census*) of ten thousand golden florins, is dated May 2 Niccolò, *de soluto genitus et soluta*, is only to succeed in t (*quod absit*) of Alberto dying without legitimate sons, legitimated (Theiner, *Codex Diplomaticus*, iii. pp. 16–21).

PRINCES AND HUMANISTS

a hard struggle to preserve the throne from the attacks of a kinsman, Azzo di Francesco d'Este, from the conspiracies hatched by the citizens themselves, and from the intrigues of his own ambitious and formidable father-in-law, Francesco Novello da Carrara, that last Lord of Padua whom the Venetian hangman strangled in 1406.

When at last the government was placed in his hands, Niccolò at the age of nineteen found himself lord of the city and territory of Ferrara, which he held from the Pope; of the imperial fiefs of Rovigo and Modena, the former including Lendinara, Adria and all the Polesine; of Comacchio, doomed to be the cause of long and frequent contentions in later years; of Argenta, Lugo and Conselice in Romagna. Seven years later, in 1409, he slew Ottobuono Terzi, the upstart Ghibelline tyrant of Parma and Reggio, at a conference beneath the walls of Rubiera, and added these two cities to his dominions. Reggio, the *giocondo*, as Ariosto called it, remained henceforth one of the choicest jewels in the crown of the Estensi—to whom, indeed, it had already belonged, as we have seen, during the latter part of the thirteenth century. Parma, which had been held by them for a few years in the middle of the fourteenth century, and had been the cause of a war with Milan, Verona and Mantua,[1] was ceded to Milan in 1420. In 1423 Rubiera was obtained from the Boiardi in exchange for Scandiano, and in 1440 Bagnacavallo and Massalombarda were purchased from Pope Eugenius IV. Thus were the dominions of the illustrious House consolidated, and from the Castello Vecchio of Ferrara, which his father Alberto had built, and which was then at the northern extremity of the city with

---

[1] The war that bore literary fruit in Petrarca's sublime canzone, *Italia mia*.

DUKES AND POETS IN FERRARA

magnificent gardens stretching down to the banks of Po, Niccolò d'Este ruled over a rich and noble State aspired, with a considerable measure of success, to the balance of power between the greater sovereigns and republics of Italy.

When once seated firmly upon the throne with his States consolidated, Niccolò was a prudent ruler, and, after the conclusion of a brief and unimportant war with Milan, which ended in 1428, and in which he had commanded the forces of the Italian League, Ferrara became the most peaceful city of Italy. He was frequently appealed to as arbitrator by other princes. At the beginning of 1424 the Florentines and Filippo Maria Visconti submitted their quarrels to him, and his instructions to his ministers for the reception of the ambassadors afford a curious picture of the homely methods of the day. On January 27, the Marquis writes to his *Fattori* from his villa at Quartisana: " On the third day of this next coming February, the Ambassadors of the Duke of Milan and those of the Florentines are to come to Ferrara, to negotiate the peace which we have in our hands. We are certain that they will not wish to stay in the same hostelry; and therefore we would have you send for Antonio Galgano, the host of the *Angel*, and for the other of the *Swan*, and arrange with them that they get ready those two or three rooms which you and they shall think necessary, or more, if they believe that more will be needed, in order that, when the said Ambassadors come, they may find in both those two hostelries the things in order, so that they may be comfortable and may have good and fine lodgings." [1]

---

[1] Letter of January 27, 1424, published by L. A. Gandini, *Saggio degli usi e delle costumanze della Corte di Ferrara al tempo di Niccolò III*, p. 163.

PRINCES AND HUMANISTS

More frequently had Niccolò to interpose between Venice and Milan, between whom in these years there was "perpetual quarrels and immortal hatreds," and on these occasions his unimpeachable impartiality excited general approval. "Thence it came about," writes Enea Silvio Piccolomini, afterwards that noblest of pontiffs, Pius II, "that although all Lombardy was ablaze with wars, Ferrara alone and the adjacent parts of its dominion enjoyed peace. For to whoso willed a passage was granted, provided that he passed through without doing harm."[1] Practically all that the Ferrarese saw of the interminable petty wars of Italy was the coming and going of the ambassadors of the various Powers, who came to Ferrara to discuss or arrange the terms of peace.

The Marquis himself is described by Enea Silvio as "a fat man, jolly, given up to lust." His character is a curious blending of mediaeval ferocity with the first germs of Renaissance culture, of apparently perfectly genuine religious feeling with the most unbridled sensuality. Like other princes of his House, his great passions were for travelling, for pageantry and gorgeous display, and for women. In the last respect, his appetite was quite insatiable. Ugo Caleffini, in his rhymed chronicle of the House of Este, says that Niccolò had eight hundred mistresses, and would have made the number a thousand, had he not died so soon.[2] This is presumably a courtly exaggeration, intended to exalt the Estense to the level of Solomon; but Enea Silvio similarly writes that the Marquis kept whole troops of concubines, and was quite indiscriminate in his choice,

---

[1] *De Viris Illustribus*, p. 15.
[2] *Cronaca di Casa d'Este*, p. 286. "L'era tropo amoroso la persona polita!"

DUKES AND POETS IN FERRARA

"plebeians and countrywomen no less than nobles."[1] He appears to have acknowledged between twenty and thirty illegitimate children.

In the spring of 1413 Niccolò undertook a pilgrimage to Jerusalem, which has been fully described for us by one of his company, a certain Luchino dal Campo, who acted as chancellor on the voyage, in a narrative which is one of the most vivid pictures extant of the delights and dangers of travelling in the early days of the fifteenth century.[2] The whole tour took exactly three months, the party starting from Ferrara on April 6, and reaching home again on July 6. They set out from Venice in a Venetian galley captained by Pietro Contarini, and, sailing or rowing as the wind was favourable or contrary, they passed down the Adriatic, and by the Ionian Islands and the islands of the Archipelago, visiting the antiquities of Pola and wondering at the stags of Cherso, delighting in the singing of the Greek monks at Corfu and in the supper given by the Venetian governor in his orange-garden; equally interested in seeing the place where Carlo Zeno defeated the Genoese and the site of the rape of Helen by Paris. They visited Rhodes, coasted Cyprus, and at last reached the coast of Syria about twenty miles from Jaffa on the morning of May 11. The Marquis passed himself off as Niccolò Contarini, brother of the captain of the galley, and their visit to the Holy City, which they reached on May 15 and left on May 19, gives occasion for a wonderfully convincing picture of the prepotency and extortion of the Turks, the devotion of the Franciscan

---

[1] *Historia Friderici III Imperatoris*, p. 95.
[2] *Viaggio a Gerusalemme di Niccolò da Este, descritto da Luchino dal Campo*, edited by G. Ghinassi for the *R. Commissione pe' testi di lingua nelle provincie dell' Emilia*. Turin, 1861.

guardians of the Holy Places, the mixture of credulity and piety in the pilgrims, as they were shown the possible and impossible sites of the scenes of sacred history and mediaeval fiction. At Mass at the Holy Sepulchre, Niccolò dubbed Alberto della Sala, Feltrino Boiardo,[1] Pietro Rossi and two others of his retinue, knights (the first-named renouncing his previous knighthood in order that he might receive it again at the sacred spot), himself girding on the swords, and on Mount Cavalry he bound on their golden spurs, bidding them ever remember where they had received the order of knighthood. "After this the aforesaid lord, who, although he also was a knight, had never borne the spurs of gold, but had ever waited until he came on this most holy voyage, willed that in this place Messer Alberto della Sala should fasten the one spur to his left foot, as being the more honourable, saying that he would go to have the right spurred at San Jacopo of Galicia."

On their return voyage, they were sumptuously entertained by the King of Cyprus, when the Marquis exhibited his great strength in drawing a mighty bow that the King had given him, past his ear, whereas ordinary men could barely draw it a span. At a solemn supper party in the house of a noble of Cyprus, peacocks were set upon the table, and upon these peacocks the newly made knights and others took vows. The Marquis himself swore to God, to the Madonna, to Saint George and to the peacock, that in the first place where he should find himself in the company of men-at-arms mounted, to the number of a hundred or more in the face of the enemy, his should be the first lance that should be broken against these enemies, and until this vow

---

[1] Whose grandson was to enshrine this pilgrimage in his *Orlando Innamorato*, II., xxv. 52.

should be accomplished, he promised to fast every Friday. Messer Pietro Rossi vowed that he would never lie, unless it were for the State of his Lord, or to save his own life or that of any intimate friend of his, and for a remembrance of this vow he undertook always to say an Ave Maria when he saw a painted picture of Our Lady. One of the household of the Marquis, Spinello, swore to aid any distressed woman who should ask him, provided that she deserved the name of woman — *alcuna donna che meriti aver nome di donna*.[1]

In the following year, apparently instead of the Compostela sanctuary, a similar pilgrimage was undertaken to the shrine of St. Anthony at Vienne, when the Marquis was attended by Feltrino Boiardo and a party of gentlemen picturesquely clad in bright green, and courteously received by the King of France at Paris. On their return, the whole party was seized by the Marchese Manfredo del Carretto di Cera, in Piedmont, who offered to sell them bodily to the Duke of Milan, who had not yet recovered Parma. The Count of Savoy promptly forced the robber noble to surrender his prey, and, in spite of Niccolò's generous intercession, he beheaded the chief criminal and razed his castle to the ground. These were by no means the only pilgrimages that Niccolò undertook—the Santa Casa of Loreto and the Annunziata of Florence likewise attracted his fitful and eccentric devotion.

But although he made these pious vows and listened gladly to the preaching of San Bernardino of Siena, he made no pretence of altering his life. His adulteries

---

[1] Cf. Dante, *Vita Nuova*, § 19, who will write his canzone " a donne in seconda persona; e non ad ogni donna, ma solamente a coloro, che sono gentili, e non sono pur femmine."

PRINCES AND HUMANISTS

appear to have continued uninterruptedly until a few months before his death.

Niccolò's first marriage with the ill-favoured Gigliola da Carrara was childless and unhappy. She died in 1416. But during her life the Marquis had a goodly family of sons born to him from other women. By the beautiful Sienese lady Stella dell' Assassino, he had Ugo Aldobrandino (born in 1405), Leonello (born in 1407), and Borso (born in 1413). Meliaduse (born in 1406, the senior of Leonello by a year) was his child by Caterina degli Albaresani, the daughter of a Ferrarese physician; Alberto (born in 1415) and Gurone Maria were the fruit of his adultery with Cammilla dalla Tavola.[1]

The three sons that Madonna Stella had borne the Marquis were treated by him as though they were his legitimate children, and were regarded by all the city in that light. The birth of Ugo Aldobrandino had been celebrated as that of an heir to the State. At his christening in the Duomo, the Cardinal Cossa, afterwards Legate of Bologna (Baldassare Cossa, afterwards Pope John XXIII) and the Lords of Rimini and Mantua had stood sponsors by their procurators and ambassadors, together with Niccolò de' Boiardi, the Bishop of Modena, in the name of the community of his city. The Arts or Guilds of Ferrara had made a great holiday, with horse-races and a sumptuous tournament; the Bishop of Ferrara (Pietro de' Boiardi), with all the clergy, had gone in solemn procession.[2] The Magnifica

[1] Cammilla, sometimes erroneously called Filippa, is named in a brief of Pope Paul II, dated April 26, 1471, which grants various spiritual favours "Alberto Estensi et Camille genitrici sue" (*Archivio Vaticano*, xxxix. 12, f. 139).
[2] Jacopo de' Delaito, *Annales Estenses*, coll. 1035, 1036. The express statement of Jacopo (writing with authority as the chan-

DUKES AND POETS IN FERRARA

Madonna Stella herself was regarded as no mere light-o'-love, but as one to be treated with all honour. Her palace is still pointed out in the Via della Tromba. It is highly probable that, on the death of the Marchesana Gigliola, Stella expected to succeed to her dignities. She was bitterly disillusioned. In April, 1418, Niccolò took another wife—that hapless heroine of romantic poetry, Madonna Parisina de' Malatesta, the daughter of Andrea de' Malatesta and Lucrezia degli Ordelaffi—and brought her in triumph from Ravenna to Ferrara. Stella's death, in the July of the following year, mercifully saved her from the sight of what followed.[1]

cellor of the Marquis and before the catastrophe of 1425) is that Ugo Aldobrandino was "the natural son, the first begotten male, of the illustrious and magnificent Lord Niccolò, Marquis of Este, by the magnificent Lady Stella dell' Assassino." And similarly, Enea Silvio Piccolomini (*Historia Friderici*, p. 94). Writing under Borso, Ugo Caleffini—for obvious reasons—implies that the hapless prince was not the brother of his sovereign, but the son of Caterina Albaresani (*Cronaca di Casa d'Este*, p. 285). It is more difficult to comprehend why Bandello (*Novelle*, i. 37) makes Niccolò's granddaughter, Bianca di Sigismondo d'Este, insist that Ugo was the legitimate son of the Marquis by his first wife, Gigliola—unless it be merely to heighten the effect of the tragedy.

[1] She was buried in state in San Francesco (*Diario Ferrarese*, col. 184). "Quanto fo bella e bona!" writes Caleffini (*loc. cit.*), "de ogni virtù la portò corona." Similarly, Enea Silvio tells us that men said she was a virtuous and wise woman, who had been corrupted by force and by the promise of marriage (*Historia Friderici*, p. 95). In the Biblioteca Estense at Modena is still preserved a Latin poem in hexameters in honour of Stella, dedicated to Giovanni degli Assassini by Galeotto Marzio da Narni (*Cod. Lat.* 66). The Assassini were a branch of the Tolomei of Siena, who changed their name when they settled in Ferrara. As the said Galeotto Marzio has it:—

"Mutantes patriam, mutabunt nomina: dicent
Namque Assassinos Ptholemea stirpe creatos."

Several members of the family frequented the Ferrarese Court during the fifteenth century (cf. Bertoni, *op. cit.* pp. 14, 25, 55, 64).

The Marchesana Parisina bore her husband one son, who lived only for a few weeks, and two twin daughters, Ginevra and Lucia. The documents still preserved in the Archivio di Stato at Modena show her to have been an ideal great lady of the Middle Ages.[1] We find her a diligent housewife, keeping strict account of the linen, taking care that the attendants of her stepsons are properly attired. She was exceedingly generous to the poor, bountiful to the churches and convents. To her *donzelle*, her maids-in-waiting, she was particularly kind and generous, finding them suitable husbands, providing each on her marriage with a dowry, with her *corredo* or trousseau, and with those richly decorated *cofani* or wedding-chests that formed such a feature in the bride's equipment in Italy and of which the panels are among the treasures of our museums and picture-galleries to-day. A certain Pellegrina, daughter of a trusted servant of the Marquis, one Giacomo Rubino known as Zoese, appears to have been specially favoured by her and treated with the utmost generosity on the occasion of her marriage at the beginning of 1423. Parisina was a lover of horses and had a notable stable; she sent them to race for the *palio* at Verona, Modena, Bologna, Milan, and Mantua; and especially in 1422 and 1423 her favourite jockey, Giovanni da Rimini, wearing her colours of red and white, carried off victory after victory.[2] Also she took pleasure in hunting and hawking. We find her

The Ferrarese chroniclers all call Stella's father Giovanni, but Count Emilio Tolomei, through Mr. Langton Douglas, informs me that, in the records of the Tolomei of Siena, his name is given as Antonio.

[1] See Gandini, *Saggio degli usi e delle costumanze*, pp. 152–157, and Angelo Solerti, *Ugo e Parisina; Storia e leggenda secondo nuovi documenti*.

[2] Cf. documents in Solerti, *op. cit.* i. pp. 614, 615.

DUKES AND POETS IN FERRARA

sending to foreign cities for choice perfumes, for rich embroideries and personal ornaments, for rare birds in cages. But of her moral qualities and mental endowments we know next to nothing. She loved music, especially the harp, upon which she had her little daughters taught to play. We read of Fra Maginardo, her chaplain, buying a psaltery for her, and of a *cartolaro* Bartolommeo selling her an office book of the Madonna covered with black velvet.[1] If she read at all in books of a lighter character, the literary fashion of her husband's Court would have led her to dwell upon the passion of Guenevere and Lancelot, the guilty loves of Tristram and Iseult.[2] And for her, like that other Romagnole spirit whom Dante met in the Hell of the Lovers, there came a day when she "read no more."

The Marquis brought up his younger sons with considerable rigidity and parsimony. Borso and Meliaduse, when studying at Bologna and Padua, were even kept short of clothes to wear. When the plague threatened Ferrara in the summer of 1424, their father sent Meliaduse to Modena and Borso to Argenta, with the strictest provisions about the number of servants and attendants that they might have about them, and with a rigid charge to the *camarlingo* of each town, in whose charge they were put, not to let them have friends to dine.[3] But for Ugo there seems to have been no restriction of any kind, and the registers of the Court expenses in these very years show Niccolò and Parisina rivalling each other in caring for his wants and pleasures, in providing him with clothes and money, horses and hawks, even with a harp—the latter, of

[1] Gandini, *op. cit.* p. 152.
[2] Cf. Bertoni, *op. cit.* p. 19.
[3] See documents quoted by Gandini, *op. cit.* pp. 158, 159.

course, being Parisina's gift.¹ In these years Leonello was away from Ferrara, having been sent in 1422, under the care of Nanni Strozzi, to study the art of war at Perugia under the famous condottiere, Braccio da Montone.

All contemporary evidence concerning the tragedy that deprived the Marchese Niccolò of his wife and heir appears to have been destroyed, and it is not easy to distinguish between fact and fiction in the story that has been handed down to us. All that is certain is that in the course of some journey that they took together—possibly to Ravenna, the city of Francesca and Samaritana—Ugo became the lover of his stepmother. One of Parisina's maids, who had been beaten by her mistress, betrayed the secret to Giacomo Rubino—that very same whose daughter had been treated with such generosity and affection by the Marchesana— and Giacomo brought the Marquis to a place where, himself unseen, he was the witness of his own dishonour. His vengeance was prompt and terrible. On the night between May 20 and May 21, 1425, the guilty pair were arrested in the Corte Vecchia, and conveyed thence to the Castello. There are two horrible dungeons shown in the Castello, beneath the Tower of the Lions. One, a little higher than the other, has a direct communication with the outer air of the court, and at times admits a faint gleam of day. The other is on the level of the moat; its floor is usually covered with muddy water; it receives air and faint light through a long aperture with treble barriers of iron bars. The tradition has it that into these ghastly cells the delicately nurtured lady and her princely young paramour were thrown; but it has recently been pointed out that the only two records that can in any sense be regarded as

¹ Solerti, *op. cit.* ii. p. 65.

DUKES AND POETS IN FERRARA

contemporary both agree that the place of their imprisonment was the so-called *Torre Marchesana*, the tower in which at the present time the great clock is placed.[1] Either way, their imprisonment was brief. The Marquis refused to admit either wife or son to his presence again, and the intercession of his most trusted advisers, Uguccione de' Contrari and Alberto della Sala, proved unavailing. On the night of May 21, Ugo and Parisina died by the headsman's axe in the Torre Marchesana. Ugo perished first. Then Parisina was led to her death by that same Giacomo Rubino by whom she had been betrayed. Thinking that she was going to be thrown into an oubliette or *trabocchetto*, she kept asking if she had yet reached the place. She asked after her lover, and, hearing that he was already dead, exclaimed, "Then I no more wish to live." When she came to the block, she laid aside her ornaments, and with her own hands prepared her neck for the stroke. The same night their bodies were brought to San Francesco and quietly buried there. Aldobrandino Rangoni, who had been Ugo's friend and accomplice, suffered the same doom at Modena.[2]

All that night the unhappy father and husband paced up and down the halls and passages of his palace in desperate grief, now gnawing his sceptre with his teeth, now calling passionately upon the name of his dead son or crying out for his own death. It is stated by Ferrarese historians

---

[1] Solerti, *op. cit.* ii. pp. 75, 76. Cf. the *Diario Ferrarese*, col. 184. In Bandello's novella, Bianca d'Este represents Ugo as imprisoned in the Torre dei Leoni and Parisina in the other tower.

[2] Fra Paolo da Lignago, *Cronaca*, ff. 114, 115; Frizzi, iii. pp. 450-453. Matteo dei Grifoni, in his Chronicle of Bologna that two of Parisina's maidens were likewise beheaded *Italicarum Scriptores*, xviii. col. 230).

PRINCES AND HUMANISTS

and chroniclers that, on the following day, he sent a written report of the tragedy to all the Courts of Italy, and that on the receipt of the news the Doge of Venice put off a State tournament that was to have been held in the Piazza di San Marco. No trace of such a document has ever been found, either in the Archives of Modena or in those of Venice or any other of the States with which Niccolò was in close relations.¹ The Marquis is said, by one of those half-mad perversions of justice habitual to Italian despots of that age, to have ordered the execution of several noble Ferrarese ladies who were notoriously serving their husbands as Parisina had served him—" in order that his wife should not be the only one to suffer," as Fra Paolo has it. One, Laodamia de' Romei, the wife of one of the judges, "who was known to him," appears to have been publicly beheaded;² but, after her, the edict went no further.

After Parisina's death, Niccolò had many bastards, male and female. A daughter, Beatrice, who was for a while the Queen of Feasts in Ferrara, was born in 1427. A Ferrarese proverb said: "Whoso would see Paradise on earth, let him see Madonna Beatrice at a festa."³ After her father's death, she was married first to Count Niccolò da Correggio and afterwards to Tristano Sforza. She bore to the Lord of Correggio a son, also named Niccolò, born in 1450, whom we shall meet many times in the course of this history. Beatrice's mother was most probably a

---
¹ Solerti, *op. cit.* ii. p. 79; but I think that the passage from the *De Politia Litteraria* (ii. 13), to be quoted presently, proves that some such step was taken by the Marquis to justify his action.

² Fra Paolo, *Cronaca*, ff. 115, 115v.

³ Cf. Luzio and Renier, *Niccolò da Correggio*, i. p. 208. They point out, however, that the saying may possibly refer to Niccolò's granddaughter, Beatrice di Ercole d'Este.

DUKES AND POETS IN FERRARA

Stimulated by Guarino's presence and his genial enthusiasm, Ferrara became one of the most cultured and learned cities of Italy. The Marquis himself gradually acquired a library which was, for the times, a not inconsiderable one. In an inventory in the year 1436 of "Libri del nostro Signore," there are 279 manuscripts set down, which were stored in the Torre di Rigobello, the chief tower of the Corte Vecchia, where the House of Este kept its secret Archives.[1] Learned men and artists flocked to Ferrara, especially in Niccolò's later years, when Leonello was in the first flower of his manhood, and were always cordially welcomed; Vittore Pisanello painted the portraits of his children and cast the sovereign's own somewhat grim features in striking bronze medals; Michele Savonarola, at his invitation, came from Padua to be his Court physician and to hold a chair at the Studio.

[1] See Adriano Cappelli, *La Biblioteca Estense nella prima metà del secolo XV*, where the complete inventory is given, pp. 12–30. Nearly 200 of these were naturally Latin, including classical writers, theologians, and mediaeval authors. There were 58 French MSS., including a great number of romances, to 23 Italian. Among these latter the minor works of Boccaccio are particularly abundant, while there are only two Dante codices, catalogued as "Libro uno chiamado Danti" and "Libro uno chiamado el scripto sovra el purgatorio de Danti" respectively. There are two French translations of the Bible, a Greek MS. and a German MS.—both unnamed. One of the treasures, which is still preserved at Modena, is a Caesar, *Commentarii de Bello Gallico*, decorated with miniatures by Giovanni Falconi of Florence and with marginal annotations from the hand of Guarino himself. That mysterious Greek manuscript seems to have disappeared, but was perhaps a Strabo, as in May, 1470, Scipio Fortuna, one of the librarians, writing to Borso in answer to his demand for "il Strabone in greco," says that he has no Greek book in the Tower and never had, but suggests that another librarian, Marco di Galaotto, may possibly have it. (Document published by Bertoni, *op. cit.* p. 259.) The famous Torre di Rigobello fell in 1553.

PRINCES AND HUMANISTS

"I verily declare," wrote that acute scholar and ardent hunter of codices, Giovanni Aurispa, who had preceded Guarino in the Court of the Estense as the *precettore* of Meliaduse, "that I love this Marquis of mine not otherwise than as a good son loves a sweet and gentle parent."[1] Nor was religion neglected. A genuine saint, Giovanni Tavelli da Tossignano, held for a while the bishopric in succession to Pietro de' Boiardi. Bernardino of Siena was heard gladly by the Court and people alike, and nowhere else, save in his own city, has he left so enduring a mark in the number of the sacred monograms that we still see in the streets of Ferrara to-day.

A gorgeous and many-coloured episode in Niccolò's long reign was the assembling of the abortive Council of Ferrara in 1438. The Holiness of Pope Eugenius, John Paleologus, Emperor of the East, the Patriarch Joseph of Constantinople, with the Latin cardinals and prelates, the Greek ecclesiastics, and representatives of the nobles of Italy, gathered together under the protection of the House of Este. Humanists swarmed, and lent their services as interpreters between East and West. Giovanni Aurispa obtained from the Holy Father the office of papal secretary, while Leon Battista Alberti mystified the Patriarch of Grado by writing the life of an imaginary child martyr whose self-abnegation and heroic constancy should bring the blush to the cheeks of these worldly prelates and fathers. Needless to say that the young princes were well to the fore. Leonello delighted the Pope's Holiness with a harangue in very choice Latin, while Borso already gave the first signs of that love for magnificent display which

[1] Letter of 1437, quoted in Sabbadini, *Biografia documentata di Giovanni Aurispa*, pp. 72-74.

became his ruling passion in later life. The Marquis himself was present at a banquet given by Ugo Benzi of Siena, " who at that time was held the prince of physicians," professor of medicine at the Studio, to a number of learned Greeks and Latin humanists. When the banquet was over, the tables were removed, and a vigorous discussion was held concerning the chief points at issue between the rival schools of the Aristotelians and Platonists, Ugo saying that he would defend whichever part the Greeks thought fit to oppose. After several hours of ardent disputation, Ugo Benzi put to silence one after another of the Greeks. It was thus made manifest, writes Enea Silvio, that " the Latins, who long ago had overcome the Greeks in the arts of war and in the glory of arms, in our age excel them also in letters and in all branches of learning." [1]

Three years later, on December 26, 1441, Niccolò died at Milan, where he had been attempting, as a generous friend to both parties, to establish peace between the Duchy and the Venetians, and to set in order the State of the last of the Visconti, Filippo Maria. In his will he named Leonello as his successor, and after Leonello's death, Borso, and only after Borso the two legitimate sons, Ercole and Sigismondo. His body was brought back to Ferrara, and buried on January 1, in Santa Maria degli Angeli; "and he was interred bare without any pomp, because he so commanded in his testament." [2]

Leonello d'Este was a scholar and a poet, "a true humanist upon the throne." [3] His military training under Braccio

[1] *Opera* (*Europa*, cap. 52), pp. 450-451.
[2] *Diario Ferrarese*, col. 191.
[3] A. Venturi, *L'Arte a Ferrara nel periodo di Borso d'Este*, p. 690.

PRINCES AND HUMANISTS

da Montone had not made a soldier of him, and he only found his real self on his return to Ferrara, being now—after the tragical death of Ugo Aldobrandino—the recognized heir to the sovereignty, when he plunged into the rapidly advancing waves of the Classical Revival. To him and to his influence was due, almost entirely, the change from mediaeval ferocity to at least the outward semblance of culture and refinement that marks the latter part of his father's reign.

Before the advent of Guarino to Ferrara, Leonello had acquired considerable culture and was already in correspondence with him. It was, indeed, an event of no small importance in the literary world that first drew the prince and the scholar together. In 1428 Nicholas of Trier, one of the papal collectors of tithes in Germany, discovered in a German convent a codex of Plautus, containing sixteen comedies, twelve of which had until then been supposed lost. The codex was purchased by the Cardinal Giordano Orsini, who, under the impression that he would thereby render his prize more precious, stubbornly refused to let either Poggio Bracciolini or Guarino himself have a copy of it, in spite of the latter's assurance that, if his request is granted, "while the Comedies are called *Plautine* from their author, they will be named *Ursine* from their restorer."[1]

When Guarino found himself installed in Ferrara as Leonello's master, he appealed to him, and the young Marquis promptly wrote to the Cardinal, to request the loan of the codex for his own use. His most reverend and illustrious Lordship deemed it not politic to refuse,

[1] Letter from Guarino to Giordano Orsini, in Pez and Hueber, *Thesaurus Anecdotorum Novissimus*, Tom. vi., pars iii. p. 165.

DUKES AND POETS IN FERRARA

and Leonello wrote exultantly to Guarino (who wa rarily absent from the city) to tell him that the p in his possession. For the gift of such "immortal Guarino wrote his pupil a letter of enthusiastic g "Greater thanks in days to come shall students whole order of lettered men pay thee. For all shall kn by thy work and intervention, Plautus has been from darkness to light, from the caverns to the from death to life." Henceforth, Leonello and were united by bonds of the warmest affection. the former was away from the city in his counti resting from his studies and engaged in hunting, h day sent the humanist presents of game in proof prowess, accompanied by elegant and spirited Latin "sweeter than honey," describing his sport; the p Guarino received with delight, as marks of his p pupil's continual recollection of him, the letters he an back in kind, with lavish praise and genuine admir For him, Leonello is his "King and Lord," the " of Princes."

A vivid picture of Leonello and his circle, in the years of the reign of the Marchese Niccolò, is given the Milanese humanist, Angelo Camillo Decembrio, curious and little-known book, *De Politia Litteraria*,[2] he undertook with the intention of dedicating it to Le himself, and, after the latter's untimely death, ins

---

[1] Thirteen letters from Guarino to Leonello (including tl quoted on the Plautine comedies) in Pez and Hueber, *op. c* 154-164. Cf. Rosmini, *op. cit.* i. pp. 62-69, and Voigt, i. pp. 56

[2] *Politiae Litterariae Angeli Decembrii Mediolanensis, O Clarissimi, ad summum Pontificem Pium II, libri septem.* I from the Augsburg edition of 1540. Neither the British M nor the Biblioteca Angelica possesses a copy of the first e printed at Basle in 1527.

to Pope Pius II instead. Angelo, who represents himself as having been present at the scenes described and listening to the discussions which he professes to report, shows us the young prince surrounded by the elect spirits of the literary society of Ferrara, gracious and genial, treating them all as friends and equals and treated by them in the same manner. In every word and action there was a certain studied refinement, revealing a thoroughly harmonious character attuned to all that was seemly and beautiful. Something of this was traced even in his dress, the fashion and colours of which were carefully sought out so as to bear some mystical correspondence with the course of the planets and the order of the days of the week. The disputations which Angelo records are practically informal lectures by Leonello or Guarino—on the formation of a library, on the great classical writers, especially the Latins, Virgil above all, and on kindred topics. Leonello is the life of the whole, and, in his absence, the discourses that Guarino delivers on Greek derivations and the like are dull in the extreme. The other interlocutors merely put in a remark at intervals, throw out an objection, or by some timely question open a new subject. Among the older men we see Feltrino Boiardo, the Lord of Scandiano, whom we have already met; Uguccione de' Contrari, still the old Marchese's most trusted adviser; Alberto Costabili, and Giovanni Gualengo. The younger men are the prince Alberto Pio da Carpi, to be more famous in a later inheritor of his name, Carlo Nuvolone, and the two sons of Nanni Strozzi, Niccolò and Tito Vespasiano. The last named, then a mere boy (he was born in 1422), was already showing himself the most apt of all Guarino's pupils; according to his son, he had digested, not merely read, at the age of thirteen, all the

chief Latin and Greek poets; even at this early
Latin lyrics were the pride and delight of Leonell
—as they were destined to be for the more modern a
of his two successors.

We see, then, in Angelo's pages this courtly and s
group, now walking together in the cool evening to
discussing as they go, now sitting under a great lau
in the garden, now meeting in the Corte Vecchia
nello's own private apartment, which was decorate
portraits of the great heroes of antiquity, now ridin;
the stars on a hot summer's night " to that castle o
palace, of all in Italy the fairest, in popular speech
Belriguardo."[1] A little volume of Sallust in Leo
hand, or a picture on the wall of a palace cham
enough to start a discussion on Roman history or F
historians, but more frequently Virgil or Terence will
the theme. Nor are the theologians denied a pla
Leonello's ideal library. And though the verna
writers are dismissed as " those books which some
on winter nights we explain before our wives and child
a sonnet of Petrarca's (the well-known *Cesare poi che'l*
tor d'Egitto) is thought worthy of more serious discus:
On one occasion the whole party sets out by ship
Venice, in attendance upon Leonello, who " in the he;
of his youth, conspicuous in his golden neck-chain and ¿
worked cloak," is going in the stead of his father to arr:
a peace between the Most Serene Republic and L
Filippo Maria of Milan. Arrived at the City of the Lago

---

[1] This palace of Belriguardo was about seven kilometers f
Ferrara, near Voghera; the other, Belfiore, was then outside the w
near the place where the Certosa still stands. Not a trace of ei
of these buildings remains to-day.

[2] *De Politia Litteraria*, i. 6, ii. 15.

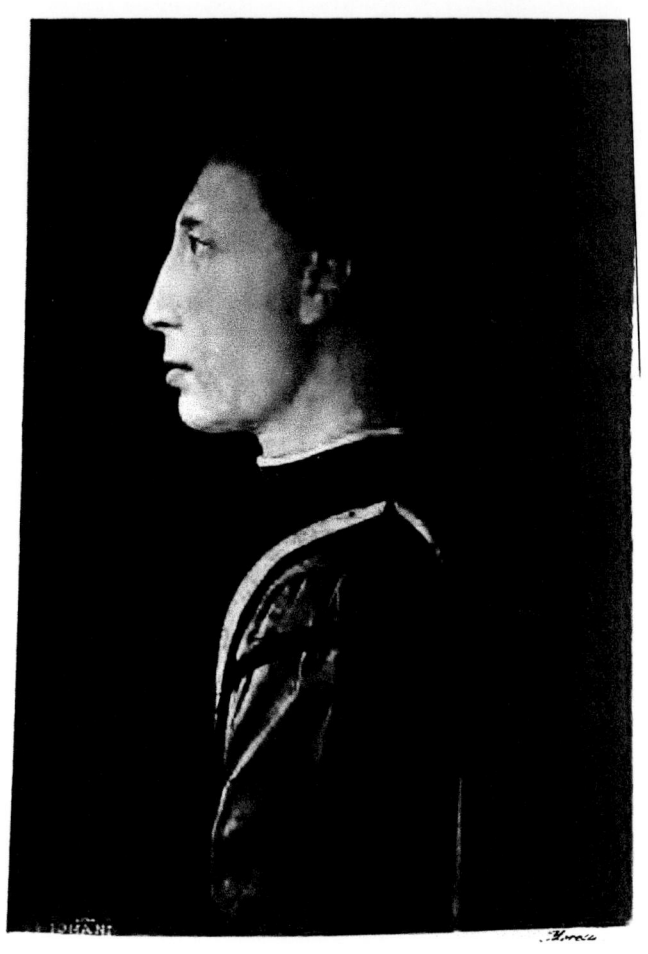

Leonello d'Este.
By Giovanni Oriolo.

PRINCES AND HUMANISTS

Leonello discourses upon Homer and Virgil with the young Venetian patricians who have come to meet him, until it is time to enter "the sublime palace of your Senate."[1] On another occasion, after hearing Mass on the feast day of St. John the Baptist at Ferrara, Leonello and his following accept the invitation of Giovanni Gualengo to taste the first ripe figs of his garden, after which they go up into his library, which he has all decorated with white and purple flowers, "diffusing grace and love with wondrous fragrance."[2]

Once, indeed, a strangely dramatic note is struck in their discussion. Leonello, with (to our modern notions) a curious lack of sensibility, defends the famous passage in the second book of the *Aeneid* where Aeneas threatens the life of Helen, by the example of the vengeance his own father had taken upon his brother and stepmother, but a few years before. "You have seen," Angelo represents him as saying, "my own father, a more recent and familiar example in this matter (concerning whom I speak not because he is my father, but as fame bears testimony), among the Italian princes by far the most famous for his observances of humanity, justice, and piety, when he saw what he would fain have not seen, put to death his wife, together with his son, the stepmother with the stepson. Was my father then condemned on account of this sort of vengeance, after the accusation was made public? By no means, but by the general opinion of all the fault remained upon the slain."[3]

[1] *De Politia Litteraria*, i. 11.
[2] *Ibid.* ii. 21.
[3] *De Politia Litteraria*, ii. 13. Very different was the judgment of the Pope to whom the book is dedicated. "He was held," writes Enea Silvio, "both by others and himself to have been cruel to his

DUKES AND POETS IN FERRARA

Although united by ties of tenderest affection to his brother Borso, whose prompt action had secured the duchies of Modena and Reggio at the outset of his reign, and who practically shared the government of the Estense dominions with him, Leonello found a more sympathetic companion in his special tastes and pursuits in the person of his elder half-brother, the bastard Meliaduse, who, on the death of Ugo Aldobrandino, had been forced into the Church by their father (a fate he had tried to escape by flight), but who seems to have shown no signs of envy towards his more favoured juniors. Meliaduse shared Leonello's friendship with humanists and artists, with Bruni and Guarino, Leon Battista Alberti and Pisanello, and there are several letters extant, written in Latin from Leonello in Ferrara to Meliaduse in Rome during their joint lifetime, which give a pleasant idea of the character and mutual relations of these two young princely students. These Latin epistles, which Leonello addressed to the distinguished humanists of Italy, do not strike us now as anything very remarkable; but they were greatly admired by his contemporaries. Guarino, in the funeral oration that he pronounced over his noble pupil's bier, cited them as extant monuments of his supereminent erudition written in such faultless and choice Latin "that he approached very near to the diction of the ancients," and Enea Silvio Piccolomini, going a little further, declared that the

son and unjust to his wife, from whom he wished to exact the faith he gave. But this was the reward of his promiscuous lust. If he kept faith to his wife, nor his wife to him. The weaker paid the penalty; the potent sinner, whom the world dared not judge, was reserved for the judgment of God." (*Historia Friderici Imperatoris*, p. 95.)

[1] See R. Sabbadini, *Biografia documentata di Giovanni Guarino*, pp. 58–61, and Mancini, *Vita di Leon Battista Alberti*.

equal to the letters of Cicero.[1] Leonello was a most ardent collector of codices of the classical authors as well as of the early Fathers, and is said to have been the first to demonstrate the apocryphal character of the supposed correspondence between St. Paul and Seneca.[2] He was emulous, his Franciscan admirer Fra Giovanni da Ferrara tells us, of the fame and glory of those ancient heroes who shone alike by the splendour of letters and of great deeds.[3] He is reported to have composed a Latin commentary upon his own actions—a species of autobiography of which no fragments are now extant. His one great hero was Julius Caesar himself, to whose name and honour he dedicated a special room in the palace. At his instigation Guarino translated the *Commentarii de Bello Gallico*, and dedicated to him a treatise against Poggio, who had exalted Scipio over Caesar among the captains of antiquity. On the occasion of Leonello's marriage with Margherita Gonzaga, Pisanello presented him with a portrait of his hero, *Divi Julii Caesaris effigies* (whether picture or medal does not appear), and Leonello was so delighted with the gift that he gave two golden ducats to the man who brought it.[4]

The diploma which the Marquis issued in 1450, shortly before his own death, in favour of Michele Savonarola—

---

[1] Rosmini, *op. cit.* i. p. 107; *Aeneae Sylvii Pii Pont. Epist.* 105 (*Opera*, p. 602). For more extravagant praise, see the passages from Poggio and Filelfo quoted by Voigt, i. p. 560. See also the poem addressed to him by the Neapolitan humanist, Porcellio, beginning, "Accipe Pieridum, Princeps Leonelle, mearum Munera" (*Carmina Illustrium Poetarum Italorum*, vii. p. 515).

[2] Cf. *De Politia Litteraria*, i. 10.

[3] Johannes Ferrariensis, *Annales*, col. 453.

[4] See Vasari, *Vita del Pisanello*, ed. Venturi, pp. 38, 39. A letter from Guarino to Leonello, encouraging him to defend the glories of Caesar, is in Pez and Hueber, *op. cit.* pp. 156-158.

DUKES AND POETS IN FERRARA

Leonello delighted in music and in the service [of the] Church. In his palace he built a beautiful chapel, [sumptu]ously furnished and decorated, and had a special [band of] singers brought from France to serve it.[1] Alth[ough he] reared few new buildings in Ferrara, he was an a[rdent and] discriminating judge of the plastic arts. The S[pedale di] Santa Anna (founded originally by the good bishop, [Giovanni] da Tossignano, who died in 1446), and the Palaz[zetto] in the Borgo Nuovo (now much modified as the S[eminario] Arcivescovile and famous for Garofolo's frescoes)[, are the] only buildings of importance that he erected. [To house] his precious manuscripts, as well as his art collec[tion, he built] Belfiore—one of those famous *delizie* or pleasure-p[alaces in] which the House of Este excelled, and which, w[ith the] solitary exception of Schifanoia, have all disap[peared,] which had been left to him unfinished and which [he com]pleted. Before and after his accession, his favourite [painter] was Vittore Pisanello. "Pisano, the most excellent [of the] painters of this age, when he came from Rome to [Ferrara] promised me of his own accord a certain picture [painted] by his own hand, in which was the image of the [Blessed] Virgin "—thus he writes to Meliaduse in 1432, ni[ne months] before his accession. "I marvellously long to [have this] picture, not only because of the excellent genius [of the] painter, but also because of my special devotion [to the] Virgin."[2] The picture is now in the National Ga[llery,] London. Pisanello cast many medals with L[eonello's] features, and painted his portrait at least twice, a [picture]

---

[1] Johannes Ferrariensis, col. 456. Cf. Ugo Caleffini in th[e] Chronicle (pp. 288, 289): "Quanto li piaceva li vespri [e le] messe!"

[2] See the letter in Sabbadini, *op. cit.* pp. 58–60.

PRINCES AND HUMANISTS

example being in the Morelli collection at Bergamo.[1] Flavio Biondo could congratulate the Marquis in 1446 that his coinage was modelled upon the style of that of the Roman Emperors.[2] When Ciriaco of Ancona, the great antiquarian traveller of that age, visited him in the summer of 1449, Leonello showed him with special pride among his pictures one by Roger Van der Weyden ("Rugerius Brugiensis") representing our first Parents and the Deposition from the Cross, which seemed to the humanist "painted by divine rather than by human art," and in the palace of Belfiore a painting of the Muses, by Angelo da Siena, adorned with a Latin epigram apparently by Guarino.[3]

The friendship between Leon Battista Alberti and Leonello seems to have begun in 1436, when Alberti dedicated his comedy *Filodossio* (*Fabula Philodoxeos*) to him, as the brother of his very dear friend, Meliaduse.[4] The occasion

[1] Shortly before Niccolò's death Jacopo Bellini and Pisanello painted rival portraits of Leonello, and the old Marquis gave the preference to the Venetian (see the sonnet by the poet Ulisse, in Venturi's edition of Vasari's *Vita del Pisanello*, p. 46). In the Louvre there is a drawing of Borso by Pisanello and also a highly finished portrait of a young lady whom Gruyer (ii. p. 29) took for Margherita Gonzaga, but whom Venturi (*loc. cit.* p. 69) is probably right in recognizing as one of the Estensian princesses, Leonello's half-sisters. Chronological considerations make it probable that she is either Isotta, who in 1444 married the Count Oddantonio of Urbino and in 1446 Stefano Frangipani, or Beatrice, who married Niccolò da Correggio in 1448.
[2] Voigt, i. p. 562.
[3] Francesco Scalamonti, *Vita di Ciriaco Anconitano*, pp. 143-145, in G. Colucci, *Delle Antichità Picene*, Tom. xv. (Fermo, 1792). Roger Van der Weyden's painting has been, rather questionably, identified with a picture now in the Uffizi. Angelo da Siena worked for both Leonello and Borso, but no Sienese influences can be traced in the Ferrarese school.
[4] *Opere volgari di Leon Batt. Alberti*, ed. A. Bonucci, vol. i. pp. cxx., cxxi.

DUKES AND POETS IN FERRARA

of the Council of Ferrara brought the architect prince together, and cemented their friendship. returned to Ferrara in 1442, and was most cordially by the Marquis. "When I came to visit thee," h "the readiness and kindness of my reception at tl showed clearly that Battista Alberti was right well to thee."¹ Alberti hesitated at first about sen works in the vernacular, written "in such wis« might be understood by my not very learned fellow-< to Leonello. "I feared that they had not as mucl as was needed to be read by a prince of such lea thyself." But the Marquis reassured him, and the tine was delighted to have such eminent suppor appeal to the vernacular. "Right glad was I, not do a thing to please thee, but also to find that thou most erudite, did not find fault with me for that fc many blame me, who say that I have offended the of literature in not writing so eloquent a matter Latin language."³

Here we see Leonello a worthy precursor of Lore Medici; but M. Gustave Gruyer notes that it was so: unfortunate for Ferrara that, less wise in this respe his Mantuan brother-in-law, he encouraged Alber man of letters rather than as architect. Leonello t utmost delight in all that he wrote, whether in Lat Italian, and kept urging him to do more. It wa instigation that Alberti's chief literary work, th "Books on Architecture," *De Re Aedificatoria*, was ¥ as Alberti himself tells Meliaduse in his *Ludi Mate*

---
¹ Dedication of the *Teogenio*, *ibid*. vol. iii. p. 159.
² *Ibid*. p. 160.
³ *Ibid*. vol. iv. p. 424. For the relations of Alberti with I cf. especially Mancini, *Vita di L. B. Alberti*, pp. 188–197.

PRINCES AND HUMANISTS

In 1444 he was invited to decide upon the merits of two rival models for the equestrian statue of Niccolò III, to be erected in front of the Corte Vecchia, the present Palazzo del Municipio (the pedestal, alas, alone remains to-day). This suggested to him his curious little treatise in Latin, *De Equo Animante*, dedicated " to Leonello, Prince of Ferrara, and delight of the human race."

"When I came to Ferrara," he says, "for the sake of seeing and saluting thee, most illustrious Prince, it is not easy to tell the great delight that detained me there, seeing thy most beautiful city, thy right modest citizens and so accomplished and kindly a Prince as thyself. Verily, I understood how important it is to spend life in a republic in which one obeys, in leisure and tranquillity of soul, an excellent father of his country and one most observant of the laws and customs. It added to this pleasure that there I met with a most pleasant and excellent occasion to exercise my intellect, as I am wont to do ; which, indeed, I took most gladly for both our sakes. For since thy citizens had decreed to set up in the Forum, with magnificent outlay, an equestrian statue of thy father, and excellent artists were contending together in the matter, they chose me, who take delight not a little in painting and modelling, as arbiter and judge. Wherefore as I again and again looked upon those works, made with admirable workmanship, it came into my mind to consider more diligently, not merely the beauty and the outward appearance of horses, but also their entire nature and habits."[1]

One of Leonello's first cares was for the Studio of Ferrara, which during the latter part of his father's reign, in spite of the presence of Guarino, had lost ground consider-

[1] *Leonis Baptistae Alberti, Opera inedita, etc.*, pp. 238–239.

ably. In this his object was not merely " to put
the clouds of ignorance and to infuse the light of
into the minds of his citizens," as the Franciscan
vanni has it, but also to promote the material well
the city by preventing promising young men from
ing elsewhere, and by attracting wealthy and
foreigners from other States. At the instance of tl
board of magistrates who were appointed to pres
the affairs of the Studio, and aided by the co
Guarino, he thoroughly reformed it in the years
1443. All incompetent teachers were banished
city, and the Marquis sent to every part of Italy
tinguished professors and lecturers in all branches
ledge, whom he rewarded with generous stipei
welcomed, as a contemporary put it, " with a mo
countenance and with sweetest words." " With th
zeal," writes Fra Giovanni, " he set himself to br
renowned and learned men in both branches of
illustrious physicians and grave philosophers (of
was one), eminent theologians likewise, poets, diale
orators skilled both in Latin and Greek eloquence
means of Aurispa a genuine Greek, Theodore Gaza,
Ferrara in 1444, to profess the language of Hoi
Sophocles. " Touching that Greek," wrote Carlo
pini to Aurispa, " who by thy doing has been su
to Italy, and especially to Ferrara, to educate yo
who have any dealings with the Muses and all w
thought for the glory of the Italians should be im
beholden to thee. In this matter all will easily

[1] Johannes Ferrariensis, col. 457 ; Borsetti, i. pp. 47–54
i. pp. 563, 564 ; Gruyer, i. p. 39. It should be observed tl
stipends were paid by the Commune during Leonello's rei

PRINCES AND HUMANISTS

how greatly the higher culture is indebted to the illustrious prince Leonello."[1] It appears questionable whether Gaza actually held a chair at Ferrara, but he was Rector of the University of Arts for the scholastic year 1448-1449.[2] These men, with others, the leaders of the literary and philosophic society of Ferrara itself, met at the table or in the gardens of the Marquis, who held a kind of informal Academy in the palace of Belfiore, a development and extension of those early literary gatherings and disputations recorded by Angelo Decembrio. Of these too we have a picture, somewhat idealized and tinged with a monkish colouring, in the *Annales* of that worthy friar who wrote himself down a "grave philosopher," Fra Giovanni.

True, it must be admitted that most of these men who thus gathered round Leonello's throne were mediocrities, that there was more pedantry than genuine scholarship, much writing of Latin verse and very little real poetry. Guarino and Aurispa are, perhaps, the only two that have left any real mark in the world of letters, though many, and notably Theodore Gaza, were instrumental in the spread of culture in Italy. Tito Vespasiano Strozzi stands alone as the one genuine poet of Leonello's circle, and his chief work belongs to a later epoch.

We must not, however, pass over in silence the name of Francesco di Princivalle Ariosti, called "Peregrinus," a figure of much interest to the student of his times.[3]

[1] Sabbadini, *op. cit.* p. 96.
[2] Segarizzi, *Michele Savonarola*, pp. 22, 67. It will be remembered that the "Studio" corresponded to our modern University, while the "Universities" were the associations of teachers and students in the different faculties.
[3] This Francesco Ariosti is not to be confused with another Francesco (di Rinaldo) Ariosti, the poet's uncle, who was *senescalco* to Duke Ercole.

DUKES AND POETS IN FERRAR

Francesco, then a very young man, composed a little dramatic idyl, the *Iside*, consisting of two Lat put into the mouths of the girl Iside and one of her r lovers. Iside has been converted from a mun(by the words of a sacred preacher, *divinus orator*, t herself henceforth to penitence and austerity. taught me to cover up my vain hair with veils, of will to put off the paint from my cheeks. Je\ gems adorned my brow; for jewels and gems the H(is given me." The representation was givei Leonello and his Court, the nobles of Ferrara anc gathering of people, and it may, perhaps, b(to speak highly for the moral tone of the Marches that this curious little play appears to have been a But the greater part of Francesco Ariosti's work that of Tito Vespasiano Strozzi, in the reign of L successors. A man of considerable scientific att: and singularly wide, if not particularly deep kn he was one of the principal personages of the Cou scientific treatises, devout brochures, Latin poe vivid descriptions of contemporary events, and evei high among the diplomatic agents of his sovereig

In foreign affairs Leonello continued the polic father. He successfully kept clear of the political and interminable wars of Italy, and throughout l reign the peace of Ferrara was not disturbed. and Latinist of Hungary, John of Csenicze (bette as Janus Pannonius), came, a mere boy, some t\

[1] Bertoni, *op. cit.* p. 178, *note*. He adds that the autho representation " fabulam veridicam." Some elegant had, perhaps, been converted in Ferrara by a popular Len of repentance.

thirteen years old, in the latter part of Leonello's reign to sit at the feet of Guarino, and in his chief poem, addressed to his master, the pacific city appears in a golden haze of ideal prosperity:—

> Pacis et aligeri Ferraria mater Amoris,
> Qua Padus in geminos iterum se dividit amnes,
> Luget et ambustum fratrem pia silva sororum.[1]

From his lofty watch-tower in the sky, Plato looks down upon the realization of his ideal, a wise State ruled by a philosopher King. Under Leonello's pacific and enlightened sway, to this one city has the golden age returned:—

> An non Saturni sunt illic secula patris,
> Bella ubi nulla fremunt, nisi quae descripta leguntur?
> Semper ubi laetas populo plaudente choreas,
> Intus festa sonant, et picta palatia surgunt,
> Arva foris gravido locupletat Copia cornu?
> Fortunati ambo, plebs praeside, plebe tyrannus.[2]

But all this, the poet continues by a pardonable and pious fiction, is the work of Guarino, whose influence had caused Leonello to be chosen prince instead of his warlike brothers and has induced him to rule in accordance with his precepts since:—

[1] "Ferrara, Mother of Peace and winged Love, where the Po into twin streams divides itself again, and the loving wood of sisters weep for their burned brother" (*Iani Pannonii, Silva Panegyrica*, 407–409). The reference is to the fable of Phaethon falling into the Po, when his wings were scorched in the sun, his sisters being changed to poplars, their tears converted into amber. Fine use of this is made by Carducci in his *Alla Città di Ferrara*.

[2] "Are not the times of father Saturn there, where no wars resound save those that are read of in books? where within is ever festal music, the crowds applauding the blithe dances, and painted palaces rise, and without Plenty enriches the fields with her loaded horn? Fortunate both, the people in its guardian, the sovereign in his people" (*ibid.* 425–430).

DUKES AND POETS IN FERRARA

Ambobus sed tu tantorum causa bonorum !
Per te, Mars alias lituis dum perstrepit oras,
Sola vacat citharis Ferraria, sola triumphat,
Principibus foecunda piis, foecunda disertis
Civibus, et pariter cunctis habitata Camenis. [1]

Unlike any other sovereign of his House, he
troubled by rival pretenders at home. The Ma
Ricciarda had retired to Saluzzo shortly after his a
and in 1445 Leonello and Borso sent her two sons
and Sigismondo, to the Court of Alfonso of Naple
brought up with Prince Ferrante at a safe distan
Ferrara. Leonello's first wife, Margherita Gon
whom he had been married in 1435, was a meet co
for her husband, a learned princess trained in the N
school of Vittorino da Feltre; she died before his a
leaving him one son, Niccolò, who was born in 14
1444, Leonello took another wife, Maria d'Aragona,
daughter to the King of Naples; Borso and M
brought her in triumph to Ferrara at the beginning
She died childless in December, 1449.

This Aragonese alliance produced a remarka
velopment of the Estensian diplomacy. Bor
carefully studied the condition of the Kingdom un
newly established Aragonese dynasty, and devised a
for the general pacification of Italy under one he
October he returned to Naples, invited by the Ki
stayed there until the end of April, 1445. In the
of Leonello and himself, speaking throughout fo

[1] "But to both art thou the cause of so great good
Through thee, while Mars makes other regions ring with t
Ferrara alone is free for lutes, triumphs alone, fruitful in 1
princes, fruitful in eloquent citizens, and at once the dwelli
of all the Muses" (*ibid.* 431, 438–441). See the whole
addressed to Guarino, lines 401–441.

lord my brother and myself," he warned Alfonso that he was bitterly hated by his new subjects, urged him to gain their love, to arrange his expenses and husband his resources, to make peace with all the Italian potentates, and especially to gain over the Pope, Eugenius IV. Borso had visited the latter at Rome on his way, and had found him in a conciliatory disposition towards the King. Duke Filippo Maria of Milan is slowly dying; the House of the Visconti in Lombardy is " hated like the Devil "; Francesco Sforza and the Venetians are preparing to seize upon his heritage. Let his Majesty prepare to make himself master of Lombardy on the Duke's death. "By means of the House of Este," said Borso, "which is loved in Lombardy like God, your Majesty will most easily enter into this state and lordship of the Duke; you will obtain it and enjoy it pacifically and with the greatest pleasure. And when you have this, your Majesty can say that you have the better part of Italy, for it is that. And there is no doubt at all that your Majesty will be King of Italy."[1]

The King proved apt, and Borso returned to Ferrara with a document empowering Leonello to arrange matters in Alfonso's name with the dying Duke. Nor did Filippo Maria evince any reluctance to the royal design; to Jacopo della Torre, Bishop of Modena, who came to him from the King, and to Luigi Mainero, Leonello's agent, in the spring of 1447, he professed himself most desirous of summoning Alfonso to Milan for the protection of his person and his states. But events moved too rapidly.

In the early summer of 1447, at the instance of Pope

[1] See the extraordinary document published by Cesare Foucard, *Proposta fatta dalla Corte Estense ad Alfonso I Re di Napoli*, pp. 708-741.

DUKES AND POETS IN FERRAR.

Nicholas V, who had succeeded to Eugenius, a
was held at Ferrara to arrange peace between ⟩
Venice. The ambassadors of the chief Italian St
under the presidency of the Cardinal of Burgu⟨
represented the Pope. The congress broke up
on the news of the death of Duke Filippo ⟩
August 12. The attempt of the Aragonese facti
occupied the Castello of Milan, to declare for
proved abortive, and the next day the Ambrosian ⟩
of Milan was proclaimed.

Pier Candido Decembrio (the elder brother of
Camillo), who had been one of the two Milanese or⟨
the congress, now entered into the service of the R⟨
and wrote the life of the late Duke, taking as his
the life of Tiberius by Suetonius. Filippo Maria ha
in August, but in October Decembrio had complet⟨
work and sent it to Leonello, as to a kind of literary di⟨
to ask his opinion of it, before publishing it. The M
professed himself much delighted with the book and fla⟨
at it having been left with him in this way, but st⟨
advised the author, seeing that his writings wou⟨
immortal, either to strike out or to veil what he hac⟨
concerning a secret vice of the Duke's. Decembrio ⟨
back that he had not mentioned this vice to bring in⟨
to his late Prince, but rather praise and glory, s⟨
that his not passing it over in silence would make p⟨
lend faith to what he reported in his favour. Neverthe⟨
he altered the passage in deference to Leonello's opi⟨
and the alteration was much commended by the lat⟨
In the general though, as it proved, temporary dissolu⟨

[1] Rosmini, *op. cit.* i, pp. 109, 110; Borsa, *Pier Candido Decen*
pp. 83, 84.

of the dominions of the Visconti, Parma—finding itself hard pressed by Alessandro Sforza, the brother of the Count Francesco—offered to return to the House of Este. But Leonello, finding Venice opposed to any annexation of this kind on his part, declined to accept it, and Parma fell into the hands of the Sforza. The Milanese Republicans somewhat resented Leonello's action, and he wrote to Decembrio on the subject, who assured him that the love of his fellow-citizens for him remained always the same.[1] This was in the spring of 1449, but before the end of the year the short-lived Ambrosian Republic was at an end, and in March, 1450, Francesco Sforza, the great condottiere, was proclaimed Duke of Milan.

On July 2 of this same year, 1450, by the intervention of Leonello and Borso, a new peace between the King of Naples and the Republic of Venice was celebrated in the Palace of Belfiore. The bringing about of this peace was Leonello's last political action.

Such then was the Marchese Leonello, as handed down to us by his contemporaries and admirers. Very probably, the smoke of so much literary incense has somewhat obscured the features of the real man, and it may possibly be, as Voigt suggests, that what by a courtly fiction passed for his own learning and his own insight was in reality Guarino's. When the courtly old humanist assures us that the Marquis placed no guards round his palace, but relied upon the love of his people, it may be a mere figure of speech; but it represents to some extent the real state of things. It is abundantly clear that he was an enlightened and popular sovereign. That he was not reputed equal to

[1] Borsa, *op. cit.* p. 84.

his father in liberality, as Enea Silvio Picc
may not be altogether to his discredit.
gitimate son, Francesco, who was older tha
in the year of his father's second marriage
under the Duke of Burgundy; but the swee
immorality brought against him rest or
authority.² Probably the Ferrarese dia
very much overstate his case: "He was a lo
of most honest life, a lover of piety, most c
divine religion, a lover of the poor, liberal
a studious hearer of the Holy Scriptures, pat
sities, moderate in prosperity. He ruled b
peace with great wisdom." ³

[1] *De Viris Illustribus*, p. 16.
[2] Giraldi, *Commentario delle cose di Ferrara*, p. 92
fini's statement about his contaminating Braccio's
zovene bona e bella" (*Cronaca di Casa d'Este*, p. 287).
sensuality are directly contradicted by Enea Silvio, *D
bus*, p. 16, and I know of no contemporary author
accusations of tyranny and cruelty (i. p. 563).
[3] *Diario Ferrarese*, col. 197.

Chapter III

THE DUKE OF MODENA

THE reigns of these two noble brothers, Leonello and Borso, the sons of Niccolò and Stella, were an age of gold for Ferrara. There was something in their character, derived perhaps from their beautiful Sienese mother, that differentiated them from their predecessors and successors of the House of Este; more blithe and genial than their kinsmen, the darker shadows in the history of Ferrara hardly appear during their reigns; conspiracies are few, and, even when they are brought to light, the repression that follows, the inevitable butchery, has not that peculiar horror and atrocity that we have noted under Alberto and shall find again when Alfonso is on the throne. No sovereigns of the fifteenth century shed so little blood as did these two. Messer Lodovico has fitly coupled them together in a much quoted stanza:—

> Vedi Leonello, e vedi il primo Duce,
> Fama de la sua età, l'inclito Borso,
> Che siede in pace, e più trionfo adduce
> Di quanti in altrui terre abbino corso.
> Chiuderà Marte ove non veggia luce,
> E stringerà al Furor le mani al dorso.
> Di questo Signor splendido ogni intento
> Sarà, che 'l popolo suo viva contento.[1]

---
[1] *Orlando Furioso*, iii. 45. "Behold Leonello; and behold the first Duke, the glory of his age, renowned Borso, who sits in peace and

DUKES AND POETS IN FE[

On October 1, 1450, Leonello died in [
riguardo. With his last breath he recom
Niccolò, then a boy at twelve years old, to [
him to secure the succession to him on his
in the meanwhile to act as father to the lad.

Michele Savonarola has left us a curiou[
Ferrarese magnates—the senate, as he calls
—gathered together in the Palazzo della R
great piazza, to elect a new sovereign a[
discuss the ideal form of government. One
government of a single man is best; a secon[
prefer an oligarchy; a third adheres to t[
propounded, provided that they get a true [
tyrant, one that will not spurn the counsels
run after his own appetite. A fourth [
the question: Is it better to have a prince
by succession? Their late prince Niccolò
sons worthy of the sovereignty, and they [
him that they are morally bound to choos[
The glorious government of Leonello has s[
Republic will be better ruled by one of his b[
any other, and, by choosing thus, both the
sion and the elective principle will be per[
Then a renowned doctor of arts and medi[
the qualities of an ideal prince, at very c[
pedantic length. A sixth speaker finds the[
and formally proposes him. A seventh s[
the motion, which is carried with acclamati[
of "Borso! Borso!" which are clamorou[

gains more triumph than all who have invaded th[
He will imprison Mars from the light of day and
hands behind her back. Of this splendid Lord e[
be that his people may live happy."

THE DUKE OF MODENA

the crowd in the piazza below. A deputation promptly goes to Belriguardo to inform Borso of his election.[1]

Thus, apparently, did the grandfather of Fra Girolamo idealize the first meeting of the Council of the Twelve Sages after Leonello's death.[2] If there was any pretence of an election, it was a mere empty form, and the people dutifully acclaimed what was already an accomplished fact. Borso entered into his brother's heritage with some show of reluctance, real or assumed; but he took care that Ercole and Sigismondo, who were still away at Naples, should not be informed of Leonello's illness until his own accession was ensured. The Marchese Lodovico Gonzaga of Mantua, Leonello's brother-in-law, had hurried to Ferrara to see if he could do anything for his young nephew Niccolò, only to find Borso's position unassailable. Still both Ercole and Niccolò had adherents in the city—known as Diamanteschi and Veleschi, respectively, from the diamond and the sail that were the crests of the rival pretenders—and a conspiracy of the Veleschi was discovered, in the following year, in consequence of which one of the Trotti and Niccolò Casari perished on the scaffold.

[1] *De felici progressu illustrissimi Borsii Estensis ad marchionatum Ferrariae, Mutinae et Regii ducatum, comitatumque Rodigii* (Biblioteca Estense, Cod. Savonarola, pp. Lat. 215). Quoted in part by Segarizzi, *Michele* 37-40.
[2] The seven speakers at the meeting are: Franciscus Mauri, Petrus Ceri, Paulus Bondenus, Nicolaus Agrippa (so at least in the codex at Modena; Segarizzi has Niccolò da Ripa), Magister Nigrisolus, Antonius Gaius, and Cato Senior. The Nigrisoli and Cato were well-known Ferrarese families. Fra Giovanni states that Agostino Valla, who was judge of the twelve Sages, called a meeting and proposed the election of Borso (*Annales*, col. 461); and from the fact that this "Augustinus Valla Pater Patriae (vel, ut nostro more loquar, Sapientum Censor)," who undoubtedly played the chief part on this occasion, is not mentioned, we may suspect that Savonarola's account is a mere literary exercise.

DUKES AND POETS IN FERRARA

Pope Nicholas V promptly renewed the investiture of the vicariate of Ferrara to Borso and to his heirs, under a considerably reduced annual tribute.

Borso raised Ferrara to its height of fame and glory. Under his rule the State assumed the aspect, acquired the peculiar characteristics that are reflected in the romance of Boiardo, the epic of Ariosto. In his fourth Latin eclogue the former poet dates the beginning of a glorious age of earthly blessedness from his accession, in words not remotely suggested by the famous fourth Virgilian eclogue, and, in another poem of the same pastoral collection, he hails his pacific rule in lines of glowing fervour:—

> Salve, Estense decus, terrarum gloria, Borsi;
> Quo duce, sideribus terras Astrea relictis
> Incolit, et prisci rursum, quo principe, mores
> Aureaque aeterni redierunt otia veris.
> Salve, Estense decus, sub quo fulgentia Martis
> Agmina et horrendo nescimus classica cantu![1]

With Borso, a new epoch begins for the House of Este. Hitherto, although usually styled "Marchese di Ferrara," the prince was, strictly speaking, only titular Marquis of Este, vicar *in temporalibus* of the Church in Ferrara, feudatory of the Empire in Modena, Reggio and Rovigo. But from 1452 dates the Duchy of Modena, which was destined to survive even the French Revolution, only to be absorbed in the new Italy of the Risorgimento.

At the beginning of 1452, Frederick of Hapsburg, King of the Romans, came to Italy for his imperial coronation,

---

[1] "Hail, honour of Este, glory of the world, Borso; under whose sway Astraea has left the stars to dwell on earth; with whom as prince, the manners of the olden time and the golden ease of eternal spring have returned. Hail, honour of Este, under whom we know not the flashing ranks of Mars, and the fearful music of the battle-trumpets!" (*Pastoralia*, vi. 65–70).

THE DUKE OF MODENA

with his brother, Duke Albert of Austria, his nephew, King Ladislaus of Hungary and Bohemia, and a train of some twelve hundred horsemen. At the passage of the Adige he found Borso waiting for him, with a number of the minor potentates of central Italy and a goodly company of Ferrarese nobles. Borso presented the monarch with a royal gift of horses and falcons, and brought him from Rovigo over a long bridge of ships to Ferrara, where for ten days he kept him and his train in a succession of festivities and sumptuous entertainments, extorting a sort of promise from him that he would consider the matter of the duchy on his return. The fact was that the Germans had not yet acquired the easy morality of Italy, and the Caesar elect had some scruples about thus elevating a bastard to the rank of a Duke of the Empire.

These scruples, however, were banished by Borso's winning personality, his universal popularity and the favour he enjoyed with the Court of Rome; and, when Frederick returned from his coronation in May, he formally raised the imperial fiefs of Modena and Reggio into a duchy. On Ascension Day, 1452, after High Mass in the Duomo, the Emperor vested himself in full imperial robes, with the crown of the Holy Roman Empire upon his head, and, surrounded by his nobles and attended by the ambassadors of the Italian powers, solemnly enthroned himself on a great platform erected in the piazza. So great was the crowd, that covered not only the square, but all the front of the Cathedral, the episcopal palace and the Palazzo della Ragione, that, Michele Savonarola assures us, nothing save human beings could be seen. "Frederick, as he gazed upon the people in their numbers, was astounded, and considering the richness of the attire of their nobles, he turned to his followers and said : ' Verily this is a city worthy of the Empire.' The other Germans too, in the tribunes away from him, were so amazed at the multitude of men, at the precious dresses of gold and silk, that they said to each other that all Germany itself did not contain so many rich robes. And they wondered at the beauty and goodliness of the men and women, which showed them that those who blamed the air of Ferrara were in the wrong." [1] A sudden burst of music, a mingling of martial trumpets with the softer strains of flutes, followed by thundering plaudits of "Borso! Borso!" and "Duca! Duca!" announced the advent of the hero of the day.

Preceded by four hundred nobles on horseback, bearing white, red and green banners, Borso rode out of the Castello Vecchio; he was dressed in red silk and cloth of gold, covered with gems, with a pointed cap equally gorgeous and round his neck a collar of jewels valued at a fabulous sum in golden ducats. The acclamations rose higher and higher as he entered the piazza. The nobles, still mounted, formed a semicircle, out of which Borso advanced alone, dismounted, ascended the platform and knelt at Caesar's feet. There he was solemnly proclaimed Duke of Modena and Reggio, Count of Rovigo; the ducal robe of crimson and ermine was placed over his shoulders; the standards of the three imperial cities and of justice, the naked sword and the golden sceptre were put into his hands. Then Borso took his seat among the princes of the Empire, next to the Duke of Austria, while the Emperor conferred the order of knighthood upon certain noble Ferrarese and

---

[1] *De felici progressu*, etc., quoted by Segarizzi, *op. cit.* pp. 73, 74. The reader will not fail to notice the professional touch in Michele's last words.

THE DUKE OF MODENA

others, including the little Niccolò da Correggio, a mere child, the Duke's nephew, and young Galeotto della Mirandola. At Caesar's special command, Monsignor Enea Silvio Piccolomini, then Bishop of Siena, delivered an address in Italian, so that the people too might understand, "in praise of the Estensi, and about the new dignity and the supreme merits of Borso," as he tells us. At the end, the Emperor rose from his throne; at once the Bishop of Ferrara and his clergy, who were present in full pontificals, intoned the *Te Deum Laudamus*, in which the whole assemblage joined, and led the procession to the Duomo, bearing the relics of St. George and St. Maurelius, the patron saints and protectors of Ferrara. Before the high altar, the newly made Duke took the oath of fidelity to the Emperor, and presented him with a rich collar or necklace adorned with jewels, which had belonged to his father and which was valued at 40,000 ducats—the whole ceremony terminating with the benediction of the Bishop of the city. "All the ambassadors who were present," writes Enea Silvio, " commended what Caesar had done, and all Italy said that it was a benefit well placed."[1]

As soon as he had dispatched the Caesar upon his homeward journey to Austria, Borso made a triumphal progress through his two newly created duchies, with the leading nobles of Ferrara and a thousand horsemen in his train. He had a sumptuous and showy reception, such as his heart loved. In each town through which he passed the inhabitants poured out to meet him with songs and flowers.

[1] *Historia Friderici Imperatoris*, pp. 94, 95 ; Frizzi, iv. pp. 20–23; *Diario Ferrarese*, coll. 198–200; Johannes Ferrariensis, coll. 463–466.

DUKES AND POETS IN FERRARA

At Modena, triumphal chariots met him at the gate of the city, with St. Geminianus surrounded by angels in one and in another the four Cardinal Virtues " adorned to the likeness of Venus " ; the streets along which he rode were carpeted with rich cloths, while scattered before him were perfumes and flowers of every kind, from which a sweet and mingled odour rose, as in Dante's Valley of the Princes. Here he stayed twelve days, in a succession of feasts and sports, and met his half-brother Ercole, who had come unexpectedly from Naples to congratulate him.

Fired by the example of their neighbour and rival, the good people of Reggio, clergy and laity alike, rose to the occasion, and gave their first Duke a greeting to be ranked (says our Fra Giovanni) " among the most rare and most lovely spectacles." When Borso, accompanied by young Ercole, approached the walls, the governor of the city came out to meet him with all the garrison in battle array, with the nobles of the district on horseback bearing branches of olive in their hands, and the multitude shouting " Duca ! Duca ! " Thousands of children were waiting for him at the gate, crowned with flowers, waving olive branches and little flags with the ducal arms, raising shrill cheers, as Borso and Ercole, preceded by Feltrino Boiardo bearing the sword of Reggio, drew near. There was a halt at the gate. A great chariot appeared, elaborately designed, upon which San Prospero, the chief patron of the city, seemed to float in air surrounded by angels, while below him was a kind of revolving wheel in which were eight other angels with musical instruments, singing Borso's praises. One of the angels turned to the Saint, courteously bade him surrender the keys of the city and the royal

THE DUKE OF MODENA

sceptre which he held, and then, with an elegant oration, solemnly delivered them to the Duke. Then came another triumphal chariot, of most gorgeous aspect, drawn by concealed horses and bearing an empty royal throne. Behind it stood Justice, with the sword and scales, attended by a beautiful boy. Angels held the canopy over her head; Regulus, Cato, Numa, and Cincinnatus sat at the corners of the chariot with angels bearing the ducal standards, while armed youths rode on either side. Admonished by Justice's attendant genius, Borso listened to the discourses of these Roman elders and edified all beholders by his attentive bearing, while they assured him that he surpassed Caesar in clemency, Octavianus in prudence, Trajan in justice, Titus in liberality, Cato in gravity, Scaevola in magnitude of soul, Antoninus in piety, and either equalled or outstripped every other famous personage in his own special virtue. Next came a car in the form of a trireme, which seemed to be rowed by ten Saracens, but was in reality drawn by concealed men. A fourth chariot was drawn by artificial unicorns, Borso's own chosen device, and bore a palm-tree, among the branches of which sat Charity with her flaming torch.

To the ringing of bells, the sound of trumpets, the music of pipes and flutes, the whole procession moved on to the church of San Pietro, where the Prince of the Apostles himself in a glory, with two angels, descended from the west front and placed a laurel crown upon Borso's head, who received it with all reverence. On two lofty pillars, set opposite each other, were Idolatry, a lay figure, and Faith, a beautiful girl who uttered a devout exhortation, at the sound of which the rival pillar fell down and was shattered to pieces. As the procession swept on towards the chief piazza, Caesar appeared with seven nymphs, representing the seven Virtues, and Borso was exhorted to pursue them. The Duke dismounted and entered the Duomo, "even as a spouse is brought to her husband" (so our good Minorite puts it). After praying for some while before the altar, he seated himself upon a throne in front of the church, and the pageant paraded before him again. Charity hailed him as the "Mirror of Christians," the "Only Delight of wretched mortals," the "Worthy Rose of the World." San Prospero offered up devout prayers to heaven for his preservation. From the top of the Palazzo del Capitano, three angels flew down and "with most sweet harmony" gave Borso a palm in sign of peace.[1]

Peace, indeed, was to be the prevailing note of Borso's government. Curiously unlike his father and brother in many other respects, he was bent upon continuing their foreign policy, of keeping Ferrara free from war and making it a common meeting-ground, as it were, for the representatives of all the Italian powers to arrange the peace of the peninsula.

A few years later, in May, 1459, Enea Silvio came again to Ferrara, but now as Pope Pius II, on his way to Mantua in that vain but heroic attempt to unite the powers of Christendom against the Turks, who, as he put it, had "taken the royal city of Constantine, slain his namesake,

[1] These pageants, which were devised by Malatesta Ariosti, are described in full by Johannes Ferrariensis, coll. 466–472. (I have not been able to consult Adolfo Levi's publication, referred to in the *Giornale Storico della Letteratura Italiana,* xxxv.) Borso was delighted at the entertainment provided for him, and testified his satisfaction by remitting, entirely or in part, a number of unpopular taxes which the citizens of Reggio had paid to the ducal chancery.

THE DUKE OF MODENA

butchered his people, profaned the temples of the high God, and defiled Santa Sophia, the noble work of Justinian, with the foul rite of Mahomet."[1] Borso expected great things from this visit; on the elevation of the Cardinal of Siena to the Pontificate, he had held public rejoicings, exulted in his kinship with the Holy Father (who acknowledged himself related to the Tolomei, the family of Borso's mother), and given thanks to God that a Pope had been elected from whom there was nothing that he could not obtain. " Nor would he have been wrong in so thinking," writes Pius, "if he had asked for things more fit for us to grant."[2]

The Duke himself rode out to meet the Pontiff, with the Lords of Forli, Cesena, Rimini, Mirandola, Correggio and Carpi, with young Niccolò di Leonello and seven bastards of the House with their attendants.[3] The streets were strewn with flowers and covered with cloths, everything rang with music and the air trembled with bells, as, in advance of the papal procession, there came, surrounded with men carrying lighted torches, a spotless white horse, upon which was the Blessed Sacrament, "the Body of Our Lord Messer Jesus Christ," Pius himself following, robed in white and with a mitre upon his head. At the Porta di San Pietro, Borso dismounted, knelt and kissed the Pope's foot, offering up to him the keys of the city.

[1] Address to the Congress at Mantua. *Opera*, p. 907.
[2] *Commentarii*, ii. p. 102.
[3] Alberto, Gurone, Rinaldo, half-brothers of the Duke; Francesco, bastard of Leonello; Niccolò, Scipione, Polidoro, bastards of Meliaduse (who had been dispensed from his ecclesiastical orders and died in 1452). Niccolò di Leonello was that rare creature an Estense born in lawful wedlock—a thing so unnatural that even Burkhardt (English translation, pp. 21, 46) and Mrs. Ady (*Beatrice d'Este*, p. 5) seem unable to realize it.

DUKES AND POETS IN FERRARA

During the eight days that Pius stayed in Ferrara, the festivities were for the most part of a religious nature; on the feast of the Corpus Domini, the Pope granted a plenary indulgence and himself carried the Blessed Sacrament in the procession. Borso was persistent in his demands. He wanted the Pope to make him Duke of Ferrara and to remit the tribute, which meant to surrender all the rights that the Church claimed in the city. Pius answered that he could not deprive the Roman Church of her tribute, but offered him the duchy with the retention of the tribute—which Borso refused. "Nevertheless he obtained other concessions of great weight, and hoped to receive greater in the future." [1] On the Pope's departure, Borso gave him "a sideboard all of silver, most worthy, which was deemed of the value of 8,000 ducats, which his Holiness accepted and then gave back to the Duke, saying that God knew to whom it would remain after his death." [2]

At the Congress at Mantua, Borso's orators, " in order," says the Pope, "that they might seem to be doing more than the rest," promised in the Duke's name the huge sum of 300,000 gold ducats for the expedition against the Turks, "not without admiration of the hearers." [3] But, on his return from the Congress in January, the Pope would not stop at Ferrara for more than one night. Borso met him on the Po near Rovigo in a Bucentaur, surrounded by a whole flotilla of gaily adorned smaller boats, with music and pageants all along the shore as they moved, so that

---

[1] *Commentarii*, ii. pp. 102, 103.
[2] *Storia di Ferrara* (apparently by Ugo Caleffini), MS. in the Biblioteca Nazionale of Florence, xxv. 8. 539, f. 40.
[3] *Commentarii*, iii. p. 169.

it made " a wondrous sight," as Pius has it. On the ship Borso signed the decree regarding the levying of tithes for the Crusade; but, in the following March, he refused to let them be collected.[1] In fact, this papal visit to Ferrara had left both parties in a bad humour with each other, and strained a friendship of fifteen years' standing. Although Borso presently furnished two (apparently Venetian) ships and a few men to the great undertaking, he was bitterly disappointed in Pius, while Pius, no less incensed against Borso, went so far as to threaten him with excommunication.[2]

Pius has left us a portrait of Borso as he first saw him in the days of Leonello, when as Enea Silvio, the imperial secretary (fresh from that interview with Pope Eugenius IV, which Pintoricchio has recorded in the fourth fresco in the Library of the Duomo at Siena), he passed through Ferrara in 1445 on his way back to the King of the Romans. "The Ferrarese," he says, "worship him almost as God. He is more handsome than words can tell, facetious and modest, distinguished for his liberality, robust in his body and without any blemish."[3] This extraordinary beauty passed off with his early manhood, and in later life he grew stout and coarsened considerably in appearance; but to the almost divine honours, apparently proceeding from sincere admiration, paid him by his courtiers and people, all the chroniclers bear ample witness. Bluff and hearty in his manners, genial and good-natured, he loved magnificent pomp and display, all things that were bright and splendid, and was passionately addicted to hunting and

[1] *Commentarii*, iv. pp. 172, 173; Pastor, ii. document 39.
[2] Pastor, ii. p. 169.
[3] *De Viris Illustribus*, p. 17.

DUKES AND POETS IN FERRARA

field-sports of all kinds. He would ride through the streets of Ferrara in gorgeous robes, covered with the costliest jewels, dazzling the eyes of all beholders. … was there a Lord who gave so much audience [?] as he did every day. He always seemed laughing, never let any one leave him discontented."[1] His generosity and liberality were more than imperial, and became proverbial in Italy: "Whoso would find Heaven open, let him experience the liberality of Duke Borso."[2] His benefactions to the Church were most lavish, and the Carthusian monastery of San Cristoforo, that he built, recalls his name even to this day. "The Signor has made it so magnificent," writes Caleffini, "that it would do for the Pope." Not only towards his courtiers and favourites—such men as Michele Savonarola, Girolamo Castelli (Savonarola's successor as chief physician of the Court), Lodovico Casella, his privy counsellor whom he called his "right eye," Teofilo Calcagnino, his handsome young companion—was he prodigal in gifts of land and palaces; but even his barber Pietro, his jester Scocola, that "nobile, facetissimo e soavissimo buffone," and the peasant woman who offered him mushrooms when out hunting, did not go without ample rewards. "Never," wrote the buffone, "has his Excellence left his poor Scocola in the

---

[1] Ugo Caleffini, *Croniche del Duca Ercole*, f. 9; *Storia di Ferrara*, f. 56v. I may here state that, when referring to Caleffini, by *Croniche del Duca Ercole* I mean the Costabili manuscript (Brit. Museum, Add. MS. 22, 324), while *Storia di Ferrara* is the codex of the National Library at Florence, and *Cronaca di Casa d'Este* the rhymed chronicle printed by Cappelli.

[2] Luzio and Renier, *Niccolò da Correggio*, i. p. 208. Cf. the long list of Borso's donations in Ugo Caleffini, *Cronaca di Casa d'Este*, pp. 293-301.

THE DUKE OF MODENA

lurch in any of his necessities."[1] The fame of Borso's magnificent proceedings and of his phenomenal lavishness passed even the bounds of Europe; eastern potentates sent embassies and offerings to him, under the impression that he was the sovereign of all Italy.

It is manifest that this magnificence bordered on prodigality, and the ducal benefactions were too frequently bestowed upon unworthy recipients. A number of corrupt and avaricious officials simply preyed upon the people, and remained as an evil legacy to Borso's successor. Even in Borso's lifetime, Michele Savonarola satirized the manners of the Court in his *De Nuptiis Battibecco et Serrabocca*, stating plainly that "the giving of robes, horses, possessions and money to buffoons and unworthy men, diminishes the love of the people."[2] The Duke coupled his lavishness in rewarding with an unbending severity in punishing, using the latter as a means to the former. The goods of aristocratic offenders—such as that Uguccione dalla Badia, one of the ducal secretaries, who in 1460, for not having revealed a conspiracy which he did not take seriously, "was accompanied by the Duke himself into Castel Vecchio to end his life"—were confiscated and given to the favourites and agents, whereby "many from servants have become gentlemen." As to minor offenders, he never once showed mercy to a thief throughout his reign.[3]

The Duke was an able administrator and, with all this external magnificence, knew how to keep his lavishness

[1] See Bertoni, *Buffoni alla Corte di Ferrara*, in the *Rivista d'Italia*, vi. fasc. iii.-iv.
[2] See Cappelli, *Fra Girolamo Savonarola*, p. 305, where an account of this curious work is given.
[3] Ugo Caleffini, *Cronaca di Casa d'Este*, p. 293; *Storia di Ferrara*, f. 56.

within bounds. Richer than his predecessors and successor, he nevertheless had recourse to strange financial methods. Not unfrequently, professors of the Studio, painters to the Court, and other creditors, were not paid in money, but by the cession to them of debts due to the ducal treasury. Throughout the duchy heavy fines were extorted for the infringement of all kinds of petty regulations, and the officials were instructed to "suck all the juice" they could get out of the ducal subjects. Blasphemy was a penal offence and a great source of income to the ducal coffers — a man being even fined for saying "God Himself could not do this." In these cases, two-thirds went to the State and a third to the informer. One result of this was that spying became a most lucrative calling in Ferrara.[1]

Nevertheless, Borso kept his popularity to the last; in many respects he was open and simple-hearted as a child, an "anima innocente," his successor called him in after years. In the midst of the moral corruption of his age, surrounded by the bastard kindred of his House, he remained sincerely and devoutly religious; almost alone among the princes of the Renaissance, his private life appears to have been pure and blameless, beyond the reach of calumny.

Leonello, with the aid of the elder Guarino, had imbued Ferrara with the humanistic spirit of the Classical Revival. Borso was devoid of all scholarship; but he continued Leonello's generous patronage to scholars and men of letters, rewarding with a lavish hand the dedications that they presented to him, and added what was needed to prepare the soil to produce the splendid flower of the Italian Romantic Epic. His very lack of scholarship stimulated vernacular

[1] Cf. A. Venturi, *L'Arte a Ferrara nel periodo di Borso*, pp. 696, 697.

literature in his circle. The Duke knew no Latin, and his wealthy favourite, Teofilo Calcagnino, shared his ignorance, the result being that those men of letters who sought their patronage were compelled to adopt the *sermone moderno*, the vulgar tongue.

"I had determined," wrote Carlo da San Giorgio to Borso, after the conspiracy of the Pio of Carpi, "for the defence of thy glorious name, as also for the information of those that come after us, to write in Latin concerning the treason that was lately plotted against thee. But Fortune, the foe of every virtuous man, hath not vouchsafed to add to thy other singular ornaments the ornament of letters, the which is the most excellent that man can have. To prove this, infinite reasons could be alleged, inasmuch as thou canst not appreciate the worth and the power of literature; but, since there is no remedy for it, we will bear it, as God wills, in peace. When I had presented my little book to thee, I was harshly and furiously abused by my magnificent and dearest gossip, Messer Teofilo, and as it were calumniated, as though I had committed an enormous error in writing such a business in Latin and not in our vulgar speech. I pardon him, seeing that also he is one of those who know not letters, which, among his other excellent virtues, would shine out like precious stones. And, wishing to do something that should please you all—thee, my dear and only Lord, and the others thy brothers and companions—as is my desire and duty, in order that thou mayest get some pleasure by reading in the vulgar tongue what thou couldst not otherwise taste by reason of thy lack of letters, I have rendered this little work of mine into the vernacular, albeit there is as much difference in sweetness and suavity between one language and the other, as there is between a sweet and delicate wine and another, rough and unpleasant, that one is compelled by thirst to drink." [1]

This writing down to poor Borso's level is delightful ; but other translators took a different tone. " Right humbly do I pray and beseech thee, my dear Lord," writes Polismagna to the Duke, in a letter accompanying his version of Pier Candido Decembrio's *Laudi della Città di Milano*, "that thou mayest deign, with thy wonted mansuetude, to excuse my ignorance with those who shall blame me, and especially concerning the words used in this translation. I know that thou art Ferrarese ; I, too, am Ferrarese ; and Ferrara, renowned city of Italy, has produced us, reared us, and brought us to our present estate ; and, therefore, I could not manage the language save in the Ferrarese idiom, the which, in my opinion, has not less elegance than any other Italian speech. So if thou art pleased, I think that every man will be satisfied." [2]

The language in question is, however, something quite distinct from the local dialect of Ferrara. It is a variety of the Lombard type of vernacular, a blending, we may say, of Dante's courtly ideal Italian with many words and forms of the Ferrarese and other Emilian or Lombard dialects ; with various local modifications, it is the language used by the literary circles and by the Courts of Mantua and the other petty states of Northern Italy. Its highest flight is

[1] Dedicatory letter prefixed to *La Congiura dei Pio contro Borso d'Este*, edited by A. Cappelli, pp. 377, 378. *Letters* is here used as the technical term for *Latin*.

[2] Bertoni, *La Biblioteca Estense*, p. 123. Against Cappelli and Venturi, Bertoni shows that this Polismagna, a Ferrarese, who appears to have been also a miniaturist, is not to be identified with Carlo da San Giorgio, who was one of Borso's chamberlains and by origin a Bolognese (*op. cit.*, p. 55, note 1). Polis magna also translated Decembrio's life of Filippo Maria Visconti.

found a quarter of a century later in the romantic poem of Boiardo.[1] Polismagna is only one of a number of similar translators seeking Borso's patronage; many men of letters in like manner presented him with translations of their own Latin books, or of those of their contemporaries, or of the classical authors; some—but comparatively few—composed original poems in Italian for his acceptance.[2] Thus "the succession of Borso to Leonello was providential, inasmuch as the former succeeded in tempering the influence of humanism by promoting and protecting vernacular literature; and so, while the classicism planted by Leonello remained and continued to flourish, the *sermone moderno* was also cultivated, to correspond with Borso's personal desires."[3]

And, together with this development and cultivation of the vernacular, a special taste and fashion for the romances of chivalry, alike in the French originals and in Italian translations, spread through the Ferrarese Court; the romances of the Carolingian cycle, or *materia di Francia*, the romances of the Arthurian cycle, or *materia di Brettagna*, which Dante had styled "the most beauteous fables of King Arthur" and Pier Candido Decembrio stigmatised as "incredible French lies."

This had begun, as we have seen, in the days of the Marchese Niccolò III; the ladies of Leonello's Court were in the habit of embroidering in gold upon their sleeves an amorous motto culled from some chivalrous French story;

[1] Bertoni, *op. cit.*, pp. 123-125.
[2] The curious anonymous capitoli in *terza rima* in the Vatican Library (Cod. Capponiano, 219) and the decidedly interesting canzone by Filippo Nuvolone, addressed to Borso at the end of a volume of erotic verse, as to one insensible to the darts of love (British Museum, Add. MS., 22, 335), are good examples. I have given some account of these, with extracts, in Appendix I.
[3] Venturi, *op. cit.*, p. 690.

but in the days of Borso it became a perfect passion. The romances, which the ducal library already possessed in good store, were perpetually being borrowed, in great request among the courtiers and ladies—those of the Arthurian cycle being especially favoured. In the winter evenings, in the warmed and brilliantly lighted halls of the gay Corte Vecchia, or during the long summer afternoons in the gardens of Belfiore or Belriguardo, to the sound of the splashing water of the marble fountains and the music of the birds among the laurels and myrtles, the princesses and their cavaliers lingered over the loves of Lancelot and Tristram, followed Merlin to his living tomb, or even at times—a touch of mysticism being inherent in the Ferrarese character—strove to ascend to the suprasensible heights attained by those who achieved the quest of the Holy Graal.[1] Borso himself loved these books. He had Italian versions of the *Merlin* and *Lancelot* richly illuminated, and we find him in 1460, while in his villeggiatura, sending to the library for a *Lancelot* in French with which to correct one in Italian.[2] Thus was the ground in Ferrara prepared for the romance of Boiardo, the epic of Ariosto.

Not that the classical studies promoted by Leonello were neglected. Little though Borso personally cared for such things, he fully realized that to promote culture of every kind tended to the glory of the sovereign. A more thorough organiser of the finances and richer than Leonello, he could afford to be no less generous than he to the University. The elder Guarino still remained, as high in honour and favour as ever, until his death at the ripe age of ninety, in

[1] Cf. Bertoni, *op. cit.*, cap. iv. ; Venturi, *op. cit.*, pp. 692, 693 ; Pio Rajna, *Le Fonti dell' Orlando Furioso*, Introduction.
[2] Venturi, *op. cit.*, p. 692.

1460; he left behind him a large family of sons, of whom one of the younger, Battista, had inherited not a little of his father's talents. Lascaris and other Greek exiles were cordially welcomed and hospitably entertained. Pier Candido Decembrio, after fishing for an invitation through Lodovico Casella, came to the Court at the beginning of 1467, and stayed on into the next reign, with a generous pension, very jealous of the great fame and reputation that Guarino had left behind him, while he himself was adulated by Tito Vespasiano Strozzi and young Niccolò da Correggio—the latter hailing him as the greatest example of virtue and glory, the most splendid light of their age that God had granted to youth.[1] And the Latin poetry that Leonello had loved continued to be the medium of courtly flattery—and, in the case of two poets, of something greater. Tito Strozzi continued singing his own loves, and celebrating the virtues of his patron, in the language and rhythms of the lyric and elegiac poets of Rome—though he felt the new impulse sufficiently to admit that books written in the vernacular, " translated in elegant and ornate language," may be read with consolation and profit, and therefore to translate at the suggestion of his brother Lorenzo, and for the benefit of Borso, the *De Vita Solitaria* of Petrarca.[2] And, both tendencies meeting in the one great poet of the day, to Borso's reign belong the first two poetic works, a book of Latin eclogues and a volume of Italian lyrics, of Messer Tito's famous nephew—the Count Matteo Maria Boiardo.

Nor was Dante neglected. In the spring of 1459 public lectures were given on the *Divina Commedia*, the commentary

[1] Borsa, *op. cit.*, pp. 129, 130.
[2] See Tito's letter to Lorenzo, prefixed to his translation (edited by Antonio Ceruti, Bologna, 1879).

DUKES AND POETS IN FERRARA

but appears to have studied under Squarcione at Padua, where he was probably Mantegna's fellow-pupil, and perhaps at Venice. Returning to his native city, he succeeded Angelo da Siena as chief painter to the Court in 1458, and was continually employed by the Duke, not only in decorating his palaces with frescoes and in painting portraits of the most noteworthy persons of his circle, but also in designing tapestries, triumphal arches and the other indispensable accessories of Estensian pomp and parade. A powerful and accurate draughtsman, Tura is a robust and original artist, peculiar and not usually attractive in his choice of types, vigorous in his execution, with angular and strongly marked folds of drapery, and with a bright scheme of colouring, which is singularly individual, if frequently hard and crude; in his altar-pieces, he adorns the Madonna's throne with classical decorations, as befits a pupil of the learned Squarcione. Francesco del Cossa was some eight years the junior of Tura, and was more directly influenced by Pietro dei Franceschi; a no less powerful, but more refined painter, as the comparison of his " St. Hyacinth " in the National Gallery with Tura's " St. Jerome " and " Madonna " in the same collection will serve to show. Borso, while bounteous to Tura, does not seem to have appreciated Cossa at his true worth. Finding himself inadequately remunerated, Francesco left Ferrara in 1470,[1] and removed to Bologna, where the Bentivoglio proved more liberal and discerning. The churches and picture-gallery still bear witness to his stay in Bologna, where he died in 1480.

[1] His letter of March 25, 1470, to Borso, complaining of his deferred payment for the frescoes in Schifanoia, and that, although he has painted the three compartments towards the ante-chamber by himself, he is receiving no more than the others, was published by A. Venturi in the *Kunstfreund* (Berlin, 1885, coll. 130, 131).

The Triumph of Minerva.
(detail)
By Francesco del Cossa.

THE DUKE OF MODENA

During the last two or three years of Borso's life, a third painter appears upon the scene in the person of the Duke's half-brother, Baldassare d'Este, sometimes called Baldassare of Reggio, who also worked as a medallist. Documentary evidence, recently brought to light, has proved that this hitherto mysterious personage was undoubtedly the son of the Marchese Niccolò III.[1] He appears to have returned from Lombardy to Ferrara about the year 1469. The famous series of portraits that he painted for Borso and his successor has entirely perished, and though a " Pietà " in a private collection at Ferrara is doubtfully ascribed to him, it is uncertain whether we have any authentic work preserved to us from his hand, save what may be regarded as his among the frescoes of Schifanoia, where, at Borso's orders, he repainted no fewer than thirty-six heads of the Duke, which were originally the work of Francesco del Cossa. It may be presumed that this slight was one of the causes that impelled the latter painter to shake the dust of Ferrara from off his feet. Baldassare was essentially a Court painter; more highly remunerated than even Cosimo Tura, he held various small offices under his reigning brothers, especially for some years that of captain of one of the gates of Reggio, in which capacity his life touched, by no means pleasantly,

---

[1] In a document of 1489, discovered by Count Ippolito Malaguzzi, and published by Venturi (*Archivio Storico dell'Arte*, i. pp. 42, 43), he is described as "Baldassare of Este, son of the late most illustrious Lord Niccolò, Marquis of Este, at present captain of the Porta Castello of the city of Reggio." I cannot, however, accept Venturi's suggestion, which is adopted by Gruyer (ii. p. 42), that his mother was Anna dei Roberti. The utterly different position at the Court held by the children of this aristocratic lady—Beatrice, Rinaldo and Bianca Maria—makes it impossible to believe that Baldassare was their full brother.

be added—the note of lubricity is not altogether absent, a note that is struck, more crudely and with less artistic skill, in the whole of the upper part of the fresco for September.

Those sections only have survived that deal with the months from March to September. The first three, the best executed and best preserved, appear to be the work of Francesco del Cossa : " I am Francesco del Cossa," he wrote to Borso, " who alone have done those three compartments towards the ante-chamber." To him is also ascribed the most noteworthy of the subsequent scenes from the life of Borso. The rest are now assigned to Tura and his assistants.[1] Doubtless, amongst those numerous figures that surround and accompany Borso, sharing in his sports and basking in his smiles, are portraits of all the leading spirits of his Court. But all the identifications that have been suggested are little else than more or less happy conjectures, with the, perhaps solitary, exception of the handsome young man with a falcon on his wrist, riding on the Duke's right in the month of March, who is plausibly recognized as Teofilo Calcagnino.

Towards the end of the series, in the portions not ascribed to Cossa, we begin to meet a new figure, younger and more sprightly than the Duke, clad like him in gold brocade, leading his troops and evidently drawing not a little of the popular favour and the courtly homage to himself. His features in the present state of the frescoes are unrecognizable, but it is hardly stretching a point to see in him the coming man, the " sole hope of our nation "—the " most illustrious Messere, Ercole d'Este."

[1] For a fuller account of these remarkable frescoes and the discussion as to their authorship, see Gruyer, i. pp. 423–468, ii. pp. 575–596 ; F. Harck, *Gli affreschi del palazzo di Schifanoia*, translated by Venturi (Ferrara, 1886) ; and Venturi, *op. cit.*, pp. 722–727.

Chapter IV
THE TRIUMPH OF DUKE BORSO

IN the latter part of Borso's splendid and peaceful reign, a dark cloud began to loom upon the horizon—the grim possibility of a disputed succession and civil war, so soon as the genial old despot should be in his grave.

The Duke, who was childless, at first treated his young nephew Niccolò as though he were his own son. The youthful prince who, like his father, had studied under Guarino, grew up beautiful and gallant, as well as highly cultured. "How he is loved by his uncle Duke Borso!" wrote Caleffini.[1] The Ferrarese began definitely to look upon him as the heir to the throne. He had been knighted by the Emperor in 1452, and, a few years later, Michele Savonarola, in dedicating to him his *De vera republica et digna seculari militia*, hinted, not obscurely, that Niccolò would in the future have an opportunity of putting these principles of good government into practice.[2] At the same time there was a strong and influential party in Ferrara that had not forgotten the exiled Ercole, and clung steadfastly to the rights of the legitimate issue of the Marchese

---

[1] *Cronaca di Casa d'Este*, p. 289. Filissetta and Lionella, the daughters of Borso pictured for us by Girolamo Bagnolino in the sixteenth century and Mr. Maurice Hewlett in our own days, are to be taken merely as poetic inventions.
[2] A. Cappelli, *Niccolò di Leonello d'Este*, p. 431; Segarizzi, *op. cit.*, p. 40.

DUKES AND POETS IN FERRARA

Niccolò III. Borso, who was a conscientious soul, was probably much perplexed in his mind, how to reconcile the promise that he had made to the dying Leonello with the more obvious claims of Ercole; it is even said that his celibacy was prompted by a desire not to add a further complication to the situation in the shape of a son of his own. "He never took a wife," writes Pope Pius II, "with the right excellent and Christian intention of leaving to the rightful heirs the sovereignty, which he had occupied in their stead while they were children."[1]

Very pleasant reading is a series of letters written in the latter part of September, 1462, by Niccolò, when on a visit to his mother's family, to Borso at Ferrara. The young prince is evidently enjoying himself immensely, but he is very anxious that his uncle should not suppose that it is that which has prevented him from writing. He has just received at Gonzaga a letter from Borso, complaining that he has not heard from him since he left Ferrara; but he assures the Duke in reply that the slackness of the messengers alone is to be blamed, not any negligence on his part, nor forgetfulness, "because of the good time that I am having here." He admits that he had not written *subito subito*, because he wanted first to have some taste of the sport prepared for him—but, as a matter of fact, the letter had been sent four days ago: "Let not your most illustrious Lordship ever believe that change of places, multiplication of pleasures, nor any imaginable delight, could equal the satisfaction that I should have in seeing your most excellent Lordship received here, as your Excellence will learn from my other letter. This illustrious lord [2] is

[1] *Commentarii*, ii. p. 102.
[2] The Marquis of Mantua, Lodovico Gonzaga.

THE TRIUMPH OF DUKE BORSO

well, and talks of nothing else but the Duke of Modena. Here they are getting up many pleasures, here they are building, here they are preparing to receive your Excellence worthily. I am still snaring quails, although very few fat ones are to be found; and I keep in good health, thanks be to God!" Then comes an account of a hawking exploit on the previous day. And more pleasures follow in the subsequent letters; fowling and fishing excursions, a great bag of fat quails, a right good take of fine pike and other fish; riding parties; courtesies from the Marquis and Marchesana; a progress through the State, ending up with a grand ceremonious entrance into Mantua. The young prince (who, from his letters, appears to be singularly young for his age—he was then twenty-four) is unaffectedly delighted at the compliments paid him; after seeing all the sights of Mantua and waiting over a great fishing party that is to be held in his honour, he will return to his Excellence next Monday.[1]

But in the meanwhile Ercole, in his banishment at Naples, was winning golden opinions from all by his gallant presence, his gracious ways and his feats of chivalry. A duel which he fought in the royal Court with Galeazzo Pandonio da Venafro, for the love of a fair Neapolitan lady, and in which he showed the utmost magnanimity in victory, long furnished a theme for the poets and novelists of Ferrara; as also did the courtesy and liberality with which he treated his former rival when the latter, in after years, passed through Ferrara as an exile.[2] After the death of King Alfonso, Ercole considered himself slighted by the

---

[1] Documents in Cappelli, *op. cit.*, pp. 429–430.
[2] Giraldi, *Ecatommiti*, vi. 1; Boiardo, *Pastoralia*, vi. 82–84, x. 76–80; Sardi, *Istorie Ferraresi*, p. 326.

DUKES AND POETS IN FERRARA

bastard Ferrante or Ferdinando, who succeeded t[...] Neapolitan throne, and in whose name he was gov[...] the province of Capitanata. When Jean, son of [...] d'Anjou, renewed the Angevin claims upon Naples, [...] went over to his party, and took the field against his [...] friend and companion. At the battle of Sarno in [...] 1460, from which Ferrante fled to Naples with only t[...] horsemen, Ercole is said to have personally encou[...] the King face to face, and to have seized and retai[...] portion of his royal mantle as a trophy in the atte[...] make him his prisoner.[1] The Angevin triumph, however, was but temporary; Ferrante speedily recovered all that he had lost, and the Aragonese dynasty seemed once more firmly established upon the throne.

At the end of 1462 Borso recalled both his brothers from the Regno to Ferrara. To Ercole he assigned the government of the duchy of Modena; to Sigismondo that of Reggio; while he kept the nephew Niccolò by his own side at Ferrara, as chief of his privy council. This move of the Duke's excited considerable satisfaction, especially among the Modenese and Reggians, who found themselves thus provided with two small Courts of their own. Francesco di Princivalle Ariosti, who was an ardent partisan of Ercole, sent Borso a Latin elegy complimenting him on this wise division of his sovereignty, and followed it up with a letter in the same language, expressing the great gratitude of Modena and Reggio, extolling the decision taken by the Duke as something quite divine, "having followed that weighty and most praiseworthy counsel of Jethro, the father-in-law of Moses."

[1] Frizzi, iv. p. 33; Boiardo, *Pastoralia*, iv. 72-75, x. 81-90; Ariosto appears to refer to this combat, *Orlando Furioso*, iii. 47.

THE TRIUMPH OF DUKE BORSO

Borso's answer is characteristically child-like and bland. "Our right well-beloved. We have received a letter from you in Latin, most worthy, elegant and moral; giving us to understand what great joy and gladness it has been to our duchies, great and small, that we have sent them our illustrious brothers to govern them, and what great thanks have been given us by all the people; and bringing into it that memorable example of Jethro, which very fittingly indeed enters into the matter. And about that we shall say nothing further, save that, as you have done the whole to a good end and with right worthy reasons, full of charity and of very good affection, we commend you very very much for your writing and for your suggestions."[1] Clearly his Ducal Excellence was not prepared to commit himself.

It was an unequal struggle for the next few years between the two claimants. While Niccolò was more addicted to pleasure than to increasing his influence and following, Ercole grasped every opportunity to make his own position more secure. He contrived at once to make himself indispensable to Borso, and to win the complete confidence of the Venetian Republic—that formidable neighbour who, by means of her Visdomino, a kind of exalted consul whom she maintained in Ferrara to protect her commercial interests and to administer justice to her subjects there, contrived to keep in unpleasantly close touch with Ferrarese matters, and who was probably already casting envious eyes upon the Polesine of Rovigo.

Although Borso was ardently bent upon preserving and

---

[1] Published by Carducci, *Delle Poesie Latine di Lodovico Ariosto*, p. 231. Borso's letter is dated from Belriguardo, February 8, 1463. The scriptural reference is, of course, to the eighteenth chapter of Exodus.

enjoying peace, he did not maintain an absolute neutrality in the politics of Italy. The accession of the Sforza to the throne of Milan, and their alliance with the Medici, had caused a new grouping among the great powers of the peninsula; Milan, Florence and Naples now formed a triple alliance, which was to some extent counterbalanced by the rapprochement between Rome and Venice. Borso had much to hope and something to fear from the two latter powers, and his sympathies were all against the triple alliance. His relations with Naples and its new sovereign were no longer what they had been in the days of the mighty Alfonso. Nor was there much love lost between the House of Este and these comparatively upstart Medicean rulers of Florence. Borso was deeply implicated in the conspiracy of the Party of the Mountain, the adherents of the Pitti and the Neroni, against the state—perhaps even the life—of Piero de' Medici in 1466. He dispatched a strong force of horse and foot under Ercole to Fontalba, to threaten the Tuscan frontier and support the conspirators. When the plot failed, he received Diotisalvi Neroni and Giovanni Francesco Strozzi in Ferrara, and used all his influence with the Doge of Venice, Cristoforo Moro, to have the skilful old condottiere, Bartolommeo Colleoni, put at the service of the exiles. To win the Doge over to his views, Borso went incognito to Venice in April, 1467, and, in jovial wise, paid him a surprise visit, while the Serenissimo was under the hands of his barber.

War broke out before the end of the spring. The Venetian object was to crush the Medici, who were the binding link in the League of Milan and Naples, that counterbalanced their power in Italy; Borso and Ercole chiefly desired to ingratiate themselves with the Pope, by supporting his

THE TRIUMPH OF DUKE BORSO

allies, and thereby to win the coveted ducal crown of Ferrara. Bartolommeo Colleoni, leading the Venetian forces in his own name and not ostensibly making war as captain-general of the Republic, Ercole d'Este with Ferrarese horse and foot, together with the petty tyrants of Pesaro, Forli and Faenza, and a number of other second-rate condottieri, advanced into the Romagna, proposing to assail Florence by way of Faenza, the Val di Lamone and the Mugello. Against them were the united forces of the Duke of Milan and King Ferrante, who were strengthened by the alliance of Giovanni Bentivoglio and Taddeo Manfredi of Imola, the whole army being under the command of Count Federigo da Montefeltro of Urbino (who was not yet Duke). The two ablest and best of the mercenary generals of Italy were thus opposed to each other, but the war was a very mean and paltry affair. The chief action of the campaign was fought at La Mulinella, near Budrio, in the plain between Bologna and Imola, on July 25, 1467. This is the regular battle engagement so derided by Machiavelli: "A parties giving, which lasted half a day, without either of the killed there way. Nevertheless, not a single man was certain prisoners only there were a few horses wounded, and fact, there were several hundred men killed on one side and the other. Bartolommeo Colleoni was forced to retire, and would have suffered a complete defeat but for the valour of Ercole who, at the head of the cavalry, stayed the Venetian rout, and covered their retreat. Ercole had two horses killed under him, was severely wounded in the foot, and walked lame for the rest of his life.[2] Peace was

[1] *Istorie Fiorentine*, vii.
[2] For this "Colleonic War," cf. Armstrong, *Lorenzo de' Medici*,

proclaimed in April, 1468, mainly through Borso's diplomacy, and Ercole, visiting Venice, had an enthusiastic reception, and probably a promise of future support in his claim to the Ferrarese crown.

Ariosto, in that scene of the *Orlando Furioso*, where Bradamante, the mythical ancestress of the House of Este, sees the long line of spirits issue from the cave of Merlin and present the forms of her descendants, refers to Ercole's heroism and the subsequent ingratitude of the Venetians :—

> Ercole or vien, ch'al suo vicin rinfaccia,
> Col piè mezzo arso e con quei debol passi,
> Come a Budrio col petto e colla faccia
> Il campo volto in fuga gli fermassi;
> Non perchè in premio poi guerra gli faccia,
> Nè, per cacciarlo, fin nel Barco passi.
> Questo è il Signor, di cui non so esplicarme
> Se fia maggior la gloria o in pace o in arme.[1]

At the beginning of 1469, the Emperor Frederick III was again in Ferrara for a few days, on his return to Germany from Rome, pouring out a profusion of diplomas, creating counts, knights, poets-laureate and doctors, literally by the score. It was a highly profitable business concern, and the amounts that he got back in fees quite refunded his royal and imperial Majesty for the costs of his journey. The Ferrarese grumbled sorely at the exorbitant sums of money demanded in payment for these luxuries by the imperial chancellor, declaring

pp. 57–71; Capponi, *Storia della Repubblica di Firenze*, v. cap. 4; Romanin, iii. pp. 326–332; Frizzi, iv. pp. 61, 62.

[1] " Now cometh Ercole, who casts in his neighbour's face, with his half-burnt foot and with those feeble paces, how at Budrio with breast and countenance he stayed for him his army turned in flight; not that in reward he should then make war upon him, nor invade even the Barco to hunt him down. This is that Lord, of whom I cannot express if his glory shall be greater in peace or in arms." (iii. 46).

THE TRIUMPH OF DUKE BORSO

that "he wanted to skin the whole lot"; and, as a matter of fact, the Emperor hurried away with a number of these newly created dignitaries in full cry after him to Venice. They had paid down their money, but got no diplomas to make good their dearly bought titles. Among those thus decorated were three brothers of the Ariosti, to whom and to their descendants the title of count was given; Francesco di Rinaldo Ariosti, seneschal to the Duke; Lodovico, an ecclesiastic, who afterwards became archpriest of the Duomo; and a third younger brother, Niccolò Ariosti, who was destined to be the father of the great poet. Presumably, their titles were fully confirmed; but Niccolò's sons do not appear to have been styled count.

This same year was marked by the darkest, almost the only tragical event of Borso's reign. The lordship of Carpi was shared by Giovanni Lodovico Pio and his brothers, the sons of Galasso Pio and Margherita d'Este (an illegitimate daughter of Niccolò III), who were thus nephews to Borso and Ercole; and by their cousins, Leonello di Alberto Pio (the son of that Alberto Pio, whom we have met in Leonello d' Este's literary circle) and Marco di Giberto Pio. The sons of Galasso are said to have imagined themselves injured by Borso in the matter of a projected marriage between one of their sisters and the Lord of Mirandola, Galeotto Pico, to whom, as we have seen, the Duke had given his own half-sister, Bianca Maria, in the previous year. Instigated possibly by Piero de' Medici, who was desirous of avenging himself upon Borso for his support of the Florentine *fuorusciti*, and with some sort of understanding with the Duke of Milan, Giovanni Lodovico—"non pio sed impio," says Carlo da San Giorgio, who paints him as a

[1] *Diario Ferrarese*, coll. 217, 218.

monster of iniquity—and, perhaps, his brothers entered into a mysterious conspiracy against Borso. According to the official Ferrarese version of the affair, they intended to murder the Duke; but it seems more probable that the idea was to dethrone him and to bind Ercole, his successor according to the plan, to the party of the triple alliance. The King of Naples was more or less privy to their design. Giovanni Lodovico himself appears to have been the connecting link with Florence, while his sister Marsibilia, the wife of Taddeo Manfredi of Imola, by means of a certain Andrea da Varegnana of Faenza, secured the co-operation of the Duke of Milan.

When the preparations had been made, Giovanni Lodovico sought an interview with Ercole at Modena, and made him the most magnificent promises on the part of the allied powers. In addition to the lordship of the three duchies, he was to have Ravenna, Forlì and Faenza, as also the baton of command (with an annual provision of 50,000 ducats) of the new League which the triple alliance was preparing to succour Roberto Malatesta, the bastard of the notorious Sigismondo Malatesta, who had died in the previous year, and whose lordship of Rimini was now being claimed by Pope Paul II as a vacant fief of the Church. Ercole pretended to assent, in order to get all the evidence of the plot into his hands, but revealed the whole thing to Borso as they rode together on a hunting expedition. On July 17, Giovanni Lodovico came again to Ercole, as had been arranged, accompanied by Andrea da Varegnana and an agent of the Duke of Milan, bringing their credentials and the clauses of the treaty as he had demanded—only to find themselves taken in a trap, and arrested as they walked with him in the garden of the castle. The Milanese agent was released, but the other two unfortunate men were brought to Ferrara by Ercole himself, bound and surrounded with troops, with their faces hidden, and the bells of the Castello ringing, "as a sign of a rich booty." The other brothers were arrested in Carpi by the soldiery of Galeotto della Mirandola; the eldest, Giovanni Marco, was brought to Ferrara to share Giovanni Lodovico's fate, the others imprisoned elsewhere.

Giovanni Lodovico Pio and Andrea da Varegnana were publicly beheaded in the piazza of Ferrara on August 12; Giovanni Marco suffered the same doom, but secretly and at night in the Castello, on September 15. The other brothers, Gian Marsilio, Gian Princivalle, Manfredo, Bernardino and Tommaso, were finally brought to Ferrara and rigorously imprisoned in the Castello Vecchio; in spite of their piteous appeals for justice and protestations of innocence, they were refused a trial and even an audience of the Duke. It is highly doubtful whether they had even known of the plot; but their cousins, Leonello and Marco, who were high in Borso's favour, were persistent in their resolution to have the whole fief; and there were other greedy courtiers who expected to derive some advantage from their disgrace. Their lordship of Carpi was made over to Leonello and Marco, and their possessions in Ferrara itself were divided among Borso's favourites.[1]

[1] A. Cappelli, *Congiura contro Borso d' Este*, pp. 368–374; *Diario Ferrarese*, coll. 222–225; Ugo Caleffini, *Storia di Ferrara*, ff. 49v–51; Frizzi, iv. pp. 67–69. The account of the "treason" by Carlo da San Giorgio, edited by Cappelli, is merely an official Court version of the matter, obscured by adulation and prejudice. A totally different story is told by Giraldi in the *Ecatommiti* (i. 8). He makes no mention of Piero de' Medici nor of the Pio of Carpi, but represents the whole as an attempt on the part of King Ferrante of Naples to be avenged upon Ercole for his share in the victory

Borso had sent an account of the whole affair to the Pope, probably representing himself as threatened in this way because of his fidelity to the interests of the Church. Paul wrote back, urging the Duke to look to it that the innocent wife and children of Giovanni Lodovico should not suffer in goods or in person for Lodovico's crime.[1] Otherwise, the Pope and Cardinals applauded Borso's wisdom and prudence in the matter. But, at the Court of Naples, it was openly said that a great injustice was being done, and that Giovanni Lodovico had never plotted against Borso's state nor his person, nor in favour of Ercole, but simply desired, in understanding with the Medici, to drive out his cousins and adhere with Carpi to the League.[2] Jacopo Trotti, the Ferrarese orator at Rome, exhorted his master to beware of Florentine poison : " I implore your Lordship most devoutly, for God's sake, to guard your person more than you are wont, even from poisons, because the Florentines are more expert in them than any other folk that live. Take care that attention is paid even to your saddles and stirrups." [3]

of the Angevins at Sarno. After an ineffectual attempt to compromise Ercole with Borso, Ferrante corrupted "certain young men in the territory of Modena, who were full of daring and had been with Ercole in Naples," to slay both Borso and Ercole together, when the latter should have given Borso into their hands. Borso magnanimously pardons the conspirators, reconciles them with Ercole, and converts the King of Naples himself.

[1] Cappelli, *op. cit.*, document iii.
[2] Cappelli, *op. cit.*, document vi.
[3] Cappelli, *op. cit.*, document iv. Trotti himself had an eye to the main chance in the ruin of the Pio. As a broad hint, he writes to Borso that he had told the Pope about the probable confiscation of their possessions, and added that, if he were near his Excellence, he too would try to get something ; " Io etiam operaria li miei ferazoli per haverne la parte mia " ; and that his Holiness had promised that he would take care that his being at Rome

THE TRIUMPH OF DUKE BORSO

Such being the mutual relations of Piero de' Medici and Borso d' Este, there is somewhat remarkable reading in the consolatory letter that the latter addressed to Lorenzo de' Medici, on the occasion of Piero's death, this same December, 1469:—

"It would be a difficult thing for us to express with letters the great grief, the great anguish and sorrow of soul that we have conceived by the death of the magnificent and most renowned Piero, your father; for, seeing that we were united continually by singular love, benevolence and close friendship with him (and first with the magnificent Cosimo, your grandfather, and with all the House of Medici, which bond of mutual charity had sweet and gracious beginning from our most illustrious predecessors, and has been preserved, and is preserved still better by us, their successors), not only through the great love we bear you, do we share with your Worship in the grief for the loss of so worthy and excellent a father, whose nobleness, marvellous intellect and admirable virtues certainly merited a longer life; but also for our own sake we grieve greatly, it seeming to us that we have suffered a grievous loss of a true and excellent friend, as was your father to us, and as we were equally to him."[1]

Such, however, was the diplomacy of the age. Each Italian prince believed that any other was capable of compassing his death, should an opportunity offer itself, while outward appearances of amity were kept up, and they wrote should not make him lose his share (*op. cit.*, document v.). Borso, however, was dissatisfied with Trotti's diplomacy, though he was *persona gratissima* with the Pope, who a few months later wrote vigorously to the Duke on his behalf (cf. Appendix II. to the present volume, document i.).

[1] Published in the *Atti e Memorie di Storia Patria per le Provincie Modenesi e Parmensi*, series i., vol. 3, p. 357.

to each other in terms not merely of courtly politeness, but of almost fraternal affection. But, perhaps alone among the sovereigns of his day, Borso was probably happier in doing such things graciously than in meeting plots and treason by counterplots and tyranny.

In the meanwhile Ercole had taken the field again. In the August of this year, 1469, he led a Venetian force to succour the papal army under Alessandro Sforza, which Roberto Malatesta had hurled back discomfited from the walls of Rimini. His intervention had the effect which Borso and he intended, of increasing still further the debt of gratitude which the Pope owed to the House of Este.

The whole Ferrarese game was now, by 1470, in Ercole's hands. Borso had completely turned against Niccolò, who, according to the partisans of Ercole, had abandoned himself to a vicious life and proved himself incapable of governing ; he kept him so short of money that the unfortunate prince had to borrow a few florins to pay the musicians of the Marquis of Mantua and of the Duke of Burgundy, who had played before him, and finally deprived him of his place of head of the privy council, installing Ercole in his stead.[1] Nevertheless, Niccolò still had partisans in Ferrara itself, and was keeping in touch with the Gonzaga at Mantua.

The old Duke was fast breaking up ; but, before his death, he was to see his dearest hope fulfilled. He felt that he had done the Church some service, and was probably insistent with the Pope that this should receive the recognition he desired.[2] As the Easter of 1471 approached, Paul II—

[1] Cappelli, *Niccolò di Leonello d' Este*, pp. 416, 417; *Diario Ferrarese*, col. 226.
[2] " The bearer of these presents, thy orator, hath set forth certain things to us faithfully in the name of thy Nobility, and albeit thy

THE TRIUMPH OF DUKE BORSO

a sovereign pontiff after Borso's own heart, one who loved the splendid appearances of things, gorgeous ceremonies, dazzling pageants, the gleaming of jewels and rich brocades—summoned him to Rome, for the purpose of creating him Duke of Ferrara, as the Emperor had already made him Duke of Modena and Reggio.

After a solemn Mass of the Holy Spirit had been offered up in the Duomo of Ferrara, Borso set out with a magnificent train, leaving the charge of his states to Ercole, Sigismondo and Rinaldo, his brothers, to Niccolò his nephew, and to Antonio Sandeo, the Judge of the Sages. With him rode two of his brothers, Guron Maria and Alberto d' Este; Marco Pio, now as Lord of Carpi, Count Galeotto Pico della Mirandola, the young Count Niccolò da Correggio; the noble poet, Count Matteo Maria Boiardo of Scandiano; and some five hundred other gentlemen in sumptuous gala attire. Their valets wore cloth of gold; their grooms shone in brocade of silver. Trumpeters and pipers followed them, with huntsmen leading packs of splendid hounds of every kind for the chase; falconers with falcons, *girifalchi*, goshawks and kites, "that were a royal thing"; and a band of oriental keepers, dressed in doublets of brocade, were in charge of a number of "tamed and most swift leopards, a thing exceedingly wondrous."[1] A long train of mules,

devotion towards the Holy Apostolic See and the Roman Church in our person hath been for a long time not unknown to us, it was, nevertheless, most grateful to us to have understood from him that it was not merely preserved but was even waxing greater with time. He now returneth with our answer to those things that he laid before us." (Brief of Paul II to Borso, December, 1470. *Archivio Vaticano*, xxxix. 12, f. 115.)

[1] *Francisci Ariosti Peregrini Iurisconsulti, De fortunati felicisque illustrissimi Ducis Borsii in Urbem Romam ingressus Dieta, ad illustrissimum et magnanimum divum Herculem Marchionem Estensem*

embraced him, not otherwise than if he had been the father of that most sapient senate of Venice." All the way between the Ponte and the Porta del Popolo was lined with people, and the crowd was so great that it grew difficult to make any progress. Dignitary after dignitary appeared, to greet Borso as he slowly rode onwards, and to join in his triumph: Costanzo Sforza, the commander of the papal troops; the ambassadors of all the foreign powers; the Roman Senator in gold brocade, "as though to a triumphal Emperor of old," with a hundred "consular patricians"; the households of the Cardinals and of Pope Paul himself. By this time, there were some eight thousand persons following the ducal pageant; but Messer Francesco remarks with delighted wonder that, in spite of all the vast number of illustrious personages, "not even one in the least intruded or was merged into the right goodly order of our most beauteous procession, as though it would have been a sacrilege to interrupt with diverse persons so admirable a company of the splendour of princes, the preserver of peace, our divine Prince."[1]

At the Porta del Popolo seventeen cardinals were waiting, headed by the Cardinal Battista Zeno, nephew to the Pope, and the Cardinal of Mantua, Francesco Gonzaga. At the sight of these princes of the Church, all the trumpeters and musicians of the ducal train sounded a blast of exultant music. Scattering silver on all sides, Borso rode through the streets of the Eternal City, flowers showering down upon him from windows, platforms, balconies and roofs, all, high and low, welcoming the Duke "as father, as most worthy prince; nay, as their own most worshipful

[1] *De fortunati felicisque illustrissimi Ducis Borsii ingressus Dieta*, ff. 39–41.

Duke Borso and his companions.
By Francesco del Cossa.

THE TRIUMPH OF DUKE BORSO

Emperor." The streets were lined with freshly planted trees, and across them, amid festoons of flowers and greenery, hung medallions with the Papal arms on one side and those of Este on the other, showing now one, now the other, as they turned round in the wind. The fountains ran with wine; everywhere were triumphal arches and music. "It was said publicly by all the Romans that never did King or Emperor enter into Rome with such great triumph and honour as this Duke."[1] At the door of the Sacred Palace the two cardinals, Zeno and Gonzaga, took Borso between them to the Pope: "Our most mild prince, all inflamed with a zealous devotion, slowly moved towards the throne, three times with fitting reverence genuflecting, before he threw himself prostrate to earth before those holy pontifical feet."[2] On the night of his arrival the weather broke up in heavy rain, the first that had fallen since his Excellence left Ferrara.

On Easter Sunday, April 14, Borso was solemnly raised to the dignity of Duke of Ferrara, with the power of disposing of the State in his will in whatever way he chose. The ceremony was carried out with every possible manifestation of honour and affection on the part of the Pope, with all the pomp and magnificence in which both Paul and Borso delighted.[3] Both the chief actors—old men, broken down

[1] Caleffini, *Croniche del Duca Ercole*, f. 4.
[2] Francesco Ariosti, *MS. cit.*, f. 45.
[3] The whole has been described in every detail by Francesco Ariosti in the second of his two letters to Ercole d'Este (in the Chigian MS. already cited), and by Borso himself in a long letter to his secretary, Giovanni di Compagno, dated April 16, 1471, prefixed in a copy by Giulio Mosti to Caleffini's *Croniche del Duca Ercole*, ff. 4v-7. The text of the latter in the British Museum MS. is fuller and better than that edited by G. Antonelli (*Lettera inedita di Borso d'Este al suo segretario Giovanni di Compagno*. Ferrara, 1869).

113

DUKES AND POETS IN FERRARA

in health and walking already in the shadow of th[...]
—entered into the spirit of the pageantry with a
mystical enthusiasm. " We refer all this our exal[...]
wrote the Duke, " to the most high God, to whom w[...]
with all submission and reverence, that, since it [...]
pleased His Majesty by means of him who holds H[...]
on earth, He may confirm this honour of ours in [...]
and that it may be a blessing for us and for all our [...]
and peoples."

Robed in a long gown of crimson cloth of gold [...]
carried the train of the Pope's cope in the mag[nificent]
procession to the Basilica of San Pietro. Before Mass,
while the papal choir sang the offices, the Pope dubbed
Borso a knight of St. Peter and gave the blessed sword into
his hands. The Despot of the Morea girded it on to the
Duke's side, while the two generals of the papal army,
Napoleone Orsini and Costanzo Sforza, buckled on the
golden spurs. " Gird on the sword to thy thigh, O most
potent one," sang the choir, " in the name of our Lord Jesus
Christ; but remember that the Saints conquered kingdoms
not by the sword, but by faith." Then, while the strains
of the *Kyrie Eleison* rose in petition from the choristers,
the Pope approached the altar for the Mass. After the
Epistle had been said in Latin and in Greek, Borso knelt
again before the Pope, and took the oath of fidelity. Pope
and Duke then prostrated themselves together before the
altar, while the Litany of the Saints was sung—his
Holiness rising in the middle to insert a novel petition of
his own for the divine blessing upon the new ducal dignity.

A much shorter letter from Borso to Giovanni di Compagno is in
Cappelli, *Ugo Caleffini, etc.*, pp. 307–308.

THE TRIUMPH OF DUKE BORSO

At the Offertory, Borso first kissed the Pope's feet and hands, and then, preceded by two archbishops and followed by Alberto d' Este and Teofilo Calcagnino, embraced all the Cardinals in turn. At the Communion, he received the Blessed Sacrament from the Pope's hands, and gave him the water at the Ablutions. Then Paul invested him with the emblems of ducal dignity—a long mantle of crimson damask brocade lined with ermine, with a long train; a great cape of ermine which covered the shoulders and arms; " in such wise," writes Borso, " that thou wouldst have thought that thou didst see a Cardinal, and we should have made thee laugh in this new dress of ours." Then the Pope blessed the pointed ducal cap, covered with pearls, and put it upon Borso's head, gave the golden sceptre into his hands, and hung a collar of precious stones round his neck. The ceremony thus concluded, the Pope exhibited the "Sudarium" or "Veronica" to the veneration of the faithful, and, attended by Borso in his full ducal robes, imparted the Apostolic benediction to the crowd in the Piazza. The vast throng, within and without the Basilica, rivalled that of a Jubilee, and many people were crushed to death. All the Sacred College, at the Pope's orders, escorted Borso back in triumph to the palace in the Piazza Venezia, while louder and louder arose the acclaiming shouts of the Roman crowd : " Duca, Duca ! Borso, Borso ! Evviva il Duca Borso ! "

On the following morning, the Pope, " imitating the customs of eternal God, who giveth all things most abundantly," summoned Borso to his presence again, to confer upon him the Golden Rose. Borso attended the Mass in San Pietro, which was sung by the Cardinal of Pavia, in his full ducal robes, sitting between the two Papal nephews, the Cardinals Zeno (of Santa Maria in Portico) and Marco Barbo :—

"When the Mass was finished and the benediction had been given in the usual way, our Lord sat down and made a fine sermon, and a long and goodly oration, in which he explained to what end the Church had invented this festivity of the Rose, and what it signified, and how it was given to one most worthy prince of this world for a similitude, to exalt every man to the desire of eternal good things, to which we all who are in this life should tend, like men, truly elect and champions, making every resistance to the things that are of the devil and contrary to the will of God. And here, right well to the point, speaking right kindly, he graciously magnified greatly both us and our House, commemorating some excellent benefits done by our House for Holy Church (albeit we could have reminded him of others), and showing clearly how we were worthy of this gift of the Rose for many reasons, which we shall pass over, and that, as we have been good up to now, so should we continue even to the end, to be hereafter crowned in our celestial country. This prayer being ended, most devoutly and with great elegance and very greatly in commendation of us, the Lord Cardinal who was on the left of his Beatitude went down to the altar to take the Rose in his hand to bring it into his sight ; and at the summons we went to kneel at his holy feet, accompanied by the Cardinal of Montferrat and him of Santa Maria in Portico ; and while we were on our knees, his Holiness gave us the Golden Rose ; which, we would have thee know, has been more worthily adorned than it has ever been before : and all this for our glory."[1]

[1] Borso's letter to Giovanni di Compagno, *MS. cit.*, f. 6*v*.

THE TRIUMPH OF DUKE BORSO

At the door of San Pietro, Paul once more gave the Rose into Borso's hands, so that the people might see; after which, attended by all the Cardinals and carrying the Rose in his hand, Borso rode in triumph through the streets to the papal palace of San Marco, tired out in body, but in a great state of mental exaltation.

In fact, beneath all this pomp, there was a serious and noble design on foot. The Pope had conceived a great idea of the renovation of the Church, and Borso seemed to him the very man among the secular princes of Italy to serve his need. He remained with his company for a month in the Eternal City, splendidly entertained by the Pope, and "so gladly welcomed by the Romans that it seemed that God had gone to Rome."[1] He was closeted for many hours in secret consultation with the Sovereign Pontiff, and openly expressed his hope of bringing the latter back with him to Ferrara. The subject of these prolonged discussions excited much curiosity among the Cardinals, and they were generally thought to refer to the future summoning of a Council at Ferrara itself.[2] Soon after the beginning of May, Borso left Rome, travelling through the territory of the Church to visit the Holy House of Loreto. On May 18 he entered Ferrara, with Ercole—who had come out to meet him—riding by his side.

Borso returned to his capital with the long-sought title of Duke of Ferrara and with the power of disposing of his duchy as he would, but utterly broken down in health. At his very entrance to the city, he refused the triumph that the people had prepared, because he felt himself unable to bear it. The annual race in honour of St. George had

---
[1] Caleffini, *Storia di Ferrara*, f. 54 v.
[2] Cf. Pastor, ii. p. 392 and document 100.

been postponed for him and his Court, and was run on May 26; but, on the next day, the Duke was seriously ill.[1] It was whispered that both he and the Pope, who showed similar symptoms, had been poisoned.

While he lay, apparently on his death-bed at Belfiore, civil war burst out in the peaceful city of Ferrara. Ercole assembled the Diamanteschi in Castello Novo, the fortress which then commanded the southern portions of the city, and appealed to Venice; Niccolò occupied the Castello Vecchio with his Veleschi, and appealed to Mantua and Milan. There was a desperate battle in the streets, in which the followers of Ercole were the aggressors and drove back their adversaries with heavy loss. An envoy from Bologna, who, after delivering his embassy to Borso, had attempted to mediate between Ercole and Niccolò, was murdered in the streets—it was said at Ercole's instigation.[2] The Marquis of Mantua sent his troops to the frontier, under the command of his son, Federigo, in support of Niccolò, and the Duke of Milan assembled a strong force of horse and foot in the district of Parma; but they were checked by the prompt action of the Venetians, who advanced upon the Polesine of Rovigo, while their ships—two galleons and five galleys—appeared upon the Po and moved up towards Ferrara, with orders to obey Borso, if he lived, and, if he died, to declare for Ercole.[3]

But a sudden rallying on the part of Borso dispelled the tempest. Carried into Castello Vecchio from Belfiore, he ordered Niccolò instantly to retire to Mantua, and Ercole to return to his government at Modena. Niccolò obeyed,

---

[1] Caleffini, *op. cit.*, f. 55; *Diario Ferrarese*, col. 229.
[2] *Cronaca di Bologna*, col. 387 (*Rerum Italicarum Scriptores*, xviii.).
[3] Cappelli, *Niccolò di Leonello d' Este*, p. 419; *Diario Ferrarese*, col. 229; Caleffini, *Croniche del Duca Ercole*, f. 8.

THE TRIUMPH OF DUKE BORSO

and left Ferrara on July 23, hastening to find the Marquis of Mantua and the Duke of Milan, who were together at Gonzaga and were profuse in their promises of assistance.[1] Ercole made a show of compliance, but soon returned and prepared the situation for taking possession of the State. On July 25 Pope Paul died, almost with his last breath inquiring anxiously after the health of his beloved Duke Borso.[2] The amelioration in the Duke's condition was only temporary. On August 5, Giovanni Stagnesio, the Florentine agent in Ferrara, wrote to Lorenzo de' Medici that Borso was dying in great suffering, and that Ercole would inevitably succeed. All his brothers, the majority of the nobles, almost the whole people both of the city and contado, were strongly on his side, and any opposition would be ineffectual against the will and power of the Venetians. All the fortresses were in the hands of his adherents, the Castello Vecchio and Castello Novo were held in force and armed with artillery, soldiers were being enrolled every day, and not the slightest chance remained for Niccolò.[3]

Borso died on August 19 in the Castello Vecchio; his half-brother Alberto watched over him till the end, and then hastened to inform Ercole in Castello Novo. Ercole kept the news secret until all his preparations were made, and summoned the Venetian ships, which arrived in the vicinity the next day, simultaneously with the meeting of the representatives of the people under the presidency of the Judge of the Sages, Antonio Sandeo, in the Palazzo della Ragione, to elect him Duke. As soon as Sandeo had

[1] Schivenoglia, *Cronaca di Mantova*, p. 166.
[2] See Pastor, ii. p. 394, and Appendix II. to present volume, document 2.
[3] Dispatch in Cappelli, *op. cit.*, p. 435.

communicated the result of the meeting to him, Ercole vested himself in the ducal robes that the Pope had given to Borso, with the cap on his head, the blessed sword by his side, and the golden spurs at his heels, and the golden sceptre in his hand. Thus attired, mounted upon a white horse, with all the members of the House of Este, with the ducal household, all bearing little banners with the crest of the *diamante* upon them, attended by several thousand armed mercenaries, Ercole rode through the streets of Ferrara to the Duomo. There, before the high altar, into the hands of Antonio Sandeo, he solemnly swore to maintain justice to the people of Ferrara.[1] Then, as "Duke of Ferrara, Modena, and Reggio, Marquis of Este, and Count of Rovigo," he announced, as though it had taken place that same day, to Lorenzo de' Medici, that Borso had died and that he had been chosen to succeed him. "May God have received his blessed and innocent soul, and placed it in Paradise. This our most faithful community and all the other peoples of our most illustrious House have unanimously elected me for their prince and lord, and given me the sceptre of the government. For which we thank and magnify the eternal and glorious God."[2]

Borso's state funeral took place on the 22nd. He was laid to rest, not with the other members of his House, but in his own special foundation of the Certosa of San Cristoforo. In that most restful and peaceful of Italian burial-grounds—at the end of one of those long, harmoniously silent ways between inclosed and fragrant gardens on either side, so characteristic of Ferrara to-day—the tomb of the "divine Borso" is still shown, while you shall seek

---

[1] Caleffini, *Croniche del Duca Ercole*, f. 8; *Diario Ferrarese*, col. 230.
[2] Letter of August 20, 1471. In Cappelli, *op. cit.*, p. 436.

THE TRIUMPH OF DUKE BORSO

elsewhere for those of the other sovereigns of his House in vain.

As the new Duke, with all his Court and a long array of poor mourners of both sexes, clad in black at his expense, followed the body in procession from the Castello Vecchio down the Via degli Angeli, the whole way was lined with the ducal mercenaries, while six hundred arquebusiers and four hundred foot-soldiers followed to guard the new sovereign—such was still the dread that he had of the fugitive Niccolò. Tito di Novello, Bishop of Adria, preached the funeral oration in the church, and, when they returned from the function, Lodovico Carbone mounted a pulpit at the entrance of the palace, and, in presence of the Duke and the people, uttered an eloquent panegyric of the dead sovereign. "It seemed," writes the chronicler, "that our Saviour God had died a second time."[1]

---

[1] Caleffini, *Croniche del Duca Ercole*, f. 8v; *Storia di Ferrara*, f. 55v *Diario Ferrarese*, coll. 231, 232, where something has clearly been borrowed from Caleffini.

Chapter V

UNDER THE SCEPTRE OF ALC

E RCOLE D'ESTE was two months under
he ascended the ducal throne of Ferrara a
He was a tall man, handsome in a somewhat
fashion, with harsh, strongly marked aquiline 1
swarthy complexion, and with something sul
scrutable in his expression. In his portrait
possibly a copy after some [lost reconstructio
sonality by Dosso Dossi, he is in armour w
one hand resting on a helmet, the other on
sword, and has an air of firm and unswervir
which the facts of his life altogether c
admirable picture at Modena, ascribed to L
reproduced in the present work, shows
softened down in later years. Here he is
in armour, wearing a black velvet bonnet
of St. Roch, leaning one arm upon a pa
study of an Italian despot of the Renais
manhood Ercole had acquired a consid
for personal valour, with which his
corresponded; although possessed of mar

[1] Chronological considerations make it im
ever sat to Dosso Dossi. If this portrait is
probably worked up from earlier materials aft

within this magnificent ducal palace, and i
humble and abject part of it, for the sacristy of
clemency." This, the pious courtier assures
mitted by the Divine Providence " for the
and instruction of her devout and pious Mes
to give him confidence in coming into his ow
Lady's patronage. She had been moved and
descend into this shrine in the palace, " for no
than more securely to protect her most devote
Lord Ercole and the right splendid city of
all the lordly barons of the most illustrious H
and to quiet henceforth the minds of the peo]
easily stirred up and divided in their wills. I
in that time not seldom did there seem fear of
than civil, in which would be such copious
blood as oft doth befall in cities and kingdom
are in doubt as to who should succeed in their

Great confidence had the new Duke of F
protection of his celestial Patroness—and :
little likewise in the assassin's dagger and
cup, no less than in the axe of the headsman.

He began his reign by showering favours
who had been assiduous on his behalf, or ha
for their fidelity to Borso; his half-brother
Borso's favourite, Teofilo Calcagnino, v
honoured, the latter being made his compa

[1] *La Origine et el Sito del novo Sacello dedicado
reverentia de la gloriosissima Vergene, Madre de Jesu
nostro, intro el magno e magnifico Pallazo Ducale d*
very curious treatise, which is dated April 22, 147
dedicated to Pope Sixtus IV. Like Francesco Arios
quoted on Borso's Roman Triumph, it is written b
in Italian. The only existing manuscript (Bibliot
a, w. 4, 4) is the copy presented by the author to Le

business, giving him a poisoned da
should lack courage to use it, a dead
the intended victim's food. But as
approached, on the evening of Decemb
with violent colic seized upon the wr
thinking that he had accidentally
that he was dying, he confessed the v
and to Federigo Gonzaga. Niccolò
self by flight, while the treacherous C
plice were publicly executed in the ma

Niccolò d' Este at once wrote to Lo
plaining bitterly that " Messer Ercole
with having occupied my State by d
but has also wickedly tried and sche
taken away by poison." Not to let
all the claim to celestial favours, h
to the intervention of God and the l
feast of her Immaculate Conception, a
to use his influence on his behalf at th
he fondly imagines that the questio
with the duchy of Ferrara is being
your Magnificence, by the right of frier
me to his most reverend Lordship, the
in order that my cause may not be los
any one to favour the justice of my c
to every reasonable man. I shall
to your Magnificence, and if ever I ha
fortune, as I hope in God, you will be
me and all my means as though they
than if we were carnal brothers."[1]

[1] Letter of Niccolò d' Este to Lorenzo de
1471, in Cappelli, *Niccolò di Leonello d' Este*

more thoroughly arranged, and, a little later, ｐ
the charge of the learned and pompous Pellegrin
who must rank as one of the great Italian １
the early Renaissance. With the utmost liber
treasures were placed at the disposal of the co
others, and the ducal library continued to be ｚ
head of culture for all the State.[1]

Magnificent pageants accompanied the state visi
to Venice in February, 1472, as soon as he foun
firmly seated on the throne, and even more sｔ
festivities welcomed the return to Ferrara in Ju
Duke's mother, Madonna Ricciarda, after her
eight years of voluntary exile at Saluzzo. Her
Rinaldo was sent to bring her from Casale di Mo
Sigismondo and Alberto welcomed her at the ｆ
and the Duke himself with all his Court came up
to meet her at Vigarano. On the day of her home-c
the law-courts and all the shops were closed; five hｔ
Ferrarese ladies waited to receive her on the river
and with bursts of music, firing of guns, clanging of
with a great company of Piedmontese and Fer
nobles riding together, she was brought to the ducal ｐ
opposite the Duomo, where, as Melissa foretells to ｋ
amante, she had for all her sorrows and vicissitud
fortune an *amplo ristoro*. "If ever honour was
to any person," says the Ferrarese Diarist, "think that
Lord Duke paid it to his mother."[2]

Henceforth every year on August 20, the anniversary

---

[1] See Bertoni, *La Biblioteca Estense*, cap. ii. and iii. *passim*.
[2] *Diario Ferrarese*, col. 241. Cf. *Orlando Furioso*, xiii. 67. Belfi
was given to her for residence, where she died in August, *1474*, S
was buried with her husband in S. Maria degli Angeli.

On other days the Duke gave a state banquet to all the chief ladies of Ferrara, "marriagea young married ladies of Ferrara fit for dan Diarist puts it, in the palace; in spite of his Excellence himself, "robed in a gown of bla with ermine, with a collar round his neck worth ducats," opened the ball with the wife of one while Sigismondo, Rinaldo, and Alberto, Teofilo Calcagnino, "his companion," Borso (first cousin to Niccolò) and the rest did the fully. The carnival of 1473 was unusually it was anticipated and prolonged from tl of January to the end of March, in honour approaching marriage. Masquerades filled its suburbs, night after night. Princes of House, nobles of the Court, private citizens v other in hospitality and display, the whole crowned by a great masked ball in the ducal last day of the carnival, when all the lords of Este appeared in masquerade.[1] Even they managed to keep it up. On March bride, Maria Lucrezia of Montferrat, cam along the Po, was met by the Duke and rod

The list occupies five pages, three columns to a pag Museum manuscript. Capons and cheeses, "form appear to have been the most usual offerings; but pheasants, partridges and other birds, even peacock A poor priest, the "capellano de Santa Maria N white torches. A Hebrew money-lender, Salomo with little tarts and candles.

[1] All these details from the *Diario Ferrarese*, co should be remembered that these festivities at this not in the Castello Vecchio, but in the present Palace c opposite the Duomo. There was a great banqueting out to the east upon the Piazza and to the north up

comber of wool—by malversation and extortio
a fortune of thirty thousand ducats. One o
married a daughter of Cammilla dalla Tavolɛ
on the mother's side of Alberto and Guron(
August, 1475, Ercole found him out. Som
shown him, because he was ready to betray hi‹
but he was sentenced to pay an enormous fin
and expelled from Ferrara. All his goods
cated, and every member of his family hunte
home. The mob was suffered to sack his l
private citizen paid the priests of the Duomc
bells all that day and night, and made a gr
front of the Castello Vecchio. "Not for two]
had the people of Ferrara received better ne\
joy." The man's wife, Giovanna Ariosti, (
Nevertheless, subsequent events showed tha
fited but little from the lesson. Another c
same type, who added hypocrisy to his attɛ
Frate Guglielmo, a Piedmontese friar who hac
confessor. He made use of his post of Rector
di Santa Anna, to extort money from the pɛ
too, Ercole sent about his business, and put m
life in his stead.²

Meanwhile in Rome, the General of the
Francesco della Rovere, had succeeded to l
the title of Sixtus IV, a Genoese thus replacii
upon the throne of the Fisherman. Moderr
cleared the memory of Sixtus from the foules
that have stained his memory, at least so far ɛ
morality is concerned. Not so, however, fron

[1] Caleffini, *Croniche del Duca Ercole*, ff. 22v
[2] Caleffini, *MS. cit.*, f. 24.

DUKES AND POETS IN FERRARA

Romagna to Ercole and his heirs, and acknowle[d] ducal title.

The time had come for the Duke's marriage [with] Princess Leonora of Aragon, the eldest daughter of hi[s] foe, King Ferrante of Naples. As the King was the spirit in the Triple Alliance, it will be seen that [by this] marriage Ercole was turning his back upon the policy of Borso, and running the risk of future compli[cations] with his formidable neighbours, Venice and Ro[me. At] present, however, neither the Most Serene Republic [nor the] Sovereign Pontiff raised any objection to the matc[h.]

A little collection of courtly and dignified love-le[tters,] still preserved in the Archivio di Stato at Modena, [written] by Ercole in his own hand to Leonora—*illustrissima [e caris-]tissima mia consorte*, as he calls her, in anticipation [of her] coming. They are mere formal courtesies for the [most] part. In one he thanks her for her letters and g[raceful] little gifts, "*le cose gentile che La me ha mandato*['; in] another, with what seems a genuine touch of passio[n, he] says: "One hour seems to me a thousand years befor[e your] Ladyship is here."[1]

In April a noble company of gentlemen left Ferr[ara to] bring Leonora to her bridegroom. The progress o[f the] bridal train up through Italy from Naples to Ferrar[a was] one continuous triumph. The countrymen of the [bride-]groom were represented by his brothers, Sigismondo [who] had acted as his procurator) and Alberto d' Este, by [Gal-]eotto Pico and Marco Pio, the Lords of Mirandola [and] Carpi, each of these two with twenty-four horsemen[; by] Borso of Correggio, Matteo Maria Boiardo, Niccolò

[1] Archivio di Modena, *Carteggio dei Principi*, letters of Jan[uary] 27, March 4, March 27, April 10, 1473.

the two Cardinals to the Vatican, to assist
Mass and have an audience of the Holy Fat
all hearts by her wisdom and her gracious
" Tully himself," said the Cardinals, " woul
quence by comparison with her." Afterwards
her back again to witness the performance o
Susanna by a Florentine company. The ne:
Monday, a sumptuous banquet was given in h
the splendour-loving Pietro Riario, in the fair
was to vanish like a dream on her departure ;
menu may be read at length in Corio's histor
modern mind its most taking feature was the
scenes set forth upon the tables in shapes of
sized. There was the story of Atalanta, the
Andromeda, the chariot of Ceres, the labours
the triumph of Venus, and many other ingeniou
the same kind—all, of course, accompanied by I
in honour of the new Alcides and his divine Pa
bride. At the end of the banquet there was a c
sixteen great lovers, men and women, of the ol
the fierce Centaurs rushed in to carry off the n
were routed and driven away by Hercules, a
" there was the representation of Bacchus an
with many other most beautiful things, of very
inestimable expense." [1]

The splendid company entered Florence on the
June 22, having spent the previous night at San
They rode through the Porta Romana across
Vecchio to the Palazzo della Signoria, where the P
waiting for them on the Ringhiera, and an expect

[1] Corio, iii. pp. 267–275 ; C. Corvisieri, *Il Trionfo*
Eleonora d'Aragona ; Pastor, ii. pp. 430–433.

festivities followed, with balls, tournament
kinds. In the ducal palace, "the Excelle
danced, with her black hair, according to th
flowing down her shoulders and a crown
Queen."[1] And the Ferrarese were not dis
magnificent, dark queenly Duchess; Leor
and virtuous as she was beautiful and ta
Messer Lodovico:—

> De l' alta stirpe d' Aragona antic;
> Non tacerò la splendida Regina,
> Di cui nè saggia sì, nè sì pudica
> Veggio istoria lodar Greca o Lati
> Nè a cui Fortuna più si mostri ;
> Poi che sarà da la Bontà divina
> Eletta madre a partorir la bella
> Progenie, Alfonso, Ippolito e Isa

On May 18, 1474, Leonora gave bi
Isabella—that Isabella in whom we nov
woman of the Italian Renaissance. Sh
Ercole's eldest child; he had already
daughter, Lucrezia, by a certain Lod
Condolmieri, born shortly before his ac
The Duchess had made a vow to the

---

[1] Caleffini, *MS. cit.*, ff. 16v, 17; *Diario*
"She surpasses the cherubim in beauty,"
from his dungeon; "never was there seen a
she will draw me out of this castle" (Bert
the previous year, the five captive Pio had c:
Bernardino and Tommaso were recapture
stricter guard. They were finally released i

[2] *Orlando Furioso*, xiii. 68. "Of the h
Aragon shall I not fail to sing the splendi
pure as she, see I neither Greek nor Latii
nor one to whom Fortune shows herself
shall be chosen by the Divine Bounty 1
progeny, Alfonso, Ippolito, and Isabella."

DUKES AND POETS IN FERR

1452, in the very year of Borso's elevation t
dignity, Girolamo Savonarola, the grandson c
Michele, was now a student of medicine at
His father Niccolò—a courtier and a spendthrift
one day in his company to assist at one of the
entertainments in the ducal palace; but he
refused ever again to cross its threshold. The
leads out from San Francesco to the shady a
poplars, laburnum and chestnut, which line the
walls of Ferrara, is now called the Via Savonarol
Via di Cisterna del Follo, and is one of the most
deserted ways of the modern city. Seldom does
more noisy pass up or down it than labouring
drawing their loaded wains. San Francesco itself
left to tell of its past glories. But in Savonaro
the street was full of gay and courtly life, and
the loud revelry in the Palazzo Strozzi, which lay
the gardens of the friars of San Francesco (
palace now called the Palazzo Pareschi was not i
Ercole until several years later), where the brothe
Vespasiano and Lorenzo di Nanni Strozzi, exercised
hospitality. A little further on, another Florentin
Diotisalvi Neroni, had built himself a palace th
stands. But, adjoining the Palazzo Strozzi, was t
pretentious house of the Savonarola, opposite the
piazza and church of San Girolamo. And here Gi
buried himself in his Thomist theology and kept hi
vigils, shutting his ears to the sound of revelry, te
convinced that the time was hopelessly out of joint.
yet, if the testimony of Fra Benedetto is to be acce

[1] In the *Vulnera Diligentis*, he professes to have had the

DUKES AND POETS IN FERRARA

fuge crudelis terras, fuge litus avarum."[1] Such seemed the Court and city of Ercole d' Este to the future prophet of righteousness.

Leonora gave birth to a second daughter, to whom the name Beatrice was given, on June 29, 1475. On this occasion "no public rejoicings were made, because they wished that it had been a boy."[2]

The year 1476 opened under favourable auspices. Pope Sixtus seemed unusually friendly. Some sixteen months before, on the death of Lorenzo Roverella, he had appointed a young nephew of his own, Fra Bartolommeo della Rovere, to the bishopric of Ferrara, and Ercole had received him graciously. The Pope now sent Monsignor Luca Pasi of Faenza, who was one of the Ferrarese agents at the Court of Rome, as special envoy; on January 21, after Mass had been sung at the high altar of the Cathedral, he presented Ercole with a silk cap adorned with pearls, and a sword of honour in a gold-worked sheath.[3] Nor did Venice prove less cordial. On February 9, Leonora went with Sigismondo and Rinaldo d' Este, Niccolò da Correggio, Bianca of Mirandola, Marietta Strozzi Calcagnino (the wife of M. Teofilo) and others, to pay a formal visit to the Doge and Signoria. She returned on the 23rd, suffering a great storm at sea on the way. The Duke went out to meet her, and it was noticed that, before she went up to her apartments, she visited the chapel of the Madonna of the Court and prayed before the miraculous image.[4]

---

[1] See whole letter in Villari, *Savonarola*, i., document 2.
[2] *Diario Ferrarese*, col. 250.
[3] Zambotto, *Silva Cronicarum* (Biblioteca di Ferrara, cod. 475).
[4] Zambotto, f. 21. The chapel had just been rebuilt. Bianca della Mirandola at Venice had astounded the Doge and Signoria by her eloquence on behalf of her husband (Caleffini, *MS. cit.*, f. 24v.).

DUKES AND POETS IN FERRARA

Paduans, under the command of Francesco and Brunoro da Groppo. Early in the afternoon, Niccolò and his men arrived at the walls of the city, beneath Castel Tedaldo, where they were being rebuilt near the church of Santa Agata. Here they easily broke through, occupied one of the smaller gates, and pressed towards the piazza, shouting "Vela! Vela!" All the bells of the churches clashed out the alarm; the people were aghast, and did not realize what was on foot; no one joined the invaders. The captain of the guard of the piazza with his soldiers rushed into the Duomo and closed the doors: "I was then with my father and with Messer Hieronymo Ferrarino, a student of law and my companion," writes Zambotto, "at the Mass at the altar of Our Lady, and we saw the priest, who was saying the Gospel, take up the chalice and missal from the altar and run away without finishing the Mass." Shouting promise after promise to the people, Niccolò rode round the piazza; his adherents burst open the prisons, roaring "Vela, Vela," and then "Marco, Marco," to make men believe that the Venetians were with them—but all in vain. Three German students, who could not understand when told to shout "Vela," were done to death. Then Niccolò took his seat as sovereign of Ferrara in front of the Palazzo della Ragione, under the impression that the people would pay him homage. A few of his partisans within the city declared themselves; one of the more prominent sat down by his side, only to be shot dead by a crossbowman from a window of the Corte Vecchia.

At the first alarm, the Duchess had caught up the new baby in her arms, and, with her women carrying the two little girls, rushed along the covered passage to the Castello Vecchio. Here Sigismondo had raised the bridges and held

DUKES AND POETS IN FERRARA

a bastard of the House. Niccolò himself escaped into the country, was found hiding in a swamp, and brought back to Ferrara the same evening.

The next day the Duke returned to Ferrara. The dead were still lying in heaps about the streets and squares; the three castles were filled with prisoners. " Messer Sigismondo and Messer Rinaldo da Este, his brothers, went to meet him," writes Zambotto, who was present, "with all the nobles of the city; and, when he arrived at the piazza, and heard all the people crying *diamante, diamante, Ercole, Ercole,* and saw his wife and children at the balcony of the Court, all weeping with gladness, he could not contain himself, but began to weep too for joy at the fidelity of the people. And straightway he dismounted and entered into the Duomo, and went to the high altar to thank God, who hath liberated him from very great peril of his life and of his State." [1]

Two days of thanksgiving and popular rejoicings followed, and then the work of vengeance began. On September 3, the condottieri and eighteen others were hanged from the balcony and windows of the Palazzo della Ragione, and five more from the battlements of the Castello Vecchio. During the night that followed, Niccolò was privately beheaded in the cortile of the Castello. On the following morning it was proclaimed on the part of the Duke that all the nobles, doctors, officials and citizens of Ferrara should go to pay honour to the body of Messer Niccolò d' Este to the tomb. The head had been sewn on to the trunk; the body was arrayed in a long robe of gold brocade, a crimson cap was placed upon the head and new gloves upon the hands; and so it was carried out of Castello Vecchio by the knights of the city, and then successively by the doctors

[1] Zambotto, f. 28v.

UNDER THE SCEPTRE OF ALCIDES

of law and the physicians to the church of San Francesco, with great pomp, attended by all the Ferrarese clergy. The Ambassador of Naples, the Visdomino of the Venetians, the Rectors of the Universities, followed as chief mourners, with Scipione d' Este (a bastard of Meliaduse) representing the kindred of the slain man, Jacopo Trotti the Judge of the twelve Sages, with the magistrates, members of the Duke's secret council and all the gentlemen of the Court. "And many could not refrain from tears, and Madama the Duchess, who was looking on from the balcony of the Court with her damsels, wept bitterly." He was laid in the red tomb of the House of Este in San Francesco, where so many of his forefathers and kindred slept.[1]

Azzo da Este had shared his fate, but was buried without any pomp or ceremony, "in his shirt all blood-stained," as Caleffini has it, in the same church. A series of hangings and beheadings followed. In compassion for his age, the deathsmen would fain have spared the life of a certain Luca, Niccolò's old cook, and on the scaffold they bade him say "Viva il Diamante," and be pardoned. The old man shouted "Viva la Vela," and died. Some two or three hundred men, who protested that they had acted in ignorance, were sentenced to lose hand or eye, but instead were made over to different courtiers and even to convents, to be put to ransom—and most of them were set free without payment. In November, the priest spy was brought out

---

[1] Caleffini, MS. cit., f. 27; Zambotto, ff. 28v, 29. Niccolò di Leonello d' Este was never married, but left three illegitimate children: Girolamo, Battista and Vincenzo (cf. I. Giorgi, *Frammento d' Iconografia Estense*, in the *Bullettino dell' Istituto Storico Italiano*, No. 2). In after years, Ercole made them a provision, and Isabella d' Este, with her characteristic generosity, took them under her protection. See Appendix II., documents 16 and 19.

upon a high scaffold erected in front of the Duomo, and there degraded. But first " there was read a brief of the Pope, which committed this punishment to the Excellence of our Duke, and, at the end of the said brief, the Pope exhorted the Duke to use pity towards him and pardon him, according to the example of the Crucified, who pardoned the Jews. The priest said that, rather than he should be degraded, Our Lady would work a miracle; but all the same he was degraded without miracles." He was taken back to the Castello Vecchio as a layman; then, a few days later, brought out again and, after his condemnation had been read, hanged from a window of the Palazzo della Ragione.[1] Alberto Masolino and Ardillaso de' Panciaticchi, Niccolò's chancellor and equerry, were beheaded in December. " They died willingly for love of their lord, and they could have saved themselves, if they had chosen, by confessing a certain thing to the Duke that he wished to know."[2] A third, Antonio di Filippo, who had influential Ferrarese connections, was pardoned on the scaffold.

Then at last the Duke gave commands that the work of blood should cease, and that no further search should be made for those implicated. On Christmas Eve one of his judges presented him with a paper upon which was written a long list of nobles and gentlemen of the duchy, with a valuation of their estates, whom he accused of having been privy to Niccolò's conspiracy, urging the Duke to put

---

[1] Zambotto, ff. 32, 32v. He states that "this priest confessed that Messer Niccolò had determined to murder Messer Sigismondo and Messer Rinaldo da Este, and to take Madama Leonora our Duchess, with the children, and send them to a city, the name of which it is better to pass over in silence." Venice is apparently meant.

[2] Caleffini, *MS. cit.*, f. 29.

UNDER THE SCEPTRE OF ALCIDES

them to death and to confiscate their goods. Ercole was standing by the side of a large fire. He took the paper from the hand of the officious judge and, without reading a single name, threw it into the flames. " Thus, with their names and their possessions which are written here, let the memory perish of all that they have thought, tried and done against me." [1]

In the meanwhile, the Most Illustrious Signoria of Venice had sent ambassadors, Messer Paolo Morosini and Messer Marco Barbarigo, to congratulate Ercole upon his triumph and to make excuses for the presence in Niccolò's attempt of men from Vicenza and Padua—all of which Ercole had received with the utmost graciousness. The ruler of Bologna, Giovanni II Bentivoglio, indignantly repelled the suggestion that he had aided Niccolò with men and horses ; and Ercole wrote to assure him that he was most ready, if necessary, to write through all Italy, that every one might know that he held him, Bentivoglio, *per suo caro e intrinseco amico*.[2] And on October 4, the feast of St. Francis, the baptism of the little Alfonso—*il nostro dolcissimo primogenito, il nostro puttino*, as the Duke calls him in his letters to his orator at Florence—had been solemnized in the Duomo by the Bishop of Chioggia, with the Republics of Venice and Florence standing god-fathers by their special envoys.[3] Thus was the future victor of Ravenna, the *uomo terribile* among the princes of the Cinquecento, born into a

[1] Cf. Giraldi, *Ecatommiti*, x. 3 ; Sardi, p. 288 ; Cappelli, *op. cit.*, p. 26.

[2] Letter of October 17, 1476. Dallari, *Carteggio tra i Bentivoglio e gli Estensi*, p. 22.

[3] See the letters from Ercole to Niccolò Bendedei, Estensian Orator in Florence, in the *Atti e Memorie di Storia Patria per le Provincie Modenesi e Parmensi*, series I., vol. 3.

heritage of sanguinary feud, at a moment when his own had been threatened in the cradle and Ferrara was still with his cousin's blood. Little wonder that, in after years, he bettered the instruction!

It was, indeed, a year of plotting and bloodshed. Two months later, on the Feast of St. Stephen, the infamous Duke of Milan—Galeazzo Maria Sforza—was stabbed to death by three noble-minded assassins in the church of San Stefano. Ercole was at Mass in the chapel of the Madonna in the Court, when the news reached Ferrara from his ambassador in Milan, Roberto Boschetti, in whose arms the Duke had breathed his last. He was prompt in rendering assistance to the widowed Duchess Bona, who was the regent for her young son, the hapless Gian Galeazzo. In the following summer, the baby prince Alfonso was solemnly betrothed to Anna Sforza, Gian Galeazzo's sister, a girl about a year older than himself. The three brothers of the late Duke—Sforza, Lodovico il Moro and Monsignor Ascanio—opposed the rule of Bona's favourite, Cecco Simonetta; they were banished from Milan in the following year, and put under bounds at Naples, Pisa and Perugia. They stayed for a few days at Ferrara in June on their ways to their places of banishment, much honoured by Ercole and lodged in Schifanoia, where on the first evening, as they sat at supper under the loggia, two blind poets, Giovanni and Francesco, who appear to have been Florentines in the Ferrarese service, sang to them. Among other things, the Duke entertained them with a race of leopards in the Barco. A month later, on July 14, the marriage of the two babies, Alfonso and Anna, was celebrated in the presence of Bona's ambassadors, "who were received in Ferrara with very great honour, and lodged in the Court of the most illustrious

Duke Ercole, and stayed there triumphantly for many days."[1]

Leonora was not present at these festivities, and did not witness the betrothal of her baby boy. She had gone to Naples in May, to visit her father, and there in September, 1477, she gave birth to a second son, Ferdinando or Ferrando, as his father always calls him in his letters. The Cardinal of San Pietro in Vincoli, Giuliano della Rovere, who was then at Naples, stood sponsor. In her absence, Ercole had relations with one of the ladies of her household, Isabella Arduino, who in March, 1478, bore him a son, Giulio.[2] This adulterous intrigue stands quite alone in Ercole's life, and we have no trace, not even the faintest suggestion, of any subsequent act of infidelity towards his wife. Leonora returned to Ferrara in November, leaving Ferrando and Beatrice at her father's Court in charge of her sister-in-law, the Duchess of Calabria. In March, 1479, the third son of Ercole and Leonora—afterwards to be famous as Ippolito—was born. The names of these three—Ferrando, Ippolito, and Giulio—were destined to be linked horribly together in after years, and with that of Alfonso.

There can be no doubt that Ercole was sincerely attached to his wife. Profoundly religious (even as he himself

---

[1] *Diario Ferrarese*, col. 254. By the *Court* is always meant the Corte Vecchia, the present Palazzo del Municipio. But in this year, 1477, probably in consequence of the alarm caused by Niccolò's attempt, Ercole began to have rooms made in the Castello Vecchio, Pietro di Benvenuto being the architect. The work was completed by the end of December, when the Duke and Duchess took up their residence there. Caleffini, *MS. cit.*, ff. 29v, 30v.

[2] This Isabella, the daughter of Niccolò d' Arduino, married a certain Jacomo Mainente of Ferrara. Three months after their marriage this child Giulio was born, whom the Duke acknowledged and brought up as his son. (Caleffini, *MS. cit.*, f. 32, the passage being apparently an interpolation by Giulio Mosti.)

DUKES AND POETS IN FERRARA

gradually grew to be), heroically brave and steadfast in times of stress and danger, a tender and affectionate mother (she treated Ercole's illegitimate daughter Lucrezia as though she were her own child, and, in later years, took care for Giulio's interests), kind and gracious to her servants and inferiors, the first Duchess of Ferrara is one of the noblest figures of women that Italian history has to show us. The Duke, as years went on, grew more and more to rely upon her, to look to her for strength and resource at his need.

It is tempting to linger over the collection of his letters to her, which are still preserved in Modena. Later chapters deal with other themes; the intrigues and perplexities of the Court of Milan; the affairs of their sons. But even those in these first years of their married life show the complete confidence the Duke had in her. In his numerous absences from the capital, she is the ruler of the State, though in difficult emergencies she has to consult her brother-in-law, the most illustrious Messer Sigismondo. "There is no need for your Ladyship to make any excuse," Ercole writes to her once, when the Duchess has forwarded a letter from Messer Alberto Cortesi, the Ferrarese orator at Venice, which she says she has opened by mistake; "you know well that you can open all our letters and do as you think fit, for we are right well content thereat; nay, you do well to send off those which you can dispatch without us."[1] As Lent comes on, being away at Reggio, he charges her to look to the protection of the Jews in Ferrara and to caution the preachers not to excite the populace against them in their sermons:—

"It sometimes happens," he writes, "in seasons like this,

[1] Letter of July 16, 1479. Archivio di Modena, Carteggio dei Principi.

that the preachers who preach in the churches of the city urge and excite the people to hunt the Jews, and to make them go to hear the Word of God against their will, in such wise that, on account of what these say, they are sometimes attacked. Therefore, your Ladyship had better have them told beforehand that they must behave themselves in their preaching in such a way that these Jews of ours who dwell in our city be not molested nor forced, by their persuasions, to go to hear sermons, and that they be not interfered with in any way through words of theirs." [1]

Little presents, too, from time to time, are exchanged between husband and wife when separated—sometimes rather quaintly. This same Lent, for instance, Leonora sends him an egg of an ostrich—perhaps a new acquisition to his menagerie in the Barco—forgetting, apparently, that the Duke keeps very strict rules about fasting. Ercole thanks her in his reply, but, because he wants her to "enjoy it for love of us," sends it back to her; "and especially because now, as you know, we do not eat eggs, and if it were kept till Easter, we believe that it would not keep good. But even if we ate them at present, we had much rather that you should enjoy it than us." [2]

Only once does the correspondence reveal a misunderstanding in these years, and then, though it appears a very

---

[1] Letter of February 26, 1479. Archivio di Modena, *Carteggio dei Principi*. Ercole took a strong line in protecting the Jews throughout his duchies. During the carnival of 1480, a scholar from Forlì mortally wounded a Jew, the son of the Salomone already mentioned, and was hanged in chains from a window of the Palazzo della Ragione, to the great indignation of the people. When in October, 1481, a report was spread that the Ferrarese Jews had crucified a Christian child, Ercole had the accusation fully investigated and proved to be false. Caleffini, *MS. cit.*, ff. 34v., 37.

[2] Letter of March 1, 1479. Archivio di Modena, *Carteggio dei Principi*.

trivial matter, the Duke thinks it of sufficient importance
to write her a letter of remonstrance—a charming letter in
its way—in his own hand :—

"Most loving Lady mine,

"I have been told that your Ladyship is angry with the
keepers of the stable, because I have brought away here to
me a palfrey of yours, without your leave. I am very sorry
to have done anything that displeases you ; but I should
never have believed that, for so little a thing, you would
have taken it ill, especially as the horse is not good for you
nor for any woman that you have. This alone grieves
me, that I believed that I had more authority with you than
I have, and that if, instead of bringing it solely for my
personal use, I had given it away, you would not have said
anything but that I had done well—as you can do with my
things. If you had taken, not merely a horse that is worth
twenty-five florins, but anything that I have, I could have
said nothing but that it was well done. However, I tell you
that the horse is here, sound, and if you want it, say so,
for I shall send it to you at once ; or if you want anything
that I have. I shall never think that I have divided
possession with you ; because I wish all that belongs to me
to be as much yours as it is mine. To your Ladyship I
commend myself. Written with my own hand at Medelana
on the twelfth day of August, 1481.

"HERCULES DUKE OF FERRARA."[1]

Meanwhile, in the general break up of the Italian peace
that followed the assassination of Giuliano de' Medici in the
Duomo of Florence on Sunday, April 26, 1478, Ercole had

[1] Archivio di Modena, *Carteggio dei Principi*.

UNDER THE SCEPTRE OF ALCIDES

taken the field against his suzerain, Pope Sixtus, and his father-in-law, King Ferrante. He accepted the baton of command from Lorenzo de' Medici, as Captain-General of the League that defended Florence from the allied powers of Rome and Naples (led by Duke Alfonso of Calabria, Leonora's brother, and Federigo da Montefeltro, Duke, since 1474, of Urbino), and he invaded the Sienese territory. Suffering from ill-health, dreading Neapolitan poison and hardly working in harmony with his colleague, the Marquis of Mantua, full of superstitious apprehensions (the sainted nun of his House, Beata Beatrice d' Este, had cried aloud from her tomb, and he himself had seen a vision while sleeping in his tent), Ercole gained but little honour in this war, and his good faith had been questioned.[1] And, in fact, save for the diplomatists on either side, there was no honour to be gained. The members of the League were divided against themselves; Mantuans and Ferrarese had come to blows in the camp, and Ercole's life had been endangered in their brawls; Venice, disliking the Florentine choice of Ercole as General, had been sparing in sending men and money; the Milanese contingent had been recalled to protect the Duchess Bona from a sudden invasion by Lodovico il Moro and Roberto da San Severino. Ercole himself was forced to hasten to Pavia to repel them; but found that Bona had made peace with Lodovico—that fatal peace which was to cost her young son his duchy, if not his life.

During Ercole's absence from the seat of war, and on precisely the same day as Bona's surrender, September 7, 1479, the only really reputable *fatto d' armi* in the campaign was fought; the Dukes of Calabria and Urbino together gained a complete victory over the Florentines and their

[1] Cf. Rosmini, *Vita di Gian Jacopo Trivulzio*, ii. p. 36; Machiavelli, *Istorie Fiorentine*, viii.

allies, under Sigismondo d' Este and Costanzo Sforza, at Poggio Imperiale near Poggibonsi. This is the battle recorded with so much mediaeval pomp and quaint circumstance in the fresco by Giovanni di Cristofano and Francesco d' Andrea in the Palazzo Pubblico at Siena, where the Sienese are represented as playing a prominent part in the storming of the camp of the League. It is somewhat exaggerated in Boiardo's Italian eclogues —in which the whole credit of the action is assigned to Alfonso of Calabria.[1] Galeotto della Mirandola, Rodolfo Gonzaga (younger brother of the Marquis Federigo of Mantua), and Niccolò da Correggio, were among the prisoners.

In the meanwhile, Leonora ruled the duchy with dexterity and ability, but appears to have leaned over much upon the four brothers Trotti—Count Paolo Antonio, the ducal secretary, Jacopo, "who is always near Madama," Galeazzo and Brandeligi. "They were at this time the chief men of Ferrara," writes Caleffini, "and almost more esteemed than our Lord Duke Messer Ercole and all the others of the most illustrious House of Este." He implies that they made themselves wealthy by unlawful means.[2] The result was that the Court split into two factions, for and against the Trotti.

A most unfortunate consequence of this war for Ercole —and one fated to prove disastrous in the future—was the

[1] " Tra tante alte vittorie una ne è tale
Che non se amenta in terra la magiore :
Il Leon vero, e questo altro da l' ale,
La Vipera sublime e il sacro Ocelo
Sconfisse insieme a Poggio Imperiale."
Ed. ii. 50-54. Cf. *Ed.* x. 121-126 ; *Orlando Innamorato*, II. xxvii. 57.

[2] *MS. cit.*, f. 34.

UNDER THE SCEPTRE OF ALCIDES

Pope's displeasure. Sixtus regarded his conduct as an act of rank rebellion in a vassal of the Church. "I know," wrote Battista Bendedei, one of Ercole's agents in Rome, "that his Holiness appears to be more wroth with your Excellence than with any one else, and even more than with the Florentines."[1] In August, the Pope prepared a tremendous Bull against "that son of iniquity, Ercole of the Marquesses of Este, whom of late we decorated with the ducal title and honour, and constituted Vicar-General in temporal things in our city of Ferrara and its county and district." In it, Ercole is declared a rebel and a perjured traitor; he has merited the major excommunication with the forfeiture of his ducal dignity, his vicariate and all his fiefs; and, with his sons and nephews, is incapable of obtaining these or similar in the future. The vicariate having thus come to an end, Ferrara and all its district has devolved to the Church. All Ercole's subjects are released from their allegiance, and bidden to recognize the Pope alone as their immediate Lord and Superior.[2]

Hearing of what was preparing, Luca Pasi sought an audience of the Pope, and, prostrate at his feet, implored him not to do the Duke this shame, urging him by every argument he could muster not to publish the Bull. "Messer Luca," said his Holiness, "the Duke could have sent his

---

[1] Dispatch to Ercole of May 28, 1479. Balan, v. p. 294.
[2] Bull of August 17, 1479, in *Archivio Vaticano*, xxxi. 62 (*Sixti quarti Bullae et Brevia diversa*), ff. 218-221v. A similar Bull of excommunication and deprivation against Roberto Malatesta, Galeotto Manfredi, Antonio Maria degli Ordelaffi and Costanzo Sforza is dated August 16 (*loc. cit.*, ff. 177-181v). The Bull against Ercole is printed by Theiner, *Codex Diplomaticus*, iii. coll. 501-503. Although never actually published, it is cited by Pope Julius II as a precedent in his famous Bull of excommunication against Alfonso I in August, 1510.

received him on May 11. His Holiness
indignation against Ercole, not so m
entered into the League, as for his ha
against him. "For myself," he said, '
the honour of God is concerned." He p
never made this war against the Florentir
Lorenzo de' Medici and his accomplice
Church and of God," and because of the
been done and said, which for the honour
been able to endure. He did not deny
times been greatly moved to anger by the
he had aided Lorenzo and assailed the Per
He could never excuse him for having, co
gation of his oath of fidelity, taken up
Church, even though he had entered the l
ever, finally accepted his excuses, pardon
gave his benediction, but added a solem
the Duke remember that the House of I
everything to the Church, and not make a
another time his Excellence made a leagu
that kind, let it always be with the stipulat
arms against the Church. Otherwise he w
evil end.[1] The same day the Pope informed
League between the Church and Venice.

Ercole had already received the notifica
League of "the Serenity of the Doge with
our Lord" from his ambassador in Venice
Cortesi, and from the beginning he realized
danger. He had sent, dated April 28, a n
Battista Bendedei, informing him of the mat

[1] Dispatch of Bendedei to Ercole, May 11, 1480.
295.

DUKES AND POETS IN

that he had better do nothing in this r
more intimate with the Pontiff and the

Meanwhile, Ercole prudently streng1
by arranging the marriages of his two le
Isabella and Beatrice, to Gian Frances
son of the Marchese Federigo of Mar
Sforza "il Moro," who was now virtual
of Milan. At the same time the young
was betrothed to Isabella of Aragon, da
of Calabria and niece of Ercole's wife.
illegitimate daughter, had been already p
Bentivoglio, the eldest son of his friend
Bentivoglio.[2] At the beginning of J
ambassador, Zaccaria Barbaro, attempt
to enter into the League with Venice
the Duke declined,[3] and, in the follo·
the post of Lieutenant-General of t
Naples, Milan and Florence, with the
50,000 ducats of gold in time of peace a
war.[4] This same summer he receivec
Edward IV of England, who invested
of the Garter. In September, Sigismor
Ercole's marriage, was born, and nam

[1] *Ibid., Minute Ducali*, May 15 and May 1ς
[2] A dispensation had to be obtained fi
marriage, because of the spiritual affinity of
having been the godfather of Annibale. S
The Bentivoglio were, strictly speaking, not
simply the chief citizens of the Bolognese
the correspondence between Ercole and (
always styled Magnificence—never Excellen
[3] " Habiamo pocha voglia de impaciarse c
Ercole to Giovanni Bentivoglio, June 3, 14!
prays Bentivoglio to keep this a strict secret
[4] Dallari, p. 41, note.

greatly appraise my words. I do not wr
seek human praises, nor because I take p;
but to show you my reason for thus kee
country, in order that you may know that
because I know that I am doing a thing 1
God, and more salutary to myself and to 1
neighbours."

Other things than preaching excited the
Ercole just then. There was marching to and
"daily cast of brazen cannon, and foreign m
ments of war," much " post-haste and romage
Yet were there some few that hearkened.
business of his Order, the young Friar was trav
Po in a small ship towards Mantua, and a par
were on board, gambling and blaspheming ;
turned to them and admonished them, whe.
fell at his feet, imploring pardon. But a terribl
war and disaster was about to burst over Ferra
House of Este ; already people were leaving tl
Studio was closing, and the convent of the Ar
then outside the walls, was threatened. Savona
vincial sent him to Florence before the end of the
he never saw Ferrara again.

[1] Letter from Pavia, January 25, 1490 (*Lettere ined;
Girolamo Savonarola*, ed. P. Vincenzo Marchese. *Archit
Italiano*, Appendix, vol. 8, p. 111).

cupidity of enriching himself at the expens
the former he was urged on by Virgini(
been deprived of his fiefs of Alba and T
Abruzzi. After the peace of 1480, Girolan
to punish Costanzo Sforza, the Lord of Pesa
ance to Lorenzo de' Medici, and Ercole's pro:
instrumental in enabling Sforza to checkma
Already master of Imola, Girolamo, after tl
degli Ordelaffi, had occupied Forlì, and ha
investiture of that papal fief from Sixtus.
successor of Pino, Antonio Maria degli Orde
mate son of Pino's brother Cecco, took refug
territory, and was kindly received by Erco
him an annual provision and left him free to g(
Bagnacavallo, whence, with the aid of Galeot:
Faenza, he could plot to recover his State.

And Girolamo could safely count on winning
second his desires. Sixtus dreaded the Aragon(
Naples; he was readily convinced that, even
had betrayed him in the matter of the separate
Lorenzo de' Medici, so now he had betrayed him
would desert him in the face of the Turk. He
forgiven Ercole d' Este for having led the Florent
late war. He was further exasperated by the fac
Duke made much difficulty about paying the annu
of 4,100 florins to the Papal Treasury, was always i:
and frequently forbade the publication of the pa)
in his dominions. Even while the forces of the Chi
the Kingdom lay together before the walls of (
Girolamo had determined that the new alliance
Rome and Venice should be turned to the destru(
Aragonese rule in Naples. And he had a temptir

in consequence excommunicated by the vic
Bartolommeo della Rovere, who was, as usu
Rome. Contarini appealed to the Duke, wh
give redress. "Then, Excellence, I shall lea
said the Venetian. "Your Magnificence will 1
open," answered Ercole. Contarini took him
upon which a ducal secretary was promptly se:
to apologise. The Doge summoned the Fe
bassador, Alberto Cortesi, to the Consiglio ‹
and gave a peremptory intimation to the Duke
revoke the excommunication and reinstate the
to compensate him and make an example of all
and to observe the conventions for the future.
of Ferrara disavowed the action of his vicar, and ;
Venetians that the Pope was very much displea
excommunication, and had professed himself on
the Republic. Ercole yielded; the Visdomino
furious and arrogant, threatening deadly vengea
Jacopo Trotti and his brothers, to whom he asc
slight that had been put upon him.[1]

These negotiations were still in progress when, i
days of the siege of Otranto, Girolamo Riario lefi
magnole dominions and set out in person for Ven
his way he visited the Duke of Urbino, who, old as
was still reckoned the first soldier of Italy, and
Malatesta, Lord of Rimini, who held the office of (
General of the Venetian army. The latter he fou
but the Duke (who was Roberto's father-in-law,
personal foe) indignantly rejected his overtures
abandoning his habitual sphinx-like calm, gave free

[1] Romanin, iv. pp. 402, 403; Frizzi, iv. pp. 117, 118
i. pp. 21-23.

DUKES AND POETS IN FERRAI

obtain a much fuller compensation from the w
Neapolitan Kingdom.¹ The more prudent men
Council misliked it, and distrusted the Pope
were overruled. It was decided to accept th
and Girolamo, loaded with honours, returned to F
Ferrarese orator informed his master that t
miserly conduct in giving no gratuities of any ki
arrogant manner in accepting the honours that th
awarded him, had displeased everybody ; ² bu1
was delighted at his nephew's reception and at 1
of the mission, and wrote an enthusiastic letter
to the Doge, hinting not obscurely that he woul
opportunity of showing his gratitude.³

In October, Antonio Maria degli Ordelaffi mac
successful attempt to surprise Forlì, with the aid o

---

¹ Cf. Sigismondo de' Conti, i. p. 119 ; Piva, i. p. 53. In
1480, Girolamo had first suggested to Zaccaria Barbaro
tian orator in Rome, his plan for the expulsion of the King
but Barbaro was told to exhort the Count to keep this
idea to himself. In the following May, it had been rum
Girolamo was coming to Venice, and Ercole had instruc
to keep his eyes open; but the Signoria, seeing that the 1
alarmed, had persuaded him to defer his visit. See the
cited by Piva, i. pp. 45, 48–50. The statement often ma·
bargain struck by the high contracting conspirators had fo
the division of the dominions of the Estensi, the Veneti
Modena and Reggio, and Riario having Ferrara itself, apj
contradicted by the documentary evidence. The Pope
were equally bent upon the destruction of the King of Na
the surrender of Ferrara to Venice was probably the nep
addition to his uncle's scheme.

² Dispatch of September 22. Piva, i. p. 53. The Count
on September 16.

³ Brief of September 19, 1481, in the codex of the
Nasionale at Florence, which Pastor (ii. p. 503, note 2) 1
must have come from the *Archivio Vaticano*. See pre
Appendix II., document 3.

it promptly and at the usual time ; he w
also about the Jews ; as to Forlì, his mas
" You can say what you like," interrupted
I am quite certain that your Duke is to b
however, ready to proceed no further in th
dition that Antonio Maria should hencefor
to remain in the Duke's dominions.[1]

Thoroughly alarmed, Ercole (who had on
been concerned in the affair of Forlì) an
and his accomplices, instructed Bendedei to
faction on every point to the Pope, and eve
self ready to hand the prisoners over to
to be examined with torture to manifest the
that their lives were spared. Girolamo dec
longer wanted them for the justification
convinced that he was innocent, but tha
them in his hands, to be put to death as
Then Ercole absolutely refused to deliver tl
have done nothing against us," he wrote, "
punishment. So that, since there is no nee
for our own justification, as the Lord Count
ledges, we must pray his Lordship to excuse
send them to have them executed, because
he would not wish us to stain our honour."
further persistence from Girolamo, Ercole d
would suffer eternal remorse in his conscien
surrendered the prisoners or put them to

[1] Dispatches of Battista Bendedei, November
ber 25, 1481. Archivio di Modena, *Carteggio degl
Roma*. The prompt aid given by Venice to the
in this affair of Forlì, had further cemented th
alliance. See brief of November 17 to the Do
document 4.

he will not have prevented, as he could have do₁
conflagration that we see is rising in Italy, that
grant that it be not the ruin of this miserable It₂
all Christendom."[1]

At the beginning of April, Roberto da San Seve
had broken with Lodovico Sforza and had been
from the Duchy of Milan, was appointed comman
Venetian land forces for the enterprise, with th
Lieutenant-General and the position which the la
lommeo Colleoni had held. The Duke of Urbino ł
ously been appointed commander-in-chief of the
the League—Naples, Milan and Florence—for th
of Ferrara, Ercole's own position being that of Li
General. The Marquis of Mantua and Giovanni B
were naturally on the same side. To the cause
and the Pope adhered the Republic of Siena, the
Savoy and the Marquis of Montferrat, the Rossi
(who had been stirred up to rebellion against Milan
hard pressed by the ducal troops under Gian Ja
vulzio), and (a little later) the Republic of Geno
when war actually broke out, practically the
Italy was involved, on one side or the other.

Hostilities began from the South. In the middle
Duke Alfonso of Calabria marched into the Stat
Church, and demanded a passage for his army to
for the defence of his sister and her husband in
simultaneously, he sent troops to occupy Marino w
held by his allies, the Colonna. On April 18,
refused the passage, and in a brief to the King ord
to withdraw his forces, lest men should say tha

[1] *Minute Ducali per Roma a Battista Bendedei*, Februar
Archivio di Modena, *loc. cit.*

under Roberto Malatesta—who was bitterly jea
honours conferred on Roberto da San Severino,
that, unless more respect was paid to his dignity
General, he might not be able to take the fi
operate in Romagna, assailing the Ferrarese te
that side and keeping the passage closed to t
the Duke of Calabria.

On May 12, all the ambassadors of the Lea
gether to the Pope, with a full statement of tl
form which amounted to a declaration of w
had been read to him, Sixtus said that the 1
therein were worthy of the greatest consi
asked for the document, in order better to ex
parts of it. The ambassadors answered th
not wait for any reply, their commission beir
leave the city. The Pope expressed his regre
his foot, and departed with his benedictic
later, Battista Bendedei and Aniello *f*
Neapolitan ambassador, left Rome togeth
Marino for supper, " where we were right g
by those Lords of the Colonna and by the M
da Gennaro, the royal commissary." [1]

The position of the Pope was, to say tl
peculiar one. He regarded himself as ass
because of his fidelity to the Venetian all
royal attack had simply forestalled his ov
the Kingdom, and the immediate occasion
been, if not his own direct permission, at l

[1] Dispatches of Battista Bendedei, May 12 an(
former inclosing a copy of the document that wa
Archivio di Modena, *Carteggio degli Ambasc*
Ferrarese orator accompanied Aniello to Naples
to Rome for a while as a private person.

claws of the winged Lion could clutch. The g
was along the Po, where the Duke of Urbino wi
of the League, including a strong Milanese cont
Trivulzio and aided by the Marquis of Mant
endeavouring to support the Ferrarese ca
definitely breaking with Venice, contested 1
advance stubbornly. Before the end of Ma
army had encamped before Ficarolo, and the \
under Damiano Moro, arrived at the point w
divides and goes towards Ferrara.

This conjunction of the fleet and army (
struck terror into the hearts of the Ferrares
famine seized upon the city. The people h
the blame for their sufferings upon the hated
Antonio and Jacopo and their brothers, to '
and policy the whole war was ascribed. "
cupidity and avarice," writes Caleffini, " {
that they would have crucified Christ anoth
money; and the Duke saw and heard nothing
wanted, and if any one of them was ill, the D
with them, and it was thought that these 1
witched him." To appease the popular fu
deprived Jacopo of his office of Judge of the
him as ambassador to Milan; but the mere
brother, Brandeligi, with the Duchess at one
of the Castello, raised a tumult which
the ambassadors of the League had only q
utmost difficulty.[1] Ercole now tried to alla
appointing six Ferrarese citizens as *Savii d*

[1] Caleffini, *Croniche del Duca Ercole*, ff. 40–4
had married a daughter of Folco da Villanova, L
and had inherited his palace in the Borgo Nuov

DUKES AND POETS IN FERRA

Milan.¹ The fighting was incessant, but less
the fever and pestilence that set in, both on t
in the camps. The Duke of Urbino broke dow
Moro and the *provveditore* with the land ar
Loredan, both sick to death, went back to V
five weeks' siege, the fortress was taken by stor
of June, in the sight of the forces of the Leagu
which were powerless to aid.² All the heroic]
perished; but, what with the fighting and t'
the place had cost the Venetians several th
In the light of his subsequent declarations, it m
that the Pope professed the utmost satisfactio
of the fall of Ficarolo.³

The whole of the Ferrarese territory be
now fell into the hands of the enemy. On A
Venetians appeared before the walls of Rov
the citadel was held by Count Niccolò Ariosti,
ducal captain of the district, with a mere ha
the greater part of them sick; resistance bei
citizens forced the Count to surrender the t
Ferrarese forces were now withdrawn from t
defence of Ferrara itself.

[1] Letter nominally from the Duke of Milan to Tr
1482, in Rosmini, *Vita di G. J. Trivulzio*, ii. p. 93.

[2] Sanudo, *op. cit.*, col. 1219, makes the Duke of
witness, but he had already left the seat of war.
de' Conti, i. pp. 128, 129, and Baldi, *Vita e fatt
Montefeltro*, 2nd edition, iii. p. 216.

[3] Brief of July 6, 1482, to the Doge of Venice, in
Biblioteca Nazionale, f. 313. In the same brief, Six
Doge's request to make Federigo da San Severino
the deadliest foe of his own nephew !) a Cardinal
1496, preaching upon Amos in S. Maria del Fior
obstinate defence of Ficarolo with the Italian collap
of Charles VIII. (Cf. Villari and Casanova, *Sc
scritti di Fra Girolamo Savonarola*, p. 223.)

seemed imminent ; the Pope was terrified ;
Rovere and the ambassadors of Ferdinand
advised him to make peace. But at length
to urgent appeals from the Pope and Girolamo
Senate ordered Roberto Malatesta to le
and set out for Rome, with all his army.[1] C
arrived in Rome, acclaimed by high and low a
of the Church: "This is he that shall d
shouted the crowd, as, handsome and smiling
figure in his glittering armour, he rode throu
to confer with the Pontiff. A few days late
forces arrived, and the banners of the Pope
floated together over the city.

Malatesta promptly took the field agai
forces. Alfonso retreated before him, and to
position with his artillery near the Pontine
so-called Campo Morto, between Velletri
Here, on August 21, he was assailed by Mala
pletely defeated, himself only saved from
valour of his Turkish followers, who fell in h
his flight, and by the heroism of Anton
Duke of Amalfi and nephew of Pius II, w
victorious forces at the head of his squadron
at bay until Alfonso had made good his esc
Riario kept out of the fighting, on the plea
standards. There was a triumphal entry

[1] On May 19, Vettor Soranzo received orders fro
his fleet to attack the Kingdom. The Republic pr
reluctance to taking Malatesta away from the en
but at length, June 8, gave him the order to go w
and a month later sent all its troops from Roma
to Rome, leaving a small guard of mercenaries
and Forlì (Piva, i. pp. 95–104).

his bedside, to administer the last sacrame
to the man to whom he owed the preserv;
and upon whom he had been building up a
triumphs in the future. The next day,
he legitimated the dead hero's sons, an
intention of investing them with the vi
under his protection.[1] There were dark w
of a deadly sequel to Count Girolamo's
victory of Campo Morto; there can, h
doubt that Roberto had died from purely

On the same day, September 10, the
of the League, Federigo da Montefeltro,
in the Duke's rooms in the garden of the
before his death, he had striven to bring
had been in negotiation with the Pope
Giuliano to that end.[2] He is said to have
heart, when he heard of the victory of C
his last hours were embittered by the be
Malatesta intended to despoil his heir, G
Duchy of Urbino. To Isabella da Mont
Federigo's daughter and Roberto's wife,
simultaneously the deaths of father and h
baldo was then a mere child, and the care of
devolved upon his uncle, Ottaviano da Mo
politician of ambiguous reputation. To
wrote, expressing great grief at the death

[1] Briefs to the Council and Commune of
Doge of Venice, September 11, 1482. *Archivio*
ff. 43-46.

[2] Brief of September 3, 1482. *Ibid.*, ff. 32,

[3] Sigismondo de' Conti, i. p. 145. Zambotto
the lying in state of Federigo at Ferrara. The u
he died at Bologna, is erroneous.

light-armed Albanians, he suffered ultimate[l]
defeat, and fled back to Argenta with a handf[u]
Venetians took seven hundred prisoners, inc[l]
San Severino (one of the condottieri of the D
and Niccolò da Correggio. These they se
paraded in triumph through the Piazza di S
kept rigorously imprisoned.

Prompt succour came from Milan in the [
Jacopo Trivulzio, in whom Leonora and E
greatest confidence. He was probably th
they could have found, to defend what re
duchy, and they were profuse in their gratitu
of Milan.[1] Trivulzio promptly strengthene
tions of Bondeno and Argenta, and w
organizing the defence. But dissensions s[
With all his undoubted valour and military
was self-sufficient and choleric, could brook
and would not work with the other Milan
who arrived upon the scene a little later.
with Sforza Secondo, an illegitimate broth
and openly showed his contempt for th[e
Sigismondo d' Este. "Let us remind y
Duke of Milan, or Lodovico in his name,
most illustrious Lord Messer Sigismondo i[s
authority that he has, you must pay him [
and generally comport yourself towards
discretion and modesty as we are certain [
in the same way with the Magnifico Sfor[za
it may be manifest that you are bent up
the benefit of that most illustrious Lord the

[1] Cf. documents in Rosmini, *op. cit.*, ii. pp. 98
[2] Letter of November 28, 1482. Rosmini, *op*

somersault, which his greater nephew was to
following century—he completely changed]
found himself threatened from the north v
of the Council of Basle—this being, in M:
phrase, "the ecclesiastical penalty of tempoi
—and realized that the Venetians were bent
acquisition of Ferrara. The orators of Lor(
and of Milan urged him to make peace be
late, and the ambassadors of the Cathol
Spain put on still stronger pressure. The C:
threw his influence into the same scale. (
held out for a while, and warned the Veneti
in progress. The Republic instructed
Francesco Diedo, to dissuade the Pope from 1
the King of Naples, and to promise the ai(
against him. But Girolamo was bought
promises of the ambassadors of the League
to have included (alas, for the Pope's ⁅
investiture of the fief of Rimini, the patrii
Malatesta.² And Sixtus gave way.

Seeing what was on foot, the Venetians
on the war with the utmost vigour, if pos
acquisition of Ferrara an accomplished
Pope's tergiversation became definite and
November 20, their army crossed the Po
by a bridge of boats. Trivulzio drove b:
guard, but was forced to retreat bef
numbers, burning the fortifications on ·

---

¹ *Lorenzo de' Medici*, p. 195.
² Sanudo, *op. cit.*, col. 1225 ; Pastor, ii. p. 52
in December, the Venetians offered **Faenza**,
vallo to Riario, to keep the Pope in their allia
but it was then too late.

room where the Duke lay upon a bed, "with
with his beard long, and he could hardly s
his eyes." For more than an hour they pa
touching his hand, going in at one door and c
in a continuous stream, many weeping and v
of consolation. At last, seeing him worn out,
that some people came through more than
had the doors closed.[1] The same afternoc
Rinaldo d' Este and Francesco Ariosti, th
into the piazza in arms, and professed the
sally out against the enemy in the Barco ; b
forbade it.

On the same day as the passage of the Ver
ber 20, Giovanni Bentivoglio wrote to F
haste and exultation, that that morning a
of the Cardinal Gonzaga had arrived at
came from Rome, and, under pretext of g
was to announce to Ercole that the peac
cluded at Rome, and to encourage him to
and defend himself vigorously, because t
his preservation and that of his Duchy.

Francesco Belvisi, a servant of the C
arrived at Bologna, and came on at one
assure the Duke of the Pope's good dis
him and his State.[2] All now depended v

---

[1] Zambotto, ff. 108–109. "Io steti sempr
vedere tale visitatione." The officials aimed at
are obviously the Trotti. A few days later, in
representations, they were secretly sent out o
laws ascribed to them were cancelled, the
property by having it conveyed to the Castle
confiscated. Caleffini, *Croniche del Duca Erco*

[2] Dallari, pp. 99, 100.

to the defence of the city itself, all the
and the other captains were devoted t
on the one side, Bondeno and Stellata
possession of these two fortresses keepin;
by which supplies and provisions could
the districts of Modena and Reggio. R
hurried forward from Milan and Bolo
who had been deputed to guard Argenta
up a party of Albanians and Slavonian
of the Venetians with Roberto himsel
their advance, but lay comparatively ina
and Pontelagoscuro.

The condition of the city was terrible,
of the Ferrarese grew intense. A lar
pleasure-loving population, which had
serious experience of war than the cc
tumults at the end of Borso's reign and tl
of Niccolò di Leonello, found itself
the walls, decimated with pestilence, r
and privation. Homeless fugitives fi
towns, starving peasants from the (
through the streets with their families,
so wasted that they seemed like pai
supplies which Leonora had obtained
Reggio, at the risk of a revolution i
altogether inadequate even for the ne
alone. Ferrara was only saved from
Pope taking the final plunge that left t
the Duke of Calabria to come to her aid.

[1] Sanudo, *op. cit.*, col. 1224 ; Sigismondo de'
two surviving mistresses of Niccolò III., Cam
Anna de' Roberti, were carried off by the pe

of Modena. To judge from the languag
Father, he has only just heard of the dar
has instantly joined the League for its def
moned the Doge of Venice to desist from
restore what he has taken, and embrace
is greatly consoled by the loyal aid of the
League and by what he has heard of the trie
Ferrarese to their Duke, whom, together w
he has taken under his special protectio
and Duke have full trust in his Legate,
them with spiritual and temporal favours, a
the Duke that he, the Pope, is entirely bent
and the reintegration of his State. " T]
salvation from the Lord," he assures Er
counsels of them that work iniquity shall no
us." If the enemy do not desist from ho
powers of the Roman Church shall be turne
Let the people of Modena and Reggio, too, k
loyal to their Prince, " whereby you will c
peace, and obtain our benediction and sp
that of the Apostolic See."[1]

On December 13, Fra Cherubino da Spol
great sanctity," announced the peace fro
the Duomo. There was a solemn servic
17th, when, in the presence of the Duche
bassadors of the League, the friar exhorte
thank God upon their knees, while the ban
was waved over their heads. The banner
in procession through the streets; bells

---

[1] Briefs of December 13 and 14, 1482. *Archiv*
15, ff. 244–248, 252, 253. See present work, A]
ments 9, 10 and 11.

DUKES AND POETS IN

so merry and jovial in his life.[1] The p
proclaimed in Rome on Christmas Eve. C
by Pontiff and people, the once hated an(
of Calabria appeared in the Eternal C
blessed sword from the hands of the Pope,
his army for Ferrara. At the beginning
Cardinal of Mantua made his state ent
in the name of the Pope, escorted from
Bentivoglio.

In the meanwhile, Sigismondo de' Con
us still in his History of his own times, a
old age was to be eternalized in Rapha
Foligno—had been sent from the Pope to
tians. He was the bearer of a brief fro
Doge and a letter from the Cardinals, in wh
were urged to accede to " this holy and (
to lay aside their arms and desist from the
in which case the Pope pledged himself to se
if they had any cause of complaint aga
Sigismondo himself spoke, drew a piteous pi
plight, assured the Senate that he had lea
to know the dignity and glory of Venice, an
diligently cultivate their friendship for the

But the Venetians remained steadfast.
that they had only entered into the war at
of the Pope himself, and that they woul

---

[1] See letter of Giovanni Sabadino degli Ari
December 20. Dallari, p. 102, note 1. Giova
fortnight previously, had been negotiating with
be taken into their pay and under their protectio

[2] Sigismondo de' Conti, i. pp. 158-164. The
ad apicem Summi Apostolatus, is printed in Raynal
Annali and elsewhere. It is dated December 1
Vaticano, xxxix. 15, ff. 239-241.

DUKES AND POETS IN F

Their ambassador, Francesco Diedo, lef
that the Republic would have recourse to
if a Crusade were proclaimed against it.
perhaps, practicable, even at that epoch ;
had sent to urge the Turk against Naples
stirring up the Swiss against the Duchy (

On January 15, the Duke of Calabria, a
of the League, entered Ferrara, follow(
which included several hundred Turks ta
of whom the greater part took the firs
deserting to the Venetians. Gathering
ties within the city that Alfonso had
again advanced in force into the Barco, ar
to battle ; but, meeting with no respons(
camp at Pontelagoscuro. Florentine and ;
came next, under the command of the Cor
and Virginio Orsini. A number of unimpor
ful actions all along the line raised the spirit
and a state ball was given in the Corte Vec
ary, the allied princes—Ercole himself, w
covered his health, the Duke of Calabria,
(acting always in the name of his helples:
the titular Duke of Milan), Lorenzo (
Marchese Federigo Gonzaga (who now first
the League), and Bentivoglio—met in the l
under the presidency of the Cardinal Gonza
preservation of Ferrara," it was said, " de
of all Italy." It was resolved immediat(
offensive, and to relieve the pressure uj

answers, the Pope's rejoinder and the Venetian rej
elegantissimae epistolae, printed by William Ca:
produced in facsimile by James Hyatt, with an
translation by G. Bullen (London, 1892).

DUKES AND POETS IN F

the League, or the reinforcements need
defence of Ferrara itself and the sec
the fortress which was regarded as the key

With all the energy of his nature, the
League against the contumacious Repu
Powers to contribute the men and mor
mised, insisting upon the equipment
of a powerful fleet to assail the Venetia
protest before God and men," he wrot
Naples, " that if anything sinister happer
in His clemency avert !), it will not ha
fault. All will impute it to thy Majest
Duke of Milan he represented Ferrara as
rest of Italy, against the insatiable lust of
Venetians. The position at Pontelago
strong to be assailed, the only chance fo
Ferrara is to take the offensive in Lombar
the Duke instantly do. Otherwise, sho
the Venetians will certainly turn their
against Milan. Let him then take the agg
all the Powers of Italy will support him, w
will pursue the Venetians, not only with
but with censures and interdict.[2]

This, indeed, was the point to whic
Arlotti, Bishop of Reggio and now Ercol
at the Vatican, and the Count Girolamo,
all his old hatred of Ferrara and Naples a
tians, were striving to bring the Pope.
decisive step. On May 24, he excommuni
put the Republic under the interdict, in the

[1] Brief of March 17, 1483. *Archivio Vaticano*,
[2] Brief of April 21, 1483. *Ibid.*, ff. 511–513.

inmost heart. And at the end you will
him that, as he does not cease from fav
with spiritual arms, he will also proceed
succour and support, even as in both resp
by sending hither his men-at-arms, and doi
that are expedient for our safety; so that
that we are aided by his Holiness in ev
held back and may know their error; an
not correct themselves, as they show th
their unbridled pride and ambition may l

The strained state of the Duke's mind a1
of his situation may excuse this somew
epistle. The Pope, now that he had onc
self, was bent upon doing the thing tho
canst be assured," he wrote to Ercole, "
upon nothing more than upon the conserv
of ours, upon which also depends the saf
Italy."² He sent corn and other sup]
kept urging on the Powers to move with
to Ercole's succour, and dispatched the
Venetians to all the sovereigns of Euro]
have it published and carried into effect
dominions. "Unless this unbridled lust
coerced," he wrote to the Emperor, "we s
that, even as they occupy our cities of Rav
Padua, and many other places of diverse
will reduce Ferrara to their tyrannical swa
rest of Italy, in order that finally they ma
Germany and the other emperies of Christ

[1] *Minute Ducali per Roma a Buonfrancesco .*
Modena, *Carteggio degli Ambasciatori—Roma.*
[2] Brief of June 8, 1483. *Archivio Vaticano,* xx

DUKES AND POETS IN FE

Venetians and that the little garrison wa
he sallied out of Ferrara at the head of his r
mounted balestrieri, took the enemy in the
them headlong in rout. The Venetian s
number of prisoners were captured. The d
had grown pressing again. The Pope, de
Stellata had fallen, it would have been all
itself, was more and more vehement and
appeals to the Powers of the League, espec
Naples, to provide Ercole with men and
urging the Duke of Savoy and King Ferr
the starving Ferrarese with corn and
insisted upon the Duke of Calabria leaving
returning in person to the defence of Fe
complied; but a general attack upon the V
at Pontelagoscuro—to which the Pope ha
generals—failed, much to the grief of his Ho

The war continued, in a half-hearted wa
any important action, alike in Lombardy an
mainland and in the Ferrarese territory,
spring of 1484, mainly to the disadvantage o
Both parties were growing weary of the wa
taken the fatal step of appealing to the
Pope had written to the King of Hunga
instantly to invade the Venetian territory wit
army.[3] The Venetians had invited the Dul
renew the claims of the Visconti upon Milar
of Bourbon in the name of Anjou to assai

[1] Various briefs of September 17, November 2, 1
Archivio Vaticano, xxxix. 16, ff. 21, 68, 84v.

[2] Briefs of November 15. *Ibid.,* f. 71.

[3] Brief of March 10, 1484. *Archivio Vatican*
49-50.

Kingdom. The Venetians took advan
secretly to offer their support to L
sum of money to further his plans
of July, Trivulzio came disguised into
and opened negotiations with Robe
on Lodovico's behalf.[1] The captains
the potentates could only send their
the conference that met at Bagnolo in
where it soon became evident that Lo
tians were working together, and tha
would have to go to the wall.

The Pope stormed against the cessat
the conditions proposed. "He uses
language in the world," wrote Arlotti t
that he has been deceived and betray
if all the allies and the captains of th
that even a dishonourable peace was
would not take the responsibility of alc

"To-day at sunset," wrote Lodovico
on August 7, "to the praise and glor
the peace has been concluded and stip
most holy and most serene League and
Signoria of Venice, which we hope is to k
and bond of perpetual quiet and rest
Italy."[3] Venice and Naples were to
places they had lost in the war, as als
possessions of the Rossi were ceded to
Roberto da San Severino was to be Cap

[1] Cf. Rosmini, *op. cit.*, i. p. 137, ii. p. 126 ; I
295, 296.
[2] Dispatches of Buonfrancesco Arlotti, Jul
1484. Archivio di Modena, *Carteggio degli Am*
[3] Rosmini, *op. cit.*, ii. p. 127.

gave evasive answers; but Arlotti passionately protested against the way in which the Duke of Ferrara had been abandoned by his allies, and that he had only yielded under compulsion. "We know," said the Pope, "the great prudence of the Majesty of the King, of the Lords of Milan, the Florentines and the Duke of Ferrara, the experience and sagacity of the Dukes of Calabria and Bari, who have brought this about. If all these have made and consented to this peace, judging it to be the better part, we, who have not such great prudence and less experience, are willing to follow them and agree to all they wish, even as we have done during the war. With great expense to ourselves have we carried on that war to save Ferrara, and to please the Majesty of the King and the other allies, and so were we ready to continue. Greatly does it grieve us that the Duke of Ferrara has not more grounds for content and satisfaction; but since he who has managed this affair thinks that it is necessary so, and that he cannot do otherwise, we, together with that Duke, shall have patience, and shall consider that everything is permitted for the best by our Lord God, from whom cometh all good and nothing evil."[1]

But Sixtus could ill dissemble his rage and indignation. When the other ambassadors left the room, Arlotti remained behind, and the Pope bade him comfort Ercole in his name, and remind him that, since Ferrara itself was saved, time would bring new remedies and resources. That same night Sixtus died, denouncing the conditions of the peace with his last breath, declaring that Lodovico Sforza was a traitor.[2]

[1] In consequence of the great interest and importance of Arlotti's dispatch of August 12, I give the full text in Appendix II., document 14.

[2] Dispatch of Buonfrancesco Arlotti, August 14, 1484 (Archivio di Modena, *loc. cit.*); Sigismondo de' Conti, i. p. 204.

DUKES AND POETS IN FERRARA

There were magnificent festivities in Venice at the beginning of February, 1485, to celebrate the peace, with many days' jousts and tournaments, at the instance of Roberto da San Severino. After some hesitation, Ercole accepted the invitation of the Signoria to be present, in sign of amity and complete reconciliation, and was greatly gratified at the cordiality of his reception. On the afternoon of February 3, he arrived by water from Corbola at Chioggia. On the way the Podestà met him, and welcomed him in the name of the Signoria, and when he landed a band of Venetian gentlemen were waiting to escort him to the palace of the town, to assure him of the great expectation that all Venice had of his coming. The next day he went on by sea to Malamocco, where he dined, and was greeted by more Venetian gentlemen from the Signoria. At San Clemente, the Doge and Senators came in the state Bucentaur, with Roberto and Leone da San Severino, to meet and embrace him. Ercole went on board the ducal vessel, and, surrounded by a flotilla of smaller ships, they brought him to his own palace in Venice, "which we have found," he wrote to Leonora, "in every part well prepared, adorned and furnished with abundance of all things meet for our reception and honourable entertainment. Verily, the demonstrations made towards us up to now could not have been greater nor more loving. We have received consolation and comfort therefrom, and we gladly share them with your Ladyship." He spent several days at Venice, using towards the Doge "those most sweet and loving words that were possible to us, to show him our filial observance." Once "we went to Murano, where they make so many kinds of right beautiful vessels of glass." Every day he was with the Doge to watch the jousts, which were of the most

Chapter VII

IN THE LULL BEFORE THE STORM

THE ten years that follow the peace of Bagnolo are the most splendid in the history of the Courts of the Italian Renaissance, before the terrible wave of ultramontane invasion had swept over the Alps. "It is manifest," writes Guicciardini in the proem to his history, "that, since the Roman Empire, weakened chiefly by reason of the mutation of its ancient customs, began more than a thousand years ago to decline from that greatness to which, with marvellous virtue and fortune, it had ascended, Italy had never felt such great prosperity, nor experienced so desirable a state, as was that in which she reposed in security, the year of Christian Salvation, 1490, and the years which immediately preceded and followed that. Everywhere she was restored to perfect peace and tranquillity;[1] the most mountainous and most barren places were cultivated, no less than the plains and more fertile regions; she was subjected to no other rule save that of her own sons. Not only was she most abundant in inhabitants and in wealth, but shone with the utmost lustre by the magnificence of many princes, by the splendour of many most noble and most beauteous cities, by the majesty of religion of which she was the seat; she

[1] Guicciardini here forgets the perpetual wars between Pope Innocent VIII and King Ferrante of Naples.

DUKES AND POETS IN FERRARA

life of the epoch, drinking in what was best in its spirit, absolutely untainted by its darker side—its cruelty and lust, its loosening of all ties and obligations, human and divine,—which, though held in check in Ferrara by the personal influence of the Duke and Duchess, was manifest enough there as elsewhere.[1] Hardly in the least exaggerated is the enthusiastic praise of the women of the House of Este, which Ariosto puts upon the lips of "the courteous enchantress" in satisfaction of Bradamante's desire to hear of the *belle e virtuose donne* to come from her race :—

> Da te uscir veggio le pudiche donne,
> Madri d'Imperatori e di gran Regi,
> Reparatrici e solide colonne
> Di case illustri e di domini egregi ;
> Che men degne non son ne le lor gonne,
> Ch'in arme i cavallier, di sommi pregi,
> Di pietà, di gran cor, di gran prudenza,
> Di somma e incomparabil continenza.[2]

The frequent absences of the Duke from his capital, and the taxes imposed to gratify his lavish spectacular and decorative tastes, aroused much discontent at times. "He just takes," says a contemporary manuscript,[3] "all the pleasures that he likes, and fills up his time with astrology and necromancy, giving very small audience to his people."

---

[1] Mrs. Ady finely remarks : "If in Isabella we have the supreme representative of Renaissance culture in its highest and most intellectual phase, Beatrice is the type of that new-found joy in life, that intoxicating rapture in the actual sense of existence, that was the heritage of her generation." (*Beatrice d' Este*, preface, p. vi.)

[2] *Orlando Furioso*, xiii. 57. "From thee I see issue the pure ladies, mothers of emperors and of great kings, that shall restore and sustain illustrious Houses and noble dominions. Not less worthy are they in their women's weeds than the knights in arms; of highest worth, pitiful and great of heart, right prudent, supreme and incomparable in virtue."

[3] Frizzi, iv. p. 147.

IN THE LULL BEFORE THE STORM

Murders and robberies with violence, even sacking of shops, took place in broad daylight.[1] The offices of State were openly sold to fill the ducal treasury, and the purchasers got back their outlay by extortion and oppression. Away from Ferrara, as at Massa Fiscaglia in 1488 and at Argenta in 1489, the people rose and took vengeance summarily upon their Podestà, and, in a subsequent chapter, we shall see an even more notable act of popular justice in Ferrara itself.

Duke Ercole had a perfect passion for the drama. Under his auspices Ferrara was now to witness what was little less than the restoration, the new birth of the theatre of the ancients, naturally followed a little later by the modern Italian comedy of the Renaissance. With the year 1486 begins the great series of dramatic representations in Ferrara, which marks an epoch in the history of the Italian stage. Nearly fifteen years before at Mantua—recent researches have shown that it was precisely in that fateful July of 1471, when Duke Borso lay on his death-bed at Ferrara, and his nephew Niccolò had fled from Ercole to seek aid from the Gonzaga and Sforza—the *Festa* or *Favola d'Orfeo* of young Angelo Poliziano had been recited under the auspices of the Marchese Lodovico and the Cardinal Francesco Gonzaga, as a part of the festivities that welcomed the Duke and Duchess of Milan.[2] This, however, as Del Lungo and D'Ancona have pointed out, does not represent the beginning of the Italian secular drama;

---

[1] Writing under 1478, Caleffini says: "In this time Ferrara was a den of thieves, and there were many murderers; every day people were killed, wounded or robbed, and never was any robber or murderer found." In 1480, it was found necessary to issue a proclamation abrogating the right of the churches to give sanctuary to criminals. *Croniche del Duca Ercole*, ff. 33, 35v.

[2] I. Del Lungo, *Florentia*, pp. 284 *et seq.*

DUKES AND POETS IN FERRARA

in spite of its mythological theme, Poliziano's *Orfeo* still retains the characteristics of the *sacra rappresentazione*; but it clearly implies " the application of the forms of the popular and religious mystery to a classical and profane subject, and, corresponding to this, the rising of an Italian theatre no longer in the squares or in a church, but in a Court."[1] For some time this stood alone, until Isabella d' Este brought the Ferrarese influence to the city of the Gonzaga; and we must look to Ferrara and the year 1486 for the real beginning of the Italian drama. " Ercole I," writes D'Ancona, " without entirely abandoning or despising the religious form, favoured and aided with his example and with his encouragement the instauration of the secular theatre, of classical character in its art and of courtly magnificence in its mounting."[2]

On January 25, 1486, the stage was set up in the cortile of the ducal palace opposite the chapel, and the series began with the *Menaechmi* of Plautus. The Marquis of Mantua had come the day before to be present, and some thousands of spectators witnessed the performance in silence, bursting out into clamorous and enthusiastic applause at the end. The scenery and the realism of a boat with sails and oars and ten persons on board, which moved across the stage, roused general admiration, and the cost is said to have amounted to more than a thousand ducats.[3] Next year, 1487, on January 21, to honour the marriage of his favourite Giulio Tassoni with Ippolita de' Contrari, the Duke had an original Italian play produced—the *Favola di Cefalo*, by that most

---

[1] Del Lungo, *op. cit.*, p. 320; A. D'Ancona, *Origini del Teatro Italiano*, ii. pp. 349, 350.
[2] *Op. cit.*, ii. p. 352.
[3] *Diario Ferrarese*, col. 278: Zambotto, f. 173.

IN THE LULL BEFORE THE STORM

perfect knight of Italian court chivalry, Niccolò da Correggio. Though not devoid of merit, the play may be described as an imitation of Poliziano's *Orfeo*, with hardly a trace of its lyrical beauty and more obviously influenced by classical models. It was on this same occasion that the Duke gave the bridegroom the magnificent new palace that he had built near San Francesco, now called the Palazzo Pareschi, and granted him the right to bear the arms of Este.

In this same month of January, 1487, the marriage was celebrated of Annibale Bentivoglio with Ercole's bastard daughter, Lucrezia. Annibale had visited Ferrara two years before, and Ercole, writing to Giovanni Bentivoglio, had expressed the great pleasure that he had derived from the visit, and assured him that the young man had won the hearts of all the Court. He painted in glowing terms the mutual affection of the two, "being both beautiful and in their first love," and suggested that the marriage had better be hurried on. Bentivoglio, however, raised some objection, and the matter had been in consequence deferred until this year.[1] To do honour to the occasion, on January 25, the *Amphitruo* of Plautus was given, with musical interludes; there was a Paradise or Olympus constructed with lamps for stars and little children dressed as planets, "that was a wondrous thing to see"; but the performance "was not finished, because there came a great rain, which fell upon the spectators, although the cortile was almost all covered over with canvas." The entertainment was repeated on February 3, for the pleasure of the Marquis of Mantua, with-

---

[1] Letters of Ercole to Giovanni II. Bentivoglio, January 8 and 14, 1485. (Dallari, pp. 108, 109). Lucrezia's dowry from her father amounted to 10,000 ducats, to which Giovanni Bentivoglio added 2,000 more (*ibid.*, p. 114, note).

out whose genial and sportive presence no festa in Ferrara seemed complete ; this time they played the whole thing through, with a pageant of the Labours of Hercules at the end.[1]

In the years that followed, Boiardo produced his *Timone*, a dramatization of a dialogue of Lucian, and Tebaldeo, whom we shall meet again, recast the *Orfeo* of Poliziano into the form of a regular tragedy. Gradually almost all the comedies of Plautus and Terence were brought upon the boards of the ducal theatre—occasionally in the original, but more usually translated or imitated—Ercole being exceedingly particular about the fidelity and accuracy of the versions provided for him. And these performances—which were held sometimes in the cortile, sometimes in the Sala Grande of the palace—were not confined to the Court. As far as space admitted, the people were allowed to assist as spectators ; and in the first printed edition of the *Cefalo* it is distinctly stated that the fable was " composed by the Lord Niccolò da Correggio for the most illustrious Duke Ercole, and by him represented to his most prosperous people of Ferrara." This was especially the case when the representation was held in the cortile ; according to Zambotto, as many as ten thousand persons witnessed the performance of the *Menaechmi*, which may be said to have inaugurated the whole.

A curious episode of the year 1487 may be mentioned. Ercole had vowed a pilgrimage to St. James of Compostela, and set out in March with a splendid company. At Milan, where he stopped for Holy Week, a message reached him from the Pope bidding him, under pain of excommunication, go no further, and commuting the matter of the vow to

[1] Zambotto, ff. 181*v*.-182*v*.

IN THE LULL BEFORE THE STORM

a visit to Rome. It seems that Innocent scented some political intrigue under this religious seeming. "Duke Ercole took it very ill," writes the Ferrarese Diarist, "but he had to obey and to go to Rome."[1] He reached the Eternal City on May 22, and had a ceremonious reception, representatives of the Pope meeting him at intervals on the way. Half a mile before reaching the Ponte Milvio, the Senator and Conservatori greeted him ; between the bridge and the gate, the households of the Cardinals and the ambassadors of the Italian sovereigns, and, a little nearer, the household of the Pope with twenty-four prelates and other dignitaries, welcomed him. The Cardinal Lorenzo Cybo and the Cardinal Ascanio Sforza awaited him, and brought him to the palace into the presence of Innocent, preceded by the ambassadors. The Pontiff received him with all the Cardinals sitting round, as is done in the Consistory, and made him sit among them under the last Cardinal Deacon, after which Cybo and Sforza brought him to his apartments.[2] On the last day of May, Ascanio Sforza gave a great hunt in the Duke's honour, six miles out of Rome, which "was a worthy and honourable thing, alike because of the equipment, which was right splendid and magnificent, and because of the banquet, which was as sumptuous and ample as could be described."[3] Ercole left Rome on June 5, and stayed some days at Urbino and Forlì on his way home. While at the latter town, he

[1] *Diario Ferrarese*, col. 279.

[2] These details of Ercole's reception are from a MS. now in the Vatican Library, *Cod. Barberini*, lvii. 44 (ff. 69v, 70).

[3] Thus Ercole to his wife, June 3, 1487. Archivio di Modena, *Carteggio dei Principi*. The Notaio di Nantiporto says: "They took only one stag ; the hunt was badly arranged ; but right well arranged was the banquet at San Giovanni della Magliana." *Rerum Italicarum Scriptores*, iii. 2, col. 1105.)

heard that Ippolito had started for Hungary, to take up his Archbishopric of Esztergom (the young prelate was not nine years old), and sent him his paternal blessing through Leonora. Count Girolamo was away at Imola, sick apparently with a diplomatic illness; but he very courteously received Alberto della Sala, whom Ercole had sent to thank him for his reception at Forlì.[1]

The next year, 1488, was one of blood and tumult for Ercole's neighbours, the tyrants of Romagna. Count Girolamo Riario was butchered in Forlì on April 14, and his corpse dragged through the streets by the populace; but prompt aid from Milan and Bologna placed the city again at the mercy of the Count's heroic widow, Caterina Sforza. On the last day of May at Faenza, Francesca, Giovanni Bentivoglio's daughter,—moved thereunto, says Machiavelli, "either by jealousy or by having been badly treated by her husband, or by her own evil nature,"—murdered her husband, Galeotto Manfredi, in their own bed-chamber. According to Machiavelli, Bentivoglio was privy to the design, in the hopes of becoming lord of Faenza. With a condottiere of the Duke of Milan and a strong force of armed men, he advanced upon Faenza and occupied it; but the men of the Val di Lamone poured into the city, shouting for young Astorre (the murdered man's son) and for the Florentines, killed the Milanese condottiere, took Bentivoglio prisoner, and handed him over, together with the place, to Antonio Boscoli, the commissary of Florence.

Informed of what had happened, the Duke of Ferrara wrote at once to Ginevra Sforza (Bentivoglio's wife) and to Annibale, offering his services on behalf of their husband and

[1] Letters of June 20 and 22, 1487, from Ercole to Leonora. Archivio di Modena, *Carteggio dei Principi*.

IN THE LULL BEFORE THE STORM

. father. Lorenzo de' Medici and the Florentines, before releasing him, required from the Duke of Milan a promise that he would interfere no more with the city and people of Faenza; and Ercole, who was insistent on Bentivoglio's behalf, alike with Lodovico Sforza and Lorenzo de' Medici, dissuaded Ginevra and Annibale from their professed intention of declaring war against Florence, if he were not instantly set free. By the end of June, Bentivoglio was back in Bologna, and took his revenge by persuading Il Moro to give an annual provision of 300 ducats to Ottaviano Manfredi, a rival claimant to Astorre's signory, who stayed under Ercole's protection at Ferrara to serve in case of need as a threat against Lorenzo and the Florentines, who by the protection of Faenza had enormously increased their influence in eastern Italy.[1]

In November, a conspiracy of the Malvezzi and Bargellini and others at Bologna, to murder Bentivoglio with all his family in their palace at a banquet and overturn the State, was discovered on the very day upon which it was to have taken effect. On December 10, Lucrezia wrote to her step-mother, the Duchess Leonora: "Now, thanks be to God, I find myself in good favour with these my magnificent parents-in-law, and they treat me very affectionately, with demonstrations of love better than in the past ; on my side I shall strive my best that these things shall last. I shall write nothing else to your Excellency, save that we have all had a great fright, and especially myself, who was never too courageous. I still cannot free me from it, for, at every

[1] See various letters interchanged between Ercole, Ginevra and Annibale, and Giovanni Bentivoglio, during June and July, 1488. Dallari, pp. 121–123. Both the Bentivoglio, father and son, were in the pay of the Duke of Milan, and Ercole had frequently, in these years, to use his influence to get their stipends regularly given to them.

little noise I hear, it seems to me that those are at hand who come to do some harm." [1]

The splendid marriages of the Duke's three eldest legitimate children lit up the years 1490 and 1491. As early as 1477, as we have seen, Alfonso d' Este, the "hereditary prince" of Ferrara, had been betrothed to the sister of Gian Galeazzo, Anna Sforza, then a child a little older than her prospective bridegroom. In 1480 Lodovico Sforza, then twenty-nine, had demanded the hand of Isabella; but, as she was already engaged to the son of the Marchese Federigo Gonzaga, Ercole offered Lodovico the hand of his second little girl, Beatrice, instead—which Il Moro promptly accepted.[2] The time had now come for these alliances to be carried into effect. In February, 1490, Isabella was taken in state to Mantua to be married to Gian Francesco Gonzaga, who had succeeded to his father as Marquis in 1484. At the end of the following December, in a winter of unusual severity, Beatrice with her mother, escorted by Galeazzo Visconti, a favourite courtier of the Duke of Bari, her brother Alfonso (who was to fetch back his own bride to Ferrara) and her uncle Sigismondo, joined on the way by Isabella, went to Pavia, where they were met by Lodovico Sforza, and the marriage was celebrated in the ducal chapel on January 17, 1491.[3] A most magnificent reception at

---

[1] Dallari, p. 126.

[2] See letter from Duke Ercole to the Marquis of Mantua, in Luzio and Renier, *Delle Relazioni di Isabella d' Este Gonzaga con Lodovico e Beatrice Sforza*, p. 77; cf. Dallari, pp. 39, 40.

[3] A full and picturesque account is given by Mrs. Ady, *op. cit.*, pp. 60-66. Leonora was a little nervous, because on the first night "that result had not followed which we naturally desired," as Ercole put it—this being a point of great importance as non-consummation of marriage in those days was a frequent pretext for a political divorce later. Ercole, however, assured her that all would

IN THE LULL BEFORE THE STORM

Milan followed, where a long series of splendid balls, with pageants and spectacles directed by no less a personage than Leonardo da Vinci himself, welcomed the young Ferrarese princess. Ercole was especially delighted to hear from his wife that Lodovico talked to her with great familiarity and affection, without using any reserve. " And when your Ladyship returns here," he writes, " we shall be glad for you to tell us by word of mouth exactly what he said, as you say that you will do." [1]

Reading between the lines of another letter from Ercole to Leonora, we gather that—not unnaturally—the daughter of King Ferrante had not been prepossessed in favour of the Duke of Bari before this visit, and that her husband was disposed to exult over her, in the testimony that she was being forced to bear to her new son-in-law's merits. Ercole has learned from her letter, he says, how Lodovico is heaping all imaginable demonstrations of affection upon her and the rest of the party, and how his Excellency, in public and in private, alike in the presence of the Venetian orator and in that of the Marquis of Mantua, has shown the cordial love he bears to him and her, and that he desires everything that is to Ercole's honour, reputation and advantage. "We have received such singular content, joy and pleasure from these things, that it is impossible for us completely to express it; for we see that the most illustrious Lord, Messer Lodovico, gives every day further proofs of the cordial love that

---

be well; Lodovico had refrained " because of the girl's inexperience and timidity, and the true love that he bears her, and because of the great desire his Excellency has had not to displease her "; he is no doubt waiting for *uno bon die a quel acto*, i.e. a day considered favourable by the astrologers. (Letter of January 21, 1491. Archivio di Modena, *Carteggio dei Principi*.)

[1] Letter of January 20, 1491. Archivio di Modena, *loc. cit.*

his Excellence bears us, and of his excellent will and disposition towards us. For this your Ladyship has to thank him, in your name and in ours, with all your power, and to make him understand that we shall always be grateful to him for so many honourable demonstrations. And right well does it please us that your Ladyship should have learned to know by true experience what we have always told you concerning the prudence and wisdom of the said Lord, his goodness, and the love that his Excellence bears us, and what we have always believed and firmly expected from him; for you will have seen and found it to be even more than we told you. And if you went over there with this good opinion, you will now return all the better edified, having seen, as you have, the excellent proofs of which you write to us, and you will think that we had formed a good and true opinion."[1]

But even then a slight cloud appeared on the horizon. At her very entry into the city, Beatrice resented having to yield precedence to her cousin, Isabella d' Aragona Sforza, the rightful Duchess of Milan, and thus began the bitter rivalry between these girls—which, it can hardly be doubted, was one of the factors in the mingled mass of motives that urged Lodovico on in his fatal course. For some while, however, all external manifestations of amity were kept up between the two Duchesses, and when once Lodovico had been induced to break off his liaison with his beloved mistress, Cecilia Gallerani, Beatrice's marriage was in most respects a happy one.[2] Dancing and riding, hawking and

[1] Letter from Ercole at Ferrara to Leonora at Milan, January 29, 1491. Archivio di Modena, *loc. cit.*
[2] For all these transactions, see Mrs. Ady, *op. cit.*, chapter viii. I can hardly follow her, however, in rejecting the story of the animosity between the two duchesses; cf. Luzio and Renier, *op. cit.*,

IN THE LULL BEFORE THE STORM

hunting, filled up her time, quaintly mingled with practical joking and horse-play of a very primitive description. "The two duchesses," wrote Jacopo Trotti to Ercole on April 28, "have been having a sparring-match, and the Duke of Bari's wife has knocked down her of Milan."[1] It is impossible not to suspect a double meaning in the Ferrarese diplomatist's report. Well had it been for Milan and the House of Sforza, if Beatrice had been content with thus knocking down her Neapolitan cousin only in sport!

Anna and Alfonso had been privately married in Milan on January 23, and at the same time the marriage had been arranged between the younger Ercole d' Este, the son of the Duke's brother Sigismondo, and Angela Sforza, one of the nieces of Gian Galeazzo. There had been some haggling—unseemly to our modern notions, but taken as a matter of course according to the feeling and fashion of that age—about Anna's jewels and Angela's dowry. Duke Ercole professed himself completely satisfied with his wife's diplomacy in these delicate matters, especially as the other side was equally pleased; right glad was he, too, to hear that Leonora had taken a liking to her new daughter-in-law. "The more the most illustrious Madonna Anna satisfies your Ladyship," he writes, "and the better she gets on with

---

p. 87. The flattering utterances of a mere Court poet like Bellincioni cannot, surely, outweigh the testimony of Bernardino Corio (iii. pp. 430, 458), and of the Ferrarese ambassador in Milan, not to speak of the bitter reference to Beatrice in Isabella's own appeal, a little later, to her father. On May 21, 1492, Jacopo Trotti wrote from Milan to Duke Ercole: "This Duchess of Milan keeps rabid and desperate with the envy that she feels more than ever towards our Duchess of Bari." (Quoted by Balan, v. p. 328, note 6).

[1] Mrs. Ady, *op. cit.*, p. 100.

you, so much the more shall we be consoled and with greater contentment."[1]

At the beginning of February Isabella d' Este accompanied Alfonso and Anna, with the Duchess, to Ferrara for the full solemnity. Escorted by two hundred knights of Milan, led by Ermes Sforza and the Count of Caiazzo, Francesco da San Severino, the bridal train came along the Po in a gaily decorated bucentaur to the Ferrarese landing-place, and passed the night in the convent of San Giorgio, Leonora and Isabella going on to the Castello. Next morning, February 12, Isabella came to fetch the bride, and the whole party entered Ferrara on horseback over the Ponte di San Giorgio and rode through the streets, greeted by pageantry in front of the Tassoni Palace, at the Schifanoia, outside San Francesco and in the chief piazza. Under a canopy of white damask, Alfonso and Anna went together up the steps of the Corte Vecchia, where Leonora was waiting in state to receive them. There was a dance in the evening, followed by the performance of the *Amphitruo* again ; on the next day, after the nuptial benediction, there was another festa in the Sala Grande of the palace, when the Duke gave them the *Menaechmi*; and at nightfall the *sposi* were brought by the covered way that connected it with the Corte Vecchia to the Castello, and there put to bed with the curious ceremonies and practical joking which the taste of the age approved.

[1] Letter from Ercole at Ferrara to Leonora at Pavia, February 1, 1491. Archivio di Modena, *Carteggio dei Principi*. In the same letter occurs a curious piece of etiquette : " As to the desire of the most illustrious Lord Lodovico, that his consort should be written to as *Illustrissima*, we say that it seems to us quite proper that, if *Illustrissimo* be written to the husband, *Illustrissima* should be written to the wife ; and we had foreseen this, because, in the letter that we wrote to the said Madama Duchessa di Bari, we wrote *Illustrissima*, as your Ladyship will have seen."

IN THE LULL BEFORE THE STORM

The Marquis of Mantua especially distinguished himself by his facetiousness on this occasion. Anna took it very quietly but Alfonso gave them back as good as he got.[1]

Isabella sent such a glowing account of their brother's wedding to Beatrice, that the Duchess of Bari wrote back that she really seemed herself to be present at it. "I am quite certain," she said, "that those parades and triumphs have been done with that mastery and gallant show that your Excellence writes me; for, since they were thought out and arranged by the most illustrious Lord our Father, there is no doubt that the whole will have been carried out with the greatest wisdom and perfection, such being the custom of his Excellence."[2]

Alfonso's secretary wrote of Anna in after years: "She was most beautiful and most gracious; and little else can be written about her, because she lived but a short while."[3] She was quiet and devout in disposition, and won her father-in-law's heart at once. Otherwise, she remains little more than a sweet and gracious shadow.

The year 1492 opened under what seemed most favourable auspices for the maintenance of the peace of Italy. In January, the long conflict between the Church and Naples was brought to an end by a treaty, practically an alliance between the Pope and the King. But the death of that merchant arbiter of the destinies of the peninsula, Lorenzo de' Medici, on April 8, changed the aspect of affairs.

---

[1] See extract from the letter from Ermes Sforza and the Count of Caiazzo to the Duke of Milan, in Luzio and Renier, *op. cit.*, p. 96. For another instance, with a serious ending, of the taste of the age in these nuptial japeries, see Giraldi, *Ecatommiti*, i. 10.
[2] Letter of February 23, 1491. Luzio and Renier, *op. cit.*, p. 97.
[3] Bonaventura Pistofilo, *Vita di Alfonso I d' Este*, p. 492.

DUKES AND POETS IN FERRARA

In the latter part of April, Ercole was in Rome, purely for his devotion and to visit the holy places, as he protested. There had been some talk of his going on to Naples; but the Pope objected on the grounds that, especially after the recent conclusion of the treaty, such a journey would wear a political aspect. The King, therefore, sent an ambassador to the Duke, to express his regret that he was unable to invite him to visit him. "We have accepted the excuse of his Majesty," writes Ercole to Leonora, "since it is caused by the above considerations; we think that it is well to guard ourselves from putting jealous ideas into the heads of others, and especially since we have neighbours of the kind that we have."[1]

On the evening of July 25, Pope Innocent VIII died; and on August 11, the infamous Cardinal Rodrigo Borgia was elected to the papacy, and took the title of Alexander VI. "With simony and a thousand rascalities and shamefulness," said the Venetian orator in Milan to Jacopo Trotti, Ercole's representative, "the Pontificate has been sold, which is an ignominious and detestable thing."[2] And his Magnificence merely voiced the common conscience of Christendom. But Manfredo Manfredi, the Ferrarese ambassador in Florence, knowing the religious susceptibilities of the Duchess Leonora, wrote to her that, in spite of the things that had been done, Alexander's elevation was to be held the work of the Holy Spirit, and that men said that he would prove a glorious Pontiff.[3] There was wild exultation at the

---
[1] Letter of April 21, 1492. Archivio di Modena, *Carteggio dei Principi*.
[2] Dispatch of Jacopo Trotti to Ercole, August 28, 1492. Pastor, iii. document 14.
[3] Letters of August 11 (?) and 17. Cappelli, *Fra Girolamo Savonarola*, pp. 322, 323.

IN THE LULL BEFORE THE STORM

Milanese Court, where the whole election was ascribed to the machinations of the Cardinal Ascanio Sforza. A few days after the news of the election had spread through Italy, Isabella d' Este went to Milan by way of Cremona and Pavia, and, from Pavia and again from the capital, she wrote to tell her husband of the universal delight. On August 19, she dined with Lodovico and Beatrice, and after dinner, in the presence of the Duke and Duchess of Milan (who appear already to have been regarded as almost negligible quantities in their own duchy) Lodovico showed a letter from the Milanese ambassador in Rome (who had, of course, written to him and not to his nominal sovereign), which he proceeded to read aloud. In this dispatch the Pope was represented as telling the ambassador that he confessed that he had been made Pope by Ascanio, " miraculously and contrary to the opinion of all the world," and that he intended to be the most grateful Pope that there ever was—with much more of the same tenor. Then Lodovico produced what purported to be a letter written in the Pope's own hand to Ascanio, in a similar tone, and declared that his Holiness had told the ambassador that, knowing the importance of his (Lodovico's) position and his prudence, he meant to rule in accordance with his views in such wise that he would practically be seated on the papal throne! Whether the luckless young Duke of Milan had enough sense to realize that this triumph of his uncle was his own ruin, we cannot say; but Isabella d' Este assured them all that she and her husband were greatly delighted, because of the affinity that they had with the Lord Lodovico.[1]

In November, Alfonso d' Este went with " a most beau-

[1] Letter of August 19 from Isabella to the Marquis of Mantua. Luzio and Renier, *op. cit.*, pp. 351–352.

teous company" to congratulate the Pope on his elevation, and to commend his father's States to his protection. Alexander received him with the utmost cordiality, and heaped honours upon him. In Alfonso's train was the new Court painter of Ferrara, Ercole de' Roberti, with a commission from the Duchess to see certain things (sculptures and pictures, presumably), and report on them to her.[1] Alfonso was back in Ferrara by December 18; and on January 3, 1493, the Duke wrote a somewhat fulsome letter to the Pope, thanking him for his "singular benignity, liberality, grace, humanity and ineffable charity."[2]

While in Rome, Don Alfonso had probably seen in the palace of S. Maria in Portico a young girl whose name was destined in after years to be linked—somewhat ambiguously— with his own: Madonna Lucrezia Borgia. We are fortunately not here concerned with the family affairs of the House of Borgia, save in so far as they touch those of the princes of the House of Este. Suffice it to say that, when her father was elected Pope, Lucrezia was between twelve and thirteen years old, four years younger than her formidable brother Cesare.[3] Her mother, the Roman Vannozza Catanei, had taken as second husband a Mantuan humanist, Carlo Canale, in 1486. The Pope had placed his daughter—whom he loved, as the Ferrarese ambassador in Rome, Gian Andrea Boccaccio, Bishop of Modena, wrote to Ercole, *in superlativo grado*—under the charge of his kinswoman, Adriana dei Mila, the widow of Lodovico Orsini. In the same palace, likewise under the protecting wing of this

---

[1] Venturi, *L'Arte Ferrarese nel periodo di Ercole I*, ii. p. 415.
[2] Gregorovius, *Lucrezia Borgia*, document 8.
[3] According to the documents found by Gregorovius, Lucrezia was born on April 18, 1480, and Cesare in 1476.

IN THE LULL BEFORE THE STORM

serviceable lady, lived a girl some four or five years older than Lucrezia, whose magnificent head of hair excited universal admiration in the Eternal City; this was Donna Giulia Farnese, ostensibly the young wife of Adriana's son Ursino, in reality the mistress of the Sovereign Pontiff himself. When a mere Cardinal, Alexander had been contented with a Spanish noble for his daughter, and had found her a prospective husband in the young Count of Aversa, Don Gasparo da Procida. But now a great Italian alliance seemed desirable. Don Gasparo came to Rome after the Pope's accession to claim his bride, only to find another competitor in the field, in the person of Giovanni, Count of Cottignola and tyrant of Pesaro, an illegitimate son of Costanzo Sforza. The Magnifico Giovanni had previously been married to Maddalena Gonzaga, sister to the Marchese Gian Francesco, who had died in childbirth. In the following June, 1493, the marriage between Giovanni Sforza and Lucrezia Borgia was formally celebrated in Rome, and the Holy Father was much delighted with the present of richly-worked plate that Ercole sent on this occasion.[1]

Even before the death of Innocent VIII, Lodovico Sforza had been in treaty with the French. Beatrice, intensely ambitious for his sake and her own, was urging him to make himself Duke of Milan in very deed, and he anticipated dire opposition from Naples. In January, 1492, he had been holding long and secret conferences with the French ambassadors, had shown great jubilation at the result, and professed a desire to speak in secret with Ercole. The concert of the Italian Powers was clearly breaking up; in May, Jacopo

[1] It was then that Boccaccio, writing to Ercole, used the oft-repeated phrase concerning Giulia Farnese: *Madonna Julia de Farnese, de qua est tantus sermo.* Gregorovius, document 10.

DUKES AND POETS IN FERRARA

Trotti, watching the game at Milan, informed Ercole that it would take little to bring about a direct rupture between Milan and Naples.[1] Under pretext of a vow, Ercole went to Milan in July, and had a long interview with Lodovico, whose ambassador in France, Carlo di Belgiojoso, was manifestly doing all in his power to bring about a French invasion of Italy—on the grounds, it will be remembered, of reviving the old claims of the House of Anjou upon the Kingdom of Naples.

The supposed slight inflicted upon Lodovico by Naples and Florence at the coronation of Pope Alexander, when King Ferrante, at the instigation of Piero de' Medici, negatived the former's proposal that one ambassador should speak for all the allied Italian Powers, did little more than increase his desire for the coming of the invader. Already, in September, he had openly told Trotti to inform Ercole that the French King had decided upon the conquest of Naples, " as a thing belonging and pertaining to his Majesty." [2] A month later, Lodovico accused the Duchess Isabella of Milan of attempting to administer a mysterious white powder to Galeazzo da San Severino and a certain Rozone, a favourite of the Duke her husband, with the ntention of diverting the Duke's affections from the latter, but which in reality was a deadly poison. Her supposed agents were imprisoned and put to the question. The Neapolitan ambassador implored Lodovico to hush the matter up, but the latter sent copies of the process to be read to the royal family of Naples and to the Pope. The old King was furious, declared that the whole process was a mere plot on

[1] Cf. Trotti's dispatches during January, February and May, 1492, cited by Balan, v. pp. 377, 378.
[2] Cf. Balan, v. p. 378, note 6.

IN THE LULL BEFORE THE STORM

the part of Lodovico to ruin his grandchild, and ordered his second son, the Prince Federigo of Altamura, who was then in Rome attempting to sow discord between the Pope and Milan, to seek an audience of the Sovereign Pontiff, and lay the whole blame upon the Duke of Bari, as he deserved.[1]

In January, 1493, Leonora went to Milan, to assist at the birth of Beatrice's first child, who was born on the 25th; named first Ercole, he is better known in history as Massimiliano Sforza. For days all the bells of Milan rang, prisoners were released, and the whole Lombard capital was gay with pageants and processions. And at Ferrara the rejoicings were scarcely less at the reception of the good tidings. Ercole wrote enthusiastically to his wife, declaring that he rejoiced at Lodovico's good fortune no less than if it had been his own. "All to-day, in token of gladness, we have had cannons fired and bells rung through all the city, with all the other demonstrations and signs of joy that befit such festive occasions, and we have ordained that to-morrow, to praise God, there be made a goodly and most solemn procession, and we shall also have a solemn Mass sung for the same intention."[2]

The birth of this little prince precipitated the catastrophe. Although the statement, sometimes repeated, that Gian Galeazzo and his wife were barely allowed the necessaries of life is absolutely contradicted by the accounts still preserved of their expenses in the Archives of Milan, it is evident that Lodovico had already usurped the State

[1] Letter from the King to the Prince of Altamura, December 26, 1492. Trinchera, *Codice Aragonese*, ii. 1, p. 229. Cf. also the extracts from Trotti's dispatches, in Balan, v. p. 378.
[2] Letters of January 26, 1493. Archivio di Modena, *Carteggio dei Principi*.

DUKES AND POETS IN FERRARA

in everything, save the title of Duke; all the fortresses of the duchy were in his hands, and the administration was absolutely his. Exasperated at the sight and sound of these rejoicings, which were far in excess of those that had welcomed the birth of her own son Francesco a few years before, Isabella wrote that piteous and passionate appeal to her father, the Duke of Calabria, which may still be read in the pages of Corio, urging him by his paternal piety, by his love for her, by her just tears, by the magnanimity of a king, to deliver his son-in-law and daughter from this shameful servitude and restore to them their rightful dominion.[1] Alfonso of Calabria lent a ready ear to his daughter's appeal and urged his father, King Ferrante, to maintain the cause of his grandchildren with arms. The rupture between the two States seemed imminent. But appearances of amity were still kept up. The King protested again and again that the Duke of Bari had no reason for suspecting his dispositions and intentions towards him, that he was absolutely contented that he should keep his position in the government of the duchy, and that he himself was disposed to do everything possible to preserve and augment his authority.[2]

But, in truth, the desires of Lodovico went far beyond the throne of Milan—concerning the investiture of which he was soon to open negotiations with Maximilian, King of the Romans. He was dreaming of the acquisition for himself of the crown of a north Italian kingdom. In the April of this year, 1493, mainly through the diplomacy of

[1] *Storia di Milano*, iii. pp. 458, 459. Is it, perhaps, possible that the letter is the rhetorical exercise of some humanist?
[2] Letter to Antonio da Gennaro, royal ambassador in Milan, of February 17, 1493. Trinchera, ii. 1, p. 288.

and improbable. It seems, however, clear that Ercole knew of all the articles of the treaty, and accepted the place reserved for him in it. Among the minor Powers, the Republic of Siena and the Marquis of Mantua adhered to the League.

The King of Naples protested against the League—and still more against what he saw lying behind it—by the mouth of Antonio da Gennaro, whom he bade use in speaking to Lodovico "that charity which is worthy of us as a father towards him whom we hold for a son." "We urge and exhort him," he wrote, "with paternal affection and most cordial intention, to continue in his ancient customs, to keep before his eyes and in his heart the assured and mutual friendships of the past, nor depart from his usual wisdom. Let him think what Italy is, where she is placed, the quality of the States that are in her and near her, and the excessive evils whereof his Excellence might be the cause, if she be divided. The blind can see whether Italy has good neighbours by sea and land."[1]

Ostensibly for pleasure, in reality for purposes connected with the new League, Lodovico and Beatrice came to Ferrara on May 18, "per puncto de astrologia," and had a most sumptuous reception. On the previous day, the news had just reached them that peace had been concluded between Charles and Maximilian, and that the former's hands were therefore free. There were races and tournaments, dances in the ducal gardens, and, of course, the inevitable Plautine comedies, without which no entertainment seemed to Ercole to be complete. A week later, the day and hour likewise chosen by astrology, Leonora and

[1] Letter of April 24, 1493. Trinchera, ii. 1, p. 376.

null and void by the Papal Court. The Marchesana Isabella came in July to be near her mother, and stayed until August 10, the Duchess being utterly unable to let her go.[1] And, indeed, Leonora was destined never to see her favourite daughter again.

A few days later, Ercole set out for Pavia, at Lodovico's invitation, with a goodly company including Don Alfonso, and a band of young men to perform a series of comedies for the Sforza's pleasure. At Pavia, which they reached on August 25, they were received by the two Duchesses, Isabella of Milan and Beatrice of Bari ; the latter was radiant with happiness and content, but her rival avoided the Ferrarese merry-makers, appearing only at the performances. Three comedies were played—the *Captivi*, the *Mercator*, and the *Poenulus*—on three successive days.[2] From Pavia, on August 30, Lodovico and Beatrice made an excursion to Milan with Ercole, to show him his little grandchild—or, as he more pompously styles it, " the most illustrious our *nipote*, son of the said Lord." They found the baby very flourishing, *tutto jocondo e piacevole*, and returned next day to join the rest at Pavia. Here they found Alfonso ill with ever, and decided, although Messer Francesco da Castello, the Court physician, did not think it was anything serious, to send him back to Ferrara in the bucentaur. But Lodovico, as usual, thought that the stars were at work, and that

---

[1] See the affectionate letter from Isabella to her sister-in-law, the Duchess Elisabetta of Urbino, July 26, 1493, in Luzio and Renier, *Mantova e Urbino*, p. 67. Elisabetta Gonzaga had married Duke Guidobaldo in 1488.

[2] Cf. Luzio and Renier, *Delle Relazioni di Isabella d' Este Gonzaga con Lodovico e Beatrice Sforza*, pp. 379, 380. As one of the actors was Lodovico Ariosto, I shall return to these festivities on another occasion.

four gentlemen " who have continually to eat with our son, because such is the custom in France and it will be an honourable thing." The numbers of attendants of all kinds are carefully defined, and the horses and mules to be appointed to each. Lodovico, indeed, had hinted that the thing was being done on too lavish a scale, and suggested that forty horses and mules would be enough; " but we thought that they should be forty-six, in order that he may go more honourably." For his own person, Ercole thinks his son is well supplied with horses; but he is content to give him two of his own, one of which, " Reale," was given him by the King [of Naples?] and the other, " Roseghino," is good for exercising in the tilt-yard. Besides all these, four Ferrarese gentlemen, including Count Giovanni Boiardo and Messer Giulio Tassoni, are to accompany him and then return, and Lodovico will send Galeazzo Visconti well attended; " so that in his going there will be about eighty horses, and in this way we think that the company will be honourable, both in respect of those who are to stay with our son, and those who are to accompany him and then to return hither." [1]

But, after this had gone on for a few days, the poor Duchess wrote piteously that she was really too ill to attend to any provision for Ferrando's departure, and Ercole put it into the hands of his brother Sigismondo instead, as he was anxious that there should be no delay. " Every day that at present is lost seems to us to be worth ten, considering that the bad weather is at hand with the winter." As to the day of the prince's starting, Leonora piously suggested that the Feast of St. Francis of Assisi would be suitable;

[1] *Minute Ducali.* Archivio di Modena, *Carteggio dei Principi.*

IN THE LULL BEFORE THE STORM

but both Ercole and Lodovico scouted the notion, and thought that a " lucky " day was needed for his affairs to prosper. Let her wait until Lodovico has heard from Maestro Ambrosio, to whom he has written to send them a good day.[1]

Meanwhile, to Ercole's unbounded delight and mainly through Lodovico's influence, Ippolito had been raised to the Cardinalate in the consistory of September 20. His most reverend and illustrious lordship was not fifteen years old, and was still in his Hungarian archbishopric. Among the Cardinals simultaneously created (not to mention our own Archbishop Morton of Canterbury and others as worthy of the purple) were Cesare Borgia and Giulia's brother, Alessandro Farnese, " il cardinale della gonnella." Ippolito was the first of the House of Este to reach this dignity, and Ercole bade Leonora have public rejoicings all over the Duchy for this good tidings. In writing to her son, he instructed her, for the honour of the House, to address the letter " Cardinali Estensi," instead of " Cardinali Strigoniensi," as the more usual custom demanded.[2]

A few days later, an urgent letter from Sigismondo reached Ercole, telling him that Leonora had been growing steadily worse for three days. Ercole would have hurried to her bedside at the reception of the news—but Lodovico interposed with his astrology : " As soon as we received your letter, we should have started to come at once to Ferrara ; but, because the conjunction of the moon will take place the day after to-morrow, it has seemed to the most illustrious

---

[1] Letters of September 21 and October 2, 1493, to Leonora. Archivio di Modena, *loc. cit.*

[2] Letters of September 22 and 26. Archivio di Modena, *Carteggio dei Principi.*

DUKES AND POETS IN FERRARA

Lord Lodovico that we ought not to set out, because of that combustion." Nevertheless, he will hasten his departure, going from Milan by Pavia to Cremona, and from Cremona to Ferrara by ship, sending the horses by land by way of Mantua. At Cremona he will take leave of Don Ferrando, who is already on his way, and then hasten to Ferrara to see his wife.[1] He came too late, arriving at Ferrara on October 12, only to find that Leonora had died on the previous day. A messenger, who had been sent to hurry him, had missed him on the way.

All Ferrara believed she had died like a saint, consoled with celestial visions. She was buried quietly in the convent of the Corpus Domini, and the funeral was followed by numerous religious services for the repose of her soul, with great donations to the poor of the city. Ferrando hurried back to Ferrara, but was too late to be present at the funeral, and left again at once.[2]

"Not without grief of heart," wrote Ercole to Ippolito, "do we inform you that your dearest mother and our most illustrious consort yesterday evening, at about the twenty-third hour, died, having first received all the sacraments of Holy Church with the greatest contrition and devotion, and in full possession of her senses, hearing and speaking of spiritual and devout things. You must this time bear yourself in such a way that you be reputed a wise and pru-

[1] Letter to Sigismondo d' Este, of October 8, 1493. Archivio di Modena, *Carteggio dei Principi*.
[2] *Diario Ferrarese*, coll. 286, 287. All contemporaries bear witness to Leonora's rare qualities of heart and mind, her boundless charity; "Acts," writes Giovanni Sabadino degli Arienti, "that would make the adamantine gates of Paradise freely open" (*Gynevera de le Clare Donne*, ed. C. Ricci and A. Bacchi della Lega, p. 401). For her library, composed almost entirely of mystical books, see Bertoni, *op. cit.*, Appendix II. (1).

IN THE LULL BEFORE THE STORM

dent Cardinal, a man and not a youth, and of a great soul and not weak, able to be steadfast in adversity as temperate in prosperity. Verily, this is a case to give evidence of the virtue of your disposition and of the constancy that a prelate of your rank should have, and one raised to such a dignity as is the Cardinalate." [1]

It is from the letters of the King of Naples that we realize what Leonora was to the State, and, indeed, in her he had lost his last friend in the counsels of the Powers of northern Italy. Besides the formal letter of condolence which he sent to the Duke, he wrote to his ambassador at Milan, Antonio da Gennaro, as though Ercole were reduced to helplessness by the loss. At the same time, reading between the lines, we see that he was prepared to take advantage of the occasion, to produce bad blood between Milan and Venice :—

" In consequence of the death of the Duchess of Ferrara, our daughter, we have thought well to speak plainly with the ducal orator concerning the peril in which Ferrara stands from the Venetians, since the Duke is of the nature and age that he is, and the Venetians have the disposition that they have to take it for themselves. And, therefore, we have spoken right clearly, that he should urge the Duke of Bari to look to it and protect it, as he ought, since he is so near and bound by the duty of blood, both as son of the Duke and as father of his children. We have enlarged much upon this, for it seems to us that there is crying need ; and, because we feel certain that the Duke of Bari will make

[1] *Minute* of October 12, Archivio di Modena, *Carteggio dei Principi*. Malipiero's story of Leonora having been poisoned at Ercole's orders is a mere Venetian calumny, as absurd as it is atrocious. It is amazing to find that it is adopted by so serious a writer as Burckhardt.

merchandise of this thing with the Venetian orator, we send you another letter together with the present, in order that you may in some discreet way come to speak with the Venetian orator in the tenor that is contained in the said letter, in order that, when he writes to Venice according to what the Duke of Bari will tell him, he may go more cautiously and not give too much faith to the words of the said Duke." [1]

The Marquis of Mantua had hurried to Ferrara on receipt of the ill tidings, but for some days the news was concealed from Isabella, who was expecting the birth of her child. On October 15, Benedetto Capilupo, her secretary, wrote to the Marquis: "She began to perceive that she was being deceived, as she kept her eye upon every one, because it was eight days to-day since she had letters from Ferrara, and also because for three nights, according to what she has said, she had dreamed of the blessed soul of Madama." [2] She heard at last by way of Milan, and controlled her grief for her child's sake, much consoled by the presence of her dearest friend and more than sister, the Duchess Elisabetta. On the last day of this year Isabella gave birth to a daughter, to whom the name Leonora was given. "I shall renew in her," wrote the Marchesana, "the name of the blessed memory of my most excellent mother;" but, in com-

---

[1] Letter of October 20, 1493. The other letter simply bids him commend Ferrara to Lodovico. Ferrante wrote similarly to Carlo Rugieri, his ambassador at Venice, bidding him recommend the affairs of Ferrara and of Alfonso to the Republic, but with dexterity, "showing that we are acting from love and confidence, not from any suspicion." Trinchera, ii. 2, pp. 282, 283, 286, 288. The thing was a clumsy piece of diplomacy, probably due to the fact that the old King himself was breaking down..

[2] Luzio and Renier, *Delle Relazioni di Isabella d' Este Gonzaga con Lodovico e Beatrice Sforza*, p. 381.

IN THE LULL BEFORE THE STORM

municating the news to her father and sister, she did not conceal her disappointment. It is ominous, in view of the great political tempest that was at hand, that the Gonzaga invited Lorenzo di Pier Francesco de' Medici—the enemy of Piero and head of the French faction in Florence—to act as godfather to "our little one," and he was represented in Mantua by his more noted brother Giovanni.[1]

On November 30 the marriage of Lodovico's niece, Bianca Maria Sforza, with Maximilian, King of the Romans, was celebrated at Milan—the bridegroom being represented by his two ambassadors, the Bishop of Brixen and Giovanni Buontempo. "All the streets from the Castle to the Duomo being decked and covered with the finest draperies," writes Corio, " Bianca with Lodovico's wife Beatrice, mounted upon a triumphal chariot drawn by four pure white horses, was brought to the Duomo accompanied by the aforesaid ambassadors, by Gian Galeazzo, Lodovico Sforza, with all the feudatories of his empery, a goodly number of damsels, and by the more notable citizens. And when they had there heard the divine offices, by the two ambassadors with the fitting ceremonies was Bianca, in the name of the most serene King Maximilian, wedded as his bride; after which, crowned as Queen and mounted on horseback, in the midst of the public joy, she returned to the Castle, and after two days she set out to go to her desired spouse in Germany."[2]

---

[1] See Luzio and Renier, *Mantova e Urbino*, pp. 68, note 3, 69, note 1. It was in this January, 1494, that Gentile Becchi from Tours wrote to Piero concerning these two: "Insino nel proprio sangue, vi trovate insidiatori" (Desjardins, i. p. 359).

[2] *Storia di Milano*, iii. p. 533. A long letter from Beatrice to the Marchesana Isabella, describing the marriage, will be found in Luzio and Renier, *Delle Relazioni di Isabella d'Este, etc.*, pp. 384-388, and is Englished by Mrs. Ady, *op. cit.*, pp. 211-216.

DUKES AND POETS IN FERRARA

Needless to say that Bianca's dowry of 400,000 ducats of gold was the bait wherewith the needy King of the Romans had been caught. Lodovico protested that by this union he himself would be *tanquam glutinum* of the peace between Charles and Maximilian.[1] But no one knew what would happen next, nor what the chief Italian States intended; no one trusted the Pope; the Florentines were anxious to keep neutral, though Piero favoured the Aragonese and there was a pro-French party; the Venetians anticipated nothing but gain to themselves from the sufferings of the rest of Italy; Ferrante still clung to the hope that Lodovico might unite with him in repelling the French invasion.

"In such disposition of men's minds and in such confusion of affairs, all tending to new perturbations, began the year 1494," writes Guicciardini, "a year most unhappy for Italy, and in very sooth the first year of miserable years; for it opened the gate to innumerable and horrible calamities, of which it can be said that, through diverse accidents, a great part of the world afterwards shared in them." On January 17, Gentile Becchi announced to Piero de' Medici that the die was cast, and that the enterprise would certainly go forward. "If this war is checked in the Milanese district (for there will be no other opposition down to Naples), all Italy will take arms with Milan, I can tell you. But it must be lost or won. If it be lost, it is all up with Italy; *tutta a bordello*."[2] "What is the use of your warning the Lord Lodovico," he wrote a few days later, "of the danger in which he is putting himself and others? Do you think that he does not know it? You will make him more

[1] Letter from Francesco della Casa to Piero de' Medici, November 9, 1493. Desjardins, i. p. 261.
[2] Letter of January 17, 1494. Desjardins, i. p. 357.

IN THE LULL BEFORE THE STORM

obstinate in his course, to make it seem that he has not made a mistake, or else he will send your letters here."[1] Sick to death with apprehension, almost with his dying hand, King Ferrante wrote the epistle which may be read at length in the "Codice Aragonese," announcing the downfall, not of his own House alone, but of all Italy: "Never did the French come into Italy without working her utter ruin, and this coming is of such a kind that it can clearly be seen to involve universal ruin, though it seems to threaten only us who are seeking, not merely to defend ourselves, but to avert the ruin."[2] He died on January 25, and was succeeded by that Alfonso, whom we have hitherto known as the Duke of Calabria. On January 30, Gentile Becchi informed Piero that the King of France was coming in person to the enterprise of Naples. "See what a stranger we shall bring you home; see what a nag the Lord Lodovico has bought for himself from over here."[3] "You are always talking to me of this Italy," quoth Il Moro, "and for my part I never saw her in the face."[4] In March, Charles arrived at Lyons, to take supreme command of the army. The Duke of Orleans with the French fleet reached Genoa; the Neapolitan fleet under the Prince of Altamura, Don Federigo, approached the Gulf of Spezia.

Nevertheless, some of the actors in this great historic drama found time for lighter amusements. "When I took leave of Madame de Bourbon," wrote Francesco della Casa to Piero de' Medici, "she called me back and told me to write to you for a civet-cat, that is the animal that makes

[1] Letter from Tours of January 22, 1494. Desjardins, i. p. 359.
[2] Letter of January 17, 1494. Trinchera, ii. 2, p. 421. The fateful word *ruina* runs through the passage like a refrain.
[3] Letter of January 30, 1494. Desjardins, i. p. 360.
[4] Villari, *Niccolò Machiavelli*, i. document 1.

civet. I answered her that it was not found in those parts, but that, if there was one in Italy or elsewhere, your Magnificence would send it her. And when I told her that I remembered having seen some at Naples, she said to me that on no account would she have the King of Naples send her any. I answered that, either from Naples or from wherever it might be, you yourself would send her one, and so she prays your Magnificence to do, and she says that she has heard that there are some in Ferrara." [1]

Ercole followed with paternal affection all his son's actions in France, and kept up a constant correspondence with him. He was delighted to hear of the gracious reception he had received from the King and Queen, and urged him to follow up this good beginning with diligence and prudence. He thanks him for the news of the Court, touching the bearing of the King towards the Spanish ambassador and his disposition to attend to the enterprise of the Kingdom of Naples. Hearing that it would be well to present some " cose odorifere " to the King and Queen, but finding himself too badly provided with such things to be able to make such a present to their Royal Majesties as would be worthy of them and him, he sends him by the Count Baldissera da Montecuccolo "three grains of musk, two small, which are set as you will see, and one large one which is not otherwise set." " We are sending them to you in order

[1] Letter of January 14, 1494, from Tours. Desjardins, i. p. 269. This "Madama de Bourbon" is, of course, Anne of Beaujeu, who, a few years before, had tried to wheedle Piero's father out of his giraffe (see Armstrong, *Lorenzo de' Medici*, pp. 232, 233). On December 3, 1493, Francesco della Casa had written from Amboise: " At this moment the Duke of Ferrara has entered, with about a hundred horses, right honourably, and the King will give him a good provision " (Desjardins, i. p. 267). This is obviously a slip for Don Ferrando.

IN THE LULL BEFORE THE STORM

that you may be able to make presents with them on your own account (*da vui ve ne potiate fare honore*), showing that you have had something from home. Those two little ones you can give, if you think fit, to two of those principal great ladies, one for instance to the Duchess of Bourbon, and the other to the Duchess of Orleans, and that bigger one you could give from yourself to that most serene Queen, without giving it in our name. We have not thought well to have it set, because we do not quite know the way they have over there of setting such things. And so, likewise, you could give to his Majesty two horns of civet, which we are sending you by the said Count Baldissera, in the way that we have told you." He sends him other odours and perfumes to dispose of as he likes; two falcons for himself; certain "goodly moulds of cheese" and salame. If he gives these latter away, he must do it as from himself, and not present them in the Duke's name.[1] But presently comes a paternal lecture. His Excellence is very much displeased to hear that his son gives himself much to ease, and does not use fitting diligence " in following and serving the Majesty of that Most Christian King." He has sent him to France that he may make himself good for something, and urges him to throw all his soul into the service of the King. "We know that you have plenty of talent and that you know what your duty is, and that, if you wish, you can do yourself credit."[2]

It was probably in April that the people of Ferrara began to realize what was on foot. A French ambassador had

[1] *Minute Ducali* to Don Ferrando, January 14, February 15, 16, 17, 1494. Archivio di Modena, *Carteggio dei Principi*. The two last may be said to give a Renaissance anticipation of the modern English schoolboy's hamper from home.
[2] Letter of April 8, 1494. Archivio di Modena, *loc. cit.*

DUKES AND POETS IN FERRARA

arrived, with some sixty persons in his train; he stayed a couple of days, the Duke escorting him on his way with great state and ceremony. "There was much talk about the war," writes the Diarist, "and it was said that this ambassador had come about it."[1]

Ercole, in spite of the Pope's threat to excommunicate him if he did so, had promised to allow the French forces with their Italian allies to pass through his duchies of Reggio and Modena, and to supply them with provisions at a suitable price. This was, however, only a small portion of the invading army—those merely who were to pass through Romagna and enter the Abruzzi across the Tronto. At the end of July, the passage began; first came five hundred Italians, under the Count of Caiazzo. They grossly maltreated the people on their way, and, when a larger force of the "men-at-arms of France and Milan" prepared to march through in August, Ercole wrote emphatically to Lodovico, describing the terror of his subjects, urging him instantly to write to the Count of Caiazzo to take measures to prevent a repetition of these outrages.[2]

In September, Charles himself arrived at Asti. Lodovico and Ercole met him, knelt and kissed his hand, while the ungainly little monarch remained mounted. At Asti the King lingered a month, laid up with what is charitably supposed to have been smallpox. In October he began his advance, Ercole presenting him with richly-worked tents and pavilions. At Pavia, the hapless Duchess Isabella threw herself at the royal feet, imploring protection for her husband, mercy for her kindred of Naples. It is too late,

[1] *Diario Ferrarese*, col. 288.
[2] He wrote also on the same day to Trotti, urging him to see that the letter to the Count was worded effectually and sent at once. Archivio di Modena, *Minutario Cronologico*, August 2, 1494.

IN THE LULL BEFORE THE STORM

muttered the Most Christian King. Hardly had he passed on, than Duke Gian Galeazzo died. Lodovico, on receipt of the tidings, left the King at Piacenza and hurried to Milan, to have himself proclaimed Duke. The King, anxious and suspicious, waited a few days at Piacenza, then proceeded on his way through Lunigiana and Tuscany. The story of his triumphal march, the collapse of the Aragonese resistance, the flight of Piero de' Medici, the entry into Florence and Rome, need not be repeated here.

On the news that Gian Galeazzo was dying, Ercole had hastened to Milan, to lend his assistance in securing the succession for Lodovico and Beatrice. On his way, he addressed a severe rebuke to Don Alfonso, whom he had left at Ferrara, as regent:—

"To-day, before we started from Ferrara, we asked for you, and had search made for you, because we wished to give you some directions and to tell you how you were to bear yourself in our absence; and we could not have you, because you had gone out of the town. This thing has greatly displeased us, because, while we were at Ferrara, you ought not to have gone away, nor done such things without our express leave. And, therefore, we have thought well to write this letter to you at once, to tell you that in this absence of ours you must govern yourself better than you did last month, when we went into Lombardy; for you did exactly the contrary to what we committed to you. Our intention was that you should give audience and that you should eat in public, in such wise that all the people could see you and speak to you; but you ate in secret and in remote places, showing that you had little care for the business that you should have had at heart, and also that you did not much esteem our commissions. You can believe that this has offended us. Therefore, while we are away, you must govern yourself properly, giving audience to the people and eating in public, and attending to the examinations ordered, and doing all those other things which are befitting to you and which you know to be our will, so that we may hear a different report of you from what we heard the other time. If you do so, you will do your duty, and a thing which will be pleasure to us and honour to yourself; whereas if you do otherwise, we shall be very angry with you and grievously offended thereat. Remember that we shall hear right well how you behave yourself, just as we heard that other time."[1]

But we must turn now to the noblest victim of this year of shame, to Ercole's Governor in Reggio, Matteo Maria Boiardo.

[1] Letter dated Finale, October 20, 1494. Archivio di Modena, *Minutario Cronologico*. Gian Galeazzo died on the morning of October 21. His contemporaries for the most part believed that he had been poisoned by Lodovico, but this is no longer accepted by modern historians.

Chapter VIII

MATTEO MARIA BOIARDO

SCANDIANO lies some eight miles south-east of Reggio, at the very foot of the Apennines, where the Tresinaro flows down from the hills to swell presently the Secchia near Rubiera. The little town itself, with its quiet streets and arcaded square, is quaint and picturesque. The whole of one corner of it is occupied by the Rocca, the great castle of its feudal counts. Built originally after the middle of the thirteenth century by Giberto Fogliani, it sheltered Petrarca in 1343, when on his way to Reggio from Parma, and in the following centuries was enlarged by the Boiardi, into whose hands it came in 1423. Scandiano is backed by pleasant hills, upon one of which stands the "Torricella," known now as the Castello Cugini, where the greatest of the Boiardi lived and wrote in the summer months. Climb a little higher, and suddenly a complete revelation breaks upon you of the whole sweeping chain of Apennines to south and west, while below your feet the great cities of the Emilian plain appear here and there, just visible in the misty distance. This enchanted spot should be visited on a bright summer morning. The whole hillside is quick with the flight of swarms of great butterflies—black and golden Machaon mingling with its swifter, paler cousin, tiger-striped Podalirius, in mimic warfare. In these paladins of the insect world a believer in the transmigration of souls might almost dream that he saw the fantastic glittering heroes of whom Reggio's two poets sang.

The Boiardi were citizens of Reggio and feudal lords of Rubiera until 1423, when Feltrino Boiardo—whom we have already met—ceded the latter lordship to the Marchese Niccolò and received Scandiano instead, with other smaller townlets and the title of Count. Feltrino married Guiduccia, the daughter of Count Gherardo da Correggio, by whom he had two sons, Giovanni and Giulio Ascanio. Giovanni married Lucia Strozzi, the sister of Tito Vespasiano, by whom he had one son, Matteo Maria, and four daughters; Giulio Ascanio married Cornelia Taddea, the sister of Marco Pio da Carpi, by whom he had a son, Giovanni. One of Feltrino's daughters, Giulia, married Gian Francesco Pico della Mirandola, who made her the mother of the famous Giovanni and of Galeotto Pico. Two others married into the Rangoni family of Modena.

Matteo Maria Boiardo was born, like Dante, under the constellation of the Gemini (as he tells us in one of his sonnets) in the early summer of 1434, probably in the castle of Scandiano, where his grandfather kept a splendid Court, the Boiardi being famous for their hospitality. The greater part of the poet's boyhood was passed in Ferrara and its neighbourhood. Leonello d' Este had made the Count Giovanni independent of his father, by granting him certain tolls and duties which had hitherto been reserved to the Crown in the townlets of Feltrino's fief; and on Giovanni's death, in 1452, Borso—who, on the occasion of his triumphal progress through his duchies, stayed at Scandiano as the guest of the Boiardi, and renewed Feltrino's investiture, adding Casalgrande and other places to his fiefs—confirmed this

MATTEO MARIA BOIARDO

privilege to Matteo Maria. The old Count and Countess appear to have resented this; and in their wills (Feltrino died in 1456, Guiduccia in 1457), on the plea that this embarrassed the feudatory, they compelled Matteo Maria to share these profits with his uncle, Giulio Ascanio, under pain of losing his portion of the inheritance.[1] Throughout the poet's life, there seems to have been this bad feeling, blazing out at intervals, at other times latent, between him and his father's family; while his relations with his mother's house, the Strozzi, were always of the most cordial character. His uncle appears to have governed the fiefs after Feltrino's death, and the young poet is completely ignored in all the official letters of the Boiardi. He probably fell much under the influence of Tito Vespasiano Strozzi, and perhaps spent these years in Ferrara, with the humanists and courtiers. In February, 1460—on the death of Giulio Ascanio—he first comes forward as the feudal lord, *Comes Scandiani et Casalgrandis*, in a letter to Count Silvio di San Bonifazio, Captain of Reggio, announcing the death of his uncle, or, as he puts it, " that it hath pleased our Creator to call to Himself the blessed soul of my good father, Messer Giulio."[2] But even now Giulio's widow, the Countess Cornelia Taddea, an ambitious and overbearing woman, shared the title and the administration of the fiefs of the House.

Boiardo appears to have passed the next eight or nine years of his life mainly at Scandiano, in the midst of the scenery he so loved, playing the part of feudal lord,

---

[1] These details from G. Ferrari, *Notizie della vita di Matteo Maria Boiardo*, in the *Studi su Matteo Maria Boiardo*, pp. 6-9.

[2] Letter of February 8, 1460. Campanini, p. 367. Casalgrande is a small place south of Scandiano, just off the road to Sassuolo, at the foot of the hills.

hunting and entertaining, and much engaged in the somewhat prosaic affairs of the waters of the Secchia—a standing source of contention between the Boiardi and the Commune of Reggio, which latter city derived its water supply from a canal from that stream. "This water is our very life," the Ancients wrote to Cornelia Taddea some years later. A further complication was added by Cornelia's kinsmen, the Pio of Carpi, who also disputed the rights of the good citizens of Reggio. There is still extant a whole series of Boiardo's letters connected with this dispute, which on his part was always conducted with the utmost generosity and courtesy. On one occasion the matter was referred to Duke Borso himself, who wrote back, somewhat sharply, that the disputants must settle the thing promptly, and not trouble him about it. Only two letters from Boiardo to Borso have been preserved. One, of September, 1462, concerns the question of the canal; the other, of February, 1466, excuses the writer for not having already gone to explain to Borso by word of mouth " about the affair of those women," on the grounds that "the Magnificent Count Giovanni Francesco della Mirandola, my uncle, has written to me that he wishes to come to Scandiano for a few days to amuse himself, and so I have been expecting him."[1] Although high in favour with the Duke, whose benign bearing towards himself he records in one of his sonnets, a far warmer devotion united Boiardo with Ercole d' Este. After the recall of the latter from Naples in 1462 and his appointment as ducal governor of the Duchy of Modena, Boiardo was a constant visitor to the latter city, as also to the smaller Court that Sigismondo held in Reggio. In January, 1469, he was summoned

[1] Letter of February 15, 1466. Campanini, p. 378.

MATTEO MARIA BOIARDO

to Ferrara to form part of the escort of the Emperor Frederick, returning to Scandiano before the beginning of April.

This appears to have been a bright and peaceful epoch in Boiardo's life. To it belong his first two works: the Latin eclogues, or *Pastoralia*; the Italian lyrics, or *Canzoniere*.

The *Pastoralia* are Boiardo's first attempts to win the Muses. They are ten in number, according to the Virgilian precedent, and show a closer imitation of Virgil's eclogues than we find in Dante's correspondence with Giovanni del Virgilio or in the Latin poetry of Petrarca. They appear to have been composed between 1458 and 1463, the latter date appearing from the references to the return of Ercole and his presence at Modena. The subjects are partly amorous, partly political and heroic, dealing with the pacific reign of Borso and the martial exploits of Ercole in Apulia. Perhaps the most remarkable is the fourth, entitled *Vasilicomantia*, a kind of imitation of Virgil's famous *Pollio*, in which the golden age of Borso's rule is depicted in glowing colours, and a glimpse is shown in the background of the struggle between Aragonese and Angevin for the possession of the Regno, with the Turkish Hydra lurking in the distance. The tenth, *Orpheus*, is in an exceedingly laudatory strain, addressed to Ercole himself, offering up the little collection to him, promising greater poetic gifts in the future. It is hard to blame adulation, when friendship and admiration alike are so genuine and sincere.

The *Canzoniere*, that comes next in the chronological order of Boiardo's work, is a far more remarkable achievement. In its rhythmic variety and lyrical beauty, it is the finest collection of love poems written by any Italian during the fifteenth century. The love that it sets forth is mainly of the most chivalrous and ideal description; there is considerably less of tangible yearning than we find, for instance, in Petrarca's *Rerum Vulgarium Fragmenta*. The object of the Count's admiration appears undoubtedly to have been a real woman, Antonia Caprara, who was probably Antonia di Bartolommeo Caprari, a girl of Reggio who was born in 1451, and whom he worships thus in song from April, 1469 (the real or fictitious date of the beginning of his love being the fourth of that month), until the spring of 1471. At times he turns to celebrating the beauties of a mysterious *Rosa*, which is most probably not the name of a woman (as some have supposed), but merely a poetic symbol for Antonia. Two other ladies are addressed in some of thè poems, as confidantes of his devotion for Antonia: Marietta and Ginevra Strozzi, the former being the wife of Teofilo Calcagnino. These lyrics are divided into three books, *Amorum Libri*; the first deals with the poet's joys in love; the second with his sorrows; in the third, old desires are overcome, and he gradually passes out of the amorous prison-house into another field. They consist of sonnets, various kinds of canzoni, different forms of madrigals, and other lyrics of peculiar metrical structure, some of them of considerable length and great originality. They show comparatively little of the frigid conventions and mannerisms of the Petrarchists, but are for the most part as fresh and musical as the best lyrical work of the poets of the *dolce stil nuovo*. And for so learned a poet and one so steeped in classicism, so in touch with the humanists, Boiardo's use of mythology is refreshingly sparing and never dragged in for mere parade. He is already dreaming of enchanted

MATTEO MARIA BOIARDO

gardens and eternal spring, in the spirit of his coming romance.

The larger lyrics are, perhaps, his greatest achievement in this kind.[1] For our present purpose it must suffice to quote two sonnets. The one gives admirable expression to the first exultation of the successful lover:—

> Qualunque più de amar fu schiffo in pria,
>   E dal camin de Amor più dilungato,
>   Cognosca l' alegreza del mio stato,
>   E tornerase a la amorosa via.
> Qualunque in terra ha più quel ch' ei disia,
>   Di forza, senno, e di belleza ornato ;
>   Qualunque sia nel mondo più beato,
>   Non se pareggia a la fortuna mia.
> Chè il legiadro desire, e la vaghezza
>   Che dentro mi riluce nel pensiero,
>   Me fan tra l' altre gente singulare.
> Tal che io non stimo la indica richeza,
>   Nè del gran re di Scyti il vasto impero,
>   Che un sol piacer de amor non può aguagliare.[2]

---

[1] See, for instance, *Canz.* lxxxii., addressed to the Strozzi ladies, and the peculiarly constructed *Canz.* civ. It may here be observed that in the British Museum MS. (*Egerton MS.*, 1999), dated January 4, 1477—a manuscript which was probably written under the poet's personal superintendence, or at least at his commands (cf. Solerti, *Le Poesie Volgari e Latine di M. M. Boiardo*, p. xiv.)—the metrical definitions and other Latin titles are not prefixed to the poems. These rubrics and headings do, however, appear in the Bodleian manuscript (No. 47 in Mortara's catalogue), as also in the *editio princeps* (Reggio, 1499), and may plausibly be referred to Boiardo himself. Besides the "esemplari rarissimi" cited by Solerti (*op. cit.*, p. xviii.), there is a copy of this edition in the Grenville Library.

[2] "Whoso before shunned loving most, and kept furthest off from the path of Love, let him know the bliss of my state, and he will return to the amorous way.

"Whoso on earth hath most what he desires, adorned with power, wisdom and beauty, whoso in the world is most blessed, cannot compare with my good fortune.

"For the gallant desire, and the loveliness that within me glows back in my thought, make me stand alone among mankind ; so that I esteem not the wealth of India, nor the vast empire of the

DUKES AND POETS IN FERRARA

The other repeats, but with an entirely different accent, a note already struck in one of the most justly celebrated canzoni of Petrarca:—

> Ecco la pastorella mena al piano
> La bianca torma ch' è sotto sua guarda,
> Vegendo il Sol calare, e l' ora tarda,
> E fumar l' alte ville di luntano.
> Erto se leva lo arratore insano,
> E il giorno fugitivo intorno guarda,
> E scioglie il jugo a' bovi, che non tarda
> Per gire al suo riposo a mano a mano.
> Et io soletto, sanza alcun sogiorno,
> De' mei pensier co' il Sol sosta non have,
> E con le stelle a sospirar ritorno.
> Dolcie affanno d' amor, quanto èi suave:
> Chè io non poso la notte e non al giorno,
> E la fatica eterna non me è grave! [1]

A religious note makes itself heard at intervals, even in the first of the three books, which, though perhaps caught from Petrarca, need not necessarily for that reason be insincere. Many of Petrarca's co-religionists, without being poets, have probably repeated to themselves his famous sonnet of *pentimento* in Holy Week. At the close of the third book comes the summons to Rome—as we know, in 1471, to attend on Borso in his coronation. The poet

---

Scythian King, that cannot equal one sole delight of Love." (*Canz.* lii.)

[1] " Lo, the shepherdess leads to the plain the white flock that is under her charge, seeing the sun sinking and the hour late, and the mountain hamlets smoking from afar.

" The wild ploughman raises himself erect, and looks round at the flying day, and loosens the oxen from the yoke, hastening at once to go to his repose.

"And I alone, without any resting-place, have no pause from my thoughts with the sun, and return to sigh with the stars. So sweet is Love's gentle torment, that I rest not night nor day, and the eternal labour is not grievous to me." (*Canz.* clii.)

professes the utmost sorrow in being thus compelled to leave *il bel volto* (Antonia) and his *signore* (Ercole), and sings the pains of parting at rather unnecessary length, consoled somewhat (so at least a sonnet says) by seeing the former turn pale and weep. But a more solemn note is struck at his first sight of the Eternal City, *in prospectu Romae* :—

> Ecco l' alma città che fu regina
> Da l' unde Caspe a la terra Sabea ;
> La triomfal città che impero avea
> Dove il Sol se alza insin là dove inchina.
> Or levo fato e sententia divina
> Sì l' han mutata a quel ch' esser solea,
> Che, dove quasi al ciel equal surgea,
> Sua grande alteza copre ogni ruina.
> Quando fia adunque più cosa terrena
> Stabile e ferma ? poi che tanta altura
> Il tempo e la fortuna a terra mena.
> Come posso io sperar già mai sicura
> La mia promessa ? Chè io non credo a pena
> Che un giorno intiero amore in donna dura.[1]

He confesses to a certain Battista that his love is unaltered and unalterable, even amidst these new surroundings and the festivities of Borso's reception. Had time or place the power to change or free him from his bonds, perchance Rome would have done so :—

> Ma nè festa regal, nè molto joco,
> Nè del mio Duca la benegna cera,

---

[1] "Behold the blessed city that was queen from the Caspian waves to the land of Saba ; the triumphant city, that held empire from where the sun rises even to where he sets.

"Now fickle fate and divine decree have changed her so from what she was wont to be, that, where she rose almost equal to Heaven, all ruin covers her mighty height.

"When then shall any earthly thing more be stable and firm, since time and fortune bring such great glory to earth ? How can I ever hope to have my promise safe ? For hardly believe I that love lasts in woman one whole day." (*Canz.* clxix.)

DUKES AND POETS IN FERRARA

> Nè in tanti giorni questa terra altera,
> M' hanno ancor tratto de l'usato foco.[1]

Presently he declares that all his hope is still in Ercole, "my gentle lord," and in "the fair face where still my heart hath rest." Then come sonnets of repentance and renunciation of love. They are somewhat conventional in expression, but there is no reason for doubting that Rome had a solemnizing effect upon the mind of the sensitive poet. And, after an allegorical canzone on the treacheries and deception of passion, he turns for aid and pardon to the "King of the stars, eternal and immortal." This concluding sonnet, however, is not in any sense a renunciation of love, but a general confession of human sin and frailty on the part of the writer. He was still to glorify love in the *Orlando* :—

> Amor primo trovò le rime e' versi,
> I suoni, i canti ed ogni melodia,
> E genti istrane e popoli dispersi
> Congiunse amore in dolce compagnia :
> Il diletto e il piacer sarian sommersi,
> Dove amor non avesse signoria ;
> Odio crudele e dispietata guerra,
> Se amor non fusse, avrian tutta la terra.[2]

A new epoch in Boiardo's life and work begins with his return from Rome and the accession to the throne of his friend Ercole, in 1471. He was probably present in Ferrara

---

[1] "But neither royal festivity, nor much delight, nor the gracious bearing of my Duke, nor in so many days this noble town, has yet drawn me from the wonted fire." (*Canz.* cixxi.)

[2] "Love first found rhymes and verses, music, songs, and all melody ; strange folk and scattered nations hath Love conjoined in sweet company. Delight and pleasure would be drowned, if Love had not his sovereignty ; cruel hate and pitiless war, if Love were not, would possess all the earth." (*Orl. Inn.*, II. iv. 2.)

MATTEO MARIA BOIARDO

at the overthrow of the Veleschi—an event which he hailed in a series of exultant epigrams.[1] His love for Antonia Caprara was now a thing of the past, and in the following year he married Taddea Gonzaga, the daughter of Count Giorgio of the Gonzaga of Novellara.

Attempts have been made to weave a romance round Boiardo's marriage. A curious allegorical poem in *terza rima*—the sixth of his Italian eclogues—undoubtedly belongs to this epoch of his life. In it an impassioned hunter is wearied to death with pursuing a *capro formoso*, a lovely goat, than which " a more beauteous never Jason saw in Crete, nor the Trojan youth in the wood on Ida," and of which he is desperately enamoured; but the fair creature proves inaccessible. " That is the goat of Pan, our god," and a shepherd shows him the way instead to a mysterious white marble fountain, where he may slake this fire in the " sweetest and clearest water of the world," though Love is hidden in the trees above it, and shoots through the boughs at all who approach. It has been plausibly suggested that this is an allegory of the poet's marriage, and that the shepherd, in whose pastoral costume the hunter is to approach the fountain, is Count Giorgio Gonzaga.[2] Be that as it may, Boiardo's bride was received in triumph

---

[1] They are eight in number (pp. 473-475) in Solerti's edition. One of the shortest will serve as example :—
    Quid juvat haec garula contendere voce profani
      Veligeri, et cunctis dicere vela viris,
    Cum tribuant regem, dyamantaque numina clament,
    Cum dominum Alcidem mundus et astra velint?

[2] Guido Mazzoni, on the *Ecloghe Volgari*, in the *Studi su M. M. Boiardo*, pp. 335-340. The poem has the rubric: " in the sixth Eclogue a wearied hunter and a shepherd speak in allegory, hiding their names even as the matter is hidden." The reference to Pan is an echo from Petrarca's sonnet, *Una candida cerva*: " Libera farmi al mio Cesare parve."

DUKES AND POETS IN FERRARA

at Scandiano; he appears to have been deeply attached to her, and the marriage proved a happy one.

In 1473, Boiardo was one of the splendid company that Ercole sent to Naples, to bring Leonora of Aragon to Ferrara. This was the first of many important affairs of State in which he was employed by his new sovereign.

In September, 1473, a violent quarrel had broken out between the municipality of Reggio and the Pio of Carpi, the subject being, of course, the endless question of the water supply of the city and the canal. The Pio even went so far as to send an armed force to cut off the water, and Boiardo, who had promptly offered his assistance to the Ancients to defend the rights of the city, appears to have driven back his aunt's kindred by force, *vi et armis.* Whether this had anything to do with what followed, or whether the Countess was actuated by the desire to secure the whole of the Boiardo fiefs and territory to her own son Giovanni (who was always hostile to his cousin and cruelly robbed his family after his death), we cannot say. But it seems fairly certain that, at the beginning of 1474, Count Marco Pio himself, her brother, with her own active connivance, suborned two men to take Matteo's life by poison. One of these two was a trusted servant of the poet, *un suo caro famiglio*; the other was a notary, Simone Boioni, either his or Giovanni's chancellor, a fellow whom Matteo Maria had loaded with benefits and marks of favour. The *famiglio*, whose name does not appear, was to go to Carpi, get the poison from Count Marco, and then, apparently, Simone was to administer it. But when the time came for the man to start, either his courage failed him or he repented, and he revealed the whole to his master, who prepared a dramatic coup worthy of the

MATTEO MARIA BOIARDO

author of the *Orlando*. He arranged things so as to overhear the instructions of the Countess to her ministers and fellow-criminals, and let the repentant servant carry out his part of the design and go to Carpi for the poison. Then, when he had all the evidence in his hands, Boiardo called to horse, and, with the servant and Simone in his train, hastened to Ferrara, and related the whole plot to the Duke. Simone was at once hurled into the dungeons of the Castle; the poison was tested and found deadly. Count Marco was summoned to the ducal presence, and placed under arrest.[1] Probably, Boiardo himself refused to take any proceedings against the Countess; there is no evidence that she was in any way called to account, though it was known and admitted that she had been her brother's accomplice.

This complete escape of the principals from chastisement was, perhaps, common enough in those aristocratic days; but Boiardo, with a magnanimity worthy of the *cortesia* of one of his own paladins, obtained that the same grace should be extended to the actual instruments. Simone's brother, Boione Boioni, who had also enjoyed his favour, was one of the Ancients of Reggio, and he prevailed upon the Commune to intercede for his brother with Matteo Maria himself and with the Duke. On February 14, the Ancients wrote to Boiardo a piteous appeal on behalf of " our poor and unhappy fellow-citizen." " It would

---

[1] Our only authority for the details of the plot is a letter dated March 23, 1474, in the Milanese Archivio di Stato, from Antonio da Correggio, " Count and ducal counsellor," brother-in-law of Feltrino Boiardo, to the Duke of Milan, Galeazzo Maria. It is given by Ferrari, *op cit.*, pp. 34-35. The other documents were first printed by A. Catelani in his pamphlet, *Sopra un attentato alla vita del Conte Matteo Maria Boiardo* (Reggio, 1891).

seem a hard thing to ordinary men to pardon so great an atrocity; but to men of the greatness and of the generosity of soul as is your Magnificence, it is a natural and easy thing to forgive the whole and consign it to oblivion." They sent another appeal for mercy to the Duke, and fervently commended their envoy and the cause of the prisoner to the clemency and mildness of Boiardo himself. The worthy citizens knew their man. The horrible penalties of the law for poisoners were commuted into banishment, and even this was soon remitted. On November 2, 1474, the would-be poisoner wrote from Bagnolo to the Ancients, expressing his ardent desire to return home. The Ancients had already petitioned Ercole for a complete pardon, and Simone implored them to write on his behalf to Boiardo, to beg him to write to the Duke and intercede for his return. This appears to have been done; Simòne was restored to his country, and allowed to fill the honourable offices of the Commune, as if nothing had happened. The Duke only insisted that he should pay the costs of one of the lawyers employed in the case! He even sat in the Council of the Forty in Reggio while Boiardo was governor of the city.[1] Nevertheless, the poet afterwards bore the legal profession a grudge:—

> Attendi a la giustizia,
> E ben ti guarda da procuratori,
> E giudici e notai; chè han gran tristizia,
> E pongono la gente in molti errori.
> Stimato assai è quel ch' ha più malizia,
> E gli avvocati sono anche peggiori,
> Che voltano le leggi a lor parere;
> Da lor ti guarda, e farai tuo dovere.[2]

---

[1] Catelani, *op. cit.*; Ferrari, *op. cit.*, pp. 31–33.
[2] "Attend to justice, and beware of procurators and judges and

MATTEO MARIA BOIARDO

The Duke, hoping to heal the feud in the family, offered to give Matteo Maria double in the Duchy of Ferrara, if he would relinquish Scandiano. But the poet naturally declined. In 1475, the dominions of the Boiardi were divided between him and Giovanni—the latter having Casalgrande and Arceto with three smaller places,[1] Matteo Maria being henceforth Count of Scandiano alone. He left the neighbourhood of Reggio for a while after this attempt on his life, and, from 1475 to 1478, stayed with his family at Ferrara, in a palace still indicated in the Via Ripa Grande, filling some position at the Court of Ercole. In his absence, the Countess Cornelia Taddea and her son made themselves disagreeable to the people of Reggio, and the question of the water supply from the Secchia pursued him even to the capital. In a letter to the Ancients of Reggio from Ferrara, on this endless theme, Boiardo professes himself entirely at their service, prays them to use the places of his dominion as though it were their own district: "If I were the Emperor, I should wish to be a Reggian, obedient to and well-loved by my native city."[2] At the same time, he was engaged in literary work, translating Herodotus from the Greek (of which he knew a little, but not enough for his task), and writing a sort of abbreviation of the *Golden Ass* of Apuleius. He had already begun his great poem of *Orlando Innamorato*, which he probably read aloud as he proceeded, canto by canto, to the Duke and the courtly gatherings of the capi-

notaries; for they are a wicked set, and lead folk into many errors; he who has most malice is much esteemed, and even worse are the lawyers, who wrest the laws to their opinion. Beware of them, and thou shalt do thy duty." (*Orl. Inn.*, II. xxviii. 51.)

[1] Arceto is down in the plain on the other side of the Tresinaro.
[2] Letter of August 2, 1477. Campanini, p. 384.

tal, the *Signori e dame e bella baronia* of his preludes.[1] To these and the few following years, before the outbreak of the disastrous Venetian war, belong the first two parts of the poetical romance.

From the beginning of 1481 to the end of 1482, Matteo Maria was ducal captain of Modena—the most turbulent and factious city of the Estensian dominions. Hardly was he arrived there when, in February, he had to put down a tumult with a strong hand, and to send for some hundred or so of his own armed retainers from Scandiano, to secure the punishment of the chief offenders, whom he had hanged from a window of the governor's palace.[2] A letter of his to the Duke on April 27 of the following year, just before the outbreak of hostilities with Venice and the Church, gives a vivid picture of the times and of the poet's own mildness of disposition. In consequence of the murder of a certain Centauro da Mocogno and his companions, the whole of the Frignano, the mountainous region to the south-west of Sassuolo, is up in arms, part on one side, part on the other, and blood has already been shed. It is useless sending the captain of the district to the disturbed area with twenty or thirty men, because the people are not afraid of him, and so many are concerned that punishment is out of the question. The writer's suggestion is that the Duke should hold out hopes of a complete pardon to every one involved, and so bring the factions to some sort of peace.

---

[1] Feltrino Boiardo had previously translated the *Golden Ass*, as we learn from the *De Politia Litteraria*, i. 6. Is Matteo Maria's version, perhaps, merely a revision of his grandfather's work? In March, 1479, according to the documents discovered by Bertoni, *op. cit.*, pp. 26, 27, the copyists of the Duke were at work upon both the *Orlando* and the translation of the *Golden Ass*.

[2] Jacopino de' Bianchi, *Cronaca Modenese*, i. pp. 47, 48.

MATTEO MARIA BOIARDO

Like the other ducal representatives, Boiardo has been examining the artillery of the various forts and castles, evidently to see what can be spared for the defence of Ferrara itself, and the singer of jousts and paladins is delightfully vague about these more modern implements of war. "In your Rocca of Castellarano your most illustrious Lordship has five or six iron cannons; very long, fine and good, according to their kind. I believe that Count Lorenzo Strozza had them made. I do not know whether I should call them *bombarde* or *spingarde*, not to make a mistake; but they seem to me good enough cannon. If you should need them, you know where they are."[1]

During the earlier stages of the war, Boiardo was certainly at Modena. He was probably still there in November and December, when serious riots broke out in the city and district, in consequence of the conveying of food stuffs by the canal in boats to famine-stricken Ferrara. A number of houses and palaces were sacked by the hungry mob, while the contadini rose in arms, plundered villas and buildings in the suburbs, and threatened the gates.[2]

The poet probably saw active service in the war. In the following year, 1483, we find him sometimes at Reggio and Scandiano, sometimes with the Duke in the capital. He had finished the first and second books of the *Orlando*, and laid down the pen with a sigh, on the outbreak of a real war instead of the mimic warfare of his song:—

> Non saran sempre i tempi sì diversi,
> Che mi traggan la mente di suo loco;
> Ma, nel presente, i canti miei son persi,
> E porvi ogni pensier mi giova poco;

---

[1] Letter of April 27, 1482. Campanini, p. 385.
[2] Jacopino de' Bianchi, pp. 67-71.

DUKES AND POETS IN FERRARA

Sentendo Italia di lamenti piena,
Non che ora canti, ma sospiro appena.

A voi, leggiadri amanti e damigelle,
Che dentro a' cor gentili avete amore,
Son scritte queste istorie tanto belle,
Di cortesia fiorite e di valore ;
Ciò non ascoltan queste anime felle,
Che fan guerra per sdegno e per furore.
Addio, amanti e dame peregrine,
A vostro onor di questo libro è il fine.[1]

But he could not quite doff his singing-robes, so turned to celebrating certain phases and episodes of the war, in Italian eclogues in *terza rima*.

Five of Boiardo's eclogues refer to the war, more particularly to the middle phase of the struggle. And we may, perhaps, imagine that their recitation enlivened the sick-room of Duke Ercole. In the first, the shepherd Tytiro —who is evidently Tito Vespasiano Strozzi—bewails the ravages of the Nemean monster and the destruction of his own beautiful villa by the sea.[2] But Mopso (Boiardo himself) reads upon the trunk of Apollo's sacred tree a prophecy, imitated in parts from Dante's of the *Veltro*. A mighty leader, *inclyto duce*, who has already delivered Italy from the Turks, shall put to flight " Dalmatians and Slavonians and their viler lords " ; with his aid, Ercole

---

[1] " Not always will the times be so discordant as to draw my mind from its place. But, at present, my songs are lost, and to devote my thoughts to them avails me little ; hearing Italy full of lamentation, I scarcely sigh now, much less sing.

" To you, winsome lovers and damsels, who have love within your gentle hearts, are written these goodly stories, adorned with courtesy and valour. Those fell souls do not hearken to them, who make war for disdain and for fury. Addio, lovers and beauteous ladies, to your honour is the end of this book." (*Orl. Inn.*, II. xxxi. 49, 50.)

[2] Cf. Mazzoni, *op. cit.*, p. 328.

shall hunt back the savage Lion to the seashore whence it came. In the second, the nymph Galatea rises up from the Po and sings a piteous lament; the royal deliverer, the victor of Otranto and Poggio Imperiale, tarries long; while " the fair land that was once full of every delight " is ravaged with fire and sword :—

>Aprete celo, e voi guardati un poco,
>   Pietosi Dei, a le isole del Pado,
>   Chè per tutto è roina e sangue e foco.
>Di corpi occisi è fatto un novo vado,
>   E fame e peste sceman tutta via
>   Ogni etade ogni sexo et ogni grado.
>È questa quella terra che solia
>   Esser spechio de Italia, anci del mondo,
>   A li omini cortesa et al cel pia ?
>Sì regal corte e stato sì jocondo,
>   Tanti trionfi e tanti cavalieri
>   Come ha sparsi fortuna e posti al fondo ?
>Le large strate or son stretti sentieri,
>   Arse le ville, e tra la gente morta
>   Stanno or le serpi, o barbari più fieri.

>Non sei del tuo periglio, Italia, accorta ?
>   Vedi che a divorarte el Leon ponge
>   In ogni parte, e bate a questa porta.
>La soglia de la intrata ha già tra ongie,
>   E ciascun passo fia soluto e piano
>   Se quel che io dico a tempo non vi gionge.
>Ogni rimedio, ogni altro ajuto è vano,
>   Però che Alcide, qual era restauro
>   Al danno immenso et al furor insano,
>Non da Getico dardo o stral di Mauro,
>   Ma da febre ferito a terra giace,
>   E sieco di vertute ogni tesauro.
>O se risurga quel spirto vivace,
>   Credèti che il Leon, che sì se afretta,
>   Non farà tal fremir, come ora face.
>Ma tu, perchè non vieni, anima eletta ?
>   Eletta in terra a possider vittoria,
>   Perchè non vieni a chi tanto t' aspetta ?
>Ove credi aquistar mai più di gloria,

DUKES AND POETS IN FERRARA

Traendo Italia languida e confusa
Fuor de la servitù di tanta boria.[1]

The third eclogue appears to be of earlier date, and has no connexion with the war; two shepherds are singing together, in somewhat Virgilian strains, in alternate song, of their loves. In the fourth, we have a lament for "the bitter capture of the son of Egeo," fallen into the hands of the horrible winged Lion—evidently Niccolò da Correggio, captured by the Venetians at Argenta, "that rare and noble spirit, the crown of virtue"—and a prophecy of his speedy deliverance and return, "like a phoenix that by

---

[1] "Open, Heaven, and ye, pitiful gods, look down upon the islands of the Po, for everywhere is ruin and blood and fire.

"A new ford is made of the bodies of the slain; famine and pest on all sides are destroying every age, each sex and every degree.

"Is this that city that used to be the mirror of Italy, nay, of the world, courteous to men and faithful to Heaven?

"Such royal Court, a state so jocund, so many triumphs and so many knights—how has fortune scattered them and cast them down?

"The broad ways are now narrow paths, the villas are burnt, and among the dead folk are now serpents or barbarians more fierce.

"Dost thou not perceive thy danger, Italy? See how the Lion prepares to devour thee in every part, and beats at this gate.

"The threshold of the entry it hath already in its claws, and each step will be free and easy, if He whom I say cometh not soon.

"Every remedy, every other aid is vain. For Alcides, he that was her protection against the immense calamity and its mad fury,

"Smitten not by Thracian dart or Moorish shaft, but by fever, lieth prone, and with him every treasure of virtue.

"Oh, if that keen spirit rises up, be sure that the Lion, who thus presses on, will not rage as now it doth.

"But thou, chosen soul, why comest not? Chosen on earth to possess victory, why dost not come to him who awaits thee so?

"Where dost thou think ever to win greater glory, than by delivering languid and harassed Italy from the servitude of such great pride?" (*Ecl.* ii. 70-105.)

burning is renewed." The fifth, again, is a love poem, in which the opening lines of the *Canzoniere* are quoted as if all the rest were a thing of the past; and the sixth, which is perhaps to be connected with it, is the poem already cited as possibly relating to Boiardo's marriage. The seventh is another pastoral *tenzone*, somewhat similar to the third. In the eighth, which is one of the finest of the series, the war is raging, but only in the background; in some peaceful spot, far from its ravages, shepherds are lamenting the death of a young girl, Nysa, who, dead on earth, lives in Heaven. There is no clue here to her identity, nor to that of her lover, Menalca; probably she was one of the victims of the pestilence that accompanied the devastation of the Ferrarese territory. The ninth eclogue, on the other hand, is a coarse piece of satire on the marriage of a beautiful girl to an old and hideous husband. In the tenth and last, "the author speaks and Orpheus sings the panegyric of the incomparable Lord Duke of Calabria." It was probably the poet's greeting to Alfonso on his entry into Ferrara, anticipating his triumphs.[1]

After the peace of Bagnolo, Boiardo formed one of the noble company that attended Ercole in his visit to Venice in February, 1485, the Count Niccolò Ariosti being also of the party.[2] The poet usually resided at this time at his

[1] Four of the eclogues referring to the war must have been written between the middle of December, 1482, and the end of January, 1483, after the papal change of policy (which is referred to in the first) and before the arrival of Alfonso. Mazzoni (*op. cit.*, pp. 333, 334, puts the tenth a little later, and finds allusions in it to the Duke's first victories over the Venetians in the spring of 1483. The other five are probably some years earlier. It is curious to note that, whereas the Latin eclogues were printed at Reggio in 1500, the ten Italian pastorals remained unedited until the nineteenth century.

[2] Ferrari, *op. cit.*, p. 40.

own castle of Scandiano, where he was probably busy preparing his book for the press; for, at the beginning of 1487, the first two books of the *Orlando Innamorato* were published in Venice, with a dedication to the Duke of Ferrara.

In January, 1487, Boiardo was appointed captain of the city and duchy of Reggio, a post which he filled for the rest of his life. On February 1, he made his state entry into his beloved *patria*, received with acclamation and enthusiasm. His residence was not the usual palace of the captain, but the great ducal citadel—the same building in which Lodovico Ariosto had been born thirteen years before. The government of Reggio was anything but a sinecure. The new captain's excessive mildness is said to have led to licence and disorder; he had a rooted objection to inflicting the death penalty (so at least says the tradition, but we have seen an instance to the contrary), and the chronicler Panciroli declares that he was more apt for composing songs than for punishing crime. The Venetians accused him of sheltering forgers and coiners. He was much harassed by a lawsuit between himself and Taddeo Manfredi, and even more by the perpetual intrigues and interference of the ducal commissary, Messer Beltramino, a Ferrarese lawyer, who tried to undermine his authority and insisted upon regarding him as a personal enemy, although Boiardo wrote to the Duke that " from me he will have nothing but kindness and good company."[1] In another strain we find him writing to Ercole, about a treatise on architecture (evidently the famous work by Leon Battista Alberti), recently published in Florence; he is unable to give his Excellence full particulars about the

[1] Letter of March 26, 1492. Campanini, p. 404.

MATTEO MARIA BOIARDO

construction of fountains without it, "because I have not my imagination too well disposed, owing to the sickness that my wife has, who is very ill indeed." [1]

There are a large number of letters, more than a hundred still extant, written by Boiardo while captain of Reggio. Most of them are addressed to the Duke himself; but a few are to the Gonzaga, to various Podestàs in the district of Reggio, and others. They are an extraordinary testimony to the minute scrutiny of Ercole's rule. Nothing is too small to be reported to the Duke—even if the writer himself desires leave of absence for a day, or the captain of the guard in the citadel wishes to go home to bring his household, or citizens have been masquerading against the regulations, or the friars have indulged in a petty squabble in some convent. Several letters refer to criminal processes. One of the most curious is the case of a Jew who has had intercourse with a Christian woman, Boiardo as captain substituting a fine for the usual death sentence, and apparently getting even the fine remitted. Another concerns three young noblemen of Reggio (including one of the Malaguzzi), who have carried off, not entirely without her own consent, and outraged a girl named Cassandra, the daughter of Messer Baldassare, the captain of Porta Castello.[2] Others deal with boundary disputes in connexion with the marchesato of Fivizzano, which was adjacent to the Duchy of Reggio, but belonged to Florence. For

[1] Letter of September 17, 1488. *Ibid.*, p. 393.
[2] Letters of November 16 and 24, and December 16, 1493. Campanini, pp. 409-412. This Messer Baldassare is, of course, the painter and medallist, Baldassare d' Este. A letter from him to the Duke, of November 3, 1493, crying out for justice upon those who had ruined his daughter, is given by Venturi, *L' Arte Ferrarese nel periodo d' Ercole I d' Este*, ii. pp. 381, 382.

DUKES AND POETS IN FERRARA

instance, a party of men from the Reggian town of Varano has gone to cut wood in a bosco on the frontier, which is also claimed by a townlet just outside the duchy called Gruppo San Pietro, and has been assailed by the folk of the latter place, shouting, "Havoc! Havoc! Marzocco! Marzocco!" Or the cattle from Varano, feeding over the boundary, have been lifted by the people of Ameglia; and in each case the poet-captain has to interfere, to prevent reprisals and political complications. Other letters deal with hawks and hounds and horses, and one is about some antique medals that have been found by a contadino, several of which are still at the command of the Duke.

But, even with all these multitudinous cares weighing upon him, Matteo Maria found time for literature. It was probably in these years at Reggio that he translated the *Vitae Excellentium Imperatorum* of Cornelius Nepos, and wrote the *Timone* for the Duke's theatre at Ferrara. The latter work, which upon a mere hypothesis is usually assigned to the year 1491, is written in *terza rima*, founded upon a Latin translation (perhaps Aurispa's) of Lucian's dialogue, and is more in the form of a miracle-play than a true drama. It has small poetic and no dramatic value; but it is naturally pleasant for English readers to see Ariosto's forerunner also heralding Shakespeare. Boiardo's supreme literary achievement of these years is the continuation, the nine cantos of the third part, of his *Orlando*, doomed to be cut short together with his life and Italy's liberty.

Probably there was no one more interested in the progress of this poem than Isabella d' Este, to whom Boiardo intended to dedicate it when completed. She wrote twice to him in the August of 1491, begging him to send her that part of the work, the *Inamoramento de Orlando*, as they called it, which he had newly composed, promising to send it back at once, as soon as she had read it. The poet answered that he had composed no more than what she had already seen, when she was at Reggio with her mother. "If your Excellence would like to see that, pray inform me, for I will have it transcribed at once and send it to you; and I am sorry, to content you, that I have not continued the work, which has been interrupted by other occupations." Of course Isabella wanted that part, as she could get nothing more, and begged him to send it to her in order that she might read it another time. "Most illustrious and worshipful Lady mine," answered Boiardo, "at present I have no copy save the original in my own hand, which would be difficult to read; but I will have a copy made of it, and send it to your Ladyship within six days by a special mounted messenger."[1] Every modern author will realize the poet's predicament.

At the end of 1493, Boiardo wrote a somewhat pitifully worded supplication to the Duke, begging him to confirm him in his offices at Reggio in the usual way. But, as a rule, his service and adulation (which was evidently quite sincere) by no means implied blind subservience. On one occasion, the Marquis of Mantua told Boiardo's brother-in-law, Count Cristoforo Gonzaga, that he had heard from the Duke of Ferrara that Boiardo had accused him (the Count Cristoforo), by letter, of secret negotiations with the Government of Milan. "If any one has told your Celsitude this," wrote Boiardo to the Marquis, "on behalf of the Lord Duke of Ferrara, he has departed from the truth. If

[1] Letters of August 8 and 17, 1491. Campanini, p. 404. See also Luzio, *Isabella d' Este e l' Orlando Innamorato*, in the *Studi su M. M. Boiardo*, pp. 149–154, where the text of Isabella's two letters is given.

his Excellence himself has said it, I keep silent and say no more."[1] A few years later, he makes a dignified answer to an accusation of the Duke himself that he has received and sheltered proclaimed criminals (*banniti*) at Scandiano and places governed by him. "Your Lordship should hold for certain that, while I am in this place, I would not keep men under ban in my house; if I did not act thus for reverence of your Lordship, I should do so for my own honour."[2]

Throughout the fatal year of 1494, we have an almost continuous series of letters from Boiardo to Ercole, in his capacity of governor of Reggio, full of the bustle and turmoil of the time. Here and there, especially in his private and confidential correspondence with the Duke, the poet-captain reveals a delightfully satirical humour. A Franciscan conventual, Frate Giovanni da Monleone, who appears on the banks of the Secchia, attended like a grand prelate rather than a religious, and professes to have been summoned by the Pope to compose the differences between the Kings of France and Spain, is a life-like portrait of the ecclesiastical political wire-puller of the epoch.[3] When "Don Juliano," captain of the French *balestrieri*, comes to Reggio with his company, Boiardo, attended by Messer Beltramino and Sigismondo Canterno, goes to drink with him in his hostelry. He describes in full the man's swagger and pretentiousness, his silk doublet all stained with soup, his black velvet cloak blazing with jewels which "Messere" thought magnificent, but which his superior perceived to be all false, his fine show of plate and silver which was of the same value as the jewels. "His conversation is exactly like his equipment,"

[1] Letter of May 7, 1489. Campanini, p. 397.
[2] Letter of May 30, 1494. *Ibid.*, p. 427.
[3] Letter of May 14, 1494. *Ibid.*, p. 424.

he writes; "your Excellence can hear all about it from Messere. I do not think that I shall light upon another Don Juliano."[1]

But the humour soon dies away. Boiardo paints with slight but firm touches the incidents in the passage of the royal and ducal troops, the difficulty of finding quarters and supplies for them, the havoc wrought in all directions, the misery of the people, the brutalities and prepotency of the French, the inability of the milder Italian officers to get their commands obeyed. Antisemitic troubles were added. The French maltreated and plundered the Jews, and on one occasion would have butchered one in the street, if certain priests had not come to the rescue; a friar (the religious of the duchy apparently differing from the secular clergy and the Duke on the Semitic question) thundered against the Hebrews from the pulpit, until Boiardo, in Ercole's name, cautioned him to moderate his eloquence.[2]

Utterly worn out by his labours, Boiardo was now rapidly breaking down in health, and the last two months of his life were occupied in a feverish attempt, as it were from his death-bed, to secure the town and marchesato of Fivizzano for Duke Ercole, in the general dissolution of the Florentine territory that seemed imminent. From Milan, on November 7, Ercole wrote cautiously both to Boiardo and to the Ancients of Reggio, giving a sort of consent to the scheme; and the inhabitants of Fivizzano itself, who had been horribly maltreated by the French in their passage, seemed to see in the sway of the House of Este their one

---

[1] Letter of August 26, 1494. *Ibid.*, pp. 444, 445. But when this showy warrior got to Modena, he made a great impression upon the people. Cf. Jacopino de' Bianchi, p. 120.
[2] Letters of October 10 and 13. Campanini, pp. 452, 453.

DUKES AND POETS I[

hope of adequate protection. Boia
at once opened a correspondence w
people of the district. But they w
Malaspina, who entered Fivizzano
were in progress; and, in the meaı
heard of what was on foot, and form;
Ferrarese ambassador, Manfredo ℕ
returned to Ferrara, and, on Decemb
Reggio received a strongly-worded
censuring them in the most severe
ignorance of the whole negotiation.
written such letters," he said, "you hɛ
and we are greatly displeased. We
recall those letters, and to write to
seem best to you, to make your exc

Thus, with his last effort to serve
and rejected, his mind full of apprel
land, Boiardo died on December 19,
hour of the night."

Unfinished though it be, the *Orlɑ*
landmark in the history of Italian litɛ
speaking, not an epic of any kind, b
in poetry. We have seen already
the legends of Charlemagne's paladins
exercised over the minds of the cava
Ferrarese Court, the zeal displayed b
lecting these romances and adven
original French or in Italian translatiᴏ
A few months before her appeal to E

[1] For the whole episode see Campanini, *l
di Reggio*, in the *Studi su M. M. Boiardo*, p
letters during October and November, pp.

MATTEO MARIA BOIARDO

the manuscript of the additions to his poem, the Marchesana Isabella had entered into a prolonged and animated discussion, both by word of mouth and by letter, with Galeazzo Visconti, as to the rival merits of Orlando and Rinaldo, —she herself persisting in her preference for the latter hero, while Galeazzo to the last professed himself ready to defend the honour of Orlando, and to prove to her Ladyship " that there has never been a man equal to him in all virtue and valour."[1] The Estensi hailed Ruggiero as their ancestor, the perfect knight and paladin of Trojan race; but their Venetian enemies professed to attribute to them a far less honourable descent, from Gano or Ganelon, and the House of Maganza (Mayence), the typical traitors of the Carolingian cycle.[2] This admiration for and interest in great Charles and his chivalry was not confined to the noble and cultured; the people loved to hear the songs that told of the doughty deeds of the paladins, just as Manzoni's immortal tailor found his intellectual food in the perusal of the *Reali di Francia*. On a historical occasion, to be described later, the street rabble of Venice assailed Duke Ercole with cat-calls and yells of " Maganzese." For the Arthurian romances, however, those *Arturi regis ambages pulcherrimae*, as Dante called them, the taste was entirely confined to the aristocracy of the epoch.

Already in Tuscany, for the delectation of Lorenzo de' Medici and his circle, Luigi Pulci had fused some of the

[1] See Luzio and Renier, *Delle Relazioni di Isabella d' Este Gonzaga con Lodovico e Beatrice Sforza*, pp. 100–107. Cf. Boiardo, *Orl. Inn.*, II. xxvi. 1 (quoted below). The letter from Borso da Correggio, given by Luzio and Renier, *op. cit.*, p. 379, and translated by Mrs. Ady, *op. cit.*, p. 206, shows that the latter is mistaken in identifying this Galeazzo Visconti with Galeazzo da San Severino.

[2] See Rajna, *Le Fonti dell' Orlando Furioso*, pp. 134–137; and cf. below, p. 319.

DUKES AND POETS

matter of the Carolingian cycle, la
a work of art. Boiardo went fur
fresh life into the stories, and tran
spirit drawn from the Arthuria
Brettagna. Taking his heroes from
figures of the personages of the
investing them with the charact
and adventures of the knights an(
Arthur, adding a strong infusion
seen as with the eyes and rendered s
of such painters as Botticelli and P
composed his poetic romance.[1]
Arthurian legends, and the new
Renaissance, are fused into a ha
fierce paladins of the Emperor are t1
errant, and Love is made the lor(
Paynim alike :—

> Non vi par già, signor, mara
> Odir contar d' Orlando inna1
> Chè qualunque nel mondo è
> È da amor vinto al tutto e :
> Nè forte braccio, nè ardire a
> Nè scudo o maglia, nè brand
> Nè altra possanza può mai f:
> Che al fin non sia da amor b

Thus the terrible Orlando himsel
cesvalles, the thunder of whose

[1] Cf. Rajna, *op. cit.*, pp. 19-25, and his :
the *Studi su M. M. Boiardo*, pp. 129-134
263-274.

[2] "Think it not marvellous, lordings,
enamoured ; for whoso in the world is haug
and subdued by Love. Nor mighty arm
shield or mail, nor sharp sword, nor any otl
him from being at the end beaten and
Inn., I. i. 2).

The Triumph of Venus.
(detail)
By Francesco del Cossa.

the literature of the Middle Ages to find an echo still in Dante's *Inferno*, becomes a Tristram or a Lancelot for the nonce; nay more, is the willing amorous slave of the lovely Saracen Angelica. The innate common-sense of the Italian genius keeps the poet from taking the more extravagant exploits and adventures too seriously, or recording them otherwise than to raise a laugh by appealing to the authority of Turpin; while his native cynicism, or perhaps that lack of genuine appreciation of mysticism which seems ingrained in the Italian character, draws him back from the dizzy ascents of the Quest of the Holy Graal. No hero of Boiardo's would have dreamed of setting foot " in the city of Sarras, in the spiritual place." The sanctity of a Galahad or a Perceval, the repentance of a Lancelot, would have introduced an utterly discordant note; and, for the same reason, we should seek in vain through his stanzas for the pity and terror of the fall of Guenevere. They are as lovers and seekers of adventure alone that the warriors of the Table Round appeal to the Count of Scandiano and his courtly audience :—

> Fu gloriosa Bertagna la grande
> Una stagion per l' arme e per l' amore,
> Onde ancor oggi il nome suo si spande
> Sì che al re Artuse fa portare onore,
> Quando i buon cavalieri a quelle bande
> Mostrarno in più battaglie il suo valore,
> Andando con lor dame in avventura,
> Ed or sua fama al nostro tempo dura.
>
> Re Carlo in Franza poi tenne gran corte,
> Ma a quella prima non fu somigliante,
> Benche assai fosse ancor robusto e forte
> Ed avesse Ranaldo e 'l Sir d' Anglante;
> Perchè tenne ad Amor chiuse le porte,
> E sol si dette a le battaglie sante,
> Non fu di quel valore o quella stima
> Qual fu quell' altra che io contava in prima.

Però che Amore è quel ch[e]
E che fa l'uomo degno ed on[orato]
Amore è quel che dona la vit[a]
E dona ardir al cavaliero arn[ato]

And again, in a passage which h[as a]
true Arthurian ring :—

Il vago amor che a sue da[me]
Portarno al tempo antico i c[avalieri]
E le battaglie e le venture is[trane]
E l' armeggiar per giostre e p[er]
Fa, che il suo nome al mondo
E ciaschedun lo ascolti volent[ieri]
E chi più l' uno e chi più l' a[ltro]
Come vivi tra noi fussero anc[ora]

E qual fia quel, che odendo
E di sua dama ciò che se ne d[ice]
Che non mova ad amarli il co[re]
Riputando il suo fin dolce e fe[lice]
Che viso a viso essendo e mar[ito]
E il cor co 'l cor più stretto a
Ne le braccia l' un l' altro, a
Ciascun di lor rimase a un pu[nto]

E Lancilotto e sua regina be[lla]
Mostrarno l' un per l' altro un
Che dove de' suoi gesti si fave[lla]
Par che d' intorno il cielo ard[a]

---

[1] " Britain the great was glorious once wit[h]
still its name resounds so that it brings hono[ur]
the good knights in those regions showed its
going on adventures with their ladies ; a[nd]
our time.

" King Charles afterwards held great Cou[rt]
not like that former one, albeit it, too, w[as]
strong, and had Rinaldo and the Lord of A[nglante]
the gates closed to Love, and only engaged
not of such worth or such renown as was th[at]
told.

" For Love it is that gives glory, and t[he]
and honoured : it is Love that gives the vi[ctory]
to the knight in arms " (*Orl. Inn.*, II. xviii.

284

MATTEO MARIA BOIARDO

Traggasi avanti adunque ogni donzella,
Ogni baron, che vuol portare onore,
Et oda nel mio canto quel che io dico
Di dame e cavalier del tempo antico.[1]

The poem opens with the great banquet given by Charlemagne at Paris to the flower of Christian and Saracen chivalry. The enchanting sorceress Angelica appears, attended by four giants and her brother Argalia; she enamours to distraction all present with her beauty, especially the paladins Orlando and Rinaldo, and the Saracen Ferraguto; her person is to be the prize of the man who shall unhorse her brother at the Rock of Merlin, the unsuccessful to remain his prisoners—the whole being a deep-laid plot of her pagan father to destroy the power of Charlemagne. For Argalia has an enchanted lance of gold, against which no knightly prowess can avail, and Angelica has a similar ring which, worn on the finger, renders all enchantment useless against the wearer, and carried in the mouth confers invisibility.

From this beginning, through varied and complicated

---

[1] "The fair love that knights bore to their sovereign ladies in the olden time, and the battles and strange adventures, and the combating in jousts and tourneys, make its name still last in the world, and each one gladly hears of it; and one honours more one and another more another, as though they were yet living among us.

"And is there a man that, hearing of Tristram and of his lady the tale that is told, is not moved in his heart to love them, deeming their end sweet and happy? For, face to face and hand to hand, heart joined to heart in close embrace, in each other's arms thus comforted they died together at one moment.

"Lancelot too and his lovely queen showed each for each such worth, that, where we speak of their deeds, it seems that the sky around burns with love. Let every damsel then come forward, every baron that would gain honour, and hear in my song what I say of ladies and knights of the olden time" (*Orl. Inn.*, II. xxvi. 1-3).

entanglement and enchantment, the
war raised upon Charlemagne by King
for the sword of Orlando and the ho
(when this is brought to a satisfactory
wrought by Argalia's lance of gold in
of England) the subsequent invasion
Agramante of Africa and the Saracen
while a third independent struggle rage
of Albracca, in which Angelica has take
she is besieged first by Agricane, King c
by the maiden warrior Marfisa, in whor
expressly so stated by Boiardo, we are
Ariosto to recognize the sister of Ruggi

This "third paladin," Ruggiero, A
is descended from Hector and Alexander
ancestor of the House of Este. He doe
the second part of the poem, when he is
about to accompany the Saracens in
France. The opening of the third part s
intended to bring the history of Rugg
treacherous murder by Gano of Magan;
As it is, he only gets as far as the hero's f
his future bride, Brandiamante or Bradama
sister of Rinaldo, who is, of course, fighting
side. Ruggiero has interrupted the single
her and Rodomonte with the news of tl
army of Charlemagne, and, as they bear
pany on their way, the youth, who sup
companion to be some Frankish knight, tell
of his family and his upbringing by the m
The girl grows madly enamoured of him as
longs to make him show her his face. In

MATTEO MARIA BOIARDO

reque[...], she tells him who she is, and suddenly lifts her helm[...]:—

Nel trar de l' elmo, si sciolse la trezza,
Ch' era di color d' oro a lo splendore:
Avea il suo viso una delicatezza
Mescolata di ardire e di vigore;
I labbri, 'l naso, i cigli e ogni fattezza
Parean dipinti per le man d' Amore,
Gli occhi avevano un dolce tanto vivo,
Che dir non puossi, ed io non lo descrivo.

Ne l' apparir de l'angelico aspetto,
Ruggier rimase e vinto e sbigottito,
E sentissi tremare il core in petto,
Parendo lui di foco esser ferito:
Non sa più che si fare il giovinetto,
Non era a pena di parlare ardito,
Con l'elmo in testa non l' avea temuta,
Smarrito è mo che in faccia l' ha veduta.

Essa poi cominciò: Deh! bel signore,
Piacciavi compiacermi solo in questo,
Se a dama alcuna mai portaste amore,
Ch' io veda il vostro viso manifesto.
Così parlando odirno un gran rumore;
Disse Ruggiero: Oh Dio! che sarà questo?
Presto si volta e vede gente armata,
Che vien correndo a lor per quella strata.[1]

---

[1] "In the drawing off her helmet her hair was loosed, which was of the colour and splendour of gold; her face had a delicacy mingled with daring and vigour; her lips, her nose, her eyebrows, and every feature seemed painted by the hands of Love. Her eyes had such living sweetness that it could not be said, and I describe it not.

"At the appearing of her angelical aspect, Ruggiero was conquered and dismayed, and he felt his heart trembling in his breast, it seeming to him that he had been wounded with fire. The youth knows no more what to do; he hardly dared to speak. With her helmet on her head, he had not feared her; fordone is he now that he has seen her in the face.

"Then she began: 'Ah! fair lord, be pleased to gratify me only in this; if you ever bore love to any lady, let me see your face

DUKES AND POETS

They have fallen into an ambush
that follows the two are separated
never see Ruggiero's face unhelm‹
his hand to finishing the poem.

It is possible,'as has been suggeste
of the poem, the struggle of Charle
assailants, may have had some ac
contemporaries, who saw their civili⸗
ened by the Mussulman. But it is tl
which the modern reader cares least.

> Strane avventure e battaglie a⸗
> Quando virtute al buon tempo
> Tra cavalieri e dame graziose,[1]

—these are what charm us in the
to-day. Boiardo finds most of his chɑ
hand in the old romances; but he in
adventures, heaps up marvellous and
ments and sorceries, some of which aɾ
air of reality that is, for the momen
ing. And he is an excellent story
poetical *novelle*, which, however, it mu
considerably more of Boccaccio's licence
of his power of characterization. He is
in words, showing us gardens and pala
find in the frescoes of Cosimo Tura a
Cossa, painting figures drawn from cla

openly.' As she spoke, they heard a great nois
'Oh God, what shall this be?' Straightway
armed men, who come rushing upon them by
Inn., III. v. 41-43.)

[1] "Strange adventures and amorous bat
flourished in the good time, among knights an‹
(*Orl. Inn.*, III. i. 4.)

with the brush of a Botticelli or Piero di Cosimo. There is absolutely no serious intention, no shadow of philosophy of any kind, to be found throughout; his one aim is to keep his hearers interested and amused, to while away the time when it hangs heavy upon the hands of the princes and nobles for whom he writes. His attitude towards women and sexual morality in general is frankly cynical. His virtue of virtues is fidelity to one's sovereign lord—though he lets even his Orlando desert Charlemagne for the love of Angelica. Friendship between man and man appeals most deeply to his inmost nature :—

> Più che il tesoro e più che forza vale,
> Più che il diletto assai, più che l' onore,
> Il buon amico e compagnia leale ;
> E a due, che insieme si portino amore,
> Maggior li pare il ben, minor il male,
> Potendo appalesar l' un l' altro il core,
> E ogni dubbio che accada, o raro o spesso,
> Poterlo ad altrui dir come a sè stesso.

> Che giova aver di perle e d' òr divizia,
> Aver alta possanza e grande stato,
> Quando si gode sol, senza amicizia ?
> Colui ch' altri non ama e non è amato,
> Non puote aver compita una letizia.[1]

The most prominent defect of the poem is its almost complete lack of effective characterization. Although Boiardo is justly entitled to the merit of having first dis-

[1] "A good friend and loyal fellowship is worth more than treasure and more than power, much more than pleasure, more than honour. To two that love each other, weal seems greater and woe seems less, since each can open his heart, and tell every doubt that rises, be it seldom or often, to another as to himself.

"What boots it to have wealth of pearls and gold, to have lofty power and great state, when they are enjoyed alone without friendship ? He who loves not another, and is not loved, cannot have one joy complete." (Orl. Inn., III. vii. 1-2.)

covered in the firmament of love '
men mad, Angelica's," he is incapable o
and self-consistent character. No do
cal analysis in the case of an Orlando
be out of place in a poem of this kind
something of it in Ariosto), but Boi
conceive of them save as puppets to be
ful game. He invests them with all
qualities from canto to canto, to suit
vellous adventures that he has found
is the same, but to a lesser extent, wit
Rinaldo, Marfisa (an invention, har
poet's own), Rodomonte, Agraman
less contradictory, because less full
appeal to us as human beings. Br
lover of Fiordelisa and the devote
the most conceivable and sympath
minor personages, and one whom B
follows with affection.

There is, however, one noticeable e
lack of characterization : the ever-d
paladin, Astolfo, though he is onl
and dainty, a mere carpet-knight
special strength or skill in arms,
good humour and dauntless coura
after danger, courting fall after fal
of Argalia falls into appropriate l
idea of its powers when, at the to

[1] G. A. Cesareo, indeed, in his spiri
tasia dell' Ariosto (in the Nuova Antc
goes so far as to assert that Boiardo
another man.

of Christendom are falling before the gigantic paynim Grandonio, and he goes out to encounter him without the slightest prospect of success:—

> Nè già si crede quel franco barone
> Aver vittoria contra del pagano;
> Ma sol con pura e buona intenzione
> Di far il suo dover per Carlo Mano.
> Stava molto atto sopra de l' arcione,
> E simigliava a cavalier soprano;
> Ma color tutti che l' han conosciuto,
> Diceano: O Dio ! deh mandaci altro aiuto ! [1]

He can hardly believe his own eyes when he sees the giant fall. But, after that, though exceedingly marvellous to every one else, it seems quite natural to him that he should overthrow everybody that ventures to break a lance with him, and his natural disposition to brag finds its justification. He harbours no resentment against the Emperor for his imprisonment, and but little against Gano for his treachery and description of him as the *buffone* of the Court; but, while Charlemagne and the rest are wild with indignation and apprehension at the way this *pazzo* has intervened and staked their liberties upon his own prowess, he unhorses the victorious Gradasso, and, after a not too prolonged jape at their expense, frees them all. And in this spirit he goes through the whole romance.

Endowed with a marvellous faculty of invention, Boiardo had neither the imagination nor the creative power of Ariosto. Morally, no less than artistically, the *Orlando Innamorato* is on a much lower plane than the *Furioso*.

---

[1] "Nor indeed does that brave baron think to have the victory against the pagan, but solely with pure and good intention to do his duty for Charlemagne. Right firmly sate he in his saddle, and seemed like a sovereign knight; but all those who recognized him said: 'Oh God, pray send us other aid !'" (*Orl. Inn.*, I. ii. 66.)

DUKES AND POETS IN

Yet there is one respect in which the
contrasts favourably with Messer]
Torquato Tasso, as also, it must be (
sage and serious poet Spenser." There
in the *Innamorato* than in their poems,
confined to three places. When youn
to cross from Africa to France with tl
King Agramante, the necromancer *t*
future glory of the House that the you
the Christians, and the mighty deeds
Estensi.[1] This is, undoubtedly, in it
with the general purpose of the fat
passages of the kind are dragged in,
without rhyme or reason. In the m
Fata Febosilla, the valiant Brandima
of his struggles with the evil enchant
sees a loggia of which the four sides
paintings representing the exploits of f
House, one side devoted to each : Aldo
the imperial armies, " at the Adda in t
Azzo Novello and the famous defeat of F
Niccolò III in his youth triumphing o
grimage to the Holy Land, his recept
France ; the early career of Ercole hims
presents his son-in-law with a pavili
Sibyl of Cumae has worked " great d
drous histories, and days present an
Here are the figures of twelve Alfonsos

[1] *Orl. Inn.*, II. xxi. 55–59.
[2] *Ibid.*, II. xxv. 42–56. Boiardo, doubtle
the style of the frescoes of the Schifanoia. H
the glories of the House of Este is somewh
old Duke's death we find no mention of hii

MATTEO MARIA BOIARDO

Castile, ancestors of the Duchess Leonora; Alfonso the Magnanimous and Alfonso of Calabria, her great-grandfather and father; the young hereditary Prince of Ferrara. The praises of King and Duke are sung in no measured terms, but there is—if I mistake not—a ring of genuine feeling in the picture of the boy, Alfonso d' Este :—

> Avanti a lui si stava inginocchiata
> Buona Ventura, lieta ne' sembianti,
> E parea dire : Dolce figliol, guata
> A le prodezze de gli avoli tanti,
> A la tua stirpe al mondo nominata ;
> Onde, fra tutti, fa che tu ti vanti
> Di cortesia, di senno e di valore,
> Sì che tu facci al tuo bel nome onore.[1]

These, however, are surely little, when compared with the extravagant flattery addressed later on by Ariosto to the Cardinal Ippolito, or with Spenser's hardly less fulsome laudations of Queen Elizabeth.

The struggle with Venice had interrupted, the French invasion now finally cut short, the *Orlando Innamorato*. A few months, or perhaps weeks, before his death, the pen had dropped from Boiardo's hand ; the noble poet was too full of apprehension for his native land, too sick at heart to carry out his story :—

> Mentre che io canto, O Dio Redentore,
> Vedo l' Italia tutta a fiamma e foco,
> Per questi Galli, che con gran valore
> Vengon, per disertar non so che loco.

---

[1] " Before him was kneeling Good Fortune, joyous in her semblance. ' Sweet son,' she seemed to say, ' look at the mighty deeds of such great ancestors, and at thy race renowned in the world. Wherefore, among all, make thyself glorious for courtesy, for wisdom and for valour ; so that thou mayst do honour to thy fair name.' " (*Orl. Inn.*, II. xxvii. 59.)

DUKES AND POETS

Però vi lascio in questo van[
Di Fiordespina ardente a po[
Un' altra fiata, se mi fia co[
Racconterovvi il tutto per e[

Harshly, indeed, did fate deal wi[
descendants and in his poetry. H[
Camillo, died in 1499. Count Gio[
out the poet's widow Taddea and [
Scandiano, and deprived them of [
" she and the daughters lack even [
them to live." [2] Some thirty years [
took the *Orlando Innamorato* in hand [
rifacimento was read in the place [
Berni diluted, altered, and utterly sp[
its pathos was lost on the men of a new[
preponderance and the presence of[
armies upon Italian soil had come [
natural order of things.

[1] " Whilst I sing, O God Redeemer, I se[
fire, through these Gauls who, with great va[
what place I know not. Wherefore I leave [
Fiordespina gradually burning. Another ti
me, I will tell you the whole in full." (*Or*[
[2] See the letter of April 13, 1504, from [
Ercole on Taddea's behalf, in Bertoni, *op. c*[

Chapter IX
THE DUKE AND THE FRIAR

"THIS friar of ours, Girolamo Savonarola," wrote the Ferrarese ambassador in Florence, Manfredo Manfredi, to Duke Ercole on December 10, 1494, "has so much influence and such great following in this city, that it is a most stupendous thing." And, a few days later, he wrote again, describing the great work that Savonarola was doing: "He aims at nothing save the good of all, seeking for union and peace, being convinced—as is the truth—that the city cannot otherwise live in tranquillity and repose."[1]

From Ferrara itself the victorious progress of the King of France through Italy had been watched with considerable popular sympathy. Ercole, perplexed and hesitating in his policy, was having artillery of all kinds cast with the utmost celerity, to be prepared for whatever emergency the morrow might bring forth. He probably dreaded an attack from Venice, and certainly knew that he was condemned by the public opinion of almost all Italy. The Pope professed himself amazed at the cowardice of the Italians. "May God pardon the Lord Lodovico and the Duke of Ferrara,"

[1] Dispatches of December 10, 15, and 20. Cappelli, *Fra Girolamo Savonarola*, p. 337.

he said to Pandolfo Collenuccio, wh
view with him in Ercole's name, " w
of this." And when Pandolfo tried
Pope showed himself convinced tha
authority could have prevented Lod
the French. Pandolfo declared that
his best, but Alexander shrugged hi
not ; all the same he is greatly blame

Ercole kept in constant touch wit
advance, through his son Ferrando, t
sent money by means of letters of
Rome, where the King stopped fro
January 28. But when Charles left
towards Naples, Don Ferrando remain
on the plea that he had not enough
to follow the Court with sufficient
had not paid him his allowance. E
sent one of his secretaries, Giovanni
Rome, provided with a letter of cr
ducats, and armed with his paternal
young prince to Naples and present h

" All these things," he wrote, " ha
ceed from your own negligence, and
give yourself to idleness and to avoi
you had followed the Most Christia
duty and our intention, you would ha
sooner ; the Majesty of the King woul
you would have given him occasion to
when Messer Sigismondo Cantelmo ar
letter of exchange for five hundred du

[1] See the long dispatch of November 6,
Ercole. Balan, v. pp. 414–415.

THE DUKE AND THE FRIAR

well follow the Most Christian King and not stay there doing nothing; and if you could not go on with all your company, you ought to have gone with four or five horsemen rather than leave him, and to have sent hither those for whom you could not provide. But you wanted to stay at Rome and take a holiday, where you have spent more than you would have done in following the King. If, by your laziness and negligence, you lose the support of the Most Christian King, you will repent of it with time, and you will wish you had not lost it. Keep well in mind what we tell you! If by your own fault you lose this opening, do not hope for anything from us, save a bad welcome and harsh treatment."[1]

On hearing the news of the flight of the young King Ferdinand—in whose favour Alfonso had abdicated—and the triumphant entry of Charles into Naples (February 22, 1495), the Diarist is immensely edified, declaring that the King has conquered thus easily "as a messenger sent from God," and that it is a just punishment for the abominable cruelties practised by the late King Ferrante and by Alfonso, the former of whom he further states was responsible for the Venetian war against Ercole and the loss of the Polesine of Rovigo, which he had caused the Venetians to retain. The turn of the Venetians will follow. "But I hope in God that, in a few days' time, they will wish that they had restored it freely to our Lord the Duke, and that they will give it back to him more than gladly; for now the time seems come when God will punish them, and the King of France will take from them what they have on the mainland and in Cyprus, and almost up to Venice, for their

[1] *Minute Ducali* to Don Ferrando, February 27, 1495. Archivio di Modena, *Carteggio dei Principi.*

inestimable pride and haughtiness,
merable vices and sins. Since this
there has always been the most bea
and there have been no snows nc
hardly any rain. Praise be to Go
Diarist written this, when the weathe
out the following month terrible st
snow swept over Italy—phenomena
explanation.

Hearing of the King's uninterru
expressed his "singular pleasure ɑ
sent Ferrando a letter of congratulɑ
Majesty, as soon as he should find
presence: "Let him understand th
surpassed in this joy and gladness."
his father a very contrite epistle a
Rome, which the Duke received kindly
"If you behave as you have behave
hope to be loved by us." However,
Ferrando and the secretary that they l
and that the former had been very k
King and Court, and expressed his
understood from the letters of our sec
Ferrando, "that you have begun to
and with diligence, and to do what pe
we have been greatly pleased and conte
commend you for it, and we tell you tha
in being diligent and assiduous in the s
and be prompt and ready at the Court,
you will do a benefit to yourself and a ɡ

[1] *Diario Ferrarese*, col. 2

THE DUKE AND THE FRIAR

as we shall be displeased if you act otherwise."[1] He bids Mariano congratulate the King on the conquest in his name, as he doubts not that Don Ferrando has already done, and is sending Bonifazio Bevilacqua and Giulio Tassoni as special envoys for the same purpose.[2] For fear of compromising himself too deeply, he recalled these latter at once, as soon as they had performed their mission.

The easy triumph of the ultramontane invader had thoroughly alarmed all the other Italian Powers, although Lodovico Sforza assured the Venetians that he "would find means to send the King home with empty hands." Ferdinand of Spain and the King of the Romans, the only foreign sovereigns who had a stake in the peninsula, began to fear, the one for Sicily and Sardinia, the other for the imperial crown. The conduct of the French had further exasperated the temper of the people. There was a general assembling of ambassadors and envoys at Venice; while Comines—who had been sent thither by Charles from Asti in the previous autumn—strove his uttermost to prevent the League from being concluded, warned the King of what was on foot, urged the Duke of Orleans (who had turned back after the capture of Rapallo in September) to be on his guard at Asti, and the Regent, the Duke of Bourbon, to send reinforcements, "because that place being lost, no aid could come to the King." Late at night, on the last day of March, the League was concluded. "The

[1] Letters of March 1, 17, and 29, 1495. In a letter of April 9, he gives him permission to tilt in a *giostra*, which is "an honourable thing and not too dangerous," but strictly forbids him to take part in any way in another which is to be held at Easter with battle-weapons, "because it is dangerous and little honourable." Archivio di Modena, *Carteggio dei Principi*.

[2] March 18, 1495. Archivio di Modena, *Minutario Cronologico*.

next morning," writes Comines, "
earlier than they were accustomed.
and set down, the Doge told me tha
Trinity, there was a League concl
Father the Pope, the Kings of th
them, and the Duke of Milan, for t
for the defence of the estate of C
Turk; the second, for the defence
for the preservation of their own es
me to advertise the King. They
number of a hundred or more, and
countenances, and sate not as they
tised me of the taking of the castl
told me, moreover, that they had
sadors that were with the King, to
return home; their names were M
and Master Dominic Trevisan. I wa
with this news, for I stood in dou
person and of all his company, su
have been readier than indeed it was
I feared further lest the Almains h
not without cause; for if they had
had never departed out of Italy." [1]

The ambassador of Naples—for tl
was still represented in Venice—
"and showed a cheerful countenance
to do, for these were good news for hii
Comines watched the procession c
ambassadors along the canal, "witl
one of the Milanese, who had hithert

[1] *Mémoires*, vii. 15. Throughout this
translation of 1596, with slight modificat

THE DUKE AND THE FRIAR

terms with him, "made a countenance now as though he knew me no more." On April 2, the Visdomino of the Venetians in Ferrara, robed in crimson velvet, formally announced to Ercole, on the part of his government, that the League was concluded, and that he and the Florentines would have to stand alone, unless they joined it. A few days later, the League was published in all the cities of the Venetian Republic, with the greatest triumph and solemnity. It was poor consolation for Comines that at night, after viewing the pageants, the ambassador of the Turk "came to talk with me by means of a certain Greek, and was with me four hours in my chamber, being very desirous that his Prince and the King my master might enter together into amity."[1]

Ercole was profoundly perplexed. In a somewhat ineffectual way, he had striven against this League from the beginning. As early as December, when the rupture between Lodovico Sforza and the Most Christian King seemed imminent (Il Moro being indignant because he had not received Sarzana and Sarzanello, for which he had lent the King a large sum, and because the latter had treated his ambassador, Galeazzo da San Severino, discourteously), Jacopo Trotti had urged the former, in Ercole's name, to keep loyal to France. The result was that Trotti had been kept in the dark, and only gathered from the long and secret interviews of the Venetian ambassadors with Lodovico that something of the kind was in progress.[2] Ercole realized that, if it came to war, the actual burden of assailing the French would fall entirely upon the Italian States of the League, and he was bent upon keeping out of it, while remaining, as far as possible, neutral. Since his wife's

---

[1] *Mémoires*, vii. 15; *Diario Ferrarese*, col. 298.
[2] Cf. Balan, v. pp. 419, 437.

DUKES AND POETS IN FER

death, he had had no one by him upon whom
he had become incapable of taking decided a(
moreover, grown scrupulously religious. Cl(
sympathy with the new theocratic republ:
Florence,[1] he was disposed to accept Fra (
phecies concerning the sacred mission of the
On April 13, the day after the public proc
League, he perplexed his subjects by or(
procession through all the city of Ferrara,
any cause or reason—though, Zambotto
guessed that it was done because of the i
thing that has not much pleased our Di
interests."[2] He kept the Ferrarese feast (
the Venetian feast of St. Mark with increase
on the latter occasion sent his trumpete
Don Alfonso, when the banner of Venice wa
to the church of the saint in Ferrara. Wl
in touch with the French King at Naples
the Doge through his ambassador at Veni
di Guidone, his great joy at the conclusion (
wrote to the same effect to the Pope, offe
in Ferrara, if the movements of the Frenc

---

[1] One of the French officers at Naples offere
Antonio Mariano, to sell Fivizzano, and the
Lunigiana that had belonged to the Florentines,
promptly revealed the whole thing to Neri Capj
ambassador with the French King, and Ercole
his action. "It seems to us," he wrote, "tha
spoken to him better than you have done ; be
friendly terms as we are with that lofty Repub.
prosperity and convenience no less than we dc
not have anything to do with matters that v
them displeasure." *Minute Ducali* of April 4
Modena, *Minutario Cronologico*.

[2] Zambotto, f. 272*v*; *Diario Ferrarese*, col.

THE DUKE AND THE FRIAR

to leave Rome.[1] Nevertheless, the people of Ferrara were enthusiastically French in their sympathies; they still affected French costumes, looked askance at the Visdomino, and shouted "Franza! Franza!" after him in the street. Reports of all kinds floated wildly through the peninsula. Venice and Milan were arming; there were rumours of stupendous preparations in France to cross the Alps in defence of the King. "The Venetians never ceased to speak evil of Duke Ercole and of his subjects, and to work them harm; and they had among themselves invented a song thereon, that ran: *O guerra o non guerra, Ferrara anderà per terra*; so great is the hatred they bear us. But I think that this present year will not pass before they will be utterly undone, by reason of their passing great and incredible pride, by the aforesaid King of France."[2]

Ercole began to realize that, in the event of the triumph of the League over France, he would be left alone among the princes of Italy, with Milan alienated, to face the hostility once more of Rome and Venice. On the evening of May 9, a secretary of the French King arrived at Ferrara, late after night-fall, and demanded an instant audience. The Duke with some difficulty put him off until the morrow, when the Frenchman gave him to understand, in the name of the King, that his Majesty intended to return peaceably to France, "without harming or injuring any person whatever," and thought of taking the route of Florence and Bologna, in which case the King requested a free passage through the Duchy of Ferrara, with provisions for his forces on the way. Ercole answered that, as to the passage, his

---

[1] *Minute Ducali* of April 14 and May 2, 1495. Archivio di Modena, *Minutario Cronologico*.
[2] *Diario Ferrarese*, col. 303.

Majesty could have it as he pleased;
it was quite impossible, because the
troops in the past year had utt
country, and left it in the greatest fa
informed Lodovico Sforza of the dema
and communicated the matter likewis
at Milan and Venice.[1]

The danger seemed imminent; from
feared lest he should be compelled to
one side or the other. At last he dec
to the man—his own subject—who was
in the counsels of the Most High than ot
to Fra Girolamo Savonarola for guidar

"We hear," he wrote to Manfredo, '
Frate Girolamo Savonarola, our Ferra
there at Florence, has said things publi
them in his sermons—things which
needs of Italy, and it seems that he thr
of Italy. And because, as you know, h
and a good religious, we greatly desire
said and is saying, and all the details up
We wish you to go to him, and, in our n
you something about these needs and
happen, and especially about our afi
diligently inform us of all that you
certain that he will willingly satisfy this
of us and because of his goodness, and
his native land, which he must still ha
will all be most grateful to us." An
adds: "Besides what we write to y

[1] Letter from Ercole to the Duke of
Archivio di Modena, *Minutario Cronologico.*

tell you to learn diligently what the said Frate Girolamo preaches, and the threats that he makes, and what he believes about our affairs, and exhort him to pray to our Lord God for us and for these our peoples, in order that His Divine Majesty may have mercy upon our errors. For we hope greatly in his holy prayers."[1]

Thus instructed, Manfredo had a long interview with Savonarola on May 17. The Friar professed himself unable to give an immediate answer to the Duke's demands. " I must first pray to our Lord God," he said, " that He may enlighten me and enable me to tell his Excellence those things which shall be to the salvation of his soul and the conservation of his State, with the satisfaction of his subjects. When I have done this, I shall write with my own hand to his Excellence." He still regarded himself as the Duke's subject and Ferrara as his native land, and seemed convinced that, with the grace of God, he could help both in this matter, " especially knowing how devout his Excellence is and of holy life, far more than any other sovereign in Italy." The ambassador could get nothing more out of him about Ferrara ; but he informs the Duke that the Friar is still keeping the Florentines on the side of France, " showing them that this Most Christian King by all means is to reform the Church, and to be most victorious in all his undertakings."[2]

The much desired letter from Savonarola to Ercole was written on May 21. It was inclosed in a dispatch from Manfredo ; its contents were to be kept a strict secret, and Ercole

---

[1] Letter of May 13, 1495. Cappelli, *op. cit.*, p. 345. Ercole speaks of his *peoples* in the plural, because he includes the inhabitants of his three duchies.

[2] Dispatch of May 18, 1495. *Ibid.*, pp. 347, 348.

probably destroyed it as soon as read
been found among the others in the
The next day, Manfredo called upon t
in Florence, who had just returned
whither he had been sent by the King
to return to the obedience and gove
tines. In answer to his inquiries as
doing, Manfredo assured his Magnifi
keeping absolutely neutral and atter
his own State. The Frenchman high
of his Excellence, adding that he kn
great love and affection. He was an
friend to both parties, should mediat
and the Duke of Milan for the peac
he said, it would be impossible to r
forcements, that were hurrying towar
King, turn back when they reached A
that the real difficulty lay in the King
the Duke of Milan and would int
intervention; but the French amb
admitting that his countrymen had
in Italy, said that they were all so
France that each one would exhort
any arrangement that might be pro
From Ercole's answer to Savonar
clear notion of what the Friar must
"We have received your letter, a
well understood what you have writ
concerning those things that we des
and we have noted the remedies t
charity and love. Your letter has

[1] Dispatch of May 22, 1495. *I*

us, and we thank you much for writing; and we are well satisfied thereat, for it seems to us that your suggestions are full of prudence and charity. And although we know ourselves to be sinners, nevertheless we shall strive with all our power to adhere to your suggestions, and to use those remedies that you propose to us. And you, for love of us and for the sake of your native land, will not fail to offer prayers to our Lord God, that He may lend us grace to be able to do all those good works that are acceptable to His Divine Majesty and for our preservation and the benefit of our peoples. Right grateful to us, too, will be that little book which you say you will send us; and so we pray you to send it to us, when you have finished it, for we are expecting it with desire."[1]

In the meanwhile, Charles had taken alarm, and decided to make his way back to France. Towards the end of May, he left Naples, leaving garrisons behind him and Gilbert de Bourbon-Montpensier as his viceroy, and entered Rome at the beginning of June, the Pope having fled from the city at his approach. Comines, who had previously been recalled from Venice, reached Ferrara on the evening of June 1. Ercole came out to meet him, and gave him a magnificent reception. The next morning, "Duke Ercole went to find the ambassador in his room, and together they went to Mass in the chapel of the Duke, which the Duke's own choristers sang. And then the Duke embraced the said ambassador, accompanied him to his room and left him there to breakfast. The ambassador was right welcome to all the Ferrarese, because the King is much loved by Duke Ercole, and the Ferrarese also are loved by the King."

---

[1] Letter of May 26, 1495. *Ibid.*, p. 351. The book in question is the Italian version of the *Compendium Revelationum*.

Ercole rode with him all over Ferrara and
Barco; they held long secret converse in tl
upon the garden, where the Duke passed th
June 4, Comines went on his way towa1
Duke and his kinsmen riding with him
" with trumpets and pipes and great love.

From Bologna Comines went to Florenc
with Savonarola : " I asked him whether
pass out of Italy without danger of his p
great preparation the Venetians made aga
he discoursed perfectlier than myself that
He answered me that the King should l
upon the way, but that the honour ther
though he were accompanied but with an
that God, who had guided him at his c
protect him at his return. Adding not
because he had not done his duty in the
Church, but had suffered his men to spoil
as well those that took his part and \
him into their cities, as his enemies : G
sentence against him, and would sh
Nevertheless, he bade me tell him that
compassion on the poor people, and er
keep his men from doing evil, and puni
he was bound by his office to do), that the
His sentence, or at the least mitigate it
that he ought not to think it a sufficiel
his own person did no harm. He said,
self would go and tell the King thus r
he did, and persuaded with him to re

[1] *Diario Ferrarese*, coll. 30<

places to them. When he spake thus of God's sentence, the death of my Lord the Dauphin came suddenly to my mind."¹

At Siena—where Comines met the King and the latter "solaced himself with the dames"—they heard news which precluded all possibility of a peaceful passage. The Duke of Orleans, who had been reinforced at Asti, had taken the offensive and occupied Novara (June 11), in spite of the express commands of the King not to attempt anything against the Duke of Milan. Charles "therefore was well assured that the Venetians would declare themselves his enemies: for they sent him word that, if he invaded the Duke of Milan, they would aid the Duke with their whole force, according to their League lately made, and their force was great and in a readiness."² He at once left Siena and moved on to Poggibonsi, where Savonarola met him and dissuaded him from his purpose of restoring Piero de' Medici. Avoiding Florence, the King pressed on to Pisa, where he left a garrison, and advanced thence through the Lunigiana towards Parma.

Ercole, under pressure from Milan, had promised to send Don Alfonso with a considerable force to the army of the League, as a kind of counterbalance to the presence of Don Ferrando on the other side.³ But the continual passing of

---

¹ *Mémoires*, viii. 2.
² *Ibid.*, viii. 3.
³ In a curious dispatch to Jacopo Trotti, of May 31, 1495, Ercole states that he cannot lend the Duke of Milan any more light horse; he has only about forty mounted *balestrieri* (crossbowmen) left, whom he always keeps near him for his personal guard when he goes out of the city or rides in the Barco, chiefly because of the machinations against his person of the Da Groppo of the Padovano, "of whom you know several were hanged here at Ferrara, when there was the affair of Messer Niccolò da Este," and the Counts of San

envoys and messengers between Ferrara
camp, the Duke's refusal to go in person to
in sending Alfonso and the hostile bearing
towards the Visdomino, had roused suspici
tion. At Venice there was much talk of
disposition and perpetual animosity towar
of his plotting with France against it; and,
Venetian ambassadors, passing through I
way to Bologna, would not leave their *carre*
respects to the Duke. "His Lordship an
were hated by all Italy universally."[1] Al
Milan at night on June 15, with the Coun
chetti and thirty-five persons of his house
soldiers to follow him. He took no subsec
campaign, but remained in Milan as lieuten
council and governor of the citadel.

Seriously alarmed at the threats of the
had put troops into the Polesine, Ercole
that he would give him every aid in the rec
and protested to Venice that he would lend
ance to the French in their passage. But
him. At the instance of Lodovico, as also
of his own subjects, he made Ferrando an
Prosperi, who was with him in the Frencl
the King from his intention of passing t
fagnana; but he kept in constant touch

Bonifazio of Verona, "who would offend us, if t
of that Count Bernardo who was executed here
Being so near the borders, they could easily
Ferrara, without his having any intimation
Modena, *Minutario Cronologico*. The Count
Bonifazio was beheaded for murder in 1473.

[1] *Diario Ferrarese*, coll. 307, 308. Cf. Sanud
Carlo VIII in Italia, pp. 380, 381, 414.

THE DUKE AND THE FRIAR

and insisted that Don Ferrando, who wished to return to Ferrara, should follow the King wherever he went. At the first news of a skirmish, he impartially congratulated the victor, no matter to which party Fortune had shown herself favourable.[1]

An ineffectual attempt had been made in Ercole's name by Antonio Costabili to make peace between France and Milan; but Lodovico had cut short the negotiations. On July 1, Ercole left Ferrara with four hundred horsemen, and went to Reggio, giving out that he was going to make a last effort to reconcile the Duke of Milan and the King. The documents in the Modena Archives make it clear that this was done under direct pressure from Lodovico;[2] but Sanudo says that Ercole took with him "many carriage-loads of tapestry and silver plate. It was rumoured that he was going to give the passage to the King, and for this he brought these trappings, to be able to receive his Majesty honourably." Before leaving Ferrara, where he left his brother

---

[1] Letters and minutes of June 26, 1495, to Alfonso at Milan and Ferrando in the French camp, concerning the proposed French passage through the Garfagnana; of June 28, to Alfonso, expressing his pleasure that the French have been beaten; of July 3, to Ferrando, bidding him tell the King how glad he is that Aubigny has been victorious, and keep near his person. Archivio di Modena, *Minutario Cronologico* and *Carteggio dei Principi*.

[2] On July 1 Ercole wrote to Lodovico: "Both by the letter of your Excellence and by the writing of Messer Jacopo Trotti our orator, we have learned how much your Excellence desires that we should go to Reggio, saying that our person in that place will assist your affairs at Parma. To this we answer that, to satisfy your Excellence, as is our desire in all that we can, we will transfer ourselves right willingly to Reggio, and, as far as it is in our power, we shall not fail to favour the affairs of your Lordship." To Trotti, he says that Lodovico has insisted that he should go in person to Reggio, "to be able to know what is going on in the Parmesano and in the army." Archivio di Modena, *Minutario Cronologico*.

DUKES AND POETS IN FEI

Sigismondo as his vicar, Ercole told the Vis
went to please the Duke of Milan and that
a good son of the Signoria, but not an
King of France. But the Venetians decla
sending powder and victuals through the
French army, and Corio accuses him of b
hearted favourer of the French, amongst
his son as hostage, desiring that Charles
arbiter of Italy."[1]

The King had passed through Pontren
entry into the mountains," where "Friar Je
proved true, which was that God would le
the hand, till he were out of danger; for it
enemies were blinded and bereft of their w
defended not this straight." Beyond Pont
five days in a valley near a small village, '
almost famished, and his battle lying thi
his vaward in the midst of huge and s
over the which such great cannons and
then, as never had passed before."[2] The
with Gian Jacopo Trivulzio—who, exile
had entered into the Neapolitan service ar
consent of King Ferdinand) into that of
for the first of many times, was leading the
his own countrymen—and the vanguard
three days before the King's main body,
great labour and difficulty were conveying
over the mountains. "Hitherto in all thi
Comines, "we had no war; but now it

[1] Sanudo, *op. cit.*, pp. 445, 460; Malipiero, *A*₁
that Ercole hoped to receive the King in Reggic
[2] Comines, viii. 4.

THE DUKE AND THE FRIAR

Fornovo the forces of the League—or, more strictly, the army of Venice with a portion of the power of Milan and a handful of Papal troops—barred their further progress The Marquis of Mantua held the supreme command; with him was his uncle, Rodolfo Gonzaga; while the Milanese contingent was captained by the Count of Caiazzo, Francesco da San Severino, the eldest of the sons of Roberto. Both Rodolfo and the Count of Caiazzo had served the French in the preceding year. With the exception of the Stradiots, light-armed Greeks and Albanians in the pay of Venice, and a company of Germans, it was an Italian army: "the finest and most potent," wrote the Marquis to Isabella, "that for a long time has been seen in Italy, fit to win honour in any great enterprise. This army alone will not only suffice to resist the French, but to extirpate them perpetually."[1]

A couple of skirmishes on July 1 and 5 with the vanguard, in which small parties of French were cut off by the Stradiots and their heads carried in triumph on lances, raised the spirits of the Italians. The Ferrarese force—six hundred horse which Ercole had been obliged to send—came into the camp on the morning of July 2; but Alfonso remained in Milan.

At about noon on Sunday, July 5, 1495, the King himself with his main body came down the mountains and took up his quarters in Fornovo. He was encamped in a valley a quarter of a league broad, between two little hills, through which runs the Taro. The enemy were on the hill to the right, hardly half a league away, " so that we were forced to pass just before them, the river running between us; for not-

[1] Letter of June 21. Luzio and Renier, *Francesco Gonzaga alla Battaglia di Fornovo*, p. 211.

withstanding that on the back side o[f
hand (underneath the which we were
another way that we might have take
do so, lest we should seem to fly."
night a terrible rain, and such lightnin
was never since the world began : so th
seemed to go together, or that this fo[r
inconvenience to ensue. For notwithst
well that the reverberation of these gre
foot of the which we lay) made this thun
indeed it was ; and further, that thun
natural in a hot country, especially in s
they at that present the more dreadful
because we saw so many enemies enca
having none other means to pass thr
battle, our force being so small as it wa
not more than nine thousand men w
weakened his power on the way by
various places and sending troops to (
the League amounted to some thirty t

Sanudo declares that, the day before
from the mountains to Fornovo, Ercole
the French camp to speak with his Maje
that the Venetians did not mean to fi
Corio, he sent letters to him to a simil

---

[1] Comines, viii. 5.
[2] *Op. cit.*, pp. 485, 517. It is worth notic
frequently accused Ercole of going about i[n
harm or to spy their proceedings. Before th
of 1482, he gave an emphatic and contemptu(
accusation that he had gone disguised to exa
forts on the frontier. *Minute Ducali per Ron
January 27, 1482. Archivio di Modena, Carte
—Roma.*

THE DUKE AND THE FRIAR

Comines gives no hint of these somewhat melodramatic proceedings, it seems fairly clear from a subsequent statement of his that, previous to the battle, Ercole had attempted some sort of mediation between the King and Lodovico;[1] and, up to the last moment, Charles was contemplating the possibility of a peaceful passage. The Duke waited at Reggio in agonized suspense, while, all night and the following morning, the rain fell in torrents, the lightning flashed over the town and the thunder reverberated among the distant hills. He had staked the safety of his Duchy upon the victory of the French, his religious hopes on the verification of Fra Girolamo's prophecy. Presently there came a rout of mounted men through the storm, clattering through Reggio's quiet streets. They were his own soldiers—Don Alfonso's company—mingled with light-armed Stradiots, flying from Fornovo, spreading the news of a royal victory of France. In his haste Ercole was for once taken off his guard. He sent towards the field of battle to gain further particulars, and then dispatched a messenger to his brother Sigismondo, informing him of the event and bidding him tell the Visdomino.

The actual facts of the battle of Fornovo are too well known to be repeated here.[2] Assailed in the van by the Count of Caiazzo, in the rear by the Marquis of Mantua with the flower of the Italian chivalry, the King had shaken off their

---

[1] Comines, when they got safe to Asti, sent to inform the Duke of Orleans of "divers treaties that were entertained between the King and the Duke of Milan, in one of the which myself negotiated by the Duke of Ferrara's means" (viii. end of 7). Cf. Ercole's letter to Lodovico of July 1, quoted above.

[2] They are superbly related from the French point of view by Comines (viii. 6), from the Italian standpoint by Corio and Sanudo. For the whole literature of the subject, see Luzio and Renier, *Francesco Gonzaga alla Battaglia di Fornovo*.

DUKES AND POETS IN I

attack, and hurled them back, broken
"Undoubtedly," says Comines, "it is i
to meet roughlier than we met." The Sti
infantry had made the merest pretence
onslaught, but had rushed "like flying
royal baggage. The whole thing had last
the utmost confusion, in thunder and ligh
of rain. Charles himself, left alone in
narrowly escaped falling into the hanc
cavalry. About three thousand Italiar
including the second in command, Rodol
was a virtuous and a wise gentleman, :
and bare arms against us with an evil w
took no prisoners, their camp-followers bi
men-at-arms with the hatchets they u
According to Comines, the French ha
hundred men, but Corio estimates the 1
thousand. The Bastard of Bourbon had
by the Marquis of Mantua, who had she
as a general, but very great personal c
the fight. The royal baggage and trea
spoils from Naples, had fallen into the h
and Italians.

A portion of the Venetian forces had
in their camp in reserve, the Provve
in Corio's phrase, "that in this battle we
fate not only of Italy but, as it were, c
because, if Charles were defeated, he lost
if the Latins lost, Italy was exposed to

[1] Comines, *loc. cit.* Rodolfo's death is
sonorous lines by Ariosto, in the poem *Ad*
i. 2).

THE DUKE AND THE FRIAR

Both sides claimed the victory. " God had performed that which Friar Jerome promised," writes Comines, " to wit, that the honour of the field should be ours ; for considering our small experience and evil government, we were unworthy of this good success that God gave us, because we could not then tell how to use it." The Marquis of Mantua wrote to his sister that he had delivered Italy, "brought forth the liberation and liberty of Italy," and when we stand in the Louvre before that most superb of votive pictures which he bade Mantegna paint for him, *La Madonna della Vittoria*, the man's self-deception seems for the nonce almost sublime. The battle, the bloodiest in Italy since two centuries, had been fought on the morning of Monday, July 6, 1495.

It must be said that Charles' behaviour was not that of a victor, but gave considerable colour to the Mantuan vaunt. The next morning, Comines crossed the river and conferred with the Marquis, the Count of Caiazzo and the two Provveditori, about an armistice. But by midnight the King had decided to retreat with all speed. Before dawn the French " turned our backs to our enemies, seeking wholly our own safety," closely followed by Caiazzo's light horsemen who harassed their rear, and at a more respectful distance by the rest of the army—which turned off to join the Milanese force that (reinforced with Germans and Flemings from Maximilian) kept Orleans besieged in Novara. Charles got safe to Asti with all his artillery, while the boastful dispatches that the captains of the Italian army sent to Lodovico roused Ercole's warmest indignation :—

" We tell you," he wrote to Jacopo Trotti from Reggio, " that verily we are much astonished that that most illustrious Lord does not perceive that the truth is very seldom

told him, and that many lies and things
to him by the Count of Caiazzo and t
you have seen, the Count of Caiazzo writ
pursuing the King of France, and repres
cally taken, and, nevertheless, he does no
do we believe that he has any wish to ca
he can capture him, seeing that his Maj
be in Asti and wherever he wishes. I
and the others write and behave in that v
of doing something, and they make that
round, and yet the things are of such a k
that his Excellence ought to perceive it h
not refrain from having these few word

It was muttered in Ferrara that Alfor
Fornovo had been purposely put into
unsupported, that French might destro
of his men-at-arms, together with the cor
da Correggio, had been killed, and the re
fled from the field, spreading the repor
defeat. The Visdomino wrote furiously f
government, complaining of the way in
announced the event and that the Ferrar
for France in the streets, showing " grea
the reported rout, and insulting his messe
itself there was great exultation at the ne
piazzas and canals blazed with festive li
of artillery thundered out the triumph of
heard in Ferrara," writes the Diarist b
Venice the Venetians had fired salvos for t
they have had, to make their subjects

[1] *Minute Ducali* of July 14, 1495. Archivio di
Cronologico. Jacopo Trotti died in the following

THE DUKE AND THE FRIAR

have been victorious, and not to forgo their custom; which always was, is, and will be, when they have lost something of theirs or had bad tidings, to have guns fired, bells rung, and to keep holiday." But there were cries of "To Ferrara! To Ferrara!" and on the Rialto the boys sang an improvised song:—

> Marchexe di Ferrara, di la caxa di Maganza,
> Tu perderà 'l stado, al dispetto dil Re di Franza.[1]

The artisans and shopkeepers offered to pay double taxes, if the Republic would assail Ferrara ; "nevertheless, the Signoria would not at this time make any demonstration against that Duke, although while he was in Reggio he had sent much victual into the camp of the King of France, and barrels of powder for his artillery, but for which the King would not have been able to use it."[2]

Ercole now realized his critical position, and, somewhat tardily, instructed his ambassador in Venice, Aldobrandino di Guidone, to congratulate the Signoria on the victory of the League. Aldobrandino was refused audience on July 13; but on the next day the Doge and Collegio received him. When he began to speak of his master's joy in the victory of the army of the League, the Doge stopped him : "What army of the League ? We say that it is ours, and we have paid for it, and not the League." Aldobrandino then said that there were reports in Venice that his master had not done his duty at this crisis; these reports were

---

[1] "Marquis of Ferrara, of the House of Maganza, thou shalt lose thy State, in spite of the King of France."

[2] Sanudo, *op. cit.*, p. 485 ; Malipiero, p. 355 ; *Diario Ferrarese*, coll. 310, 311. It is quite evident from Comines that these Venetian accusations were false. But Malipiero (p. 363) says : "Some carts of the Duke of Ferrara have been taken, which were going to the French army with victuals and powder."

false, and Ercole was ready to stand the
the Doge had the letters of the Visdo
expressed his great dissatisfaction with t
missed the orator.[1] "And in Ferrara the
Duke Ercole, there was made a public p
no one should dare to speak against the Ve
had complained to the Duke that it seem
looked upon badly by the Ferrarese—as
pride and haughtiness."[2] Nevertheless, th
oured for war; a crowd of three hundred
night to Aldobrandino's house, and ma
uproar under his windows.

The Pope had by now excommunicated t
King. A papal envoy was at Florenc
insistence with the Signoria, telling them
resolved to join the League, the whole of
against them with good cause, seeing that
they were working the ruin of Italy. F
professed itself unable to break with the
sador," said this wily prelate to Manfredo
well to induce the Excellence of your Lo
declare himself openly on the side of the
Powers of Italy should complain that
Frenchman than Italian. Far better for h
in the sight of all Italy, than his wishing t
as he has done up to now; for *he that is
against me*." To this scarcely veiled
Pope, which was made in the presence
ambassador, Manfredo answered that
enough to know his own business, and tha

[1] Sanudo, *op. cit.*, p. 486; Malipiero, p
[2] *Diario Ferrarese*, col. 311.

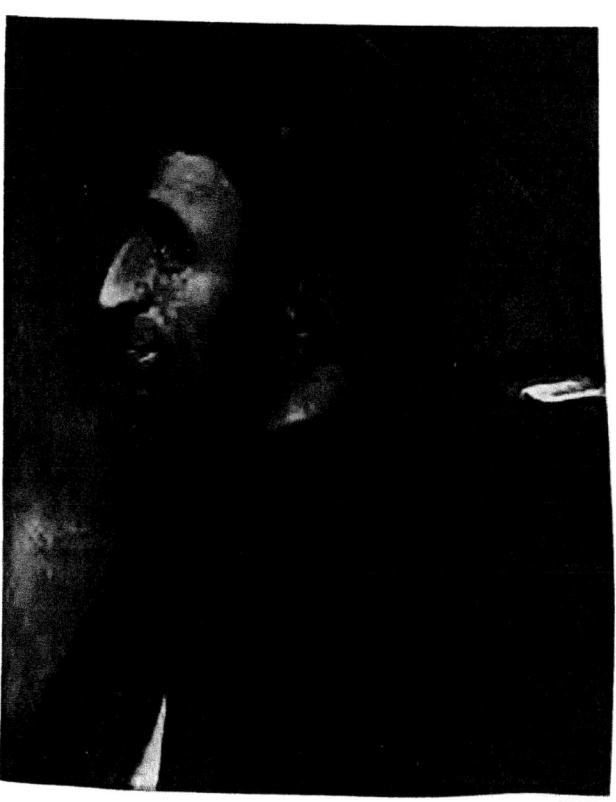

Girolamo Savonarola.
(in the character of St. Peter Martyr)
By Fra Bartolommeo

THE DUKE AND THE FRIAR

serve the cause of the Duke of Milan and the other potentates of Italy, by thus remaining neutral, than he could do if he declared himself entirely on the side of the League.[1]

Ercole was exceedingly impatient to see the book that Savonarola had promised him, the *Compendium Revelationum*, from which he anticipated much spiritual guidance in this present crisis. He bade Manfredo go to the Friar and implore him to let him have it; if it was not yet printed, he wanted to have a copy taken of the manuscript and sent to him at once. "If necessary, we will keep it secret as long as he shall wish, and we will not show it nor make it known in any way." Savonarola told Manfredo that the book would be ready next week, and that he had ordered a copy to be printed on special paper for the Duke; if he had known how eager the latter was, he would have had it transcribed by hand. And, sure enough, next week the long-expected book arrived at Ferrara, in two copies—one on special paper for the Duke, the other for his physician, Lodovico de' Carri. Manfredo, in forwarding them, explained that, seeing that the Duke's copy was something special, he had tried to pay for the expense of the paper; but the Friar would not hear of it. Ercole eagerly and instantly read the little book through, and wrote an enthusiastic letter of thanks to the author. He did not, however, commit himself in any way to the theories expressed in the work, but again earnestly implored Savonarola to pray to God for him and for Ferrara, "that our affairs and those of our native land may pass well, and be under the protection of the Divine Majesty."[2]

[1] Dispatch from Florence of July 26, 1495. Cappelli, *op. cit.*, pp. 360, 361.
[2] Letters of August 10 and 15, 1495, from Ercole to Manfredo

DUKES AND POETS IN F

The Duke of Orleans was now hard pres
men reduced to the utmost extremities
response to a pressing invitation from the]
forward again as peacemaker and mediat
September, passing to and fro between M
vico kept with his power, and Vercelli, whe
lay. Pandolfo Collenuccio, whose genius
would put the most enterprising of modern
blush, had been holding high talk wit
Florence. On his return to Ferrara, he wr
of the expectations which all Italy had in
influence with the King of France, but un
in silence the fact that the Friar was very
the reality of this peace:—

"When I took leave of his Paternity, I
conclusion I should bear away with me a
He said to me: 'Messer Pandolfo, I shall
the words of Ezekiel the Prophet: *And ye
I am the Lord God. Because they have dec
saying: Peace, peace; and there is no peace ;
a wall, and others daubed it with untempered t
them that daub without tempering, that it shall*
the reply that he gave me, which I have af
Ezekiel, and it is in the thirteenth chapter.
to tell this to your Lordship, because it cou
that you, with your goodness and with

(Villari, *Savonarola*, i. appendix, doc. xxxvi. 1, 2
patches of August 13 and 20; letters dated Com:
from Ercole to Manfredo and to Savonarola (Cappe
363). The book in question was the Italian vei
pendium of Revelations. In October, Savonarola
Duke the Latin version with a short letter (Vill
xxx. 1), which Ercole gratefully acknowledged (le
24, Cappelli, *op. cit.*, p. 366).

THE DUKE AND THE FRIAR

your heart and devotion to God, will be the cause of this decree being changed, as in His wisdom God did in Isaiah and Jonah. However, *the hearts of kings are in the hand of God.*"[1]

Notwithstanding Savonarola's forebodings, the peace was concluded in October at Vercelli, between Charles and Lodovico. Novara was surrendered, Milan paying an indemnity to the Duke of Orleans; the French ships taken at Genoa were to be restored, and Lodovico was to aid Charles against Naples, if the latter returned in person to the enterprise (Ferdinand had re-entered his capital in the very month of the battle of Fornovo); the castelletto of Genoa (which city, it will be remembered, the French claimed as a fief), as a pledge of Lodovico's fidelity, was to be put into Ercole's hands as neutral for two years. It was an insincere peace on both sides, and the attitude of the Venetians, who had two months given them in which to enter into it, but to whom Ferdinand had consigned six coast towns in Apulia, was questionable. But Charles was only anxious to return to France, and left his garrisons in Apulia and the Abruzzi to their fate.

Ercole, through Manfredo, had promptly informed the "Ten of the War" at Florence of the arrangement about Genoa. In November, he took possession of the castelletto and garrisoned it with men and artillery—though he experienced the utmost difficulty in getting the necessary funds, which he understood had been promised, from either of the high contracting parties.[2] Then he returned to Ferrara, his

---
[1] Dispatch of October 12, 1495. Cappelli, *op. cit.*, p. 406.
[2] Letters of October 27 and December 10, 1495, dated Milan and Ferrara respectively, to Don Ferrando. Archivio di Modena, *Carteggio dei Principi*. After the battle of Fornovo, Charles had

faithful subjects noting with approval th[e]
good health and decidedly well pleased
molto di bona voglia e grasso, as the Diaris[t]

Savonarola had already expressed to M[a]
tion of appealing to the Duke to take up
event of the Pope forbidding him to pr[each]
1496 found Ercole completely under his
attempting to transform Ferrara into an id[eal]
ance with the Friar's precepts. He be[gan]
proclaiming a black fast of two days throu[gh]
in consequence of an alleged apparition of
in Rome, to avert the fearful scourges o[f]
that were said to be about to fall upon Ital[y]
the example by fasting rigidly with all
days later, the Friar sent the Duke what
been a printed first draft of his book
Christianae Vitae, with a letter full of h[o]
soon see my earthly country, by virtue o[f]
bring forth some spiritual fruit." He beg[ged]
little book secret for the present, or at
others read it with him in his own room
revise it. In view of the terrible trib
rapidly approaching, let his Excellence b
divine things; especially let him purge
men, and put the offices into the hands o[f]
away all power from the evil and infamou[s]
greatly provoke the anger of God." [2]

made Ferrando Duke of Amalfi; but Mont[p]
disregarding the young Ferrarese prince, confe[rred]
a French noble.

[1] Dispatch of October 26, 1495. Cappelli, *op*
[2] Letter of January 10, 1496. Villari, *op. cit.,*
The first published edition of the *De Simplicit[e]*

THE DUKE AND THE FRIAR

At Easter, Ercole made a vigorous effort to begin this reformation of Ferrara, according to Savonarola's exhortations. A strongly-worded edict was published from the balcony of the Palazzo della Ragione against blasphemy, unlawful gaming, sodomy, married men keeping concubines in public or private, letting houses to harlots or their panders; and steps were taken to see that it was carried out. All shops were to be shut on feast-days, and nothing was to be sold on these days in the piazza, save what was really necessary. Unfortunately, the Duke went further, and abandoned his former enlightened policy towards the Jews. All the "Hebrews and Marrani" living in Ferrara and the Ferrarese territory were to be compelled to wear the yellow badge of shame sewn on to the front of their dresses, and on Low Sunday all the Jews in Ferrara were obliged to attend a sermon in the Duomo, at which Ercole himself and Anna were present.[1]

Hearing of all these measures from Ercole's Dominican confessor, Fra Tommaso, Savonarola expressed the utmost satisfaction; but he exhorted the Duke not to rest there. "Let your Lordship especially set diligent watch, supervision and restraint upon your ministers and officials, which matters more than all the rest. These are often wont to derogate the clemency, goodness and reputation of the Sovereign by perverse suggestions, and wicked and impious exactions; and by fraudulent adulation; wherefore such men should be abhorred as enemies of your

is dated August 28, 1496; an Italian version, by Girolamo Benivieni, followed in October.

[1] *Diario Ferrarese*, coll. 322, 323. The worthy preacher's eloquence, however, was wasted: "On that day one Hebrew was baptized, after the sermon in the Vescovado; but he was not one of those who had been to hear the sermon."

Excellence."[1] Unfortunately, Ercole co[n]
pably lax on this point, until a severe lesso[n]
Gregorio Zampante of Lucca, his capta[in]
Ferrara, was universally and justly hate[d]
unlimited confidence that the Duke had [in]
pante " cared not for any man in the w[orld]
the sons and brothers of his ducal Lords
all the subjects of the Lord tremble," w[ith]
and cruel tortures; he lived luxuriously, a[nd]
sum of money from his extortions. Erc[ole]
him and would hear nothing against him,
hated this " enemy of God and man "
hatred that he dared not cross the road o[r]
the Duke, without an escort of soldier[s]
July 18 of this year, while Ercole was at
to arbitrate between the Pio who were,
other's throats, two medical students an[d]
entered Zampante's house after dinner at
and disembowelled him with a dagger.
they rode furiously through the quiet s[treets]
claiming what they had done, and escape[d]
frontier, all the people helping them on
Duke, on his return, made no attempt t[o]
but took the lesson to heart. A few mon[ths]
an example of Count Niccolò Ariost[i]
guilty of cruelty and oppression in his
commissary at Lugo; he was fined fiv[e]
ducats, deprived of his post, and declared
again holding office in the Duchy.[3]

[1] Letter of April 27, 1496. Villari, *op. cit.*,
[2] *Diario Ferrarese*, coll. 330–333. Cf. chapte[r]
[3] *Ibid.*, coll. 337, 338.

THE DUKE AND THE FRIAR

In the meanwhile, Lodovico Sforza was plying the Friar with honeyed words, while his agents were intercepting his letters and endeavouring to compromise him with the Pope and the King of France. He produced faked letters, either written in Savonarola's name by his foes in Florence or composed for the occasion by his own agents, and sent copies to Ercole, who promptly placed them in Savonarola's hands, through Manfredo, and received the Friar's assurance that they were forgeries. Manfredo still pressed the latter for advice to Ercole, in the growing rumours of a new French invasion, to which the Friar could only answer that he would not fail to pray continually to God that He would illumine the Duke as to the best course for him to pursue.[1]

The situation, indeed, was growing more difficult every day. Throughout 1496, there were perpetual rumours of a French expedition to support the claims of the Duke of Orleans upon Milan and to reconquer the Kingdom of Naples, where the House of Aragon was rapidly winning back all that it had lost. Comines tells us that the French were assured of the Duke of Ferrara's friendship and aid.[2] Trivulzio was actually at Asti in May, and a French ambassador, who came to Ferrara at the end of the month,

---

[1] Dispatch of April 28, 1496. Cappelli, *op. cit.*, pp. 369, 370. Communications between Ercole and Savonarola continued uninterruptedly throughout this year. Besides constant advice, the Friar sent the Duke a rosary. " We have received," writes Ercole to Manfredo, " the rosary which you have sent us in the name of our venerable Fra Girolamo, the which has been as acceptable to us as any other thing that we could have received, and therefore we would have you take an occasion greatly to thank him for it in our name." Archivio di Modena, *Minutario Cronologico* (May 17, 1496).

[2] *Mémoires*, viii. 15. He says that Ercole had promised to aid them with five hundred men-at-arms and two thousand foot-soldiers.

DUKES AND POETS IN FE

received a popular ovation. The Venetian
the Ferrarese frontier, alike on the Polesin
though Ercole assured them that he was
boundaries should extend to the piazza o

The hesitancy of the Duke of Orlean
Dauphin having died at the beginning o
himself the heir to the French throne,
delayed the invasion. But the French
their alliance with the Swiss had ala
Lodovico Sforza and the Pope, supp
induced the King of the Romans to con
plea of taking the imperial crown—in r
than the condottiere of the League for
In July, Lodovico and Beatrice met th
in the Tyrol, whither most of the Italia
bassadors. Some of the imperial min
the presence of the Ferrarese envoy,
had not joined the League; and Maxin
when he arrived in Italy, he would e
Ferrara to come to him in person, to swe
reinvested with the imperial fiefs of M
The envoy protested his master's devo
that no renewal of the investiture was

Maximilian arrived in Italy in Aug
greeted by the Cardinal Carvajal in the na
der. Venice and Milan were growing c
each other's designs concerning Pisa, w
to keep firm in his alliance with Franc

---

[1] *Diario Ferrarese*, col. 326.
[2] Dispatch of Dandolo and Foscari, July
*Senato Veneto di Francesco Foscari e di altri ora
Massimiliano*, pp. 784, 785.

THE DUKE AND THE FRIAR

after excuse for not coming to see the Emperor at Vigevano in the Milanese. "He cannot come," said Antonio Costabili, who had succeeded Trotti as Ferrarese ambassador at Milan, "because he is old and absorbed in his devotions; but he will send Don Alfonso, his son." The Duke feared lest he should be bidden surrender the castelletto of Genoa and break faith with France. Maximilian was indignant at the suggestion that Ercole was bound to write to the King of France for direction, and bade the ambassador order him absolutely to come to him. The Moro sent Antonio Costabili to Ferrara to urge him to obey, but Ercole for once was unshaken. When Maximilian entered Genoa on September 27, the Ferrarese garrison in the castelletto fired a few salvos in salute—but only under compulsion from the governor of the town.[1] The story of Maximilian's abortive siege of Leghorn, the timely succour of the French fleet, and the would-be Caesar's retreat to the Tyrol in December, need not be retold here.

Ercole's bearing throughout this episode had estranged Milan, and increased the suspicion of the League against him. Lodovico's agents professed to have intercepted incriminating dispatches from the Ferrarese ambassador in France,[2] and it was universally believed that Savonarola and Ercole were working hand in hand to bring the King back to Italy. Ercole, however, bade Manfredo warn the Friar in his name to be on his guard against circumvention and treachery, since "from afar they cast the nets to bring the fish to shore."[3] To add to his perplexities, the Pope

---

[1] Foscari's dispatches of September 9, 13, 14, 27. *Ibid.*, pp. 856, 877, 882, 896.
[2] Foscari's dispatch of September 11. *Ibid.*, p. 870.
[3] Letter of November 17, 1496. Cappelli, *op. cit.*, p. 373. The warning is, for once, against the French.

had attempted to appoint his own
the Cardinal of Monreale, to the E
when the Duke, who desired this,
dominions, for his son Ippolito,
possession, Ferrara was put und
death of the Duchess Beatrice, on
tically severed all the ties that bou
and, when Alfonso's young wife Ar
grave on November 30, there was
two Dukes united.

Very early in the morning on Ma
sought out Savonarola in the name
him of the affection and love that th
him, and the faith he had in the th
prophesied. He exhorted him to p
and implored him to give him som
what he believed was going to happer
he should do at this crisis. Savona
thanked the Duke much for the love
he had no need to remind him perpe
for him, as he did so continually, and
as he knew that he was praying for a

[1] Although it was not until September,
interdicted, this trouble had begun in 1494
December 12) to the Cardinal Borgia him:
son who was a Cardinal, verily we could
Bishopric should be bestowed upon another
Lordship, both because of your own virtu
as also in respect of the Holiness of our L
and son we are. But since we have the m
Este our son, who has need of benefices, an
the first benefice and the most important
dominion, it seems to us fitting and perfec
retain that benefice for our son rather th
Archivio di Modena, *Minutario Cronologico*.

who lived like a Christian and a Catholic. As to Manfredo's last request, he would pray to God for inspiration to be able to give Ercole the light he needed. On the following evening, the Friar suddenly sent for Manfredo, and gave him a slip of paper, written in his own hand, to convey with the utmost security to Ercole, on the understanding that the latter would keep most secret this inspiration of his, which he revealed to him "under the seal of confession." On the slip of paper which Manfredo forwarded to Ercole, after solemnly pledging both the Duke and himself to absolute secrecy, were these words:—

"The *Friend* is not rejected, but he is deceived by his own; if he choose, he will still do great things and get rid of every one; and, therefore, it is a dangerous thing to leave him. I do not think, however,—and this I say of myself—that it would be bad to use some astuteness with our enemies, in order not to enter into any danger, until God opens his eyes. We shall aid the affair with our prayers. On the other hand, it would be good to aid it with prudence, by some trusty person who could speak to him securely and open his eyes. It should be a religious and wise person, and one who believed in these things. This must not be communicated to any one, because I have not yet divulged this thing to any here; but your faith has merited this secret from the Lord, in Whom alone you must trust, taking opportune measures for your own right living and that of your subjects, for *cursed be the man that trusteth in man, and maketh flesh his arm*." [1]

[1] This note accompanied Manfredo's dispatch of March 7, 1497. Cappelli, *op. cit.*, pp. 374, 375. Ercole's bastard, Don Giulio, was in Florence, and had been present at the Friar's sermon in the Duomo. Savonarola was also in correspondence with the younger

The mysterious friend, the *ami*
and the hint—which goes perilou
—is obviously that Ercole should
until he comes, temporize with
urged him to adopt the suggestion,
but wise person to urge up " tl
adequacy of such a message, prof
a chill to the Duke's heart, and i
faith in the prophet wavered. In
the Duomo at Florence, followed by
excommunication against Savonarol.
at Milan Antonio Costabili vigorous
tine ambassador in defending the
cause to the face of Lodovico him
conceal his anxiety and perplexity.
his circle, probably the Fra Tomm;
informed Savonarola that the Duke
at the tardiness of the fulfilment o
Friar at once wrote an impassioned
to persevere in the faith. God is n
like man, but sometimes proceeds s;
of the elect and to make more mani
the reprobate. "Similarly the Jews
prophets, because it seemed to them

Ercole d' Este (the Duke's nephew) and
Cf. Mansi's Appendix to Baluze, *Miscel*
Angela is wrongly styled " Duchess of Ferra:
Paolo Somenzi, the Milanese orator at Fl
March 5, it is stated that this Ercole di Sigis:
on the previous day to Florence, disguised, t
Villari, *op. cit.*, ii. p. 6, note 3. Father Lu
appears to have confused the uncle and the
F ¹ Dispatch of Antonio Costabili to E:
Villari, *op. cit.*, ii. document vi.

THE DUKE AND THE FRIAR

foretold were long in coming, and so at last they were deceived every time, until their final destruction by the Romans." Let him have lively faith, and in the meantime reform whatever is wrong in his household and Court. In spite of his tribulations, the Friar professes himself confident, and urges Ercole to have no fear. " Read the Holy Scriptures, or have them read to you, and especially the Prophets, as Jeremiah and Ezekiel; and you will find almost everything similar to these times."[1]

" With all our power do we thank you," wrote Ercole in reply, "for your affectionate treatment of us and for the good suggestions that you charitably offer us, because we see that they are worthy of your goodness and corresponding to the love that you bear us, and we are extraordinarily obliged to you for it. Verily, for your satisfaction, we assure you that we have hitherto never doubted that those things are to ensue which have been foretold by you, and more than ever are we of this firm opinion and faith that not one iota shall be omitted of what you have prophesied. It is quite true that, seeing the delay and negligence of the King of France, and the little care that he has had for his own honour and for the weal of his friends, we have doubted —and do doubt very much—lest he should not be the man who is to do any notable and eminent achievement; and this doubt of ours is not alien from our faith and belief

[1] Letter of August 1, 1497, in Mansi's Appendix to Baluze, *Miscellanea*, i. pp. 585, 586. In this same month of August, Sanudo describes Ercole as having become " very Catholic," and going about in a carriage with his doctor, Francesco da Castello, who follows him everywhere. Also his half-brother Rinaldo " is entirely given to devotion ;" but it is reported that, a few days ago, "Don Alfonxo fece in Ferrara cossa assa' liziera, che andoe nudo per Ferrara, con alcuni zoveni in compagnia, di mezo zorno." *Diarii*, i. coll. 706, 707.

DUKES AND POETS

in what concerns you, because ir
seen that the King of France of 1
does the things that are to follow ;
been foretold by you and if we had
not have failed to believe it also,
others. And since you have been
this your sweet letter, we should be
earnestly, if you would reveal and
think and what is your opinion to
aforesaid King of France, and wha
we esteem you so, that all that y(
believed by us as a thing certain ; a
desire, we shall take such good care
us that it will not come to the knowl(
for our greater content, shall receive in
from and shall be greatly obliged t
selves continually ready to serve you :
you to be pleased to be a good aml
presence of our Lord God." [1]

Savonarola delayed some while in
praying for many days for light to sa
at length he could only say that the el
of God had always been revealed to
that he still saw no signs that the King
they must trust in God.[2] In the mean
Nero and his four associates had be(
courtyard of the Bargello's quarters a(
Vecchio, for their complicity in the plot
Medici. Ercole had instructed Manfred(

[1] Letter dated Modena, August 8, 1497. Cap
383.
[2] Letter of August 29, 1497. Villari, *op. cit.*,

THE DUKE AND THE FRIAR

the Signoria for their lives, but the sentence had been carried out before the ambassador's instructions reached him. The Florentines had been bitterly offended at the interference of the Duke of Milan—indeed, Manfredo thought that it had hastened the prisoners' deaths—but they were gratified by the terms of the Ferrarese message. In answer to questions as to what his Duke thought of the executions, Manfredo answered in effect that his master had every confidence in the prudence of the people of Florence.[1]

But, in spite of his assurances to Savonarola, Ercole was wavering. The Venetian forces from Ravenna were threatening Bagnacavallo, and, Charles not having returned, the time for surrendering the castelletto of Genoa to Milan was at hand. At Rome, the orators of Venice and Milan were openly declaring that, to protect Italy from a new French invasion, the only way was to crush the Italian rebels—the Florentines and the Duke of Ferrara. "They are the cause of the ruin of Italy," they said; "it is they alone who keep the Most Christian King in hope and in thinking of the affairs of Italy."[2] Don Ferrando had returned from France, and the Venetians expressed a wish to take him into their service. He had visited Venice *incognito* at the beginning of November, but the Republic had, against Ercole's will, published the fact. Ercole was at length forced to give way and humble himself again before the great Republic, and go in person to Venice. But before going, he assured Manfredo that this visit of reconciliation was only for purposes of self-protection, and instructed him to inform the Signoria of Florence that his friendship to-

---

[1] Dispatch of August 29, 1497. Cappelli, *op. cit.*, p. 389.
[2] Manfredo's dispatch of September 9, 1497. Cappelli, *op. cit.*, p. 392.

wards them was unbroken and un
ber 16, with his son Don Ferran
Venetian Visdomino, Ercole left
subjects liking his journey as little
The Doge received him most graciou
the conclusion of Ferrando's *condotte*
Duke, "that we may verily learn, an
the love and affection that this most
bears us," and made fullest profess
good will towards the House of Este

The surrender of the castelletto of
visit to Venice roused a suspicion in Fl
adhered to the League, without pre
Florentine allies. Manfredo found it
long interview with Savonarola, who p
justice of the Duke's conduct. A fev
professed themselves more than satisf
the Duke to mediate on behalf of Flor
the restitution of Pisa; which he did in
without result.

But, in the meanwhile, the Cardin
having yielded in the matter of the Ferr
Ippolito being made Archbishop of Mil
Rome, intriguing in his father's interests

[1] Letter from Ercole to Manfredo, Novem
op. cit., pp. 392, 393; letter from Ercole to
from Venice, November 25, Archivio di M
Principi; *Diario Ferrarese*, col. 341; Malipi
497. "To many it seemed strange," writes]
Signoria should have wished to give its arms in
chief of its enemies; but with this appointmer
rulers of Italy to their duty, and especially the]
The Gonzaga, whose secret dealings with Franc
Chiara, the widow of Montpensier) had been d
cashiered from the Venetian service in the prece

THE DUKE AND THE FRIAR

and especially, according to the paternal instructions, currying favour with the Venetian Cardinal Grimani. Ercole was greatly gratified at his conduct. " Your excellent bearing in that Court," he wrote, " has satisfied us so much that, if there could be obligations between father and son, we should consider ourselves to be much obliged to you." And again, a few days later : " It seems to us that our Lord God is directing and governing well the affairs of your most reverend Lordship, and that you are deporting yourself in all your actions with such dexterity and maturity that you facilitate every arduous undertaking and bring it to a successful end."[1] At the end of February, 1498, Ippolito went to enter upon his new office at Milan ; but the result of his stay in Rome had been to draw Ercole still more from Savonarola and towards the Pope. It was, indeed, the beginning of the end, so far as the Duke's relations with Fra Girolamo were concerned.

Hearing that, in spite of the excommunication, the Friar was going to preach the Lent in the Duomo, Manfredo sought him on January 31, and talked to him for a long while upon the subject. Savonarola told him that he most certainly was resolved to preach this Lent, and perhaps even sooner, if it were intimated to him by those who could command him. The ambassador was puzzled. " Do you mean that you expect a commission from the Pope, or from the Signoria here ? " " Not from the Signoria nor even from the Pope, seeing that he is continuing in his usual mode of life, besides that I know he certainly does not intend to remove from me the excommunication ; but from One who is higher than the Pope and all other creatures." Manfredo tried in vain to

[1] Letters of January 10 and 22, 1498. Archivio di Modena, *Carteggio dei Principi*.

dissuade him. "We shall wait for t]
affair," he wrote to Ercole, "by w]
better to judge what foundation it is
whether it be divine or human."¹ O1
came the famous sermon declaring
invalid and the Pope a broken tool.
diligently informed; but the Duke's m
dared go no further.

An opportunity soon came for him
licly. In March, Count Gian Franc
published at Florence a defence of Savo
it to Ercole, implying that he had writ
of a conversation that he had had v
request.² Monsignor Felino Sandeo, o
prelates of the Curia, urged the Duke to t
himself. The latter at once wrote back,
entirely from Gian Francesco, protestin
consulted him as to the validity of th
He inclosed a letter to the Pope himself
calling God to witness that he had noth
publication, and that he had never c
authority and power of the Sovereign P(

[1] Dispatches of February 1 and 8. Cappell
[2] *Joannis Francisci Pici Mirandulae Op*
excommunicationis injusta pro Hieronymi Savo
innocentia. This Gian Francesco was Ercole's
the Galeotto della Mirandola we have so often
the famous scholar), had been urged to repen
in two letters (Marchese, *Lettere inedite di*
124-126), but in vain. Galeotto died in April
excommunicated for sixteen years and Miran(
interdict, but Alexander gave the widowed Bi;
to bury him in church. *Diario Ferrarese*, col.
[3] Letters from Ercole to Felino Sandeo and
March 26, 1498. Cappelli, *op. cit.*, pp. 399, 400.

THE DUKE AND THE FRIAR

observed that this letter does little credit to the Duke and shows how impossible a religious reformation was, at that epoch, in Italy; but to me, unless I read the man's character wrong, it appears a perfectly sincere utterance on Ercole's part. He conscientiously believed that even the Borgia held the keys of Heaven and Hell.

Nevertheless, Ercole followed closely every detail in the closing scenes of the tragedy that ended in front of the Palazzo Vecchio on the morning of May 23, 1498. It is uncertain whether he made any effort to save the Friar from his fate; but it would, in any case, have been in vain. At least, he did not sink to dissimulating his heartfelt sorrow.

Chapter X

IN THE CLOSE OF THE TROCENTO

FOR all in Ferrara, high and low alik
had remained a saint and prophet
was whispered that, in the hour that the
immured in a column in a church in Viterb
souls of the three martyrs—Savonarola, Fr
Fra Silvestro—carried up into Paradise by
that a blind man had recovered his sight
eyes with their ashes, that devils had been
nuns in a convent at Florence, and th
miracles had been wrought after their deatl
in Ferrara grew very bitter for a while ag
Dominican order, which had deserted Fra
especially against its general, Fra Giovac
of Venice, who, together with Monsignor
delivered him over to the secular arm. Wher
ing June, the general chapter of the Friars
held in Ferrara, the people murmured aga
refused them their usual alms.[1] Ercole hin
remained devoted to the Order and on most

---

[1] *Diario Ferrarese*, coll. 353, 354. Zambotto (f
Paolo da Lignago (f. 160) similarly bear witness
sanctity, the latter exulting in the evil end of all hi

IN THE CLOSE OF THE QUATTROCENTO

with Fra Giovacchino, who had, for the rest, acted in good faith. But, indeed, the Duke had abandoned the cause of the prophet, even as his brethren in religion.

On the very same Saturday, April 7, 1498, that the miserable fiasco of the ordeal by fire in the Piazza della Signoria at Florence had brought Fra Girolamo's career to so ignominious an end, Charles VIII of France—the new Cyrus of his prophetic dreams, the *Amico* who, he had assured Ercole, had not been cast off by God—had been struck down by an apopletic stroke at Amboise, and " ended in a few hours the life with which he had, with more impetuosity than ability, disturbed the world, and there was great danger lest he should disturb it anew."[1]

But, with the death of Charles, the danger was by no means averted. The Duke of Orleans succeeded to the throne as Louis XII, and promptly " made known to every one what his inclination was to the affairs of Italy," by assuming not only the title of King of France, but also those of Duke of Milan and King of Jerusalem and the Two Sicilies, thus reviving at once in his person the claims of the Visconti on Milan and the Angevins on Naples. Borso da Correggio, " with a goodly company of horse and foot," went as special ambassador of Ercole to France, to congratulate the new sovereign.

There was, however, a short breathing-space, during which war raged, not very fiercely, in Tuscany concerning the liberation of Pisa. The Venetians, under pretext of freeing the beleaguered city from the Florentines, were preparing " a very great war," as the Ferrarese Diarist has it, and invaded the Casentino. Their forces were commanded by Duke Guidobalddo of Urbino, Astorre Baglioni (who was to fall a

[1] Guicciardini, iii. 6.

victim in the famous tragedy of the
Bartolommeo d'Alviano and others. 1
saw, in their proposed zeal for the libe
intention of taking the place for them
extending their power on the Mediterr;
the Florentines. " It is not true," he :
ambassador, Marco Lippomano, " that]
Pisa in liberty ; you want to subdue it ;
got Pisa, you will wish for Leghorn
jealous for my State, as you are for yours
you to have it."¹ He refused a passage
sent money and men to the Florentines

Ercole kept strictly neutral in this w
Ferrando, as a condottiere of the Most Se
been forced to march his troops towards
his will ; another, Don Sigismondo, was
Milan as a sort of counterpoise ; while A]
holiday, *si dava piacere*, in Ferrara. We
neither the soldiering nor the enjoymen
very effectual in this year, as all three
penalty of their vices, and suffering mor
from the unmentionable disease that was r;
of Italy at this time.²

Don Ferrando was as troublesome ar
source of anxiety to his father in the servic
had been when following the banner of Fra
given passage through his territory to the
to which Lodovico Sforza's hostility had c
and easier way of Parma and Pontre

¹ Malipiero, p. 506.
² On this unsavoury theme, cf. *Diario Ferrar*
362, and Lucrezia Bentivoglio's letter to Sigismonc

IN THE CLOSE OF THE QUATTROCENTO

marched his men through the Garfagnana, and the Venetian Provveditore ordered him to lay waste the country near Barga, which belonged to Florence. But Ercole wrote him a forcibly worded letter, intended to be shown to the Provveditore, forbidding him to do this, as, Barga lying so near his own territory, it would seem an act of hostility on his part towards his friends the Florentines, especially as these latter had complained at his letting his son go against them and having given him the passage.[1] Ferrando's soldiers, over whom he appears to have had no control, threatened to plunder the Pisans and grumbled against the Signoria, and Ercole suggested that he should hang one, "to give an example to the others that they be wise," as the Signoria had heard a great deal of their bad behaviour.[2] Although he acquitted himself creditably and the Signoria professed themselves convinced of his faith, Ferrando was as usual very discontented, complained that he was kept short of means, and threatened to return home. Ercole was aghast. "We are much amazed," he wrote to his son, "that you have had the presumption to say that you will go away, for we should not have believed that you would even have dared to think of it. And, therefore, we expressly command you, that on no account must you go away. For, if you were to depart thence without the good leave of the most illustrious Signoria, and it were to be displeased at your departure, as it would be, you would not be welcomed by us, and we should not receive you here in our house nor give you anything; but we should drive you away, as one who had entirely disobeyed our will and commandments, nor ever

---

[1] *Minute Ducali* to Don Ferrando, July 1, 1498. Archivio di Modena, *Carteggio dei Principi*.

[2] *Minute Ducali*, August 23, 1498. Archivio di Modena, *loc. cit.*

more should we see you gladly, bec͟ too great and presumptuous."[1]

For the rest, Ercole seemed absorb͟ his buildings. Every day he rode sung, now in one church and now more bent than ever upon his put͟ quarter of the city, where preparatio͟ erecting the great equestrian statue ͟ where the rather insignificant monum͟ now rises; he redecorated and resto͟ churches and monasteries. "He k͟ writes the Diarist, "by going every Mass, now to one, now to another ch͟ them to be decorated; and then he͟ boys, sons of different gentlemen, from͟ years old, whom he keeps in his house, letters and singing by a master, and he everything for them, and he brings th͟ room, when he has nothing to do, and them."[2]

The carnival of 1499 was brilliant peace, with the usual dances and dram͟ the Sala Grande of the Corte Vecchia, Mirandola (destined in two months to t͟ chief hostess and queen of the revels. Terence was first played, with entirely decorations; nearly three hundred acto͟ comedy and interludes together; in one of pantomime raised much applause, in wl͟

[1] *Minute Ducali*, December 14, 1498. Arc͟ cit.
[2] *Diario Ferrarese*, col. 359.

while feasting was attacked by a bear, "who played his part so excellently that many thought he was real." On subsequent days two Plautine comedies, the *Trinummus* and the *Poenulus*, were performed, with morris-dances, one of which represented an allegory of the pursuit of Fortune. On February 12, which was Shrove Tuesday, they danced till dark; then the torches were lit and the windows closed, and the *Eunuchus* was played again with new morris-dances, including a masque of wild men and nymphs hunting a bear, a panther and an ape (that is, men dressed in the skins of these beasts), which somewhat primitive amusement appears to have pleased the learned Zambotto immensely. The Marchesana Isabella arrived a few days later. The three comedies were repeated in private for her to see, and, on the second Sunday of Lent, the Duke gave a great ball in her honour, after which the *Eunuchus*, the one that pleased her most, was performed again.[1] In the following night, a number of things that had been used for the decorations were stolen; but the Duke, who had been in unusual pleasure this carnival and did not wish to have to punish any one, would have no inquiry made.[2] It was noticed that, during the fortnight that she stayed in Ferrara, Isabella gave public dances in her father's palace, notwithstanding that Lent had begun.[3]

Ercole had already attempted to bring about peace

---

[1] This carnival, especially with reference to the entertainments, is fully described in four letters from Giovanni Pencaro, a native of Parma attached to the Ferrarese Court, to Isabella d'Este Gonzaga, published by Luzio and Renier, *Commedie classiche in Ferrara nel 1499*, pp. 182–189. There is a slighter account, in which the names of the Plautine comedies are not given, in Zambotto, f. 327v.
[2] Zambotto, f. 328.
[3] *Diario Ferrarese*, col. 361.

DUKES AND POETS

between Florence and Venice ; bu
result. During the winter, howev
on both sides ; and Lodovico Sfo
at the alliance which was in prepar
France. After some three months'
at Ferrara, Lodovico prevailed up
invitation of the Venetians, and go
mediator—though he seems to hav
inducing the Florentines to consent t
to Guicciardini, the Moro hoped tha
about and by his means, the Venetia
of the coming of the French and l
himself ; while the Florentines were
pronounced judgment in Venice, wou
a decision more favourable to the V
have done of his own accord.

On March 15, 1499, Ercole with
Milanese ambassador set out for V
sumptuously received and entertai
palace of his House. The Florentine
Giovanni Battista Ridolfi and Paolo
Venice, on March 25, Ercole witness
son-in-law of Milan had striven to av
clamation of the new League betweer
The ducal palace and the piazza were su
a great wind was blowing, and a ban
missed killing the Doge himself.

[1] The alliance had been concluded at Ang
February 21, while Isabella was at Ferrara, t
came to announce the fact to the Duke, in th
and Isabella had instantly written to infor
and Renier, *Delle Relazioni di Isabella d' Est*
Beatrice Sforza, p. 664. This son of the
bella does not name in her letter, is young Pi

IN THE CLOSE OF THE QUATTROCENTO

After much difficulty and discussion, the matter was absolutely committed to Ercole's arbitration. On April 6, he read his decision to the Collegio. He had had a very difficult task, and undeniably showed an unusual degree of moral courage. His decision was a compromise, but very decidedly in favour of the Florentines. The Venetians were to evacuate the Pisan territory and to restore Bibbiena to the Florentines, with the other places which they had taken; in compensation, however, for the costs of the war, the Florentines were to pay them 100,000 ducats in twelve annual payments; the Florentines were to have back their old rights over Pisa and its territory, but to give the Pisans a complete amnesty for the past, as well as to grant them a number of fresh privileges and liberties, both political and commercial.

Though the Doge and the Collegio maintained a correct and courteous bearing as long as Ercole was present, the Venetians, high and low, were furious at his decision. That night a mob gathered round his palace, hooting and hissing, shouting abuse and calling him a traitor. He was insulted in the streets, until neither he nor the ambassadors of Milan and Florence dared to appear in public. To appease in some part the piteous appeals of the Pisan envoys, the chief Venetian senators induced Ercole to make a few additions, which did not, however, materially alter the decision. In fact, no one was satisfied. The Pisans declared that they were more enslaved than ever; the Florentines said that they got nothing but the bare name of dominion, and were being forced to pay the expenses of those who had unjustly assailed them. Nevertheless, after a long discussion in the Pregadi, it was decided by a large majority of votes that Venice would abide by the Duke's arbitration, and

DUKES AND POETS

recall her army and Provveditor
larly ratified the peace and sentenc
which had been made without their
determined to resist to the last, ratl
Florentine yoke.[1]

Ercole left Venice "with the mal
as Malipiero has it. When he got l
13, the officials of the Visdomino to
insisting upon searching the baggag
plea that the conditions of the Venet
observed.[2] The Ferrarese ambassador
fredi, wrote that the Pope was am
Ercole's conduct.[3] Nevertheless, to
it must be perfectly obvious that he h
without human respect, endeavoure
difficult duty for the peace and welfa
in this negotiation for an agreemen
decision," he wrote to Don Ferrandc
very best for that magnificent commu
because of our respect for the most
Venice, which has it under its protectie
the love and benevolence that we have
Pisans, and because of the desire that
peace and quiet of that city and of the
although the Pisans are perchance aggr
our decision, yet we doubt not that, if t
whole, they will be quite satisfied; and

[1] Guicciardini, iv 3, 4; Malipiero, pp. 53
Machiavelli, i. pp. 328, 329. This general di
may be taken as fair evidence in favour of
of Ercole's decision; but Pisa held out until r
[2] *Diario Ferrarese*, col. 363.
[3] Balan, v. p. 498.

IN THE CLOSE OF THE QUATTROCENTO

recognize more that we have fully considered their interests, and so also for the future we shall not fail to give them every benefit and favour. If we could have done more for their advantage, we would have done it right gladly. But it was also necessary to act in such a way that the result should be an effectual peace."[1]

In the meanwhile the alliance between France and Venice, for the division of the Duchy of Milan between them, had been solemnly ratified. The adhesion of Alexander VI had been procured, not without difficulty, by the exaltation of Cesare Borgia—who was, as his Holiness assured the French King, the dearest thing that he possessed on earth.[2] Cesare had abjured the Cardinalate, and had received from Louis the Duchy of Valence, with a princess of Navarre, Charlotte d'Albret, for wife, and probably a promise of effectual support in his designs of building himself up a vast principality in Italy itself.

Lodovico Sforza found himself left alone to face the storm. He had hoped to assail the Venetians first; but all his prospective allies failed him. Maximilian would willingly have helped, but his hands were tied by his own struggle with the Swiss. The King of Naples promised to send a force under Prospero Colonna and to assail the Papal States, but did neither. The Turk alone was in arms in his favour. As to the minor Powers, the Florentines remained neutral, and continued the siege of Pisa.

Ercole, since the death of Beatrice, had grown more and more alienated from the Sforza; to the Moro's appeal for aid, he answered that the frontiers of Venice were too near

---
[1] Letter of April 19, 1499. Archivio di Modena, *Carteggio dei Principi*. See Appendix II. document 18.
[2] Brief of September 28, 1498. Pastor, iii. p. 417.

DUKES AND POETS

the gates of Ferrara, and that he r
In spite of a request from Ippolit
in his diocese of Milan and warml
the Sforza—he refused to allow Gi
Lodovico's condottieri, a safe-conc
the Modenese.[1] He was aghast
Ippolito was having a suit of whit
the intention of personally fighting
professed himself exceedingly scan
conduct in a prelate of the Church

"If we still have any paternal au
ship, we command you to desist fr
and to strive to live like a good *
reverend Cardinal. If, perchance,
you that, by arming, you could give
illustrious Lord Duke of Milan or bene
that he who gave such advice loves
your Lordship less. For your taking
our Lord God and provoke Him to a
Him contrary to the side for which y
you wish to help the said most excel
all should wish), let your Lordship
Pray to our Lord God for the safe
Excellence and of his armies, and mal
secular clergy throughout your provin
yourself at these prayers, as is your
mission. These will be good white an
irregularity and with great merit. If y
commit a mortal sin and be worthy
And if you were present when any one

[1] Letter of August 7, 1499. Archivio d
Principi.

IN THE CLOSE OF THE QUATTROCENTO

be irregular; because it is not lawful for simple clerics to combat, save for the necessary defence of their persons, when they are assailed by others and cannot otherwise escape; much less is it lawful for a Cardinal and Archbishop. And you must consider that every little unpopularity which you have at Rome will, in these cases (as could easily happen), exaggerate your sin; besides the infamy and the indelible stain which you would acquire from it, and the danger of your life or of the mutilation of some limb. Then fear our Lord God and acknowledge His benefits; remember that, if you do not keep His commandments and if you are not grateful to Him, He will make you recognize your error by the sword of His justice. And if it seems to Him that your excess does not merit mercy (as this would not merit it, being only too contrary to the Christian faith and religion), He will do worse to you." [1]

The French army under Trivulzio and Ligny had crossed the Alps in July, and begun hostilities in August. Lodovico's resistance collapsed. Fortress after fortress fell before them, and the surrender of Alessandria showed that all was lost. Although the Turk was preparing to assail them in the Friuli, the Venetians crossed the Adda and occupied Lodi. Deserted by the Marquis of Mantua and by the Count of Caiazzo, Lodovico fled from Milan to Como, and thence made his way to join Maximilian in the Tyrol. On September 6, Trivulzio and the royal army entered Milan without any resistance; "and of the Duke of Milan men spoke no more, even as though he had never been in the

[1] Letter of August 19, 1499. Archivio di Modena, *Carteggio dei Principi*. As this long letter is a characteristic example of the tortuous and strange ways in which Ercole's mind and heart worked to what was, no doubt, a perfectly just and proper conclusion, I give the full text in Appendix II. document 20.

world."[1] Cremona surrendered to th
later, King Louis himself made his
the Lombard capital.

On the news of the fall of Milan,
his ambassador, Ettore Berlinghieri,
assure him of his fidelity to the cause
alleged to the contrary are mere fictit
Venetians, "in order that they may m‹
according to their appetite, although fr
received any offence or injury." "B
lent us grace that, also in this enterpri
Most Christian King for the Duchy of
severed in the devotion that we have a
his Majesty and towards the Crown of]
lent any aid to the most illustrious Lor
anything—not of our men-at-arms, n‹
not of cannons nor of shot, for which t]
many times besought us; and because
him, he complained of us publicly, as ca
hundred gentlemen in Milan." It is tru‹
who was in the Duke's service before th‹
between him and the Crown of France, k
to send his soldiers who were in Lodovico
is convinced that neither the King nor
sider that he has failed in his duty to his]
this, especially as he has not allowed Dc
to serve his enemy. He has postponed
Lodovico for his faith and devotion t‹
Christian Majesty; and if the latter and
judge his actions fairly, they must not l
what they hear from Venice against him,

[1] *Diario Ferrarese*, col. 369.

IN THE CLOSE OF THE QUATTROCENTO

firmed from another source. In answer, Trivulzio strongly advised Ercole to come in person and do reverence to the King on his arrival in Milan; which the Duke decided to do, especially as he heard that Louis was going to take Ferrara under his protection. "When we shall find ourselves in the presence of his Majesty," he wrote to Manfredo Manfredi, who was still his orator to the Republic of Florence, " while we act for ourselves, we shall not omit likewise to do all we can for the benefit of that lofty Signoria." [1]

Accordingly, Ercole, with his sons Alfonso and Ferrando, hastened to meet the King, and accompanied him in his triumphal entrance into Milan. The Cardinal Ippolito had shared Lodovico's flight into the Tyrol. With the exception of King Federigo of Naples, all the Italian princes, either in person or by their ambassadors, had come to congratulate the French conqueror, or to make their peace with him. The Florentines found the greatest difficulty in this respect; but Ercole, who stayed in Milan nearly a month and was treated by the King with special marks of confidence and esteem, found that he, too, had to pay a large sum of money before he could get his duchy taken under the royal protection—his conduct, since he had consigned the castelletto of Genoa into the hands of Lodovico Sforza, being regarded as unsatisfactory.[2] His Majesty took particular exception to the fact that Ippolito was still with the fugitive Duke, and Ercole dispatched one of his chancellors, Gian Giorgio Seregnio, with an imperative letter to the Cardinal, bidding him return without delay, "come flying," to Italy. "If

---

[1] *Minute Ducali* of September 14 and 21, 1499, to Ettore Berlinghieri, and of September 23 to Manfredo Manfredi. Archivio di Modena, *Minutario Cronologico*.

[2] So at least Guicciardini, iv. 4.

you do not return, you will lose your t
in this dominion, and will put us int(
our State, without any fruit or benefi1
illustrious Lord Duke. And, therefc
command you by our paternal author:
excuses or delay or any loss of time, yo
and as quickly as Gian Giorgio himsel
your return imports more than we can

Giovanni Bentivoglio, who was rej
Annibale, was compelled to obtain the
for his House for a similar financial cor
of his previous oscillations between Fr
the Marquis of Mantua, who had met
appears to have experienced less diffic
honours upon him, and took him into
stipend of twelve thousand francs.[2]

But, indeed, the royal protection was
tively needed by both Ferrara and Bolog
henceforth in virtue of his new French
Il Valentino, was in the company of th
his favour. He had large schemes on h

The Pope had resolved to take this
alliance with France to build up for his s
—to develope, perhaps, into a kingdon
feudatories of Romagna, the petty tyra
Romagnole cities as vicars of the Chur
lished Bulls declaring that Pandolfo Ma
Giovanni Sforza of Pesaro (but lately

---

[1] Letter dated Milan, October 21, 1499. *A*
Carteggio dei Principi. Ippolito returned to Fe.
[2] Cf. L. G. Pélissier, *La Politique du Marquis
la lutte de Louis XII et de Ludovic Sforza*, pp. 9.

son-in-law), Caterina Sforza Riario and her young sons who ruled Imola and Forlì, Astorre Manfredi of Faenza, Duke Guidobaldo of Urbino, and the Varani of Camerino had forfeited their fiefs, for not having paid the tributes due to the Holy See. According to the promise he had made, the French King put at Cesare's disposal 300 lances under Yves d'Allègre, at his own cost, and 4,000 Swiss to be paid by the Pope—nominally to recover those revolted cities for the Holy See, in reality to conquer them for the Borgia.

Included likewise in Romagna were Ravenna and Cervia; but these had passed in the earlier part of the century into the hands of Venice, the ally of France, against whose power nothing could be attempted. His ducal rank and his position among the princes of Italy differentiated Ercole d' Este from his Romagnole neighbours. Alexander seems, indeed, for a moment to have contemplated the possibility of grasping Ferrara for his son; but the opposition of Venice and the protection of France compelled him to abandon the project.[1] Bologna also, strictly speaking, was a city of the Papal States; Giovanni Bentivoglio ruled it, not as vicar of the Church, but as a sort of informal head of the Republic; it seemed an equally tempting prize, and one far easier of acquisition than Ferrara. Here, too, however, there was the newly acquired French protectorate in the way. Nevertheless, both Ercole and the Bentivoglio realized their danger.

But neither of them ventured to cross the dreaded Borgia's path. Ercole gave Cesare's French and papal auxiliaries the passage through his dominions, both through Ferrara and the Modenese—Cesare himself with the main body taking the latter course. This was in November. At Bon-

[1] Cf. Pastor, iii. p. 425, note 5.

deno, in the Ferrarese territory, a p
the place, murdered the ducal Pod
Bendedei, with several ecclesiastics a1
persons, and hung out the banners of t
of France on the castle; and they repea
or worse, a few hours later in the Borgo
was helpless: "we had to have pati
rendered to the Borgia at the end o
weeks later, he was lord of Forlì, and M
sent as prisoner to Rome. His further
by the recall of his French troops. 1
brutalities of the French and the prep
whom the King had left in his stead, the
at the approach of Lodovico and the Ca1
a hastily collected force of Swiss and
February, 1500, the Sforza were once mo

Two days before Lodovico re-entere
news of the revolution in Milan reached
of Ercole's French policy, the Moro h
in Ferrara (his conduct in the matter of the
had been forgotten), and there was much
evening a mad Servite monk, Fra Marcell
the streets, beating a drum and followed by
Shouting " Moro ! Moro ! " they went to
Venetian Visdomino, and made a tremendo
door. The outraged functionary protested
there were hints of possible complications
Venice. On the following afternoon, first fi
of the Palazzo della Ragione and afterwards
city, it was solemnly proclaimed to the sou

[1] *Diario Ferrarese*, col. 373.

IN THE CLOSE OF THE QUATTROCENTO

that the Duke's Excellence was greatly displeased at what had happened, and that he commanded that for the future, in Ferrara and its suburbs, no one should dare to name or talk of any Lords or Kings whatever, under penalty of a fine of a hundred gold ducats for each adult offender, or more according to his Lordship's discretion, and, in the case of boys, a sound whipping, twenty-five *staffilate*, for each of them.[1]

Ercole, realizing the purely ephemeral character of Lodovico's success, sent Giovanni Valla as special envoy to the French King. Avoiding the towns obedient to Milan, he was to go, with all possible diligence and speed, into the presence of the Most Christian King, to assure him that the Duke had abstained from rendering favour or aid of any kind to Lodovico, " although he is our son-in-law and his sons are our grand-children." He was to lay stress upon the kind reception and treatment that the French troops had experienced in passing through the ducal territory, although, for the abominable cruelties and atrocities that they committed, " they would deservedly have all been cut to pieces by our subjects." He was to deny emphatically that Ercole had held any communication with Lodovico before the latter returned into Italy, or that he had sent any ambassador to the King of the Romans, or ever sent to Lodovico the least invitation to come back ; he had not lent him the slightest assistance in his return. But the Duke complained bitterly of the way in which the Venetians had calumniated him, both with the King and with his ministers, and of the unfriendly attitude of the Cardinal of Rouen. " We have persevered in our faith with his Majesty,

[1] *Diario Ferrarese*, col. 378.

both before and after the return of th
Italy, as is notorious to all Italy. So
severe, if his Majesty perseveres in l
protection truly and sincerely, as is a
Majesty, and not in words only and wi

The triumph of the Moro was brief
ments and a new general, la Trémoill
fresh heart into the royal army. At
Swiss refused to fight against their count
army, and, on April 10, the hapless Du
the French, as he passed out of the city c
as a Swiss. Sent as a prisoner to France
to the King's presence, he expiated his
that long living death in the castle of l
prison thus inclosing the thoughts and
whom first the boundaries of all Italy coul
Betrayed to the Venetians and by
to the French, the Cardinal Ascanio fou
prisonment at Bourges, and was released
to take part in the Conclave on the death

Ercole had carefully abstained from rend
assistance to Lodovico in his restoration, ai
nothing to fear from his fall. Giovanni Va
the King on his victory, and assured him t
favoured and assisted him in his affairs mor
done who had shared in the gains [i.e. the V
that he had persuaded all those who could in
not to lend aid to the Lord Lodovico, of
Lodovico had himself publicly complaine

---

[1] *Istruzione a Giovanni Valla*, March 2, 1500. An *Carteggio degli Ambasciatori—Francia*.
[2] Guicciardini, iv. 5.

Pope Alexander VI.
By Pinturicchio

IN THE CLOSE OF THE QUATTROCENTO

answered that he held Ercole "for his good friend, and for a wise and excellent Lord;" but he complained of the bearing of the Marquis of Mantua.[1]

It was the year of Jubilee, and the corruption in the Church and the Curia had reached its height. The pilgrims, who flocked to Rome for the indulgences, saw with amazement Cesare Borgia triumphing as the conqueror of Forlì and Imola, and receiving the Golden Rose from the hands of the Pope. Frantic papal rejoicings hailed the overthrow of the House of Sforza. In August, Lucrezia Borgia's second husband, the young Alfonso of Bisceglie, was strangled in the Vatican by Cesare's orders. The scandal of the Pope's private life was renewed.[2] "The Pope," said Paolo Capello, one of the Venetian ambassadors, on his return to Venice, a month after young Alfonso's murder, "grows younger every day; his reflections do not last a night; he wants to live, and is of a happy nature, and only does what is to his own advantage; his whole thought is to make his children great, and he cares about nothing else."[3] Yet there were some that, with a full knowledge of all that was in progress and though themselves in personal danger, came to the Eternal City, rather than lose the indulgence of the

---

[1] Dispatch of Giovanni Valla, May 20, 1500. Archivio di Modena, Carteggio degli Ambasciatori—Francia. In spite of his alliance with France, Gonzaga had been treating with both Maximilian and Lodovico Sforza, and had sent his brother, Giovanni Gonzaga, to fight in the latter's army. Louis at first thought of depriving him of Mantua, and making it over to the Venetians in exchange for Cremona and the Gera d' Adda, but ultimately contented himself with inflicting a heavy pecuniary fine. See Pélissier, *op. cit.*, pp. 103-115.
[2] Cf. Pastor, iii. p. 431, note 2. Giulia Farnese resumed relations with the Pope, who also "favoured" one of Lucrezia's damsels.
[3] *Relatione fata im pregadi, per Sier Polo Capelo.* Sanudo, *Diarii*, iii. coll. 846, 847.

DUKES AND POETS IN

Jubilee though granted by a Borgi
betta of Urbino, though her House v
out by Cesare for destruction, came
fitting visitation of the churches or(
Jubilee," as she herself puts it in h
the Marquis of Mantua, who ha
dissuade her from going.[1] Under
Colonna, she fulfilled the conditions, ;
to Urbino. The alms of the pilgri
Cesare Borgia, for his projected
The one papal action during the ye
lutely unworthy of a Christian sov
one who claimed to be the Vicar of
of Peter, was the attempt to or
against the Turks—who were beati
land. But here, too, it is impossible
Pope was moved, in part at least, t
support of the Venetians for the de

"As I doubt not that your n
knows well," wrote Giovanni Bent
infirmity has need of a better and 1
and it would be necessary that ou
pertains the government of our]
Christ did, when He said : *For I ha*:
And this would be more to the poi
to disturb the poor lords of Roma,
keeping this harassed Italy in so
some are induced rather to desire tl

[1] Cf. Gian Francesco's letter, of Mar(
Renier, *Mantova e Urbino*, p. 105, and
from Assisi, March 21, in Gregorovius,
20.

than to think of opposing them in any way. But if this private passion be put aside, and thought be taken for the universal good and for the conservation of the Faith and our Religion, I am certain that lords and communes and all men will be found excellently disposed to do all that shall be needed."[1]

At the beginning of the year, Ercole had announced his intention of going in person to Rome for the Jubilee. "For many years," he wrote to the Marchesana Isabella, "we have thought and almost firmly intended to go to Rome for this Jubilee, if our Lord God in His grace allowed us to reach this year. And so we have decided to depart at once and to go with a small company, with the intention of returning quickly to avoid the concourse of the multitude. We have wished to give particular notice of this thing to your Ladyship, in order that you may know this deliberation of ours, and can tell us if you desire anything from us in this our voyage. Do not omit to pray, and to have prayers offered up to our Lord God, for our safety."[2] But a fall from his horse had delayed his departure, and subsequent events—the Borgian invasion of Romagna and the

[1] Letter of September 19, 1500. Dallari, pp. 192, 193.

[2] Letter of January 1, 1500. The same day he gave notice to the Pope, to his various ambassadors and others, of his intention of going immediately to Rome, " to satisfy a singular devotion of ours, and to gain the indulgence and plenary remission of our sins." He had previously, on December 29, been in negotiation with the Cardinal of San Giorgio, who was then in Florence, to borrow his palace in Rome, the present Palazzo della Cancelleria, "for ten days at the longest, with the beds and all the things of the kitchen. We shall go with few persons and not more than fifty horses, because, as we are making this journey for our devotion, we wish to go as pilgrims." *Minute Ducali* of December 29, 1499, and January 1, 1500. Archivio di Modena, *Minutario Cronologico*.

DUKES AND POETS

fate of the Milanese duchy—ind
idea.

Instead, he had solemn process
cities of his duchies in March, to
upon Italy and the liberation
Turks; and he had them repeated
good reasons known to him and
to keep on good terms with God,
put it. On the latter occasion,
place one on every third day in Fer
in front, with more than four tho
white, each bearing a banner up
image of Christ. Then came t
Bishop of Ferrara, followed by th
Duke on foot, and, at the last, Er
because he was still unable to
thousand persons took part i
Whitsuntide a revivalist preache
from the convent of the Angeli,
the Duomo, and exhorted the p
consequence of his eloquence,
solemnly proclaimed from the win
Ragione, to forbid the keeping
forbidden games, blaspheming G
Saints, openly or in secret, con
difficult to imagine that the dec
effect in an Italian city of that

---

[1] *Diario Ferrarese*, coll. 385, 386; 194, 195. Tomasino de' Bianchi give procession in June at Modena, in a chronicle, pp. 269–273.

[2] *Diario Ferrarese*, col. 387.

IN THE CLOSE OF THE QUATTROCENTO

The fact was that Ercole himself was at this time in bad health, very anxious about all things, and much concerned with the affairs of his soul. Disappointed at the failure of the reforms that seemed promised by Savonarola, disillusioned by the nonfulfilment or the method of fulfilment of the Friar's prophecies, he had thrown himself heart and soul into a very remarkable religious movement—a movement too little noticed by Church historians—which may be said to have come to a head in this year.

The chief aim of this movement was to fight the corruption in the Church and in human society, to oppose the degradation and immorality of the Curia, no longer by the violent tirades of a Savonarola, but by a revival of the cult of St. Catherine of Siena. More than a hundred years before, she had striven to heal the wounds of Italy; she had attempted to unite the Powers of Christendom against the Turk; she had bidden high and low strip themselves of self-love, enter the cell of self-knowledge; she had denounced in burning words the corruption of the clergy; she had urged the Pope, in Christ's name, to think of souls and not of cities, to choose between the Temporal Power and the salvation of souls. In her words seemed to many the very remedy for the malady of these new times. And this year of Jubilee was chosen by "certain devout servants of God" to bring out her letters, as a protest against the hideous state of things in the Church. Aldo Manuzio, the publisher, made himself their spokesman, in a letter dated from Venice, September 19, 1500, to Francesco Piccolomini, the Cardinal Archbishop of Siena. "I pray you," he writes, "to communicate these sacred epistles to the Holiness of the Pope, in order that he may consider the epistles sent to Pope Gregory XI and Pope Urban VI as

written to his Holiness. Moreover
Lordship show those that were sen
the Cardinals of our own time, in ord
by that Sacred Virgin, inspired by
carried out for the reformation of
the Crusade may be made against
viour promised this to her, when
ardent prayers, and, since it has
all means, because God cannot lie

But this movement had a far m
tation than in letters alone. Whi
day crucifying Christ anew in Ro
over Italy, robed in the black a
Catherine had worn, bearing in t
and feet and side—the wounds of
of them professed to be in cons
with Catherine herself, and all, to
imitated her mode of life, had id
renew her work. Even as God
sent holy men and prophets—thus
little tract in the publication o
doubtedly concerned ²—" so, in th
extreme daily adversity, He would
people ; but now, for the joy of t
the wicked and the strengthening

---

¹ Letter prefixed to the first Aldine
tissime de Sancta Catharina da Siena,

² *Spiritualium personarum feminei s*
a tract of six leaves without paginatio
name, but apparently printed in 150
letters of Ercole and others concerning
frontispiece represents three nuns kn

IN THE CLOSE OF THE QUATTROCENTO

these tempests, He wondrously manifests Himself in many spiritual, pious and religious persons, especially of the feminine sex. Most seasonably doth He now stretch forth His hand, that man may rise again out of this ruin to sublime things, that all may know God more clearly and love Him more ardently, may imitate Him more diligently and become more blessed. Concerning which things the most illustrious and serene prince and lord, the Lord Hercules, Duke of Ferrara, beareth witness."

Ercole diligently collected information from all sources concerning the lives these women lived and the miracles they were said to have wrought. Three were especially famous. Colomba of Rieti lived in the convent of the Dominican nuns at Perugia, took no apparent nourishment, but was sustained (so the Duke said) by the Blessed Sacrament miraculously conveyed to her by the hands of an Angel; she had raised up a dead child to life, almost in the presence of Cesare Borgia, and preached repentance (not very effectually, we should say) to the fierce Baglioni. Osanna Andreassi, of Mantua, was an older woman than the others (she was born in 1449) and a stronger, more independent spirit; related on her mother's side to the Gonzaga, she was held in the utmost reverence by the rulers and people of Mantua, and frequently consulted by the Marquis and Isabella. She was in correspondence with many of the sovereigns of Italy, notably with the Duke of Urbino and Ercole himself. She had fed her soul upon the writings of St. Catherine and of Savonarola, but did not share the political theories of the latter; at the Battle of Fornovo all her sympathies had been with the army of the League, and she professed to know by revelation that the souls of almost all who fell fighting for the independence

DUKES AND POETS I[N]

of Italy against the foreign invad[er]
girl compared to these two, but
nected with Ferrara, was Lucia Br[ocadelli]
had probably heard in the first in[stance]
Niccolò Maria d' Este, the Bishop
papal service.

Lucia Brocadelli was born at Na[rni]
Lucia, December 13, 1476. Her fa[ther]
was a child, was Treasurer of the C[ommune]
of his brothers was attached to the
Datario to Alexander VI. Fanta[stic]
her childhood. St. Catherine he[rself]
cradle; Christ espoused her myst[ically]
the Angels, practised strange au[sterities]
perpetual chastity. Then St. Ca[therine]
taught her to read and write, bade
Dominicans. After her father's d[eath]
her to marry a young Milanese ge[ntleman]
lived in virginity, until at the age

[1] Our chief authorities for the lives a[nd]
are: Leandro degli Alberti, *La Vita*
(Bologna, 1521); Fra Francesco da [
Osanna da Mantova, written immediat[ely]
to Gian Francesco Gonzaga and Isabella
1590); Girolamo da Monte Oliveto, *L*[
della Beata Osanna da Mantova, includi[ng]
and her letters to the writer (second edit[ion]
Marcianese, *Narratione della Nascita*, *V*
da Narni (Ferrara, 1616); Domenico [
(Rome, 1711); and the more recent w[orks]
Gandini, *Sulla venuta in Ferrara della*
and *Lucrezia Borgia nell' imminenza*
d' Este. I hope, on another occasion,
of the Beata Osanna.

IN THE CLOSE OF THE QUATTROCENTO

left him and took the habit of St. Dominic in her mother's house—to the fury of her husband, who is said to have attempted to burn down the convent where her confessor lived. The next year she went to Rome, to the monastery in which St. Catherine had died in the Via Santa Chiara, where a basrelief in the chapel (originally St. Catherine's cell) still records her presence. In January, 1496, the General of the Dominicans—that same Frate Giovacchino Turriani who, a little later, was compelled by the Pope to play the part of Savonarola's executioner—sent her to Viterbo, to direct a house of Dominican tertiaries there. There, on the night of February 24, the second Thursday in Lent, while between Suora Diambra, the Prioress, and Suora Leonarda (both of whom we shall meet again presently) in choir at Matins, she received the Stigmata. In spite of the agony they gave her, the wounds remained invisible until Passion Week, when they became visible and bled terribly. Her mother, Madonna Gentilina, and Fra Martino da Tivoli, her former confessor, were summoned to the convent, as the nuns believed she was dying.

Catholics and Protestants are nowadays agreed that the reception of the Stigmata is a question to be dealt with by the psychologist and the physician, rather than by the theologian and hagiologist. But it was naturally not so then. The matter seemed a new manifestation of the mystery of Christ's Passion. "These things," writes Ercole, "are shown by the Supreme Craftsman in the bodies of His servants to confirm and strengthen our Faith, and to remove the incredulity of impious men and hard of heart."[1] The Pope sent his physician, Berardo da Re-

[1] Letter of March 4, 1500, in the *Spiritualium personarum facta admirationi digna*, and in part published by Ponsi, *op. cit.*, pp. 205-207.

DUKES AND POETS

canati, with a Franciscan bishop a1
of the Sacred Palace, to investig
report, even as he had personally
Colomba; but these things impres
the mysterious warnings were to do
A little later, the local Father Inqu
a prolonged examination, to which
"St. Catherine of Siena by her pray
our Lord Jesus Christ that the Stigr
and palpable in me, as a pledge and
mata of St. Catherine herself."

Her life at Viterbo seemed to becc
tery.[1] Before the Crucifix and at Ma
ecstasies, in which she cried, *Fuoco*,
Her face appeared like that of a ser;
grew stiff and rigid as a statue. She
and suffered His Passion, and reveale
celestial mysteries, such that the nuns
in which to record them. All these thi
were collected a little later at Ercole's
"beyond measure desirous to hear t
mundane and well-nigh celestial "—by l
Maria d' Este, who was then filling the
of the Patrimony. "I send them to yo
Lordship," writes Niccolò Maria, "in o
read so many miraculous actions, you m
day more the love and benevolence whicl
aforesaid Suora Lucia; who seemeth to n

[1] Could she have been the nun in that town wl
apotheosis of Fra Girolamo and his fellow-marty
there is no hint of anything like the column to
refers (*Diario Ferrarese*, col. 353).

this fragile and corruptible world of ours, but of the celestial and most blessed Hierarchies."[1]

Full of his desire to make Ferrara a kind of centre of religious life in Italy, Ercole in the summer of 1497—before his rupture with Savonarola—invited Lucia to his city, promising to build for her a convent of nuns of her own Order. Lucia accepted with alacrity; her mother, Gentilina, was profuse in her gratitude to the Duke for having "set such great love upon my own flesh and blood."[2] But the nuns and the authorities of Viterbo flatly refused to let her go. One of her uncles, Antonio Mei, went to Viterbo to fetch her, on the pretext that her mother was dying; a nun overheard their conversation and raised the town upon him, with the result that the worthy man was arrested and sent about his business. Before he went, he arranged with the confessor, Fra Martino, that Lucia should continue every day to visit for her devotions the sanctuary of the Madonna della Quercia, outside Viterbo. But an attempt during the winter by Alessandro da Fiorano, captain of the Duke's *balestrieri*, to carry her off on the occasion of one of these visits, failed. The people shut the gates in her face, and utterly refused to let her pass out to keep the appointment with Alessandro, of which they appear to have had some inkling from Fra Martino.

Throughout the greater part of 1498, the people of Viterbo and Ercole's agents struggled together in the Papal Court for the possession of Lucia. The General of the Dominicans, who was naturally anxious to gratify so eminent and generous a benefactor of his Order, was entirely on

[1] Letter of March 5, 1503, from Viterbo. In Giacomo Marcianese, *Narratione*, pp. 104, 105.
[2] Gandini, *Sulla venuta in Ferrara della Beata Suor Lucia*, Letter 2.

Ercole's side ; Alessandro da Fio
money lavishly in all directions, a
action rather than a diplomatist,
" I am not a chancellor nor an am
Ercole, " but I am a very faithful
lence and desirous of doing always
industry the thing that you want,
business, since your most illustrious I
to understand how much you have t
The Cardinal Ippolito and Monsignor
their influence with the Pope to induc
briefs to Viterbo, threatening excomn
unless Lucia was sent to Rome. A c
da Modena, also a Dominican, push
affair, presented himself to the General
Ercole's permission or knowledge) as t
and tried to work a little scheme of his
Lucia from Viterbo and bringing her to
permission of the Father Inquisitor of
gave the over-zealous friar a spell in t
Castle for his trouble, until he was " mo
molto " (as Monsignor Felino put it),
him from Ferrara.[2]

The whole thing, in fact, grew excee
Ercole himself was perfectly sincere and
his devotion to one whom he believed
favoured by God and to bear in her bo
Christ's Passion. Alessandro da Fioranc
honest fellow, bent on pleasing his master.
with the exception of poor Lucia, evidentl

[1] Gandini, *op. cit.*, Letter 9.
[2] Gandini, *op. cit.*, pp. 25, 27,

IN THE CLOSE OF THE QUATTROCENTO

what they can for themselves out of the situation. Even Frate Martino, whose own conduct had been rather dubious, professed to be shocked at the sums of money that Lucia's uncle Antonio was demanding: "I fear," he said, "that, if Antonio makes merchandise of this holy thing, we shall lose the credit in Heaven and on earth."[1] The people of Viterbo hunted Antonio and Gentilina out of the place.

Lucia appears to have left the convent, and to be very lonely and miserable, longing for Ferrara as a place of rest and peace. "I have no consolation, neither of soul nor of body," she writes to her uncle, "and cannot stay any longer in this Hell. I pray you again to do all you can to take me away." And to Ercole himself she wrote, somewhat bitterly, complaining that they had taken her mother from her, and that it seemed more impossible than ever for her to get away from Viterbo. "My Lord and Father, I have no other hope on earth than your most illustrious Lordship. You ask me to pray for you. My Lord and Father, you know that I continually pray to that sweet Jesus that He may preserve you in this mortal world with health of soul and body."[2] Her sadness and perplexity were, perhaps, increased by the fact that Suora Colomba of Rieti—whom she venerated as a mother—had sent her confessor from Perugia to advise her not to go, but "to console with her presence that city in which she had received so manifest and excellent a gift."[3] The uncle, Antonio, wrote to assure the Duke that Lucia had told him that she was longing to come and stay with his Lordship, "and she

[1] Gandini, *op. cit.*, Letter 48 (from Felino Sandeo to the Duke).
[2] Gandini, *op. cit.*, Letters 36 and 37.
[3] So at least Ponsi, *op. cit.*, p. 106.

told me that, when she had spoken with
the most contented religious that the
earth." [1]

Finally, Monsignor Felino went secretl
bought the Podestà of the town, with th
the thing succeeded, the Duke would give
lucrative and honourable position in F
them and Gentilina and the uncle, they
a certain day Lucia should be carried ou
mule, hidden in a basket of linen. On A
plot succeeded, and Lucia was brought safe
house at Narni, whence Alessandro da Fior
conducted her through the states of the
to Ferrara. She arrived at Ferrara on
mother Gentilina, a young cousin (Suora C
Order, who died shortly after), and Fra Cris
who had succeeded Fra Martino as her co

Ercole himself came out to meet Lucia
make enough of her. He declared that I
the wonderful things that he found in her
report, and wrote enthusiastic letters of
one concerned. Fra Timoteo turned u
midst of all these rejoicings, very anxio
and bringing a letter from Monsignor Fel
haves himself like a good religious," said th
not lack favour from us." Seeing that L
tressed and evidently uneasy in her co
with almost womanly tact and considerat
General of the Dominicans : " In order
may stay here with her mind at rest and wit

[1] Gandini, *op. cit.*, Letter 4.

IN THE CLOSE OF THE QUATTROCENTO

we pray your most reverend Lordship to be good enough to write her a kind letter to praise her for coming here, and to tell her that your Lordship is very pleased that she has come, and that she could not have done better. Such a letter will be a great comfort to her and a singular pleasure to us." He cordially invited Fra Martino to Ferrara, to take up his old duties of confessor to the Suora, and obtained from the General that he should be relieved of the office of prior of the convent at Foligno for this purpose. We may, in fact, hazard a guess that the ordinary clergy of the city would have found Lucia a terribly difficult penitent, for we find Ercole assuring the General that he is much edified by Fra Martino, and that "his coming was more necessary."[1] There was nothing that the Duke would not have done for Lucia, to ensure her happiness under his protection, or for the Dominicans, to show his gratitude to them for having given this jewel of their Order into his hands. He had, indeed, fallen completely under their spiritual guidance.

"I congratulate your most illustrious Lordship much," wrote Fra Bonaventura da Como, one of the numerous members of the Order who seem to have had a share in the management of his conscience, "and I have the greatest pleasure that you have been given as confessor and spiritual father of your soul this venerable father Frate Giovanni da Tabia, a master in theology, a man most religious and of great perfection; the more your most excellent Lordship experiences his devotion and goodness together with the sufficiency of his learning, I am certain that your Lordship will be so much the more consoled thereat. Further, I rejoice greatly that the Divine Goodness hath sent thither

[1] Gandini, *op. cit.*, Letters 52, 53, 54, 60.

to Ferrara that most devout handmaid of His, Suora Lucia, of whom I hear stupendous things. It would be a great happiness to me to be able to come so far to see this miraculous thing, and I assure your most illustrious Lordship that this is a great argument for our faith, because it is not possible by human means to preserve those wounds in the state in which they are. May the sweet Lord Jesus Christ ever be praised, Who has deigned for your very great consolation to lead thither this His humble spouse."[1]

Ercole lost no time. On June 2, 1499, less than a month after Lucia's arrival, he laid the first stone of the monastery he had promised to build for her. It was situated near the Dominican convent of the Angeli, more to the east of the Certosa, but not a stone of it remains to-day.[2] In the meanwhile, he found her a suitable house, in which she received a first band of young Ferrarese girls to train in the footsteps of St. Catherine—but, within a few days, the majority of them left, finding her rule too hard. We have some indications, indeed, that Lucia was lacking in the sweetness of disposition, in the lovable and winning nature that was so conspicuous in the character of her great Sienese prototype. But she believed herself in direct spiritual intercourse with her, and went unshaken on her way. One evening, as she watched the progress of the building, St. Catherine appeared to her and led her round the whole, blessing every room, the two singing together Savonarola's favourite hymn, *Ave maris Stella*; and Lucia imagined that, when the Saint left, she gave her a rod in token of command and government. Another time, she saw her hastening along a path paved with thorns, and call-

[1] Gandini, *op. cit.*, Letter 56 (dated Piacenza, July 3, 1499).
[2] See below, Chapter xii.

IN THE CLOSE OF THE QUATTROCENTO

ing her to follow. And yet again, the Madonna and Angels seemed to her ecstatic gaze to take possession of the place. In consequence of these visions, the convent was dedicated to St. Catherine, its church retaining the original title of the Annunziata.

Lucia communicated all these visions to Ercole, to whom they meant much. He passed hours in mystical conversation with her; heaped favours of all kinds upon her. Not only did he diligently collect all the evidence of her past life, for the confusion of the incredulous, but he himself—shortly after her coming and while the building of the convent was in progress—wrote the long letter in her honour which has been already mentioned.

The letter is dated from Ferrara, March 4, 1500, and must be regarded as another of the strange fruits in which that amazing Jubilee of Pope Alexander was so prolific. After describing at length Lucia's condition, her sufferings from these wounds and her holy life, Ercole goes on to relate, " for the devotion of the faithful of Christ and the confirmation of the good," the things that he has heard from his messengers and witnesses concerning a certain Suora Steffana, a nun of the same Order in Crema, who has similar revelations and ecstasies, and who on Fridays endures the whole of the Passion in her body, stage by stage, from the Flagellation to the Deposition from the Cross. He then touches more slightly upon the miraculous communions of Suora Colomba at Perugia and the sanctity of Suora Osanna at Mantua: "And in this our city of Ferrara," he concludes, "there are many other nuns of the same Order, who are often rapt in ecstasy by the Divine Spirit and are redolent of sanctity; as also we have heard of many in many other places in Italy, who, inspired by the God of Heaven, bear witness to us that this our Catholic Faith is true, and that the Holy Roman Church is the Mother of the Faith, and to be followed in all things that pertain to salvation and good morals." [1] Clearly, it is a tacit protest against the corruption of the Curia, in the same spirit as the Venetian publisher's letter dedicating the Epistles of St. Catherine to the Cardinal of Siena.

Pope Alexander took little heed of all this. Had Lucia or Colomba been possessed of Catherine's literary gifts, and written letters touching him personally to the quick, or bidding him renounce the temporal power for the salvation of souls, it would have been another thing. Osanna, indeed, the only one of the group who appears to have been a really strong spirit, prophesied the downfall of Cesare Borgia and the speedy death of the Pope himself, and had such a fearful vision of the damnation of the latter and his Cardinals, *povere anime*, unless they changed their works, that she made the blood of her friends run cold with terror when she related it. But she kept very quiet at Mantua, and probably reserved these revelations for the sympathetic ears of such choice spirits as the Duchess Elisabetta of Urbino and her own spiritual son, Fra Girolamo of Monte Oliveto, who has recorded them for us.[2] As it was, Pope Alexander saw no danger in the movement.

[1] This letter is printed in full in the *Spiritualium personarum facta admiratione digna*, mutilated and abbreviated in Ponsi and elsewhere. Certain persons still refusing to credit his report, Ercole wrote another letter to the consuls of Nuremberg on January 23, 1501, in a similar strain, urging them to force those who had slandered Lucia to retract what they had said. It is printed with the former one in the tract quoted, as also by Giacomo Marcianese and Ponsi.

[2] *Libretto della Vita et Transito della Beata Osanna*, pp. 50v, 51, 97

IN THE CLOSE OF THE QUATTROCENTO

The Duke had interested Isabella in his mystical desires, but did not succeed in inducing his favourite daughter either to go to Rome for the Jubilee or to bring Osanna to Ferrara. In a curious reply to a letter in which Ercole had exhorted her to make the journey to the Eternal City, Isabella pleads that she finds that it would cost her not less than a thousand or eight hundred ducats, doing it as cheaply as possible, and she is too heavily in debt to undertake it. His Excellence and God will, therefore, hold her excused, and the Pope is so generous with his indulgences that she hopes that, in the coming Lent, he will grant her the complete absolution through her ordinary confessor, whereby, adds the practical and economical Marchesana, " I shall gain the same merit with less expense " :—

" If I had come, I would have done everything to bring the venerable Suora Osanna. I have talked with her about it, and she says that, to visit the venerable Suora Lucia and do a thing pleasing to your Excellence and to me, she would make every effort ; albeit unwillingly, because several years ago she resolved and made a vow not to leave Mantua, it seeming to her (to use her own words) that she is such a mournful person that she ought not to go about. Nevertheless if I had come, in obedience to the summons of your Excellence, I should have persuaded her and brought her." [1]

" Oh how many things did she prophesy to me concerning Italy ; and especially of the Duke Valentino ! When he was in his greatest state and prosperity in the Marches, she said to me these very words : ' The lordship of the Duke Valentino is a fire of straw that soon passes ; so will be his State ; it will soon be dispersed, and the Pope shall remain short while upon the earth.' "

[1] Letter of November 27, 1500. Archivio di Modena, Cancelleria Ducale, *Lettere di Isabella d' Este Gonzaga*. A passage from this

DUKES AND POETS IN FERRARA

In the meanwhile, the new convent was rapidly approaching completion. "Since we have in great veneration the glorious St. Catherine of Siena," wrote Ercole on April 7, 1501, to the Cardinal of Modena, Giovanni Battista Ferrari, then filling the office of Datario at the Papal Court, "whom among all the Saints we hold for our special advocate, we have decided to dedicate and entitle to her a monastery which we are having newly built in this our city, not very far from the monastery of Santa Maria degli Angeli of the Friars Preachers of the Observance; and this monastery, with a certain endowment, we wish to consign to the venerable sisters of the third habit of St. Dominic, as to those who are the daughters and imitators of the said St. Catherine." Hearing that the authority of the Pope is necessary, he asks the Cardinal to consult with the vicar of the Order and arrange the matter with his Holiness. He explains that these sisters are to have the rules and privileges of the "cloistered" nuns of St. Dominic, but that, if "the venerable Suora Lucia da Narni, who is to be the guide and ruler of the said sisters and for whose sake we are so much the

letter is quoted by Bertoni, *op. cit.*, p. 207. For the full text, see Appendix II. of present work, document 22. Although Osanna never met Lucia, she refers to her once in her colloquies with Fra Girolamo of Monte Oliveto (concerning the wound in her side), and once incidentally in a letter to him (*Libretto della Vita et Transito della Beata Osanna*, pp. 78v, 122). On Whitsunday of this year, 1500, there had arrived in Ferrara "a live saintly nun, named Suora Colomba, of whom it was said that every day she received Communion from an Angel and that she lived on this Communion alone." The Duke lodged her in the house where Lucia was, until the monastery was ready (*Diario Ferrarese*, col. 387). This Colomba must have been an imitator and namesake of the more famous Colomba of Rieti, who certainly did not leave Perugia.

IN THE CLOSE OF THE QUATTROCENTO

more gladly having the said building built," wishes it to be so, they are to be allowed sometimes to go out of the convent, under certain conditions and restrictions, " in order to retain in some part the custom and way of their Mother, St. Catherine of Siena, who was of the same Order with this liberty."[1]

The matter was soon settled. The Pope, by a Bull of May 29 of the same year, gave the Duke leave to do all that he wished, and conferred various privileges and an indefinite chief authority (even over the prioress) upon " our beloved daughter in Christ, Lucia da Narni, sister of the said third Order, who (as it is asserted) devotes herself as far as she can to following the footsteps of the Blessed Catherine."[2] On August 5, Lucia made her solemn entry into the new convent, and Ercole naturally made a great function of the event and formally consigned the keys to her charge. He heaped favours of all kinds upon her, great and small. The convent was richly endowed, and he exempted her from giving any account to the ducal Camera of what she received from him. We have curious records of painters set to work for her at his expense, of religious books given to her from the ducal library.[3] He sought out rare relics of Dominican martyrs, to comfort her when she was ill. Her slightest wish to him was law. He ordered that peculiar honours and respect should be paid to her and to her confessors by all his subjects. The cloths in which her hands and feet were wrapped on the days upon

---

[1] Gandini, *Lucrezia Borgia*, Document 1.
[2] In Ponsi, *op. cit.*, pp. 227, 228.
[3] Gandini, *op. cit.*, pp. 7, 8 ; Bertoni, *op. cit.*, pp. 206, 237. The Duke gave her from his library a Bible in the vernacular. For the pictorial decorations of her convent, see below, in Chapter xii.

which the blood gushed out anew, Wednesdays and Fridays and all the feasts consecrated to the Passion, were to him sacred objects, endowed with rare healing powers.[1]

Nevertheless, the new institution was not a complete success. Lucia was too young for the responsibility thrust upon her, and it was difficult to get women of the kind the Duke wanted to subject themselves to her rule. Her mother, Gentilina, had returned to her own home at Narni. Not content with transferring nuns from other convents in Ferrara, Ercole acceded to Lucia's ardent desire and decided to obtain a number of her former friends and associates from Umbria, to place them under her in Santa Caterina. This, however, was easier said than done.

In May, 1501, before the place was finished, Ercole sent Bartolommeo Bresciano, the messenger of the ducal chancellors, to Narni and Viterbo for the purpose. The mission was unsuccessful. At Narni, the fathers of Tomasa and Beatrice, two girls (cousins) whom Lucia particularly wanted to have, used *male parole*. "We should like to see," said they, "who will take away our daughters by force." They received Bresciano courteously enough, and let him talk with Beatrice for an hour. He reported to Ercole that she seemed *una santarella* and evidently loved Lucia cordially; but, all the same, he could not get either her or her cousin to come. Lucia's relations, however sent grateful messages to his Excellence, and offered him at his need, fifty armed men at their own expenses; Gentilina and two nuns with her would be most happy to come At Viterbo the nuns wept together when they remembered

---

[1] Giacomo Marcianese, *passim*. She was said to have healed Don Alfonso in a dangerous illness by one of these cloths.

IN THE CLOSE OF THE QUATTROCENTO

the past, and Diambra, the Prioress, told Bresciano of many good works that Lucia had done; but the Prior of the Dominicans absolutely refused to let him have the four nuns that he wanted. "It is quite enough for his Excellence," quoth this very reverend father, "to have robbed us of Suora Lucia, which hath been a great loss to this city of Viterbo."[1]

The convent being finished, Ercole returned to the charge. This time, however, "for our complete satisfaction and the perfect contentment of Suora Lucia," as his Excellence put it, at least eight women were required—two from Narni and six from Viterbo, including Diambra and Leonarda, the two who had been with Lucia at the moment of her reception of the Stigmata. Bartolommeo Bresciano was sent post-haste to Rome at the end of September, "in the name of God and with the aid of the glorious Saint Catherine of Siena," bearing a letter from Ercole to a lady remarkably unlike Saint Catherine, but in whose assistance he had reason to place unbounded confidence at that moment—Lucrezia Borgia.

---

[1] Gandini, *op. cit.*, Documents 2 and 3, being letters from Bartolommeo Bresciano to the Duke.

Chapter XI

THE COMING OF MADONNA LUCREZIA

THE Holy Year of Jubilee had nearly three months still to run, when Cesare Borgia, well supplied with money from the offerings of the pilgrims and from the sale of twelve elevations to the cardinalate at the September consistory, and backed by the consent of Venice, which the Pope had bought by his demonstration of crusading zeal against the Turk, took the field again against the petty tyrants of Romagna at the beginning of October. His own forces amounted to some seven hundred men-at-arms and six thousand infantry, with Paolo Orsini, Giampaolo Baglioni, Ercole di Sante Bentivoglio, and other condottieri, and he had a promise of a well-equipped body of French horse and foot under Allègre, which would bring his whole army up to some ten thousand men.

To this overwhelming force the luckless potentates of Romagna could offer no effectual resistance. Rimini surrendered as soon as Ercole Bentivoglio appeared before its walls in the name of Cesare, Pandolfo Malatesta escaping to Bologna. Giovanni Sforza, too, fled " the hydra's fiery breath," and, on the evening of October 27, the Borgia made his triumphal entry into Pesaro.

At the outset of this Borgian and Papal advance, Giovanni Bentivoglio saw his own rule in Bologna threatened,

THE COMING OF MADONNA LUCREZIA

and had appealed to Duke Ercole for aid. The latter had written earnestly, to both Beltrando Costabili and Giovanni Valla, his resident orators in Milan and France respectively, urging them to point out to the King and his representatives that the royal interests in Italy would be seriously compromised, if Cesare Borgia or the Church got possession of Faenza, Rimini, and Pesaro, let alone Bologna. "If the Duke Valentino or the Church have these towns," Ercole writes to Costabili, "together with Forlì, Cesena, and Imola, they will be not less powerful in Italy than is the State of Milan, and, therefore, the most illustrious Lords Dukes of Milan have never consented that the Church should undo all the lords of those towns, nor that they should be given to one man; nay, they have done all they could to preserve each of those lords in his State; and to avail themselves the better of them, they have also taken them into their pay. So, in all the enterprises that they [the Dukes of Milan] have undertaken in Italy, they have made great use of the lords and cities of Romagna, since it is a convenient place and very handy for all the campaigns that are made in Italy; as was seen, for instance, in the war waged against the Florentines in the time of the magnificent Bartolommeo of Bergamo, and afterwards in the time of the most serene King Charles, and lastly when the Venetians wished to send succour to Pisa by the Val di Lamone. Therefore, not only should the Most Christian Majesty not suffer that Bologna should come into the hands of Duke Valentino, but he should not even permit him to acquire more than he already has in Romagna; besides that it would be very wrong that these lawful lords should be undone and hunted out of their homes, without any just cause." Let the ambassador, then, urge the royal lieutenants in his name

DUKES AND POETS IN FERRARA

not to suffer Bentivoglio to be molested, not only in consideration of the protection that the King has promised him, but also seeing that, as long as Bologna is in his hands, the King will be able to dispose of its resources as he chooses, which he certainly cannot do if it falls into the power of Cesare or the Pope. Let him not omit to make them realize that the writer's own interests will be seriously prejudiced if Cesare gets more in Romagna than he has, and especially in Bologna. He suggests that the King and his lieutenants should warn the Pope not to attend to wars in Italy at a time when Christendom is threatened by the Turk, and concludes by urging the utmost secrecy with respect to these communications of his. The letter to Valla is in nearly the same words.[1]

The royal lieutenants in Milan made the most ample assurances and promises in favour of Bentivoglio; but no reply was forthcoming from France. "His Majesty," wrote Machiavelli to the Ten, "in the things that can arise in Italy, makes more account of the Pope than of any other Italian potentate." The King gave the Ferrarese and Bolognese envoys to understand that he would not interfere with the affairs of the Church, nor allow his Italian confederates to help the Romagnole despots. If the Pope actually attempted to do anything against the Bentivoglio, his Majesty would hear both sides of the question and condemn whichever was in the wrong.[2] Ercole was forced to dissemble.

[1] Archivio di Modena, *Minutario Cronologico, Minute Ducali* of October 5, 1500. See Appendix II., document 21.

[2] Letter from Ercole to Giovanni Bentivoglio, October 14, 1500 (Dallari, p. 193); Machiavelli's dispatch from Nantes, October 25, in his First Legation to the Court of France.

THE COMING OF MADONNA LUCREZIA

As Cesare was entering Pesaro, Pandolfo Collenuccio arrived upon the scene—sent by the Duke of Ferrara to congratulate the conqueror, who had already written to inform him of his progress. Pandolfo did not succeed in getting an audience until the twenty-ninth; but then he found the Borgia most affable. "In substance," writes Pandolfo to the Duke, " he told me that, knowing the prudence and goodness of your Lordship, he has always loved you and desired to have dealings with your Excellence; and that, when you were at Milan,[1] he wished to have done so ; but that time and those affairs that were then in progress did not permit of it. And so, now that he has come into these parts, following up this desire of his, he wrote you that letter about his progress, as a beginning and demonstration of his mind and to show you that he is your son, holding for certain that your Lordship would be pleased thereat. And he is going to do the same also for the future, because he desires to have more intrinsic friendship with your Excellence, to whom he offered all his faculty and all that he could do, saying that in every need your Lordship should see the proofs. And he bade me commend him much to you, because he would have you as a brother. Also he thanked your Lordship for the reply that you had made him by letter, and for having sent a special messenger, but said that there was really no need ; for that, even without this, he was quite certain that your Lordship would take keen pleasure in every good thing that befell him. In fine, he could not have used better nor more suitable words than he did, always speaking of you like a brother and himself as a son. And for my part, putting the affair and all his

[1] On the occasion of the triumphal entry of Louis XII.

words together, I understand that he would be very glad to have more dealings with your Lordship and good friendship."

The interview lasted a good half hour, Cesare expressing great desire to be on friendly terms with Ferrara. They talked of Faenza, which he declared he would storm fiercely if it did not do as the other cities had done. Not a word of Bologna. He was delighted to receive friendly messages from Alfonso and Ippolito, above all from the latter, of whom he spoke most affectionately. "They say," adds the envoy, "that the Pope is going to give this town as a dowry to Madonna Lucrezia, and to give her an Italian for husband who will always be a good friend of the Valentino. If it be true, I know not; so it is thought."[1]

A little later, to his disgust and indignation, Ercole found that his own eldest son, Don Alfonso, was the person upon whom the Pope's choice had fallen.

Lucrezia Borgia was then in her twenty-first year, radiantly lovely and with a certain degree of cleverness, but destitute of the finer spirit that shines out in other women of that epoch, such as Isabella d' Este or Elisabetta Gonzaga. Hitherto, she had been simply a pawn in the great game her father and brother were playing. They had married her to Giovanni Sforza (in whose very palace the above recorded conversation had been held), when the star of the Sforza seemed in the ascendant; they had dissolved the marriage in December, 1497, when a different political combination seemed desirable, and had married her to the young Alfonso of Bisceglie, nephew of the King of Naples, in July, 1498. Alfonso's life had ended at Cesare's

[1] Letter from Pandolfo Collenuccio to Ercole of October 29, 1500, Gregorovius, document 25.

THE COMING OF MADONNA LUCREZIA

bidding, barely two months before this new marriage was proposed, when the Aragonese alliance was no longer needed. In all these infamies Lucrezia had been to a certain extent passive. She had, on one occasion, saved Giovanni Sforza from Cesare's assassins; possibly, the oath that she declared herself ready to take, to have her marriage with him annulled, would not have been perjury. Hideous reports were spread by Giovanni Sforza and others whom Cesare had injured, concerning relations between her and other members of the Borgia family as the real motive for the divorce. They had been duly reported to Ercole by Antonio Costabili and Pandolfo Collenuccio; but, probably, were as little credited by him as by the serious student of history to-day. According to another scandal of the time, she had had a lover of plebeian origin in the interval between the dissolution of her first and the effectuation of her second marriage.[1] Be that as it may, Lucrezia had passionately loved her second husband (who had married her most unwillingly), and had borne him a son, Rodrigo. She had sincerely wept his untimely death, perhaps for a month, in her retirement at Nepi; but had returned, smiling and serene as ever, to Rome, looking, with her sweet innocent girl-like face, ready—over ready, in fact—to accept the new and greater fortune that was preparing for her.

[1] According to a dispatch from Bologna to the Marquis of Mantua, of March 2, 1498, a favourite papal *cameriere*, Pierotto, was imprisoned " per haver ingravidato la figliola de sua Santità, Madonna Lucretia " (Pastor, iii. p. 288, note 1). In Paolo Cappello's famous report to the Pregadi, it is stated that Cesare stabbed Pierotto to death with his own hands, while he clung to the Pope's mantle, so that his blood splashed over Alexander's face (Sanudo, *Diarii*, iii. col. 846). Pastor (iii. p. 429, note 3) regards this latter story as incredible.

DUKES AND POETS IN FERRARA

The Pope, in the meantime, was doing all that he could to isolate Ercole from his allies and make it impossible for him to escape out of his net. The latter had resolved not to get involved in the affairs of Faenza, where young Astorre Manfredi, loyally supported by his subjects, was holding out manfully against Cesare's overwhelming forces. Both in the Venetian Senate and in the French Court, the papal orators were intriguing against the Duke, attempting to make Venice and the King believe that Florence, Bologna, Mantua, and Ferrara were going to declare against France and for Maximilian, the Pope's idea being to restore Piero de' Medici to Florence, take Bologna for Cesare Borgia, and make Ferrara and Mantua completely subservient. "The design," wrote Machiavelli, "seemed to me to be worthy of the Holiness of our Lord"; and he spoke to the Cardinal of Rouen, pointing out that the Florentines could not possibly expect the Emperor to help them, seeing that he had done nothing for Milan that was his, and that neither Bologna nor Ferrara could have any hope in any one save the King, for protection from the Pope and Venice. Let his Majesty beware of those who were seeking the destruction of his friends, only to make themselves more potent and more easily to take Italy out of his hands. "The Majesty of the King," answered the Cardinal, "is very prudent, and has long ears and short belief; he hears everything, but only lends faith to what he finds by actual proof to be true."[1]

When, in December, the French troops under Yves d' Allègre, whose uncle Aubigny was royal governor of

---

[1] Letter from Machiavelli at Tours to the Ten of Liberty and Peace, November 21, 1500, in his First Legation to the Court of France.

THE COMING OF MADONNA LUCREZIA

Milan, passed through the districts of Modena and Reggio to aid Cesare Borgia in the conquest of Faenza, Ercole directed his ducal captains of those cities to provide them with lodgings and victuals at a just price, to pay all honour to Allègre, and to take care that the men-at-arms were well treated for their money, "taking precautions wisely among your other measures that they cannot say that the gates are shut against them, nor that they are mistrusted in any way."[1] Needless to say, the French repaid this confidence with brutality and outrage. Against one specially overbearing party, the people of Modena, "down to the priests," rose in arms. They killed six in the piazza and two more in San Domenico, closed the gates of the city and would have cut all the rest to pieces, if Count Gerardo Rangoni and the ducal *fattore*, Niccolò Sadoleto, had not come to the rescue and persuaded the indignant populace to let them go.[2]

Before the end of the year 1500, Alexander had formally proposed to Ercole that Lucrezia should be married to the hereditary prince of Ferrara, Don Alfonso; and, as early as November 26, the Venetian ambassador at Rome, Marino Gorzi, had informed his government that such a marriage was on foot.[3] The idea was intensely repugnant to the House of Este; Ercole, who had hoped to make a great French match for his son, attempted to gain time by pleading that he was already negotiating a marriage elsewhere and could not draw back. In February, 1501, the papal insist-

[1] Archivio di Modena. *Minutario Cronologico*, December 21, 1500.
[2] *Diario Ferrarese*, coll. 393, 394. This was at the beginning of April, 1501.
[3] Sanudo, *Diarii*, iii. col. 1130.

ence was renewed. Hearing that the matter of Alfonso's projected marriage had been put by the Duke into the hands of the King of France, Alexander was sending another papal envoy to the latter sovereign to induce him to support his proposal. Ercole at once wrote to Bartolommeo de' Cavallieri, his ambassador at the French Court, to beg the King not to give way. "We trust that his Majesty will not write to us according to the desire of the Pope. We shall take it as a singular favour if he will represent that he has already quite decided for another marriage. Beseech him, in our name, with the greatest efficacy that you can, that at least he will not write to urge us to contract this affinity with the Pope, nor say that he leaves us free in the matter. Because, to speak freely with his Majesty, we shall never yield nor consent to give Madonna Lucrezia to Don Alfonso; nor could Don Alfonso himself be ever induced to take her."[1]

But the Pope insisted. Cardinal Ferrari wrote from Rome to urge Ercole to consent, and the apostolic commissary from Cesare Borgia's army came in person to Ferrara. Dire consequences to the whole State of the Estensi were threatened, if they persisted in their refusal. The only hope that remained was to get the French marriage settled before the papal envoy arrived. Ercole instantly wrote to Cavallieri, telling him that he remembered two ladies who had been suggested as suitable brides, the daughter of the Comte de Foix and Madame d'Angou-

[1] *Minute di dispacci per Francia a Bartolommeo de' Cavallieri*, February 14, 1501. Archivio di Modena, *Carteggio degli Ambasciatori —Francia.* The opening words of the dispatch, "già son più mesi," show clearly that Gregorovius is mistaken in supposing that the negotiations began with Cardinal Ferrari's letter of February 18.

THE COMING OF MADONNA LUCREZIA

lême. Let him try to get the first from the King and the Cardinal of Rouen; but if " quella de Foys " cannot be had, " you will give us information clearly as to the qualities of Madame d'Angoulême, in such wise that we may understand well about her age, and if she has been married again or not, and in what degree of affinity she stands conjoint with the Most Christian Majesty; because, when we have learned all, we shall then answer you as to whether we think that you should open any negotiations about her. We should also much like you to inform us of the qualities of the Foix lady and her age, and the beauty of both of them, and also the dowry of each, if you can find it out." And, the same day, he sent him another letter, bidding him instantly inform the King of the coming of the apostolic commissary and of the papal threats, and beseech him, if he is urged by the Pope in this matter, to tell him that he has already engaged Don Alfonso, and cannot therefore set the Duke at liberty; " or whatever will seem best to his Majesty, provided that he relieves us from this persecution of the Pope, and that he delivers us from his hatred, the which without doubt we should incur very greatly, if we repulsed his overtures although we were at liberty to satisfy him, and every day would he attempt something against us. This we have to consider and estimate very much; but the Most Christian King need reck little if he does not gratify the Pope in this, since the Pope has more need of him than he of the Pope." [1]

The Duke, however, had reckoned without his host. Louis was counting upon the Pope's support in his designs

[1] *Minute di dispacci per Francia a Bartolommeo de' Cavallieri*, February 25 (two dispatches of same date), 1501. Archivio di Modena, *loc. cit*

upon Naples, and had no intention of offending him for the sake of a mere feudatory of the Church. Cardinal Ferrari in the Pope's name represented to Ercole the advantages of this union, and the enmity of the Pope and Cesare, perhaps also of France, if he refused; and Alexander already flattered himself that the day was won.[1] On May 26, Bartolommeo de' Cavallieri wrote from Châlons that, on the previous evening, the Cardinal of Rouen had told him that the Pope had sent one of his secretaries to ask the King to write and urge Ercole to consent to the marriage, and that the King, "having at present need of the Pope," had been unable not to write about it to the Duke. Bartolommeo saw the King that morning. His Majesty professed himself favourable to the marriage of Alfonso and the daughter of the Comte de Foix, but said that the Pope had pressed him to write to Ercole in support of the Borgia marriage, "and that already he had written to your Excellence, who was prudent and wise, and who would not, because of his letter, do anything save what you thought fit, adding that his intention is, in case this negotiation does not proceed, to give him the Foix lady."[2] Thus the responsibility for further resistance was thrown upon Ercole's own shoulders.

The Duke, who had continually answered the importunity of the Pope by pleading that he could not enter into the question, because he had entirely resigned his liberty in this matter to King Louis, was aghast, and saw his game played out. "Where we believed and held for certain," he wrote back, "that we were delivered and liberated from this business by the authority of the Most Christian Majesty,

[1] Gregorovius, p. 160.
[2] *Dispacci da Francia di Bartolommeo de' Cavallieri.* Archivio di Modena, *loc. cit.*

THE COMING OF MADONNA LUCREZIA

we see ourselves entangled in it more than ever, by his means and his work. Wherefore, we cannot refrain from remonstrating with his Majesty concerning this thing. We trusted in the words and promise of his Majesty, who in writing to us affirmed that he would never write to us about this matter and that he would make an opportune reply to the Pope. And we, trusting in the grace and wisdom of his Majesty, felt quite certain of this thing; and we replied continually to the Pope's importunity that we could not enter into this business with him, because we had given up our faculty and liberty to the Most Christian Majesty; which we should not have said, nor written, if we could have imagined that the said Majesty would have changed, and consented to have such a letter written to us as he has done. This seems to us so much the more grievous, as his Majesty with one tiny little word could satisfy the Pope, by giving him to understand that already there had been so much spoken of the other marriage, and that his faith had been given to such an extent, that he could not change it nor intervene in favour of this affinity with the Pontiff. Nor should it be taken into consideration that his Majesty at present has need of the Pope, as the most illustrious and reverend Monsignor of Rouen has said to you; for the Pope has much greater need of his Majesty, without whose favour he could not stay in Rome nor in Italy. And if the Most Christian King had used those terms with the Pope that perhaps would have been not unfitting but universally commended, he could have much more securely disposed of this, or of another better Pontiff, than he can at present.

But we cannot do so; we must needs temporise, and avoid all occasions of angering the mind of the Pope, and especially at present, since we have seen that the Most Christian

Majesty, because he has some small need of the Pope, grants him what he wants, paying no heed to our concerns and needs. And if, perchance, his Majesty deemed that we were of such great cleverness and prudence as to know how to get out of this difficulty (and this may be the cause that has induced him to write to us !), you can assure him that we were never so industrious nor so wise that we should know how to vary or contradict what we have said and written. Since, therefore, we have always affirmed to the messengers of the Pope that this affair of ours was in the hands of the Most Christian King (trusting in him, as we said above), and now his Majesty writes to us according to the Pope's desire, we are reduced to so great perplexity that we do not know what line of conduct to adopt. For, in the first place, we are resolved never to contract this relationship with the Pontiff. It does not appear to us advisable to tell him absolutely that we will not; because such a repulse would make him an even bitterer enemy to us than he is now. Neither will we say that the Most Christian Majesty does not wish it, albeit he writes to us in another tone in order not to offend him. He, therefore, can judge right well the great difficulty to which we are reduced; from which we see no way of escape, save by the means and aid of his Most Christian Majesty."[1]

But these were mere words, and Ercole soon found that further resistance was useless. The Pope threatened him with the loss of his duchy unless he consented, and, although the King told Cavallieri that Ferrara was under his special protection and could only fall if France fell, the

---

[1] Original letter of June 9, 1501. *Istruzione a Bartolommeo de' Cavallieri*. Archivio di Modena, *loc. cit.*

THE COMING OF MADONNA LUCREZIA

French ministers urged the Duke to yield on advantageous conditions for Ferrara and the House of Este. The Cardinal of Rouen sent the Archbishop of Narbonne to Ferrara to counsel compliance.[1] Ercole gave way with some dignity, declaring that he was postponing his own will and the dignity of his House for the desires and interests of the King of France. He was ready, he told the envoys of Alexander and Cesare, to do what the King and Cardinal desired, provided that a satisfactory agreement could be made about the details and conditions. To the Cardinal of Rouen himself he wrote : " Having postponed the honesty of my most ancient House, I have decided to yield." [2]

So pleased was the Sovereign Pontiff at Ercole's surrender, that he promptly took a holiday, leaving Lucrezia in the Vatican as regent of the Papal States. He was not so pleased a little later, when he heard of the conditions upon which Ercole insisted. These included 200,000 ducats as Lucrezia's dowry, liberation from the annual tribute that was paid to the Holy See, the concession to himself of the right of patronage of the bishopric of Ferrara, the cession to Ferrara of Cento and La Pieve (small towns included in the archbishopric of Bologna, and therefore a part of the Papal States), and a number of benefices for members of the House of Este. Alexander offered half the dowry demanded. The French King advised Ercole, if the thing had to be done, to get the biggest profit out of it that he could; in case it fell through, he was still ready to find a French bride for Alfonso.[3] But he thought that the ducal demands

[1] Gregorovius, pp. 169, 170.
[2] *Minute Ducali* of July 8, 1501, to Giovanni Valla and the Cardinal of Rouen. Archivio di Modena, *Minutario Cronologico*.
[3] Gregorovius, pp. 172, 173.

were excessive. Ercole indignantly protested that he was only asking what was reasonable, " in such wise that it can be understood that we make more account of honour than of money." If there should be any further delay, he assured the King, or any rupture in the negotiations, it would proceed entirely from the Pope. He wrote to Cesare Borgia that he had agreed to this marriage, " because of the reverence which we bear to the Holiness of our Lord, and the excellent qualities of the most illustrious Madonna Lucrezia ; but much more because of the love and affection which we bear towards your Excellence." [1] Cesare and Lucrezia—the latter being the one person most bent upon the marriage, and showing her wishes without the slightest delicacy—persuaded the Pope to give the Duke what he wanted. Venice misliked the affair, as tending to increase Cesare's power in Italy. The King of the Romans urged Ercole not to make this alliance. But the ill-humour of the one Power and the interference of the other merely strengthened the Duke's hands. On September 1, 1501, the marriage was contracted *per verba* in the palace of Belfiore, the Pope having previously conferred on the Cardinal Ippolito the dignity of Archpriest of San Pietro.[2] The Duke wrote to Lucrezia on the same day :—

"Most illustrious and noble lady, our daughter-in-law and dearest daughter. Your Ladyship will hear from Messer Guglielmo, Archdeacon of Châlons, the present bearer, how to-day by the Divine grace the marriage has been contracted *per verba de presenti* between yourself, by means of your

[1] *Minute* to Bartolommeo de' Cavallieri and the Most Christian King, of August 11, to " the Duke of Romagna " [i.e. Cesare Borgia], of August 6. Archivio di Modena, *Minutario Cronologico*.

[2] Gregorovius, pp. 174, 175.

THE COMING OF MADONNA LUCREZIA

two procurators, and the most illustrious Don Alfonso, our first-begotten. To us this thing has been a supreme satisfaction and very great consolation in our old age. We rejoice thereat with your Ladyship, whom we first loved in no ordinary wise because of your own singular virtues, our reverence for the Holiness of our Lord, and because you are the sister of the most illustrious Duke of Romagna, whom we hold as our honoured brother. Now we love you intimately more than a daughter, hoping that from you will result the conservation of our posterity; and we shall endeavour to have you near us as soon as possible, according to our desire."[1]

But in his communication the next day to the Marquis of Mantua, to his ambassadors in France, Venice and Florence, and to Bentivoglio, he simply stated that he had yielded to the exhortations of the Most Christian King, now that the Pope had agreed to his conditions. Indeed, he originally intended to say that he "had condescended" to arrange this relationship with the Pope, but thought better of it, and altered the word to "consented" before the dispatch was sent.[2]

There were wild rejoicings in the Papal Court at the news that the fish had at last been brought to land. The Vatican was illuminated; cannons thundered from Sant' Angelo. Lucrezia could not contain herself for delight. She went through Rome in state to give thanks in Santa Maria del Popolo, and her Spanish buffoon danced through the streets, cheering for "the most illustrious Duchess of Ferrara." The Pope, losing what little dignity he had left to him,

[1] *Minute Ducali* of September 1, 1501. Archivio di Modena, *Minutario Cronologico*.
[2] *Minute Ducali* of September 2. *Ibid.*

assembled the Cardinals in consistory, and harangued them about the virtues and prudence of Duke Ercole, the excellent qualities of Don Alfonso, the ancestral glories of the House of Este.

On September 15 two Ferrarese envoys, Gerardo Saraceni and Ettore Berlinghieri, arrived in Rome. Their object was to secure the papal Bulls required, before their master committed himself further—Bartolommeo de' Cavallieri having warned him not to trust the Pope further than was necessary. Lucrezia received them enthusiastically, and showed herself the most zealous supporter of the Ferrarese claims. "She already seems to us an excellent Ferrarese," wrote the ambassadors. Festivities fast and furious followed in the Vatican, some of them far exceeding the bounds of propriety.[1] Lucrezia danced night after night, to the huge edification of his Holiness and the admiration of the Ferrarese envoys, until she made herself quite ill. A few little complications remained. One was the personage whom the unsophisticated reader of these events might have imagined to be the bride's lawful husband, Giovanni Sforza of Pesaro, who was supposed to be lurking in Mantua. The Pope made the ambassadors write to Ercole that the unlucky man must be kept out of the way, and not allowed to come to Ferrara at the time of the wedding. Another was the little boy, Rodrigo, her son by Sforza's even more unfortunate successor; but Lucrezia assured Gerardo Saraceni that he would stay in Rome and that ample provision would be made for him. "Rome seems to me a prison," said the gay young lady, and she urged the Pope to do everything that Ercole wanted.[2] She had already

[1] Cf. below, p. 402, note 2.
[2] The Bull, reinvesting Ercole and Alfonso and their descendants

THE COMING OF MADONNA LUCREZIA

begun an affectionate and confidential correspondence with her prospective father-in-law. The envoys assured him that she had nearly fainted when she heard that he was ill, and had expressed her ardent wish that she could have come to Ferrara to heal him with her own hands, as she had done the Pope on a similar occasion.[1] With his usual anxiety that the dramatic and spectacular entertainments in the coming celebrations should be worthy of his reputation, Ercole wanted to hear all about the mighty deeds of the ancestors of the Borgias in past ages, in order that they might be worked up for artistic purposes. But his ambassadors found it difficult to satisfy him. "Up to now," they wrote, "it is only of Calixtus that something worthy is found, especially his own achievements, of which Platina writes much. For the rest, it is generally known what this Pope has done, so that whoso has to make the oration will have a wide field open before him."[2] This was perfectly true, though not quite in the sense in which the writers ostensibly meant it.

Don Alfonso still maintained a sullen silence. The Emperor Maximilian continued to abuse the Pope and to blame the marriage, urging the Duke to draw back before it was too late. Ercole promptly informed the Pope of this " evil disposition " of the King of the Romans, and had his letters read to the papal orators at Ferrara. "Although as far as it concerns us," he wrote to his ambassadors

---

with the Dukedom of Ferrara, is dated September 17, 1501 (Theiner, iii. pp. 511-513). The tribute is reduced to one hundred golden florins annually, or, in case of the direct issue of Alfonso and Lucrezia failing, to one thousand.

[1] Gregorovius, p. 190.
[2] Dispatch of October 18. Gregorovius, pp. 192, 193.

DUKES AND POETS IN FERRARA

in Rome, "we do not make much account of this opinion of his Majesty, since we have done what we have with reason and feel every day greater satisfaction of soul thereat; nevertheless, because of the tie that binds us to his Holiness, and in order that with his wisdom he may be able to judge of this demonstration for his other needs and affairs, we have thought that we ought to inform him of what we hear. We are persuaded that, with his prudence, he will examine and judge right well how far this evil disposition of the said Majesty can matter to him."[1] The imperial opposition was for Ercole simply an excellent instrument with which to reduce his Holiness to docility. Alexander was profuse in his panegyrics of Lucrezia, her beauty, her graciousness and prudence. Cesare, who was now in Rome (Faenza had capitulated in April, and the partition of the Neapolitan Kingdom between France and Spain had been practically effected in July), also approved, but was "not at home" to the Ferrarese ambassadors—a thing which the Pope declared grieved him to the very heart.[2] There were still some weeks of negotiation and haggling; Ercole would not send to fetch the bride until he got his Bulls and her dowry paid down in hard cash, but professed himself insulted when Alexander said that he was acting like a merchant. Lucrezia continued to urge the Pope to yield in every particular, while Maximilian put all the pressure he could upon the Duke to delay. But, on November 14, Ercole wrote to the Marchesana Isabella (who had been the most emphatic of all the family against Lucrezia when it had been first proposed), that he had decided to send the

[1] Letter of October 23, 1501, to Saraceni and Berlinghieri. Archivio di Modena, *Carteggio degli Ambasciatori—Roma.*
[2] Dispatch of Saraceni, October 26. Gregorovius, p. 191.

Saint Catherine of Alexandria.
(a supposed portrait of Lucrezia Borgia)
By Pinturicchio.

THE COMING OF MADONNA LUCREZIA

company to Rome to fetch Lucrezia at the beginning of December, and that the marriage would be celebrated as soon as she arrived in Ferrara :—

"Since you are our daughter, it is proper that you should be present at this wedding, and so we exhort you to come. And we are certain that the most illustrious Lord Marquis, your consort and our most beloved brother, will be most pleased at your coming hither, as he is always desirous to do whatever pleases us. And although we should not be less desirous that his Lordship also should be present at it, nevertheless, for every sufficient reason, it seems to us better that he should not come, taking into account the condition of the present times—all of which we believe that his Lordship, too, in his prudence right well considers and knows. And so your Ladyship can give him to understand." [1]

At the same time, a very different transaction was in progress between Ercole and Lucrezia. He had interested his Borgia daughter-in-law in his mystical aspirations, and especially in his cult of St. Catherine of Siena. As we saw, he had sent Bartolommeo Bresciano to Rome, to induce her to use her influence with the Pope to get the nuns that Lucia wanted sent from Viterbo and Narni to the new convent of Ferrara. "We desire greatly," he wrote to Lucrezia, " that an excellent beginning should be given to that monastery with these nuns, who are full of supreme goodness and charity. It will be easy for your Ladyship to obtain that we have what we desire, and you will give us as great a pleasure as you could possibly give us by any other action that at present we could expect from you. As soon as we thought of using the means and favour of your Ladyship in this, we thought that we had gained our object.

[1] Archivio di Modena, *Minutario Cronologico*.

DUKES AND POETS IN FERRARA

And let not your Ladyship wonder at this solicitation of ours, because, since we are in the state that we are, we attend more to affairs of the soul (like this is) than to other matters, and the affairs of the soul should be embraced with all possible fervour and efficacy." [1]

With this letter, Bresciano reached Rome on the evening of October 11, not without running considerable risk on the way from bands of French and Gascon soldiers who were marching from Lombardy to join the royal forces in the newly conquered Neapolitan provinces. He was delighted at his reception by Lucrezia, who promised to do all that the Duke wanted and induced the Pope to send messengers to the governors of Viterbo and Narni with papal briefs and letters from the General of the Dominicans, threatening the nuns with excommunication unless they came to Rome within six days. "So I live in hopes," wrote Bresciano to Ercole, "that her Ladyship will bring them with her to Ferrara, to make a desired present of them to your Excellence and to the venerable Suora Lucia; and I shall not abandon the undertaking, as your Lordship has committed it to me, but shall keep continually near this most illustrious Madonna until we are brought to Ferrara. Verily, this lady has taken up this thing with all her powers to get your Lordship gratified, and I find her Ladyship so well disposed towards you that she could not be more. I hope that your Excellence will be right well satisfied with this most illustrious Madonna, for she is endowed with so much graciousness and goodness that she continually thinks of nothing else, save how to serve you." [2]

[1] Letter dated Comacchio, September 28, 1501. Gandini, *Lucrezia Borgia*, document 6.
[2] Dispatch of October 31. Gandini, *op. cit.*, document 14. This

THE COMING OF MADONNA LUCREZIA

Early in November, Suora Diambra and Suora Leonarda came to Rome, accompanied by our old friend, the redoubtable Fra Martino. Their appeals to the General of the Dominicans and to the Pope himself were of no avail. His Holiness, without further words, told them that they were sent to Ferrara. Lucrezia was more kind, but equally firm, and told them plainly that, unless they produced those other nuns that Ercole and Lucia wanted, she would herself send and fetch them on her own account. All sorts of excuses were now trumped up by these pious dames. "For my part," said Leonarda, "I cannot come, because I have my old mother who is infirm. If only my brother were alive, I could say that I would come, but never will I abandon my mother." "You must obey the commands of the Pope," answered Bresciano severely. Then Diambra the prioress, whom Bresciano had previously noted as a woman of few words, suddenly gave tongue. "Suora Beatrice," she said, "is so lame that she cannot move without two crutches. As to Suora Felicità, we shall never give her to Suora Lucia, because she has the dropsy so badly that it would not do to put her with the other sisters. Her family will never let Suora Appolonia come to Ferrara. Let us go home, and we shall choose four nuns so good and sufficient that the venerable Suora Lucia will be contented and well satisfied."[1]

---

last day of October, 1501, is the date of the notorious supper said by Johannes Burchardus (*Diarium*, ed. Thuasne, iii. p. 167) to have been given by Cesare in his apartment in the Vatican to fifty harlots —the Pope and Lucrezia being present—and followed by an orgie of the most obscene description. For a discussion of this unpleasant topic, see Pastor, iii. p. 452, note 1. It seems quite incredible, in the face of the laudatory epistles about Lucrezia's goodness and virtues that the Ferrarese agents were sending at this very time to the Duke.

[1] Bresciano's dispatches of November 12 and 18, 1501. Gandini, *op.*

Ercole, however, persisted that he must have the women Lucia wanted; *seven* from Viterbo, two from Narni, and two other young girls who were not nuns. He professed himself certain that Lucrezia would see the thing through. He declined to believe in Beatrice's lameness or in Felicità's dropsy (though he was ready to dispense with Leonarda herself, if necessary), and suggested that Lucrezia should tell the Governor of Viterbo to speak with them. In the presence of Fra Martino and Bresciano, the Pope's daughter gave a thorough scolding to Diambra and Leonarda, whom she found "more obstinate than the devil," as Bresciano put it. The heads of the Dominican Order, understanding that Lucrezia had taken the matter in hand and that the nuns would be properly looked after until they got to Ferrara, made them give way. Bresciano went to Viterbo, with a commissary of the Pope, and brought the nuns wanted safely to Rome on December 21, the contingent from Narni coming in a few days later. The original idea had been for Lucrezia to bring them with her to Ferrara; but this being obviously unsuitable, Ercole decided that his sacred prize —which was regarded as a present to him and Lucia from Lucrezia—should set out a day or two in advance of the bridal party, Lucrezia herself taking care that they were properly housed and provided for on the way with all possible comfort in the cold winter weather. Hearing that there were a number of relations of the nuns who wanted to

---

cit., documents 18 and 19. In the latter document I have corrected an evident error in the text. Gandini (pp. 15, 42) reads "*Se sore Biatrice la priora dice essere siancata*"; but it should obviously be "*De sore Biatrice la priora dice,*" the speaker being the prioress Diambra, as is quite clear from the context and from Ercole's answer (document 21).

THE COMING OF MADONNA LUCREZIA

come to Ferrara with them, Ercole professed himself well pleased: "Let all come who want to come, and caress them and use every kindness towards them," he wrote to Bresciano, " because also by us they will be well received and caressed."[1] At the last, Suora Beatrice began to make fresh difficulties, but was apparently overcome by Bresciano hinting that, with her spirit and cleverness, she would certainly be one of those who would govern the monastery. Right glad was the worthy fellow when, on the last day of the year, he mustered his troublesome flock and found that not one of those his master wanted was missing. " My lord," he wrote, " I never knew what labour was until I had to make so many heads agree. I thank our Lord God who has got me through it with credit, but there was a time when I doubted."[2]

In the meanwhile, the splendid cortège of princes and nobles of Ferrara had come to Rome to fetch Don Alfonso's bride. All the noblest families in the Estensian duchies were represented. The Cardinal Ippolito was the presiding genius; with him were his brothers Ferrando and the younger Sigismondo, his cousin the younger Ercole, Niccolò Maria and Meliaduse d' Este (bastards of the House, and bishops respectively of Adria and Comacchio), Niccolò da Correggio and Federigo della Mirandola, representatives of the Pio, Rangoni, Strozzi and the like; as special ducal ambassadors came Gian Luca Pozzi of Pontremoli and Gerardo Saraceni, as before, while a number of ecclesiastics and religious were headed by Maestro Zanetto, the Inquisitor of San Domenico.[3] With them rode young Annibale Bentivoglio, whose presence

[1] Gandini, *op. cit.*, document 28.
[2] Dispatch of December 31. Gandini, *op. cit.*, document 30.
[3] The whole list is given by Zambotto in his *Silva Cronicarum*, and in the *Diario Ferrarese*.

in Rome, according to the hopes of his father and Ercole, would augment the good dispositions of the Pope towards the Lords of Bologna.[1] The whole cavalcade consisted of more than five hundred persons, superbly mounted and gorgeously arrayed, preceded by pipers and trumpeters; but the weather was fearful and the journey, in the utmost discomfort, took thirteen days.

On the morning of December 23, they made their state approach to the Eternal City. There were the usual receptions at intervals along the way. At the Ponte Milvio, the Senator of Rome and other civic dignitaries met them with two thousand men; further on, they were greeted by Cesare Borgia and the French ambassador, with the Swiss guard. It was nearly evening when they reached the Porta del Popolo, where nineteen Cardinals awaited them; a united procession was formed, Romans and Ferrarese together passing in triumph through the streets towards the Vatican, while the cannons of Sant' Angelo thundered out their welcome. After a most cordial reception by the Pope, Cesare brought the Princes of Este to be introduced to his sister. Lucrezia appeared in a wonderful costume of white and gold, with a green headdress, all studded with the famous pearls that she so loved. It was noticed that Cardinal Ippolito's eyes flashed when he saw her, and the others were equally delighted. The same evening Messer Gian Luca went with Saraceni to interview her, on behalf of Ercole and Alfonso, and sent the former a glowing account of her beauty and her piety—upon the latter point, seeing that she had promised him the reversion of the bishopric of Reggio, he was surely a competent judge. Nevertheless, the tone of his dispatch shows that apprehensions had still

[1] Cf. letters in Dallari, pp. 205, 206.

been entertained at the Ferrarese Court. "Altogether," he wrote, "she seems to me of so excellent a condition that there is no need or possibility of fearing anything sinister from her, but we may rather presume, believe and hope always the best conduct." [1]

By a decree of the Pope, the carnival now began, and for more than a week Rome was the scene of the wildest festivities. Lucrezia gave balls in her own palace, at which she danced specially with Don Ferrando, "gentilmente e con grazia singolare," while the Ferrarese and Mantuan guests eyed her damsels and judged that, with a few exceptions, they could show fairer at home. The public ways swarmed with masked courtesans. The Cardinal and Ferrando went with Cesare masked through the streets, while all Rome seemed rejoicing, though—as we learn from "El Prete," a dependant of Niccolò da Correggio and correspondent of the Marchesana Isabella—*brutti giochi* were played after dark.[2] On the evening of December 30, Lucrezia, in a magnificent costume of crimson and gold brocade, blazing, as usual, with pearls, emeralds and rubies, with a long retinue of cavaliers and ladies, was escorted in state by Ferrando and Sigismondo to the Vatican. In the Sala Paolina the Pope sat enthroned with the Cardinals and Cesare, the ambassadors of France, Spain and Venice being present. Here the marriage by proxy was celebrated; Ferrando gave the bride the ring in the name of his brother, the Cardinal Ippolito presenting her with a superb casket of jewels, of the value of 70,000 ducats, the gift of Duke Ercole to his daughter-in-law. Races and a sham fight were exhibited in the Piazza beneath the windows, after which Lucrezia's damsels danced

---

[1] Dispatch of December 23, 1501. Gregorovius, document 31.
[2] Gregorovius, pp. 204, 205.

for an hour before the Pope, she and Cesare opening the ball. Alexander was nearly crazy with delight and fondness, and laughed continually. Then there were comedies played, with allegorical pastorals, upon the conclusion of which the gathering broke up, leaving the Borgias and Estensian princes together to sup quietly with the Pope.[1]

But the Duke of Ferrara by no means trusted either Alexander or his daughter completely. He had given Messer Gian Luca minute directions, before he left Ferrara and by letter since, as to the way in which Ippolito was to present the jewels to Lucrezia, and he charged the Cardinal strictly not to deviate in the slightest degree from these instructions, " in order that, in case the Duchess should fail in her duty towards the most illustrious Don Alfonso, we may not be more obliged than we wish to be, concerning these jewels." He was not to make an unconditional present of them to her, and there was to be no mention of them in the notary's instrument.[2] The ambassadors, in a similar spirit, declined to give the papal authorities a receipt for the dowry, until every penny of it had been paid, and Ercole warmly commended their prudent conduct.[3] They had previously assured him that Lucrezia had told the Pope himself that she would never give his Holiness cause to blush for her conduct, and of this, " so far as we can judge," they declared themselves convinced, being much edified by her bearing and the life of her household.[4]

---

[1] Gregorovius, pp. 205-207.
[2] Gregorovius, p. 206 ; *Minute Ducali* to Cardinal Ippolito, December 21, 1501. Archivio di Modena, *Carteggio dei Principi.*
[3] *Minute Ducali* to Pozzi and Saraceni, December 31. Archivio di Modena, *Minutario Cronologico.*
[4] Dispatch of December 28. Gregorovius, p. 213.

THE COMING OF MADONNA LUCREZIA

The festivities reached their height on the first two days of the new year, 1502. On January 1, there was a great pageant in the Piazza San Pietro, given by the Roman municipality. Thirteen triumphal chariots, accompanied by a thousand men on horse and foot, with music and preceded by the banner of the City, came from the Piazza Navona to the Vatican and moved round the square, setting forth the triumphs of Hercules and of Caesar and the heroes of ancient Rome, while the Pope and his guests looked on from the windows. Then, in the Vatican, there were comedies and morris-dances; shepherds recited the praises of Lucrezia, who sat at the Pope's right hand, surrounded by the Cardinals. A buffoon danced before the Pope, dressed as a woman, the courtiers joining in, masked, with Cesare himself conspicuous among them by his splendid attire and noble figure. To the sound of trumpets, a tree appeared, out of which came a child who sang verses and threw cords of silk to the merrymakers, who whirled round it as they danced. Finally, at the Pope's command, Lucrezia descended from her throne and led out another dance with one of her Spanish ladies.

The next day opened with a great bull-fight in front of San Pietro, in which Cesare took part and killed the most furious bull with his lance. In the evening there was a dramatic representation in the Pope's chamber, the whole being designed to glorify the new alliance between Este and Borgia. Virtue and Fortune strove together for precedence, until Glory appeared upon a triumphal car with the world beneath her feet, declaring that Caesar and Hercules had overcome fortune by virtue, relating the deeds of the Duke of Romagna. Hercules followed and fought with Fortune, whom he took and bound, releasing her only on Juno's promise that neither would ever do anything against the Houses of Este and Borgia, but would favour this new relationship. Afterwards came Rome, on a triumphal chariot, and bewailed that Alexander, who held the place of Jove, should deprive her of Lucrezia, who was the refuge of all Rome. Ferrara followed, without a triumphal chariot, declaring that Madonna was going to no unworthy place, and that Rome was not losing her. Then appeared Mercury, sent to establish concord between the two cities, announcing that it was the will of the Gods that Madonna Lucrezia should go to Ferrara, and he made Ferrara ascend upon a triumphal chariot and pass in honour across the stage. This being concluded, the *Menaechmi* of Plautus was played, and, in the scene where one of the twins is seized by order of his father-in-law, the actor cried out that he marvelled that they dared to use such violence to him, when Caesar and Hercules were on his side, and Jove propitious. This topical allusion, of course, raised much applause, and the preceding allegory inspired the Ferrarese agents with great hopes that, in the future, Ercole could count upon the aid of the Borgia against his enemies.[1]

---

[1] These festivities are fully described in dispatches from Pozzi and Saraceni to Duke Ercole, and from El Prete to Isabella d' Este, both of January 2, 1502; documents 34 and 35 in Gregorovius, pp. 414-417 (also in his text, pp. 208-211). "All these things," wrote Gian Luca and his colleague, waxing eloquent over the allegorical portion of the entertainment, " were recited in heroic verse, right elegantly, always celebrating greatly the conjunction between Caesar and Hercules, manifestly intending us to infer that together they should do great deeds against the enemies of Hercules, in such wise that, if the results corresponded with these prognostications, our affairs would come to a right good termination." The hint is directed against Venice. In a previous dispatch, of December 28, the envoys had seen grounds for hope that the Pope would help

THE COMING OF MADONNA LUCREZIA

Amidst her preparations for starting, Lucrezia did not forget to further Duke Ercole's rather numerous interests. She had already procured from the Pope the promise of the reversion of the bishopric of Reggio for Gian Luca Pozzi, and was exerting herself also on behalf of Don Giulio. "Since we greatly desire the honour and weal of the most illustrious Don Giulio, our son," wrote the Duke, "we pray your Ladyship, before you leave Rome, to be good enough to obtain from the Holiness of our Lord this other grace, that his Beatitude promise, as soon as an occasion presents itself, to confer a good benefice upon the said Don Giulio, such as a bishopric or a good abbey, as we believe that your Ladyship will easily obtain, through your influence, as also because of the excellent dispositions that the Holiness of our Lord bears towards us and our sons."[1] She was indefatigable in providing for the captured nuns, whom she dispatched upon their journey on January 4, giving Bartolommeo Bresciano an escort of crossbowmen and bidding him wait for her at Bologna, in order that she herself might bring them thence to Ferrara. This latter part of the plan fell through, as Ercole obviously thought it unsuitable and was anxious that the nuns should arrive some days before the bridal cortège. At Cesena, the troublesome Suora Beatrice fell ill; but, by feeding her up with marchpane and bread sopped in chicken-broth, Bartolommeo brought her round; and, avoiding Bologna, they went on to Ferrara from Faenza, by way of Lugo and Argenta. The city was already in festal array to

Ercole to recover the Polesine of Rovigo, and that, if a safe occasion presented itself, he would drive the Venetians from Ravenna and Cervia to give these places to Cesare (Balan, v. p. 524, note 2).

[1] *Minute Ducali*, undated, to Lucrezia. Archivio di Modena, *Carteggio dei Principi*.

greet Lucrezia, when they arrived.[1] The Duke himself came out to meet them. The same day he wrote to Lucrezia, explaining that he had instructed Bartolommeo not to wait, but to bring them on by the shorter way of Lugo and Argenta, because he thought it would be inconvenient to her to have the nuns in her train, and because he was anxious to have them with him as soon as possible. " You will be pleased that, without putting your cortège to any inconvenience, these sisters have arrived here with celerity to satisfy our desire." [2]

In the meanwhile, Lucrezia had turned her back for ever upon the Eternal City. She left Rome on January 6, riding a white mule covered with gold and silver trappings, all the Cardinals, ambassadors and magistrates accompanying her to the Porta del Popolo. The Pope rushed from window to window of the Vatican to follow her with his eyes as far as possible—perhaps some instinct told him that he was never to see his daughter again—and consoled himself with sending letters, both from himself and through the Cardinal of Modena, urging Ercole and Alfonso to treat her kindly. Cesare Borgia and the Cardinal Ippolito rode with her a little way, and then turned back together; an imaginary conversation between these two worthies on their return would have furnished a fitting subject for Walter Savage Landor.

The noble cavalcade of Romans and Ferrarese moved slowly through the Papal States, the people headed by their magistrates pouring out in gala attire to greet the new Duchess as she passed. In Foligno, they performed a pageant in her honour. The Lucrezia of old Rome was

[1] Gandini, *op. cit.*, pp. 18-20.
[2] *Minute Ducali* of January 23, 1502. Archivio di Modena, *Carteggio dei Principi.*

THE COMING OF MADONNA LUCREZIA

surpassed in virtue by her namesake and successor; Paris revoked his sentence and gave the golden apple to her, as eclipsing all the ancient goddesses; the Sultan appeared in a galley of Turks, and assured her that he would restore all the conquered Christian lands. The Ferrarese ambassadors found it stupid; the verses, they said, were scarcely those of Petrarca, and there was no point in the whole performance.[1] Two miles from Gubbio, the Duchess Elisabetta joined them, and accompanied Lucrezia all the rest of the way. Guidobaldo himself, marked out for destruction by her House, met them near Urbino and made over his own palace to Lucrezia. Thence, on January 20, they moved slowly down to Pesaro—the city in which Lucrezia had lived as the wife of its now exiled lord, Giovanni Sforza,—where Cesare's agents received her. Here, practically for the first time, Lucrezia showed some signs of sensibility; in her former husband's palace she kept to herself and, although she allowed a dance, was not present at it. Thence she passed on to Cesare's recent conquests of Cesena, Faenza and Imola; at the time of her jubilant entering into the two latter towns, their dispossessed rulers, the beautiful young Astorre Manfredi and Caterina Sforza Riario, were being kept closely imprisoned in Rome, and the former was doomed to meet a fate of appalling atrocity, a few months later, by her brother's orders. At Bologna, the Bentivoglio, anxious to ingratiate themselves with the dreaded Cesare, gave her a sumptuous reception. Thence, on the morning of January 31, the bridal party started on their way to Ferrara by canal and river.[2]

[1] Dispatch of Pozzi and Saraceni, January 13, 1502. Gregorovius, document 37.
[2] It will be remembered that the courses of the Reno and Po have

DUKES AND POETS IN FERRARA

On the evening of the same day, they arrived at Castello Bentivoglio, about twenty miles from Ferrara. Here the bridegroom, Don Alfonso, suddenly appeared upon the scene. He had come disguised with four horsemen to see his bride, stayed with her for a couple of hours, and then went back to Ferrara. This surprise visit of his, which was quite contrary to the usual ceremonial etiquette on these occasions, made an excellent impression. "It pleased all the people," writes Zambotto, "and much more the bride and all her friends, that his lordship should desire to see her and that he should be taking her with good heart, for it was a sign that she would be well received and better treated."[1]

Isabella had come from Mantua to do the honours of Ferrara to Lucrezia, and with the old Duke she arranged the whole thing. In her letters to her husband, she describes every detail in the pageantry and festivities, with many pretty little messages to him and to the children, especially the *puttino* Federigo, but shows clearly that she misliked the situation and was not over pleased at her brother's wedding. Still her bearing towards the bride was cordiality itself. On February 1, she met her in her barge at Malalbergo; and together with the Duchess Elisabetta, Don Ferrando and Sigismondo, they went on to Torre della Fossa, the point where the canal joined the Po di Ferrara or Canale di Cento, which thence led to Ferrara itself. Cloth of gold and crimson silk, with profusion of pearls, was the distinguishing feature in the dress of Lucrezia; Isabella wore a robe of green velvet worked with gold; the more sober-minded

been completely altered since those days. A canal then ran from Bologna to join the Po di Primaro near Ferrara itself.

[1] *Lucrezia Borgia in Ferrara, sposa a Don Alfonso d' Este*, pp. 12, 13 (Ferrara, 1867. Cf. below, p. 418, note 1).

THE COMING OF MADONNA LUCREZIA

Elisabetta was clad in black velvet covered with golden devices. At Torre, the ducal bucentaur was in readiness, with the ambassadors of France and all the Italian Powers on board ; Ercole and Alfonso, with their Court, were waiting on foot on the shore, and the mounted crossbowmen, *balestrieri*, in their gala dress of red and white, drawn up behind them. Lucrezia sprang to shore and was embraced by Ercole (it was the first time that they had seen each other), who attempted to prevent her kissing his hand. Then they all entered the great bucentaur, where the ambassadors were presented, and Lucrezia took her seat between the representatives of France and Venice, Ercole and Alfonso going up on the poop and amusing themselves with the bride's Spanish buffoons, who sang her praises. Amidst popular acclamation and salvos of artillery, they landed near the Porta San Paolo, and Lucrezia was brought for the night to the palace of Alberto d' Este in the Borgo San Luca, where Lucrezia d' Este Bentivoglio did the honours.

On February 2, the Feast of the Purification of the Madonna, this new Roman Lucrezia made her state entry into Ferrara. After hearing Mass and having dinner, Ercole and Alfonso, with Alberto d' Este and the French ambassador, Monsignor Filippo della Rocca Berti, came to fetch her. They entered the city by the Ponte del Castel Tedaldo, Lucrezia, a mass of superb jewels and gems, in every sense mistress of herself and of the situation. A beautiful white horse, the Duke's gift, had been brought her, covered with crimson cloth with most sumptuous ornaments of gold and pearls. At the entrance to the city, the sudden discharge of artillery frightened the animal, which reared and threw her. There was general consternation for a moment; but she landed on her feet, laughing gaily, and the Duke made her mount a mule instead. Looking round, she saw the French ambassador between the two Venetian envoys, and at once summoned him to her side, a position of honour which he retained for the rest of that day.

The procession was headed by three squadrons of mounted *balestrieri* of the ducal guard, in red and white uniforms with white French hats and huge plumes, followed by more than a hundred trumpeters, pipers, and drummers. Then came all the courtiers and nobles of Ferrara, gorgeously arrayed and wearing massive gold chains and necklaces, attending upon Don Alfonso himself, who, mounted upon a superb bay horse, dressed in dark velvet covered with scales of beaten gold and wearing a black and gold velvet cap with white feathers, rode slowly forward, accompanied by Annibale Bentivoglio. The attendants of the Duchess of Urbino followed. Next came the bridal cortège proper: twenty Spanish and Roman gentlemen, riding two and two; five bishops, to wit, the Estensi of Adria and Comacchio, the Bishop of Cervia, and two sent by the Pope, who, in spite of Ercole's solicitation, had declared that it would not be possible to allow a Cardinal to accompany the bride on this occasion; and the ambassadors of the Tuscan Republics, of Venice and of Rome, in crimson mantles and brocade of gold. More musicians followed, with Lucrezia's two buffoons, to introduce a lighter note. Then, under a canopy of crimson silk carried by the doctors of the universities, appeared Lucrezia herself, riding her mule (the restive horse being led along in front), waited upon by six of her husband's chamberlains, and with the French ambassador riding alone by her side under the canopy. Isabella, in describing the pageant to the Marquis, noted that among the magnificent jewels blazing all over her were those that

THE COMING OF MADONNA LUCREZIA

Ercole had sent to Rome, including the ones that had belonged to the writer's own mother, "the blessed memory of Madama of Ferrara." Radiant with exultation, her sweet girl-like face and slender figure making her appear even younger than she really was, Lucrezia won the hearts of her future subjects on the very day she entered the city, and had already almost reconciled the House of Este to the relationship. Side by side, Ercole himself and the Duchess Elisabetta followed after the canopy. A troop of " gentlewomen and fair damosels," led by Angela and Girolama Borgia, the Pope's nieces, Adriana dei Mila and one of the Orsini, rode next, with Lucrezia Bentivoglio and many others following in fourteen chariots, of which the first two were drawn by white horses and covered with gold brocade. Then followed some two hundred more *balestrieri*, partly mounted, partly marching on foot. A long array of mules, decked in *morello* and yellow, the bride's colours, brought up the rear, carrying her goods and treasures.

At intervals along the way were the inevitable triumphal arches, painted with allegorical devices and mythological scenes. At four places were representations and recitations, which to Niccolò Cagnolo, who was in the suite of the French ambassador, seemed "most worthy," but Isabella, writing to her husband, declared them not worth mention. The three goddesses with the golden apple, Hercules with the god of Love, Mercury with nymphs appeared in succession, singing verses in honour of the bride and bridegroom ; nymphs and bucephalous men, with satyrs, danced and gamboled round Europa mounted upon the red bull of the House of Borgia. It was evening by the time that the procession reached the great piazza. Instantly all the prisoners in the city were released, while from the Torre di Rigobello and the tower of the Palazzo della Ragione two acrobats flew down on ropes, amidst the applause of the vast crowd that had gathered together in Ferrara from every province of Italy to see the wedding. "So full was the piazza in every part," writes the Ferrarese Diarist, "that if a grain of millet had fallen to earth, it would not have reached the ground." At the head of the great stairway of the palace (the Corte Vecchia), Isabella, in a marvellous robe embroidered over with notes of music, with Laura Gonzaga and the Estensian ladies, received the bride; while, without in the piazza, all the musicians gathered together and played a long harmonious welcome, the *balestrieri* seized the baldacchino, and the servants of Ercole and of Alfonso fought together for the possession of Lucrezia's mule.[1]

Six days of festivities followed, with a series of dramatic representations from Plautus, lightened by masques and morris dances. In the afternoon of the day after Lucrezia's arrival, February 3, there was a great ball in the Sala Grande of the Corte. Lucrezia appeared in all her glory, and "danced many dances in the Roman and Spanish fashion to the sound of her tambourine-players." The crowd was so great that, after the bride had danced her dances alone, there was no room for much general dancing. Then came the comedies. First the Duke exhibited to his guests all the costumes that

---

[1] Our chief contemporary sources for this "most happy and most fortunate" bringing of Lucrezia to Ferrara, and the "pomps and spectacles" of her wedding, are: the *relazione* of Niccolò Cagnolo of Parma, inserted by Zambotto into his chronicle and printed by Antonelli, *Lucrezia Borgia in Ferrara* (an excerpt from Zambotto corresponding to ff. 359-380v of his chronicle); Sanudo, *Diarii*, iv. coll. 222-230; the letters of Isabella d'Este to her husband, in D'Arco, *Notizie di Isabella d' Este*, pp. 303-309; the *Diario Ferrarese*, coll. 410-413.

THE COMING OF MADONNA LUCREZIA

were to be worn by the actors in all the performances, "in order," Isabella wrote to her husband, "that it might be known that these dresses were made on purpose, and that those of one comedy would not have to serve for the others." Then an actor came forward in the person of Plautus, and recited a prologue explaining the arguments of all the five comedies that were to be played during the week. On this first night, the *Epidicus* was represented, with five *bellissime moresche* between the acts, including a mock fight of gladiators and a somewhat trivial allegory of the triumph of virtue. After the dance, on the next evening, the *Bacchides* was given, which, with its *moresche*, lasted five hours. One of these morris-dances included a dance of wild men, with horns of plenty full of some inflammable stuff that blazed up as they moved, and the deliverance of a distressed maiden from a voracious dragon by a knight. The *Miles Gloriosus* was represented on the evening of February 6, with dances of men covered with blazing torches so that they seemed all on fire, horned shepherds butting against each other as they danced, a triumph of Cupid, a dance of jugglers with darts and daggers. The next evening they had the *Asinaria*, with new *moresche* between the acts, dances of satyrs, mimic hunts of beasts and birds, and, at the end, the triumph of Agriculture, a symbolical pageant of the whole life of the fields from sowing to harvest. Women took part in these entertainments as well as men and boys, the total number of actors being over a hundred. On the last day of the festivities, February 8, which happened to be Shrove Tuesday, after the dance in the Sala Grande, there was a sumptuous performance of the *Casina* in another room, at which more than three thousand persons were present. The interludes were especially admired, though to-day they appear somewhat pointless. One apparently symbolized the victory of Love and Music over rude and savage natures, while in another twelve Swiss danced a *moresca*, fighting with their halberds in time to the orchestra.[1]

Isabella's daily letters to the Marquis of Mantua give us a vivid picture of these days, not untinged with a touch of malice. The ladies have always to wait for Lucrezia, because she lingers for hours over her toilet, in order to surpass the Duchess of Urbino and the writer, whereas " I will not pass over in silence, in my own praises, that I am always the first up and dressed." As for the plays and interludes, they bored the Marchesana terribly, and the whole marriage seemed to her to be very cold. " I will not deny," she says, " that your Excellence is taking more pleasure in seeing my little boy every day than I am getting out of these festivities," and she consoles herself by sending kiss after kiss to their *puttino*. As to the *Bacchides*, she found it so long and tedious that she wished herself many times at Mantua. " It seems to me a thousand years till I am there again, both to see your Lordship and my little son, and to get away from here, where there is no pleasure in the world. Your Excellence need not envy me for having come to this wedding, because it has been so cold an affair that I envy those who have remained at Mantua."[2] The *Casina*, she said, " was as lascivious and impure as one can say " ; and indeed her secretary, Benedetto Capilupo, writing to the Marquis, assured him that she had openly shown her displeasure during the performance, and had forbidden any of her damsels to be present at it.[3]

---

[1] Cagnolo, *loc. cit.*, pp. 48–65; Sanudo, *op. cit.*, iv. coll. 225, 226; Gregorovius, pp. 238–250.
[2] Letters of February 3 and 5. D'Arco, *op. cit.*, pp. 307, 308.
[3] Luzio, *I Precettori d'Isabella d'Este*, pp. 36, 37.

THE COMING OF MADONNA LUCREZIA

There was, however, one personage who enjoyed himself immensely throughout these days, and that was Monsignor the ambassador of the Most Christian King. Every one, but especially the ladies, courted him and heaped attentions upon him. On the Friday, February 4, Ercole came with a great train to the Palazzo Bentivoglio, where he was lodged, and took him to Santa Caterina, where, after hearing Mass, they had mystical talk with Lucia, whose wounds were that day gushing out blood afresh. She gave him some pieces of cloth which she had held over them, and then the Duke took him away to inspect his artillery. The next day, Monsignor gave rich presents; to the Duke, a shield of gold enamelled with a St. Francis, "of very subtle workmanship of Paris"; to Lucrezia, a golden rosary exquisitely wrought; to Alfonso and Ferrando, shields like the Duke's, with St. Mary Magdalene and St. Francis, respectively; and "to the most illustrious Madonna Angela Borgia, a most elegant damosel," he gave "a chain or collar of gold, most subtly worked and of notable value." That evening, there being no state ball or performance, Isabella gave a little supper in his honour, the Duchess of Urbino being the chief guest. After supper, "the Lady Marchesana herself with her lute in hand sang several canzonette, with the greatest melody and sweetness"; and when, after an hour's secret talk in her chamber in the presence of two of her damsels, he rose to take his leave, she gave him the gloves which she had on her hands, "which the Lord Ambassador accepted with reverence and love, as proceeding from that most sweet fountain. Verily, they will be preserved by him in a holy place even unto the consummation of the world." [1]

[1] Cagnolo, *loc. cit.*, pp. 52, 54–57.

DUKES AND POETS IN FERRARA

The next morning, the Sunday of the carnival, the Duke sent him a magnificent golden collar, with golden pendants set with rubies, diamonds and large pearls. At High Mass in the Duomo he was the chief personage when the Bishop of Carniola, specially deputed from Rome for the purpose, confirmed the Ferrarese duchy to Don Alfonso, placing the ducal cap upon his head and the blessed sword in his hands in the name of the Pope. It was noticed that neither Duke Ercole himself nor the Venetian orators were present.

On the day after the performance of the last comedy (Ash Wednesday, February 9), the Venetian orators came to take their leave of Lucrezia. They found the Marchesana of Mantua and the Duchess of Urbino with her, and took the occasion to pay their farewell visits to them too, with the usual ceremonious observances and speeches in the name of the Republic. Isabella promptly answered them back in kind, "with such great elegance and prudence that it would have sufficed for every consummate orator," and sounded her husband's praises so eloquently that all that heard were astounded. Elisabetta answered wisely in her turn. But poor Lucrezia, probably painfully conscious that she had neither the wit nor talent of her two rivals, was not equally successful. "Although she has had to do with more men than have your wife and sister," wrote Capilupo to the Marquis, "she got nowhere near their prudent replies."[1]

Duke Ercole, however, appeared more than satisfied with the way the whole affair of the marriage had been carried

---

[1] Letter of February 9 from Capilupo to the Marquis of Mantua. Luzio, *I Precettori d'Isabella d'Este*, pp. 36, 37. By a printer's error, it is dated February 17, in *Mantova e Urbino*, pp. 114, 115. The secretary's equivoque, *ha praticato più homini*, etc., is of course intentional and malicious.

THE COMING OF MADONNA LUCREZIA

through, and his letter to the Pope may be taken as the final reception of Alexander's bastard daughter into the noblest and proudest House of Italy:—

"Before the most illustrious Duchess, our common daughter, arrived here, my firm intention was to caress her and honour her, as is fitting, and not to fail in anything pertaining to singular affection. Now that her Ladyship has come here, she has so satisfied me, by the virtues and worthy qualities that I find in her, that not only am I confirmed in this good disposition, but the desire and intention to do so have greatly increased in me; and so much the more as I see your Holiness, by a brief in your own hand, lovingly suggests this to me. Let your Holiness be of good cheer, because I shall treat the said Duchess in such wise that your Beatitude may know that I hold her Ladyship for the dearest thing that I have in the world." [1]

---

[1] Letter of February 14, 1502. Gregorovius, document 38.

Chapter XII

THE LAST YEARS OF DUKE ERCOLE

THE coming of the Duchess Lucrezia was the last great pageant that Ferrara saw for more than a quarter of a century. It was the turning point in this strange woman's life. Henceforth she appears as a model of propriety, and no breath of scandal again soils her name. She had already completely gained the heart of the old Duke and the enthusiastic admiration of her new subjects. She conquered the aversion of her husband and even, to some extent, won his affection. A little later, that model of Christian chivalry, the chevalier Bayard, and his French knights exalted her as the ideal of noble womanhood. When, after seventeen years, Alfonso announced her death to Federigo Gonzaga, there can be no question of the heartfelt sincerity of his grief for the loss " of so sweet and dear a companion, for such was she to me, by reason of her gracious character and the tender love that there was betwixt us."[1]

Not that this happy result was immediately obtained. Alfonso at first made no pretence of being faithful to his Borgian bride, nor did the Pope expect it of him. Once satisfied that the two continually slept together—the Borgias evidently dreading lest the same trick should be

---

[1] Letter of June 24, 1519. Gregorovius, p. 336. Cf. Yriarte, *Autour des Borgia*, p. 139.

THE LAST YEARS OF DUKE ERCOLE

played upon them as they had served Giovanni Sforza—his Holiness professed himself perfectly contented, and saw no objection to Alfonso, for the rest, taking his pleasure where he chose.[1] And, as a matter of fact, Lucrezia saw but little of her formidable husband in these first years of her married life in Ferrara. Alfonso was either absorbed in his favourite mechanical pursuits, or else absent from the city, travelling in Italy and France, which gave him a wider outlook upon the world than had most of his Italian contemporaries, but naturally did not tend to make him popular with his future subjects.

We have already met the son of the Venetian Visdomino, who had come to inform Ercole and Isabella of the alliance between France and the Signoria.[2] This youth, then nineteen years old, was no other than Pietro Bembo, whose father had represented Venice in Ferrara since 1497, and who was destined in after years to play the part by turns of the Socrates and the literary dictator of the sixteenth century. Young though he was, he was already a leading figure in the literary circles of the city, when the new Duchess came to Ferrara. He fell madly in love with her, and she encouraged his devotion. On Lucrezia's part, indeed, it seems to have been nothing more than an acceptance of the courtly service of the latter-day troubadour to his lady; but it is clear that Bembo's worship was more passionate,

---

[1] Cf. the extract from Beltrando Costabili's dispatch of April 1, 1502. Gregorovius, p. 267. But, after an illness of Lucrezia's in the summer of this year, Alfonso went to Loreto to satisfy a vow made to the Madonna for her recovery. He had vowed to go on foot, but Ercole had him dispensed and sent in a ship. *Minute Ducali* to Beltrando Costabili, October 9, 1502. Archivio di Modena, *Minutario Cronologico*.

[2] See above, p. 346, note.

and Lucrezia seems to have received letters from him which would have seriously compromised both, if they had fallen into the hands of her husband.[1] More frequently, however, Angela Borgia, her cousin and favourite lady-in-waiting, appears to have been at once the screen of the poet's love and his emissary in approaching the Duchess. "They say," wrote the daring lover, when absent from Ferrara, probably at Venice, "that each one has a good Angel who prays for him. I pray that Angel, who can pray for me, that he pray to FF for what he knows that I need. This much know I, that my steadfast and pure faith deserves that you should be the friend of pity towards me. For if I were an Angel, as he is, I should be seized with much pity for each one who loved in the way that I love. With my heart do I now kiss that hand of yours which I shall soon come to kiss with the mouth that ever has your fair name upon it—nay, rather, with this soul, that would in that moment come to my lips to take in this wise a sweet vengeance for its sweet wound."[2] But though Lucrezia accepted his homage and even came to his bedside to visit him in an illness, she had no thought of playing Guenevere to his Lancelot.

[1] Bembo's letters to Lucrezia are contained in vol. viii. of the collected edition of his works (Milan, 1805-13), those openly addressed to her being among the letters " a Principesse e Signore ed altre Gentili Donne scritte," the others (numbered only) among the "lettere giovenili e amorose." Can the compromising letter 91, dated Venice, February 10, 1503, be really to her?

[2] Letter 84. FF is Lucrezia; the allusion to an Angel in the masculine, as a different person from the recipient of the letter, is an intentional piece of mystification. A comparison of this with the other letters (e.g. 86) makes it clear that it is addressed, not to Lucrezia herself, but to Angela. We may here remark that Angela Borgia was a grand-daughter of the Pope's sister, Juana, and therefore second cousin to the Duchess.

THE LAST YEARS OF DUKE ERCOLE

In the meanwhile, Cesare Borgia was not hiding his one talent in the earth. At the beginning of June, 1502, he had young Astorre Manfredi and his boy brother brutally murdered, and their bodies flung into the Tiber. Having thus brought the succession of Faenza to a satisfactory conclusion, he suddenly and treacherously invaded the Duchy of Urbino. The whole duchy was lost in a day, the fortress of San Leo alone holding out for a few weeks, while Duke Guidobaldo, flying for his life with his adopted nephew and heir, the little Francesco Maria della Rovere, and hunted from place to place like a felon, escaped to Ravenna, and thence, through the Ferrarese territory, to Mantua. There he found the Marquis "so affectionate that one could not desire more."[1] Isabella indeed, on the first news of the conquest of Urbino, attempted to obtain for herself a share of the spoils, in the shape of a marble Venus and a Cupid, which, she said, she was sure that Cesare could spare her, "understanding that his Excellence does not take much delight in antiquities";[2] but she was most kind to both Guidobaldo and Elisabetta, and put pressure upon her husband to use all his influence with the King of France on their behalf, while he was in attendance upon him at Milan. A few days later she wrote, wild with sudden terror, hearing that he had spoken ill of the Borgia in the presence of the King and of some of the papal agents, to implore him to take all possible precautions lest Cesare should have him poisoned for his words. For her sake and for that of their child (Cesare's own god-son, be it observed!), let him be more

---

[1] Guidobaldo describes his escape in a long letter of June 28, 1502, from Mantua to the Cardinal Giuliano. Alvisi, document 60.
[2] Letter of June 30, 1502, to the Cardinal Ippolito. *Ibid.*, document 61.

careful at table and have his food properly tasted. "My Lord, do not make mock of this letter of mine, nor say that women are cowardly and always afraid; for the malignity of these men is far greater than my fear or your Lordship's courage."[1]

Remembering her own happy visit to Urbino on her way to Ferrara a few months before, Lucrezia expressed the greatest sorrow at the misfortunes of Guidobaldo and Elisabetta, and protested that, to the utmost of her power, she would never fail them.[2] Ercole, however, would not commit himself. " You will have heard," he wrote to Alfonso, who, like the Marquis of Mantua, was with the King at Milan, " of the acquisition which the most illustrious Duke of Romagna has made of the Duchy of Urbino. It can well be that men speak variously of this affair there, as also they do here. We have therefore thought well to warn you that, if you speak about it, you speak in such a way that you do not offend the Most Christian Majesty or any of his friends, nor the said most illustrious Duke of Romagna; but with modesty and wisely, so that no one can take exception to what you say, and according as in your prudence you shall know what to do, you being there on the spot."[3]

France and Spain were now about to rend each other for the spoils of conquered Naples. Ercole, who, besides sending Alfonso and Sigismondo, had personally met and paid his homage to King Louis in the short visit that the latter had made to the Milanese duchy this summer, natur-

---

[1] Letter of July 23, 1502. Luzio and Renier, *Mantova e Urbino*, pp. 136, 137.
[2] Luzio and Renier, *op. cit.*, p. 125.
[3] *Minute Ducali* of June 30, 1502. Archivio di Modena, *Carteggi dei Principi*.

THE LAST YEARS OF DUKE ERCOLE

ally attached himself to the side of France. By a letter dated from Milan, on September 22, the King invested " our well-beloved kinsman, the Duke of Ferrara," with the town of Cottignola—very much against the will of the inhabitants. They made a hostile demonstration against the ducal commissary when he entered the town, on October 25; the contadini joined with the townsfolk, men, women and children, in shouting " Franza, Franza," until the royal procurator, Cesare Guaschi, reassured them by a glowing account of the clemency and benignity of Ercole's rule.[1] Their special fear seems to have been lest they should be put under the commissary of Lugo, or some other Ferrarese official in Romagna. In the following year, Ercole sent some six thousand *balestrieri* and men-at-arms to Mantua, to join the royal army that was being gathered in Lombardy under Gonzaga's command; and, although broken in health, he went himself to Parma to confer with the commander-in-chief, la Trémoille. The Ferrarese contingent, under Giulio Tassoni and others, was in the French army that, at the end of 1503, Gonsalvo crushed at the Garigliano.

Lucrezia had by this time completely settled down in her position as Duchess of Ferrara—the title already given to her in anticipation by all the Court and by Duke Ercole himself. At the carnival of 1503, when the *Menaechmi* was represented, the chroniclers describe her as sitting by the Duke's side, "most ornately attired, with great jewels."

---

[1] See documents in Alvisi, pp. 540, 541. Ercole had previously instructed his envoy to ask the King for Cottignola, on the plea that, although it was held by the Duchy of Milan, it had paid no taxes to Milan, and had formerly belonged to the Estensi. *Istruzione per Francia a Giovanni Valla*, August 29, 1500. Archivio di Modena, *Carteggio degli Ambasciatori—Francia.*

DUKES AND POETS IN FERRARA

The Holy Week of this year was celebrated with much solemnity, as was always done in Ferrara when the conditions of Italy were more than usually disturbed and threatening. On Maundy Thursday, April 13, the Duke gave a sumptuous dinner to a hundred and fifty poor men in the Sala Grande of the Palace, himself with his sons and chief courtiers waiting upon them at table. Afterwards, on his knees, he washed and wiped the feet of all, and gave them presents of clothes and money, while his choristers sang the antiphons prescribed by the Church, beginning with the *mandatum novum* : " A new commandment I give unto you : that you love one another, as I have loved you, saith the Lord." On Good Friday, after the sermon and Mass, the whole Passion of Christ was represented on a great stage erected in the Duomo, Lucrezia and her ladies sitting with Ercole on a raised platform opposite. Near the roof a Heaven had been constructed, which opened and from which an Angel descended with the chalice to Christ who prayed in the Garden. Before the high altar was Mount Calvary, with the Crucifixion. At the other end of the stage was the mouth of Hell, in the form of the head of a gigantic serpent, out of which trooped the ducal choristers, robed as the fathers in Limbo, " sweetly singing lauds." " Everything was done in praiseworthy fashion. It lasted five hours, with much devotion."[1]

A few days after Easter, Isabella came from Mantua, received by Lucrezia with all possible demonstrations of love and affection. There were more miracle-plays performed in the Duomo, at which the two ladies and the Duke were present. The Annunciation, in which the Angel Gabriel

[1] Zambotto, ff. 389*v*, 390.

descended to the Blessed Virgin in a wonderful rain of light, especially moved Isabella's not too facile admiration, and it was followed by the Visitation to St. Elizabeth and the Dream of Joseph. The whole was in much the same style as the representation on Good Friday had been. On another day, they had the Adoration of the Magi and the Massacre of the Innocents.[1] In consequence of the recent death of the Duke's half-brother, Rinaldo d' Este, the customary horse-race for the feast of St. George, April 24, was not run; but Ercole instead gave the prize, the *palio* of gold brocade, " to the monastery of the sisters of Santa Caterina where Suora Lucia of the Stigmata lives."[2] The Duke was much concerned with Lucia's wants and wishes in this year, and was in correspondence with his nephew, the Bishop of Adria, on the subject. On June 18, we find him writing to the latter at Viterbo, inclosing a communication "which is of very great importance," to be sent on instantly with all speed to Bartolommeo Bresciano at Narni. The mysterious inclosure, treated thus as though it were an urgent political document, is simply this:—

" Herewith we send thee a letter that the mother Suora Lucia writes to Suora Anna; we would have thee give it to her instantly, and from it you will see all that she writes

[1] Letter from Isabella d' Este to the Marquis of Mantua, April 24, 1503. D'Arco, *Notizie*, pp. 310, 311; Zambotto, ff. 391*v*, 392.
[2] Zambotto, f. 392. In the previous February, Berardo da Recanati, physician of the Pope and bishop-elect of Venosa, had examined the stigmata in the presence of Ercole, Lucrezia, the papal vicar-general Pietro Gambo, and Guglielmo Raimondo (a nephew of Alexander), and reported that they had all been profoundly edified by Lucia's conversation. Document in Giacomo Marcianese, *Narratione*, pp. 204–207, and Ponsi, *op. cit.*, pp. 216–219.

to her. Wherefore, we will and commit to you that you should execute all that is contained in that letter."[1]

Although the Cardinal Juan Borgia held the Bishopric of Ferrara, he never set foot in the city. On bad terms with his papal uncle, he still remained in Rome, heaping up wealth. Paolo Cappello had told the Venetians that the Cardinal " would gladly lead the life of a merchant; he would like to have thirty thousand ducats on his desk, and lend them out at usury. He is most miserly; he thinks much of a ducat."[2] This was a dangerous kind of life to lead in the Rome of the Borgias, especially when the Pope was your heir and Cesare needed money for his mercenary soldiers, to complete his conquest of the rebellious feudatories of the Church. At the beginning of August, the Cardinal suddenly died, and the Pope succeeded to the vast wealth that he had left behind him. Antonio Giustinian, who had replaced Cappello as Venetian orator in Rome, wrote to the Doge that it was believed that the Cardinal had been poisoned by Cesare.[3] His nephew, Guglielmo Raimondo, the captain of the Palatine Guard, died about the same time. From a window of the Vatican, Alexander watched

---

[1] Archivio di Modena, *Minutario Cronologico*, June 18, 1503. The phrasing is a little ambiguous, but I take it that it is from the letter and not from Anna that Bresciano is to have the explanation. Lucia's letter has not been preserved, but presumably it was about getting more nuns, as there had been fresh desertions from the convent.

[2] Sanudo, *Diarii*, iii. col. 843.

[3] Dispatches of August 2 and 3, 1503. *Dispacci di Antonio Giustinian*, ii. pp. 92-94. " It is publicly affirmed that he, too, has been sent by the way along which have gone all the others, after they have grown right plump, and the fault of this is laid to the Duke's door." The Cardinal Michiel had certainly been poisoned by Cesare in the previous year, and possibly the Cardinal Ferrari. Cf. Pastor, iii. pp. 464-466.

the funeral procession. "This month is deadly for fat people," he muttered. A dark bird of some kind flew in to the room, and fell down at his feet. The terrified Pontiff fled into his bedroom, repeating again and again : " An evil omen, an evil omen is this."[1]

A fortnight later, a thrill of exultation ran through all in Italy who looked for righteousness. Pope Alexander VI was dead. He died on August 18, of a fever contracted at the famous supper at the villa of the Cardinal of Corneto; and Cesare himself lay at death's door. The contemporary legend of the two, father and son, having been poisoned by the wine that they had prepared for their host, is now rejected by all serious historians—relegated to the same category as the wonderful account given by the Marquis of Mantua to Isabella of how the devil in person had come to claim the soul of his creature, who had sold himself to him for the Popedom and whose time was now expired.[2]

Ercole was usually cautious in his written utterances, but this time he spoke plainly. " To make thee clear about that which thou art asked by many," he wrote to Gian Giorgio Seregnio, his ambassador at Milan, " whether we are sorry for the death of the Pope, we assure thee that it does not displease us in any respect ; on the contrary, for the honour of our Lord God and for the universal utility of Christendom, we have for a long while desired that the Divine goodness and providence should give us a good and exemplary pastor, and that so great a scandal should be taken away from the Church. Nor could our own private interests make us desire otherwise, because the honour of God and the universal weal will preponderate with us. But we tell thee

[1] Sigismondo de' Conti, ii. p. 267 ; Yriarte, *César Borgia*, ii. p: 152.
[2] Gregorovius, document 49.

further that never was there a Pope from whom we had not more favour and satisfaction than from this, even after the affinity contracted with him ; we have only and hardly had what he was bound to, for which we did not depend upon his faith; in nothing else, great or small, have we been gratified by him. This we believe to have come about in great part through the fault of the Duke of Romagna, who, because he could not use us as he would have wished, has treated us as a stranger, nor ever been open with us nor communicated his proceedings to us; neither have we communicated ours to him. And latterly, since he inclines to the Spaniards and sees us loyal to France, we have never hoped for any advantage either from the Pope or from his Lordship. Therefore we are not sorry for this death, and were expecting nothing but evil from the greatness of the said Lord Duke. We wish you to communicate this our secret exactly to the Lord Grand Master,[1] as we would not have our mind concealed from his Lordship; but speak discreetly about it to others, and then send back this letter to the reverend Messer Gian Luca our counsellor."[2]

Lucrezia's position at Ferrara was not a pleasant one at this juncture—and was only rendered tolerable by the tact and kindness of Ercole. The King of France openly hinted that she might be repudiated. "I know," he said to the Ferrarese ambassador, "that you have never been pleased at that marriage; this Madama Lucrezia is not even the effective wife of Don Alfonso."[3] She probably heard something of the horrible stories of her father's death that spread through Italy, and certainly realized the danger in which

---

[1] Chaumont, the French governor of Milan.
[2] Letter of August 24, 1503. Gregorovius, document 46.
[3] Gregorovius, pp. 274, 275.

THE LAST YEARS OF DUKE ERCOLE

her brother was. Bembo has painted in touching words her appearance in the first burst of her misery, in her darkened room, robed in black and with the marks of abundant weeping on her face.[1] But no ungenerous thoughts seem to have found place in the hearts of the Estensian sovereigns. In spite of what he had written to Milan, Ercole lent ear to Cesare's appeal through the Ferrarese ambassador in Rome, and—seeing that the only choice was between him and the Venetians—sent Pandolfo Collenuccio into Romagna to prevail upon his subjects to remain faithful. Nevertheless, Duke Guidobaldo returned to Urbino and Giovanni Sforza re-entered Pesaro in triumph. At the beginning of September, Cesare was conveyed in a litter to Nepi, where he put himself under the protection of the army of France, which was in the neighbourhood under the nominal command of the Marquis of Mantua. A few days later, Ercole wrote to congratulate him on his convalescence and on his wisdom in throwing in his lot with the French. "As to your affairs in Romagna," he wrote, "we have sent a suitable person to those peoples, to do what your Lordship, before you left Rome, had us besought by the letters of our ambassador there, to keep their minds well disposed and steadfast in their devotion to your Excellence. As you will have heard, our men-at-arms are in the camp of the Most Christian King. We are certain that the authority and will of his Most Christian Majesty will make such provision that your Lordship, where need shall arise, will be succoured by his protection."[2]

[1] Letter to the Duchess, of August 22, 1503 (*Opere*, vol. viii. pp. 5–7). Cf. Canello, *Storia della Letteratura Italiana nel secolo xvi.*, p. 24, for real date of the letter.

[2] Letter of September 15, 1503, from Codigoro. Alvisi, *op. cit.*, pp. 581, 582.

DUKES AND POETS IN FERRARA

In the downfall of her House, Lucrezia's little son Rodrigo had lost his duchy, and even his life was threatened. The Cardinal of Cosenza, his guardian, proposed to sell all his goods and convey him in safety to Spain. Ercole, in a very kind and fatherly letter, urged Lucrezia to agree to the Cardinal's proposals :—

"We have had the letter of your Ladyship, together with that of Monsignor the most reverend Cardinal of Cosenza directed to you, which you have sent us, which we send back to you with this of ours, and which has not been read by any person save by us; and we have noted the very prudent writing of your Ladyship and of the said most reverend Cardinal, who is moved by so many good reasons that one cannot but judge that he is loving and wise. Wherefore, after considering the whole, it seems to us that your Ladyship can and ought to consent to all that the said most reverend Monsignor proposes to do. We think that your Ladyship owes him some gratitude, for the demonstration and proof of so much cordial love that he clearly bears to you and to the most illustrious Don Rodorico your son, who, one can say, has been preserved in life by his means. And although Don Rodorico will be somewhat severed from your Ladyship, it is better to be so far away and safe, than near with the danger in which he evidently would be; nor, because of this distance, will the love between you be at all diminished. When he has grown up, he will be able according to the condition of the times to decide on his own course, whether to return to Italy or to stay; and it is a good provision which Monsignor the Cardinal suggests, to sell his movable goods and purchase there, to supply his needs, increasing his income, as he says he will do. Wherefore, on every consideration, as we have said, it seems to us

THE LAST YEARS OF DUKE ERCOLE

that it is well to agree to his will. Nevertheless if to your Ladyship, who is most prudent, it should seem otherwise, we yield to your better judgment."[1]

Needless to say that Ercole was profoundly interested in the election of a successor to Pope Alexander. It would have been the first conclave in which a member of the House of Este had taken part; but Ippolito fell from his horse on the way to Rome, and was laid up at Florence. Ercole, by letters to Bartolommeo de' Cavallieri and to King Louis himself, pledged his son to do his utmost for the election of " a good pastor and one that would please the Most Christian Majesty," but regretted that Ippolito's fall would make it impossible for him actually to vote.[2] He wrote to him from Belriguardo, that he had heard from the Grand Master (Chaumont) at Milan that the King wished to do all that was possible to secure the election of the Cardinal of Rouen, " in which his Majesty and the said Grand Master desire your vote and your work." Although the news of his accident has reached Milan, Chaumont still seems to hope that Ippolito can have himself brought to Rome in time for the conclave. " It would please us much if your most reverend Lordship were in such a state that you could do it, because this is a very great occasion to be able to satisfy the Most Christian Majesty and the most reverend and most illustrious Monsignor the Legate." But, if he really cannot move, let him pay all the honour that he possibly can to the Cardinals of the French faction (the Legate Amboise himself,

---

[1] Letter of October 4, from Codigoro. Archivio di Modena, *Carteggio dei Principi*. It is not quite accurately transcribed in Gregorovius, document 50.

[2] *Minute Ducali* of August 28, 1503. Archivio di Modena, *Minutario Cronologico*.

DUKES AND POETS IN FERRARA

Ascanio Sforza, who had been released from his French captivity on condition of supporting Amboise's candidature, and the Cardinal of Aragon) when they pass through Florence, "not omitting to inform his most illustrious and most reverend Lordship of what you were going to do in favour of his election, and also that you had been exhorted about this by us, and that we had bidden you follow and do all that you understood to be the will of the Most Christian King."[1]

Finding his own elevation impossible, the Cardinal of Rouen supported the nomination of the excellent old Cardinal of Siena, Francesco Piccolomini, who was elected Pope on September 22, and took the title of Pius III, in memory of his uncle. The new Pontiff had always shown himself most friendly towards the Estensi, and the Duke and Cardinal shared in the general satisfaction. Ercole wrote to implore Ippolito to send him every minute detail of the way in which the election had been carried out. "Suppose that we know nothing about it, and that we would fain understand it and see it as if we had been present. Assume that we are entirely ignorant of this elevation, and that we must needs be informed about it from the alpha to the omega."[2] By a brief dated October 8, the day of his own coronation, the new Pontiff conferred upon Ippolito the vacant bishopric of Ferrara. Ten days later, to the genuine grief of all Rome, Pius died.

Ercole was quite resolved, for once, to have a voice in the election of the new Pontiff. He dispatched a long letter to Ippolito—who was, by now, sufficiently recovered from

[1] *Minute* to Ippolito of August 29, 1503. Archivio di Modena, *Carteggio dei Principi*. It will be remembered that the Cardinal Amboise of Rouen was Papal Legate in France.
[2] *Minute Ducali* of September 24, 1503. Archivio di Modena, *Carteggio dei Principi*.

his fall—concerning the vote he was to give in the coming conclave. "We make first a general presupposition," he writes, " that we should not be pleased at the election of a Cardinal who was not an Italian; and, therefore, your Lordship, if you wish to conform with our views, must not give your voice to any one who is not an Italian, excepting the most reverend Cardinal of Rouen, who, it cannot be denied, is out of the question for the causes known to your Lordship." Among the Italians, he would greatly like Naples (Caraffa), Santa Prassede (Pallavicino), or the Cardinal of Alessandria (San Giorgio); but Ippolito must be careful not to offend Amboise by his vote. He is to do what he can, in an underhand way, against the Cardinal of San Pietro in Vincoli, Giuliano della Rovere. "If Rouen should use his power for San Pietro in Vincoli, you can warn him that San Pietro in Vincoli has always been most friendly to the Venetians, and they have more confidence in him and would favour him more than any other Cardinal, and they have had the votes of Grimani and Cornaro given him, as you know, and that therefore it is to be feared that, if he be made Pope, he will not be a good Frenchman, but rather a Venetian." He is, therefore, to dissuade Amboise from this course—as also because Giuliano is opposed to Ercole himself in the matter of Cento and Pieve (which the Duke was still trying to get separated from the diocese of Bologna). But " in the case that your Lordship should see that the lot has to fall to him, and that your vote could not prevent it, we should praise you if you could give what you could not sell, that is, if you should gratify him by voting for him." But he must first speak with the Cardinal of Rouen, and be guided by his wishes and intentions.[1]

[1] *Minute* of October 23, 1503. Archivio di Modena, *Minutario*

DUKES AND POETS IN FERRARA

Ippolito, however, had but one course open to him.]
conclave was the shortest in the whole history of the Papa
On the very day that it opened, October 31, Giuliano de
Rovere was practically unanimously elected Pope, and to
the title of Julius II. By magnanimous promises (which,
we shall see, he did not keep), he had bought the support
Cesare Borgia, who commanded the votes of the Spani
Cardinals, and the election, though less scandalously cc
ducted, was hardly less simoniacal than had been that
Giuliano's hated enemy, Alexander VI.[1] Ippolito had giv
his vote with such grace and dexterity, that all parties ha
been pleased, and his father was greatly delighted with h
entire conduct in this emergency. " We could not hav
felt greater satisfaction," he writes, " and we think tha
your Lordship has this time shown the good talent an
dexterity that you have. We commend you, and, if ou
interests were not yours, and yours ours, we should than
you."[2]

The newly created Pontiff received Ippolito's first act c
homage with much graciousness, and declared that he ha
always been a staunch friend to the Estensi. He professe
special anxiety to see his godson, Don Ferrando, who ha
indeed started from Ferrara for Rome with a few horseme

Cronologico. The next day, Ercole sent an urgent message, pos
haste, to Ippolito, bidding him by all means go to the conclav
" especially as the Cardinal of Rouen urges you to this," and carr
out the instructions in his former letter. Letter of October 24. *Ibid*
Carteggio dei Principi. Outside, to encourage the couriers, a gallow
is drawn, with the suggestive words *sub poena furcarum, cito—cit*
—cito.

[1] See Pastor, iii. pp. 520-522.
[2] Letter of November 5, 1503. Archivio di Modena, *Carteggi*
dei Principi.

THE LAST YEARS OF DUKE ERCOLE

as soon as the news of the election had reached him. The official Ferrarese embassy, to join with Beltrando Costabili, the ordinary ambassador at the Papal Court, in presenting the Duke's congratulations, arrived a little later; it included Gian Luca Pozzi, Antonio Costabili, and Giovanni Francesco Maria Rangoni.

The Venetians had taken advantage of Cesare's broken fortunes to occupy as many towns in Romagna as they could lay hands on, under the plea of liberating these places from the tyranny of the Borgia; "with great offence to God," as the Pope put it, "and injury to us and to this Holy See." Fano, Faenza and Rimini surrendered to their forces in succession, while Cesare's agents still held Forlimpopoli and the citadels of Bertinoro, Forlì and Cesena. The Pope remonstrated with the Venetian ambassador, Antonio Giustinian, insisting that all those places must be restored to the Church; in a strongly-worded letter to the Doge, Leonardo Loredan, he declared that nothing could make him swerve from this resolution, and that no composition was possible.[1] When Cesare refused to surrender what was left to him, he had him arrested and brought to Rome as a prisoner. Julius at first appears to have thought of handing him over to Ercole, to be kept at Ferrara until he had the citadels in his hands. But Ercole gave an evasive answer, said that he must first know what he would have to do if the Valentino did not yield up the fortresses in accordance with his promise—his real motive being, according to the Venetian ambassador, that he wished to delay his decision until he could hear from the King of France and be guided

---

[1] Giustinian, *Dispacci*, ii. pp. 285, 288-292; Brief of January 10, 1504, *Archivio Vaticano*, xxxix. 22, ff. 7v, 8.

by his Majesty's wishes in the matter.¹ Julius then i[m]
prisoned the fallen terror in the Borgia Tower, in the ve[ry]
rooms in which he had murdered Alfonso of Biscegl[ie]
and only released him on the condition that the citadels [in]
question should be surrendered within forty days. [By]
March, all had been recovered, excepting that of Fo[rlì]
where the castellano—in secret understanding with Cesare—
still flaunted the banner of the Borgia Bull, imperturbab[le]
alike to papal threats and proffered papal bribes. T[he]
Venetians and the last descendant of the former rulers [of]
the place, Lodovico degli Ordelaffi, were likewise treati[ng]
with him, each trying to outbid the other in their attemp[ts]
to purchase the citadel.² Peaceable measures being u[n]
availing, Julius demanded artillery from Ercole, a[nd]
announced his intention of taking the rebellious fortress b[y]
storm.

May saw the close of Cesare's career in Italy. On h[is]
release from Rome he had gone to Naples, which had by no[w]
fallen into the hands of the Spaniards, with a safe condu[ct]
from Gonsalvo de Cordova, the great captain. There, at [the]
Pope's instigation, he was made a prisoner. In a brief [to]
Gonsalvo, dated May 11, 1504, the Pope, hearing that [he]
has been sending money to the castellano of Forlì, whom h[e]
had secretly exhorted not to restore the fortress, and tha[t]
the latter " has begun to bombard our city of Forlì with h[is]
artillery, and does not cease from acclaiming the name of th[e]

¹ Giustinian, *loc. cit.*, ii. pp. 364, 366, 378.
² "It is grievous to us to buy this citadel which is ours," wrot[e]
the Pope on March 9 to his commissaries, the Archbishop of Ragus[a]
and Pietro Paolo de Callio, " but we think that lighter than to allo[w]
it to pass into the hands of others. Wherefore, if it cannot be don[e]
otherwise, you may promise him in our name 15,000 golden ducats.'
Archivio Vaticano, xxxix. 22, f. 30.

THE LAST YEARS OF DUKE ERCOLE

Duke in contempt and hatred of us," urges him " so to confine and coerce the Duke, who has been received under thy protection, that he may be unable to compass anything against our state and that of the Holy Roman Church," and to force him to have the citadel surrendered without any excuse or delay, " for it lies in the will and power of the Duke." [1]

For a while the castellano proved obdurate. Ercole himself now interposed, urging him to yield; but the man professed himself sceptical as to Cesare's captivity, and made difficulties about surrendering into Ercole's hands. Duke Guidobaldo advanced with the papal troops, and at length in August, by Ercole's intervention, backed up by an order from Cesare (extorted by Gonsalvo with a promise of his liberation), the citadel was surrendered to the papal authorities.[2] In spite of Gonsalvo's pledge, the Borgia was sent as a prisoner to Spain. Lucrezia was wild with apprehension for her brother's safety, fearing even for his life. " Be of good heart," wrote Ercole to her, " for even as we love you sincerely and with every tenderness of heart as our daughter, so shall we never fail him, and we wish to be to him a good father and good brother in everything." But he could only give her vague expectations, and bid her " hope

---

[1] Brief to Gonsalvo de Cordova, May 11, 1504. *Archivio Vaticano* xxxix. 22, ff. 51*v*, 52. In part published by Pastor, iii. doc. 69.

[2] In a brief to Ercole, of June 19, the Pope thanks him for what he is doing, and expresses his astonishment that the castellano does not believe his (Ercole's) assertion concerning the arrest of Cesare; he says that Gonsalvo will send a man to Forlì to order him to surrender, in the name of the King and Queen of Spain, and urges Ercole to continue what he has begun, so that the said citadel may be restored to the Church through him. *Archivio Vaticano*, xxxix. 22, f. 100.

in our Lord God who does not abandon whoso trusts Him."[1]

Things had not hitherto run quite smoothly between the Duke of Ferrara and the new Pontiff. The concession made to the former by Pope Alexander, on the occasion of Lucrezia's marriage, were only recognized under protest by the Roman Curia. Ercole had still to labour to get the complete cession of Cento and La Pieve, with the separation of these places from the diocese of Bologna, confirmed. When on the vigil of the Feast of the Apostles, June 28, 1504—the first occasion since the death of Alexander—Beltrando Costabili went at the hour of vespers to the Camera Apostolica, to present the hundred gold ducats of the tribute and demand the receipt, he had a bad reception from the Cardinal Camarlingo and the other papal officials. The Fiscal Procurator said that the Duke was wont to pay 4,150 ducats as tribute, and professed to know nothing about the reduction to one hundred. Costabili answered that the Duke had the reduction granted by a very full apostolical Bull, and showed the receipt for last year's tribute, which he had brought with him. The Auditor of the Camera, " who is a terrible man," wanted to see it, and then, turning to the Camarlingo, made some frivolous objections to its validity. Finally, however, the Cardinal accepted the money under protest, " without prejudice of the Camera Apostolica," as the reduction had not been confirmed by the Pope.[2] Julius had even suspected that Ercole was favouring Lodovico degli Ordelaffi in his

---

[1] *Minute Ducali* of October 20 (year illegible, but presumably 1504). Archivio di Modena, *Carteggio dei Principi*.
[2] Dispatches of B. Costabili to Ercole, June 28 and August 4, 1504. Archivio di Modena, *Carteggio degli Ambasciatori—Roma*.

THE LAST YEARS OF DUKE ERCOLE

designs upon Forlì.[1] But the Duke's good offices in getting the obstinate citadel surrendered to the papal forces, and his promises of artillery and ammunition to the Duke of Urbino, completely changed the situation, and the Pope expressed his warmest gratitude. "Write to his Excellence," he said to Monsignor Beltrando, "that we are obliged to him, and that, should the chance arise, we shall do the same for him. Others, indeed, have promised to do things and have said words; but his Excellence has both said and done. Right glad are we that this occasion has arisen, to let us know upon whom we can rely in our needs."[2]

The chief dramatic novelty of this year in Ferrara had been the *Jacob et Joseph*, which had been written for the purpose by Pandolfo Collenuccio. It was played in Lent, on the Thursday in Passion Week and on Palm Sunday, in the Duomo, with unusually elaborate mountings and with a representation of Paradise in which the ducal choristers filled the parts of Angels.[3] This was Pandolfo's last achievement. The restored Giovanni Sforza (whose natural subject he was) regarded him as a traitor for his adherence

[1] Hearing that Giovanni Francesco Maria Rangoni had gone to Forlì and offered financial assistance to the Ordelaffi, the Pope had sent a strongly-worded brief to Ercole, bidding him clear himself from the suspicion—which, said his Holiness, everybody but himself entertained—that he was privy to the transaction, by recalling Rangoni at once, and either not allow him to give the money to Lodovico or, if given, make him take it back as soon as possible. He followed it up by a furious order to Rangoni himself to leave Forlì instantly. Briefs of March 12 and 18, 1504. *Archivio Vaticano*, xxxix. 22, ff. 31v, 32. Lodovico died at Ravenna at the end of May; he was a bastard brother of that Antonio Maria degli Ordelaffi whom Ercole had befriended in the days of Sixtus IV.

[2] Dispatch of B. Costabili to Ercole, August 20, 1504. Archivio di Modena, *Carteggio degli Ambasciatori—Roma*.

[3] Zambotto, f. 400; Gaspary, ii. part i. p. 205.

to Cesare Borgia. In July, he lured him to Pesaro; and, o[n] the plea that Pandolfo had slandered him in order to cur[ry] favour with the Borgia, in spite of the intervention of t[he] Marquis of Mantua, he had him cruelly and perfidious[ly] strangled.

Since the accession of Pope Julius, Ercole had grown di[s]satisfied with the conduct of the Cardinal Ippolito. H[e] considered that his son was neglecting his interests at th[e] Papal Court, and, in December, had written him a strongly worded letter of rebuke. Things grew more serious in th[e] spring, when Ippolito was at Ferrara. A messenger fro[m] Rome penetrated into the Cardinal's room, to deliver [a] papal brief or admonition concerning the surrendering o[f] certain benefices which the Pope had conferred upon one o[f] his favourites; Ippolito was furious, and had the unfortunate messenger soundly beaten. The Duke ordered him instantly to write to Rome and apologize, under pain of banishment from his duchies. The Cardinal haughtily refused, and, on April 9, left Ferrara and fled to Mantua. The next day, Ercole sent a letter after him. He had heard, he said. that he talked of going to Spain. If he really means this, " as we look more to your interests than at your conduct towards us," he reminds him that he must pay his respects to the King of France on the way; otherwise, he will run great risk of losing his archbishopric of Milan (which Ippolito still held in addition to the see of Ferrara), as the King will think himself slighted. " After that, you can go to Spain or wherever you like." The Cardinal is to answer by the same messenger, as to what he intends to do in the matter.[1]

In answer to this, Ercole got a letter in Ippolito's own

[1] *Minute Ducali* of April 10, 1504. Archivio di Modena, *Carteggio dei Principi*. Cf. Zambotto, f. 400v.

THE LAST YEARS OF DUKE ERCOLE

hand, and "full of insolence," as he said. The Cardinal begins by declaring that he had intended to hold no further communications with his father. It was most presumptuous of those persons who had spoken of his intention of going to Spain. He thanks the Duke for his suggestion about going first to the Court of the Most Christian King, but, not having made up his mind, he cannot for the present give him a definite answer. "I am greatly astonished that in this matter your Excellence has made a show of caring for my interests, if not for my honour (which is a thing of much greater importance than seven churches of Milan); whereas you have done your best to make every manifestation of the opposite. As to what you say concerning my bearing towards you, I say that—as any one, who wishes to judge this without passion, can see clearly and perceive the effects —it has always been good, and typical of a good son. In everything that has happened, I have always postponed my own private advantage for your service and benefit."
He complains bitterly of the Duke's injustice in thus banishing him from his State. "Although you could have accomplished what you wanted, without doing me shame and damage, you have sought my dishonour with as much diligence as though you were going to gain a State for yourself, not taking into consideration who it is that you are treating in this way and for what cause. You do not care for what every one will say who shall hear this, nor for the bad example that you have given your successors, to treat their sons and brothers in the same fashion for every trivial difference and trumpery disagreement. If this thing were done in the future, it could easily result in the total ruin of the State; which, however, would be caused only by the example that in your time you have given. Since

it is your desire that I should never see you again, I w
satisfy your wish nor offend your eyes in any way; for yo
have made me of such a nature that I should not desire
go into the presence of Christ, unless I hoped to be welcome
by Him." Let his Excellence take care of his health, an
forgive him if, in his own defence, he is compelled to tell th
whole truth about their quarrel, wherever he goes. "Witl
all my power, I pray you to deign to give me your blessin
for this my journey."[1]

"In the first line of your letter," wrote the Duke i
reply, "you say that, in spite of what you had resolved
you have written. Verily, it seems to us that the beginning
of your letter corresponds with the rest, and that you wish
to show us at the outset your bad will. We know not which
would be worse, to have written to us in the way you have
or not to have deigned to answer us." "We are astonished
at these impertinent words of yours. The favour that we
asked of you, to write to Rome, was not in the least against
your honour. Nay, we should have believed that, not
merely in a tiny thing like this was, but if we had urged
you to renounce this bishopric of Ferrara, you would have
done it to please us, right willingly." It is not true that he
has behaved like a good son. "Excepting the vote that
you gave to the Holiness of the Pope, with the will of the
most reverend Cardinal of Rouen, which was well done, you
have never satisfied us in anything of importance. And
if, indeed, it seemed that you began to favour our interests
in Cento and La Pieve, you then suddenly departed from
Rome, without our leave, and in spite of the need of those
affairs of ours." Ippolito has always been retrograde to

[1] Autograph letter of the Cardinal Ippolito, dated Mantua, April 12, 1504. Archivio di Modena, *Carteggio dei Principi*.

his wishes, although Ercole has got him the cardinalate and almost all the benefices that he has. "Since you have been disobedient and ungrateful towards us, you need not wonder that we have dismissed you from our State; because, bearing yourself towards us as you do, we do not think that you are worthy to be near us. As to your saying that, by our treatment of you, we have given a bad example to our successors, and that from such a thing the ruin of the State could follow: we say that we are, nevertheless, content to have done this, and that it should pass as an example for our successors—for those of them, at least, who have sons that are not obedient." "We know not how it befits a Cardinal to say that you would not desire to go into the presence of Christ, unless you hoped to be welcomed by Him. But we understand that you wish to behave towards our Lord God as you do towards us, and towards the others in this world. You do evil to take Christ's name in vain, with small reverence and with such haughtiness as you do." As to his threat of speaking out, let him tell the truth wherever he goes, and every one will judge that he is in the wrong. "As to our benediction, which in the end you pray us to give you for this journey of yours, we tell you that we do not deny it you; nay, we give it to you willingly, and we would that it had the power to make you bring forth good fruit. But, since virtue cannot operate well in things that are ill disposed, we know not what effect it can have upon you—although we would that it were good. And we fear that our Lord God, since you do not reverence His Majesty and are disobedient to your father, will give you some fitting chastisement, although we should be very sorry for it."[1]

[1] *Minute Ducali* of April 14, 1504. Archivio di Modena, *Carteggio dei*

DUKES AND POETS IN FERRARA

But the storm soon subsided. On Sunday, April 14, (the very day on which Ercole was dictating this letter), the Marquis of Mantua arrived unexpectedly at the palace at the hour of Mass. He had come down the Po in a gondola with twelve oars, to reconcile the Cardinal with the Duke, in which he succeeded without difficulty. Ippolito returned to Ferrara, and the festivities for the feast of San Giorgio passed off with exceptional success. The horse-race was run in the presence of the Duke, the Marquis and the Marchesana Isabella, the *palio* being given to the latter, one of whose horses had come in first, " with very great gladness of the people; and after dinner were recited comedies." [1] This was the last festivity and entertainment of Duke Ercole's reign.

In this April, before their father's reconciliation with Ippolito, Don Alfonso had started upon a tour, accompanied by Antonio Costabili and others, to make acquaintance with various European sovereigns. From Paris he went to Brussels, where he met the future Emperor Charles, and thence he came to England and was kindly received by our Henry VII.[2] On his return to France, an urgent summons reached him to hasten back to Italy, for that his father was dying. In the light of future events, the entry in Sanudo's

Principi. The reader by this time will have had enough of Ercole's correspondence with his sons, but I have printed another letter from the Modena Archives in Appendix II., document 15, written at an earlier date to Ippolito on the duties of a Cardinal, because of the instructive contrast that it affords with the famous advice of Lorenzo de' Medici to the young Cardinal Giovanni.

[1] Zambotto, f. 400v.
[2] "From an English courtier, who had been informed of it by letters of the 15th of the past month from England, I hear that the most illustrious Don Alfonso has been much caressed and honoured in England by that most serene King." Dispatch of Beltrando Costabili of August 4, 1504. Archivio di Modena, *Carteggio degli Ambasciatori—Roma.*

THE LAST YEARS OF DUKE ERCOLE

Diary for June 7 reads ominously: "From Ferrara the news comes that the Duke is ill; Don Alfonso is in France and is going to England, so that a messenger has been sent after him for him to return, because his father is in great danger; and if at his death he should not be found in Ferrara, the second brother, Don Ferrando, who is loved by the people, could be made Lord." Similarly, Zambotto tells us that Alfonso hurried back, "thinking that he was in danger of not succeeding to the lordship of Ferrara, if his father died in his absence, although he had been already invested by Pope Alexander VI with the duchy and its dominion; nevertheless, he hoped in the people who loved him."[1] Zambotto, it will be observed, gives no hint as to which of the brothers it was from whom the opposition should come. There was much discussion in the Papal Court as to the future of Ferrara. "This morning," wrote Antonio Giustinian to the Doge of Venice, on June 29, "it was said that there were letters from Ferrara that the Lord Duke had had a return of his malady and was in great danger of his life. As to what will happen in the event of his death, various judgments are passed, and all conclude that there must be great dissensions among his sons, and that the absence of Don Alfonso will be greatly to his disadvantage, since the Cardinal, who is popular with the people, is in Ferrara. But they all seem to be not a little jealous of your Celsitude, whose conduct is watched more than ever, since all think that you are aspiring to the monarchy of Italy."[2]

Ippolito ruled the State while Ercole, devout to the last, had himself conveyed to Florence in a litter drawn by

---
[1] Sanudo, *Diarii*, vi. col. 30; Zambotto, f. 402v.
[2] Giustinian, *Dispacci*, iii. p. 162.

mules, to keep a vow that he had made to the Madonna of the Annunziata. "This morning," he wrote to the Cardinal, on July 7, " early, with the grace of our Lord God we have arrived here at Florence safely ; and we have been to the Mass at the Annunziata. To-morrow morning we shall go to San Giovanni, and then, the next morning, we shall start on our return home, and we shall return by the way that we have come. We have thought well to give you notice of this, in order that you may know our progress in this voyage, and we add that, at present, we feel ourself really convalescent." So much was he recovered that he ultimately decided to go on from Bologna to Modena and Reggio, " to visit those peoples and cities of ours." [1]

Alfonso reached Ferrara on August 8, and found his father had rallied. Realizing that the situation might become critical, he resolved to make friends with the Venetians, and, with the consent of Ercole, who remembered how they had secured his own accession, went to Venice. To Beltrando Costabili, the Pope expressed mild displeasure at this step. It was too much submission to the Venetians, he said ; it would make the Venetians prouder than ever and more bent upon the acquisition of Ferrara. He had heard of the excessive homage that Alfonso had paid to the Signoria ; the Nuncio there had warned him that it was too much submission, but Alfonso had answered that he thought the times demanded it of him, especially as the power of France was on the wane. " Even if the affairs of France are not firm," said his Holiness, "there is no need to fear the Venetians, so long as we are here. We

[1] Letters of July 7 and 10, 1504, from Florence and Appiano respectively. Archivio di Modena, *Carteggio dei Principi*.

THE LAST YEARS OF DUKE ERCOLE

shall never suffer that they do him any injury."[1] Remarkable words as coming from Pope Julius, and which he was destined in a few years completely to belie.

The old Duke grew worse again in September, and, although he rallied temporarily, it was clear that the end was not far off. Don Ferrando kept quiet, but a furious quarrel arose between Alfonso and Ippolito. Their followers armed themselves; there was a free fight outside the Cardinal's palace one day, and near Alfonso's palace on the next. At Rome, the Cardinal Soderini assured the Pope that the Venetians were stirring up this discord among the Estensian princes, in order to make themselves masters of Ferrara on the Duke's death, and suggested that Giovanni Bentivoglio, being the nearest potentate, should interpose and make peace. "The Venetians are never contented," he said; "when they have that State, they will want Bologna also, and then it will be our turn at Florence." A similar warning reached the Pope from his Nuncio at Venice.[2] Julius sent briefs to Ercole promising him all the aid in his power, and to Alfonso declaring that, in every event, he would take him under his protection.[3]

Ercole's last cares were for the spiritual needs of his people. In what appears to be the last of his letters that has been preserved to us, we find him writing to the Cardinal of San Giorgio, as the protector of the Augustinians, to have Frate Egidio da Viterbo of that Order sent to preach the coming Lent in the Duomo of Ferrara, and asking that the

---

[1] Dispatch from Beltrando Costabili to Ercole, September 3, 1504. Archivio di Modena, *Carteggio degli Ambasciatori—Roma.*
[2] Giustinian, Dispatches of September 13 and 20, 1504. *Dispacci* iii. pp. 229, 236.
[3] Briefs of September 18, 1504, from Ostia. *Archivio Vaticano.* xxxix. 22, f. 179.

friar should be commanded by a brief from the Pope, if he refuse. "For this good work we shall be as much obliged to your most reverend Lordship as for any other thing which at present we could receive from you, because, since that Frate Egidio is of the learning and sufficiency that he is, we cannot but hope that all those good fruits will follow that are desired."[1] But the Duke himself was not to see this Lent.

Both Venice and Rome were on the alert. On December 7, the Venetians heard that Ercole was at the point of death, and that Don Alfonso had sent to tell the Visdomino, Ser Alvise da Mula, "that he recommended himself to our Signoria and wished to be its good son." The Pope, understanding the Duke's critical condition and mistrusting the intentions of the Republic, used "strange words" (the recognized euphemism of the epoch for undiplomatical language), and talked of sending the Cardinal of Volterra (Soderini) to Ferrara, as legate. To this, however, Beltrando Costabili objected, and used all his powers of persuasion with different Cardinals to prevent, or at least to delay it, until he could hear from Alfonso.[2] A most amazing story was sent by Giustinian from Rome to Venice to the effect that the chief reason for which Julius intended to send a legate to Ferrara, in case of Ercole's death, was that the Cardinal Ippolito had promised to keep the duchy loyal to the Pope, if the latter helped him to become Lord of it instead of Alfonso, whom he represented as entirely Venetian in his sympathies and as having pledged himself to complete

[1] *Minute Ducali* of November 16, 1504. Archivio di Modena, *Minutario Cronologico*.
[2] Sanudo, *op. cit.*, vi. coll. 110, 114. Giustinian, *Dispatch of December 9, Dispacci*, iii. p. 330.

subordination to Venice. It was asserted that the Cardinal felt himself strong in the affection of the people and was in good understanding with Don Ferrando; if the thing came off, he would lay down his red hat and marry the daughter of his Holiness.[1] This must have been the merest canard, for it would rather seem that Ippolito had been completely reconciled to his brother. Nevertheless, the proposed coming of the legate made Alfonso uneasy, and he bade the ambassador do his best to prevent it:—

"Messer Beltrando. We have seen and right well noted all that you tell us in your letters, about the decision that the Holiness of our Lord had taken to send hither the most reverend Cardinal of Volterra, in the case of the death of the Lord our Father. In reply, we tell you that, in this case, we would have the Pope, as a demonstration of the love that we know he bears us, do only as much as we shall request from his Beatitude, and nothing beyond. Wherefore we wish you, if you hear at any time in the future that he is thinking of sending us the said most reverend Monsignor or another, to do your best to prevent his Holiness from sending any one. We do not think that he ought to send a legate here, unless we demand it, especially as we see no obvious need of one; so, as you are on the spot and understand that this is our will, you will strive that it be done as we have said. Do not believe that we are led to this thought and determination in order to escape the expense which we should incur through the coming hither of a legate, or to oppose the will that our Lord has to honour and protect us,

[1] Dispatch of December 13, 1504. *Dispacci*, iii. p. 334. The daughter in question is the famous Madonna Felice della Rovere. The thing, adds the writer, is being kept a strict secret by the Pope, and will not be disclosed at all, unless there is a further change in the state of affairs.

the which we hold more **dear than ou**
that infinite and important **considera**
and if we made them **known to you by**
letters, you yourself **would urge us to**
Ferrara, January 20, 1505. **Alfonso.**'

Five days later, on **January 25,**
d' Este, the man who, **in spite of** mai
had truly striven to tread in the path
beacon-light of the martyred Fra Gir
passed away peacefully in the Castello Ve

His last Will and Testament is still
Archives of Modena.² It is a noteworthy de
ting both the mystical side of his character
with his children. It begins: " Even as
Christ before He suffered called His disciple
founded a new Testament, in which He made u
His heirs; so hath He set us an example, that
of Him, before we pass out of this present wor.
make a disposition of those things which we wou
after our death. Therefore should each one
that, before the hour of death overtake him, he se
himself and his possessions that after his death l
seen to have done all things prudently." He com.
soul to God's mercy, his body to be buried at Sar
degli Angeli, before the high altar of the new chur
each of a number of monasteries and religious bo
leaves one hundred *lire marchesane* annually in perp
with minute instructions concerning *monthly Mas*

¹ *Minute Ducali per Roma a Beltrando Costabili.* Archi
Modena, *Carteggio degli Ambasciatori—Roma.*

² *Cancelleria Ducale, Documenti spettanti a Principi Estens*
take this opportunity of thanking Dr. Giulio Bertoni for calling
attention to this document.

THE LAST YEARS OF DUKE ERCOLE

perpetuity for his soul, the legacies to be paid immediately after his death and afterwards at the beginning of each year : " in order that the soul of the testator may more swiftly feel their suffrages, and more easily be delivered from the pains of Purgatory." Moreover, he leaves another hundred *lire marchesane* to the "chaplains and college of the chaplains of the Cathedral of Ferrara," in order that, in addition to the obligation of saying the above Masses, they may be bound every Saturday, in perpetuity, in the morning to say and celebrate a solemn Mass in honour of the Blessed Virgin Mary, and in the evening to sing the Rosary of the Blessed Virgin before the Lady-altar of the Cathedral.[1] Then follow the legacies to his sons. To Ippolito, he simply leaves four cardinal's rochets, considering that he is sufficiently provided for, "by so many benefices which he possesses and holds." To Ferrando, besides the palace near San Francesco (the present Palazzo Pareschi) in which he is living, he leaves a number of possessions in the Ferrarese and Modenese and in the district of Carpi, the annual income from which together amounts to 14,992 *lire marchesane* ; in addition to this, Don Alfonso is to give him an annual salary and provision of 3,000 *lire marchesane*, "so long as he follows the Court, and remains in obedience and devotion to that most illustrious Don Alfonso." To the younger Sigismondo, besides the Palazzo Schifanoia in which he lives at present, with all that it contains, he leaves a number of possessions and customs, more especially in Romagna, amounting to an annual income of some 11,000 *lire marchesane*, and the additional 3,000

[1] The whole of these pious bequests comes to 1,200 *lire marchesane* a year. In 1504, the *lira marchesana* was a sum of money equivalent to about 10 *lire* of modern Italian coinage.

from Don Alfonso under the sam
of Don Ferrando. Small legacies
d' Este Gonzaga, who has her d(
grandsons, Maximilian and Fr;
the dowry of their mother Beatri
the palace in the Via degli Angeli
possessions and customs bringin;
4,500 *lire marchesane*, and an add
provision from Don Alfonso, und
Ferrando. No mention is made
voglio. Don Alfonso is made
cessor in all the rest, and in all
The Testament is drawn up by
notary Lodovico Bonamelli, in the
da Siena, on July 1, 1504, and
Giovanni da Tabia, prior of the
Santa Maria degli Angeli of the
fessor of the Lord testator," Fra
five other friars of the Angeli, Don
" called and specially requested
mouth of the most illustrious Lo
aforesaid."

It is not too much to say that, (
in the epoch of the Borgia, Ercole
thetic, almost the only not ignobl(
rest upon his reputation : his cru
towards his nephew, Niccolò di
Italy in abetting the disastrous p
which brought the French invader
first, in any other of the contem
be excused on the plea of the poli
but not so in the case of Ercole, wh

THE LAST YEARS OF DUKE ERCOLE

of morals and undoubtedly held higher ideals. In palliation of the second might be urged the lack of genuine national sentiment among the Italians of the early Renaissance; but, at the best, it was treason, and as treason all the more enlightened spirits even of that age stigmatized it. Ercole's religious fervour was intense and genuine; to the best of his abilities, he strove to follow where the light of the truth seemed to shine. Want of moral courage and a certain spirit of time-serving kept him back from the heights. He loved his people, and was, on the whole, a good lord to his subjects; the faults of his administration were many and grievous, but they were due more to the general condition of the times, and to the low and sordid conception then prevalent as to the art of government and the duties of a sovereign, than to any lack of noble qualities of heart and mind.

Ercole must be regarded as the maker of modern Ferrara. "The Duke desires nothing else," writes a discontented contemporary and subject, "save every day to decorate and magnify this his city of Ferrara with new edifices and palaces."[1] He was much concerned in draining and fertilising the country, and undertook considerable public works in this direction in 1486 and subsequent years. In the adorning and embellishing of the capital, Pietro di Benvenuto—who had, it will be remembered, finished the Schifanoia for Borso—appears to have been the principal architect employed in the earlier part of his reign; it was he who adapted the Castello Vecchio for a ducal residence, and to him is due the marble stairway, still standing, of the Corte Vecchia. After his death in 1483, the Duke

[1] Document quoted by Frizzi, iv. p. 148.

chiefly relied upon the services
and of Biagio Rossetti. Under
1492, Ercole began the great wc
magnificent aspect that it still ret:
the enlargement of the city and
a new district on the northern sic
Erculea or *Terra Nova*. Ferrara
The smaller Barco, Belfiore, the
degli Angeli were included in the
Herculean ramparts along which
to wander hour by hour. Broa
down, such as the Corso di Porta
the Corso di Porta Mare, that seem
Strada del Borgo Leone. The St
fresh importance, while the trer
city-walls became the Strada dell
few animated streets of the mode
quarter magnificent palaces beg:
and courtiers threw themselve
scheme. Sigismondo d' Este, the
Palazzo de' Diamanti begun by
to be finished later by Girolan
Borgognoni, upon the façade of w
still recall the Herculean badge; w
the chief physician of the Court
palace reared by its side, the

[1] Cf. Frizzi, iv. pp. 165–168, and es]
in Solerti, *Ferrara e la Corte Este*
describes the beginning of the new w
" and the Venetians, hearing this, se
why he was making those excavations
he wanted to enlarge Ferrara." Cf.
al suo mantello aggiunge panno.

THE LAST YEARS OF DUKE ERCOLE

All the landowners of the duchy were compelled to send *contadini* to labour on the walls and the laying out of the new district; a special tax was levied upon all the Ferrarese territory; the salaries of the servants of the Court and the stipends of the professors of the Studio were reduced, to find funds.[1] The building of this Herculean quarter was completed about the year 1501. In the centre of his creation the Duke desired to raise an equestrian statue of himself, and he attempted to obtain from Milan, which had by then fallen into the hands of the French, the model which Leonardo da Vinci had made in 1493 for the monument of Francesco Sforza. In this he was unsuccessful.[2] The work was never executed, and, upon the column which the Duke had prepared for himself, stands now—not unfittingly—the statue of the great poet who was to be the supreme glory of Ferrara.

Many of the works that Rossetti carried out for his ducal patron have perished. But there still stands San Francesco, the most noteworthy ecclesiastical building of the early

---

[1] Frizzi, iv. p. 166.

[2] On September 19, 1501, Ercole wrote to Giovanni Valla, his ambassador in Milan, that the master who was to have made the model of the horse to be cast in metal to be put up in the piazza of *Terra Nova* had died, and no one here could finish it. Remembering that in Milan there is the model made of a horse that the Lord Lodovico had in mind to have cast, "which model was made by a Master Leonardo, who is a good master in things of this kind," as it is not being used and is getting more spoilt every day by neglect, he bids him ask the Cardinal of Rouen for it. On September 24, Valla answered that the Cardinal would be delighted to let the Duke have it; but that, since the King has seen it, he cannot give it without a word to his Majesty. Valla advises the Duke to instruct Bartolommeo de' Cavallieri to speak to the King about it. G. Campori, *Nuovi documenti per la vita di Leonardo da Vinci* (Modena, 1865), pp. 6, 7.

Renaissance in Ferrara, with its
which he began in 1494; the c
Vado, one of the oldest and m(
the duchy with its chapel of t
rebuilt by him a little later (fr(
Grandi), but has been entirely rec(
campanile of San Giorgio is his.
choir of the Duomo, also, is Ro:
the most beautiful private pala
and now abandoned to squalid p(
bili—now more usually called th
which Lodovico il Moro once hop(
in the approaching ruin of his
reared for Ercole the princely
cesco, completed the Certosa, l
Benedetto. There was, indeed, h
in the city that the Duke did nc

The decoration of these new bu
former princes had reared, the
portraits of members of the reign
marriages and betrothals, the s
ducal theatre, afforded occupati
artists and craftsmen, great and :
of Ercole's reign, the prince of
Cosimo Tura, as in the days of I
marriage, Ercole commissioned l
himself and (amazing example o:
of that age in these matters)
Lucrezia, to send as presents to l
likewise designed the nuptial be(

[1] A. Venturi, *L'Arte Ferrarese nel p*

THE LAST YEARS OF DUKE ERCOLE

with its canopy and coverings, and a wonderful silver sideboard. He painted a Madonna for the Duke's private apartment in 1475. A few years later, he decorated his study with seven panels representing naked women, *figure nude di femmine*, probably intended for the three theological and four cardinal virtues.[1] He painted the little Alfonso's portrait to send to the Duchess Bona in 1477, and, later on, those of the princesses, Lucrezia, Isabella and Beatrice, to be sent to their future husbands. He died in 1495. It is doubtful if a single work that Tura painted for Ercole has survived, and if there still exist any authentic portraits (save those executed for Borso in the Schifanoia) from his hand. The same applies to Baldassare d' Este, who lived through the greater part of Ercole's reign; all that he produced during this epoch has perished, with the doubtful exception of one medal.

To Cosimo Tura as chief Court painter succeeded his pupil, Ercole de' Roberti, a member of that noble Reggian family that had given a mistress to the Marchese Niccolò III and a mother to Rinaldo and Bianca Maria. Born some time after 1450, his earlier work appears to have been done at Bologna, and it is to this epoch that his most important extant picture belongs: the Madonna with Pietro degli Onesti, painted for a church at Ravenna and now in the Brera at Milan. He took Cosimo Tura's place at Ferrara in 1487. A little later he visited Venice, and learned to temper the harsh style of his master with the softer influence of the young Giambellino. He was the leading artist in the festivities for the marriage of Isabella d' Este, painting the chests that were to convey her belongings to Mantua,

[1] Venturi, *op. cit.*, ii. pp. 362, 363.

DUKES AND POETS IN F[

designing and directing the constructio[
and of the triumphal chariot upon wl
husband's city. We have seen him
to Rome on the accession of Alexanc
of Roberti's death in 1496, he was engag
the Duke for Isabella, which was sent u
Very few of his works have been preser
Gallery possesses a most beautiful exar
in the "Gathering of Manna in the
Dudley collection.

Lorenzo Costa, the connecting li
and Bologna in painting, although a
was but little employed by Duke E
would have thought, such works as
pieces with which he filled the church
have strongly appealed. What wo
student of Ferrara give for some pic
Herculean circle, analogous to that p
with which Costa adorned the stud
Isabella and which is now one of
Louvre ? The most important work
or follower, Ercole di Giulio Cesare (
in the frescoed ceilings of the Palaz;
not belong to Ercole's reign. Wit
Mazzolino begins a new generation
which lies outside the scope of th
already, though no extant picture c
to a date earlier than some five year
the one great master of Ferrarese pa
known as Dosso Dossi, had been bo

Not a trace of the Duke's favouri
vent of Santa Caterina da Siena, r

Two Ferrarese Ladies.
By Ercole Grandi.

THE LAST YEARS OF DUKE ERCOLE

we can still trace its site on the northern side of the Via Aria Nuova, the road that once bore the name of St. Catherine. It is uncertain who was the architect whom Ercole employed to give the design of the church and convent; but we have many records of the pictures that adorned it. They almost all referred to the life of the Seraphic Virgin of Siena. The decoration was carried out mainly in the years 1503 and 1504, by Antonio Aleotti, Geminiano di Bongiovanni and Ettore de' Bonacossi, painters of small importance whose works have perished, but of whom the last named is interesting, as he appears to have belonged to the family of Savonarola's mother. Outside the convent was a fresco of St. Catherine receiving the Stigmata, and another of her holding a Crucifix; various scenes from her life, in one of which she was represented as kissing the feet of her Divine Spouse, were represented in *tondi* in the cortile. In Lucia's private loggietta were the "Agony in the Garden," the "Madonna inspiring St. Bernard," "St. Jerome in the Desert," while, in another part of the convent, there was a large fresco of St. Catherine taking a number of nuns under her mantle.[1] We have also records, in the account of the ducal expenses, of pictures (no longer extant) specially painted as presents from Ercole to Lucia in 1502; a head of St. John the Baptist, by Francesco de' Maineri of Parma; an altar-piece, by a certain Niccolò of Pisa, representing St. Catherine of Siena with other saints, worshipped by the Duke himself and others of her clients of the time.[2] There are few of the many lost Ferrarese pictures that the lover of Ercole could not have spared rather than that.

---

[1] A. Venturi, *op. cit.*, ii. (2) pp. 373–375; Gandini, *Lucrezia Borgia*, pp. 7, 8.

[2] A. Venturi, *op. cit.*, ii. (2) pp. 385 note 1, 394.

DUKES AND F'

The death of Ercole invo
There had already been dis
of the new comers had left,
it is even said that one of t.
her. Her absolute power in
Duke showed her, certain r
of the black veil, all combi
disliked. No sooner was the
and malice of these women bla
of artificially renewing the wo
had healed or, at least, become
that Pope Alexander had gra
she was deprived of all autho
convent, even of the consolatic
fessor. She was then not twenty
age of sixty-eight—that is, for ne
nuns kept her a close prisoner ir
her in every possible way, treatin
criminal. But she bore it all w
and patience, comforted still by .
with St. Catherine. She died on]
soled with celestial visions and
"Having obtained from the Lord
some souls from the pains of Purgat
biographer, "before she received the
of the Eucharist, she asked for the
of Duke Ercole her benefactor, of on
a brother, the state of whose souls sh
special revelation."[1] When dead, the

[1] Giacomo Marcianese, *Narrationi*, pp.
recent biographers pass over the alleged ca
of Lucia, nor have we any record as to whicl

THE LAST YEARS OF DUKE ERCOLE

revulsion of feeling, acclaimed her as a saint, and to this day her body, strange relic of a stranger time, is venerated in the Cathedral of the city that had seen her its sovereign's Egeria and afterwards a despised captive.

in it. A certain Suora Maria of Parma was made superior, and the majority of the nuns renewed their vows to her.

Chapt(

THE POETS OF THE

THE one supreme poet in
Ercole's reign is Mattec
we have already considered a
Tito Vespasiano di Messer Nanr
the poets who sang in the Lati
even more prominent figure in ι
capital. Messer Tito lived in
giving lavish entertainments to
sovereign's efforts in the restorat
hospitality to foreign potentates
that of the princes of the House of I
splendid and magnificent," writes
Lorenzo di Filippo Strozzi, "in h
tions in his house, with royal mou
the presence of the Lord Duke and
rara."[1] Unfortunately, he played
the administration of the city. Ha
the Duke as commissary in Romagna
posts, he was made Judge of the Twelν
1497, and entered into office "with v
perhaps, greater than any other had ev
Strozzi would have us believe that the

[1] *Vite degli uomini illustri della Casa S*
[2] *Diario Ferrarese*, col. 347.

THE POETS OF THE HERCULEAN CIRCLE

to this office "more for his own advantage than for the benefit of the said Messer Tito," and that " he administered the public affairs with the good will of the people and to the profit of his sovereign." But his Ferrarese contemporaries tell us a very different story. Probably, like many other Ferrarese magnates, he used his official position as a means of amassing wealth, especially in his old age, when his poetical work was practically done. " Messer Tito and his sons," writes the Diarist in March, 1500, " are universally detested by every person for their devouring of the people and for their cruel oppression "; and again, a little later: " Messer Tito Strozza is hated by the people worse than the Devil is."[1]

By his wife, Domitilla de' Rangoni of Modena, Tito had three sons: Ercole, Guido and the younger Lorenzo. Ercole —who, like his father, latinised their surname from Strozzi to Strozza (on the same principle as Petrarca calling himself Francesco Petrarca instead of Francesco di Petracco)— succeeded him as the chief Latin poet of the Court. Lame from his birth, always over-dressed and perfumed, this scholarly dandy at one time thought of entering the Church. When Lucrezia Borgia came to Ferrara, he attached himself to her service, partly because he hoped to gain a Cardinal's hat through her influence with her father, Pope Alexander.[2] For the rest, he strove to follow in his father's footsteps, with scantier means at his disposal but no less hated by the people. Of his vernacular poetry, the one great passion that inspired it and, perhaps, led him to his death, something will be said in the next chapter. A selection of the Latin lyrics of father and son was collected

[1] *Diario Ferrarese*, coll. 382, 401.
[2] Lorenzo Strozzi, *op. cit.*, p. 77.

DUKES AND

and published together
the latter's tragic end, b
 Coupled by Ariosto v
chief singer of Lucrezia'
Antonio Tebaldi, who si
Tebaldeo. He was born ;
time instructed Isabella d'
her marriage, he left Ferra
Bentivoglio at Bologna,
adulatory poetry on the b
in 1496 invited him to Man
much favour. Thence he ·
1499, entering first the servi
afterwards that of Lucrezia
morals and great personal be
he wandered back to Mantua
for libelling a rival poet and ;
Court of Leo X. He lived l
Raphael and to lose all he had
theless, almost all his poetry l
and was written before the end
 This poetical work of Tebal
a number of epistles, *capitoli*
They are partly amorous, pa;

---

[1] *Orlando Furioso*, xlii. 83.
[2] For Tebaldeo, see especially Lu;
Relazioni Letterarie di Isabella d'Esl
V. Rossi, *Il Quattrocento*, pp. 206, 2
312–314. My quotations are fron
printed at Modena, 1500. The first e
his consent) by the poet's cousin
with a dedication to the Marchesana Is
loc. cit., p. 204).

THE POETS OF THE HERCULEAN CIRCLE

are especially remarkable for their exaggeration of the traditional conceits of the Petrarchists, whose imagery is materialised often to an absurd degree. The lover's tears become a torrent and cause the floods of the Po; Love riddles him with his darts, until he can use him as his quiver; he needs no mask in carnival time, because his amorous troubles have made him such a walking death that only Love and his lady, Flavia, can recognize him. Flavia's house catches fire, but her beauty inflames the firemen so that they must use the water for themselves. When she slips on the ice on her way to church, an analogous explanation is forthcoming:—

> Che non po invidia ? invidia dispersa erra,
> Hor questo cor et hor quello altro speza,
> Nè sol intrar ne gli animanti è aveza,
> Ma in le cose insensate anchor si serra.
> Sendo la neve qua discesa in terra,
> E vedendose vincer di biancheza
> Da Madonna; disdegno, ira e tristeza
> Aghiazossi per farli ingiuria e guerra;
> E vedendola un giorno andare al tempio,
> Cader la fe: sì che gli mosse un braccio;
> Ma forsi il ciel dar vuole a l'altre exempio,
> Che se Madonna ardea sì come io faccio
> Gionta mai non serebbe a tal caso empio,
> Chè, a chi ama, sotto i piè se strugge il ghiaccio.[1]

---

[1] "What cannot envy do? Envy wanders everywhere, breaks now this heart and now that other; nor only into living beings is it wont to enter, but even incloses itself in senseless things.

"The snow, having descended here on earth and seeing itself surpassed by my lady in whiteness, froze with disdain, anger and sorrow, to injure and make war upon her.

"And seeing her one day going to church, it made her fall, so that she sprained her arm; but, perchance, Heaven wished to give an example to the others;

"For if my lady burned as I do, she would never have come to so cruel a plight, for ice is melted beneath the feet of those that love." (Sonnet 101.)

DUKES AND

But at times he can

  Simplice aventu[
   Che il dì ti st[
   Poi quando l'[
   Torni a posar[
  Lasso, che spers[
   Senza quiete a[
   Vassene la mi[
   Come dal mar[
  Tu sol temi del[
   Per te sta vigil[
   Che fa l' insid[
  Et io temo del c[
   Contra ho fort[
   Nè l' arme alc[

Those of his sonnets [
subjects, though somew[
undoubted interest for th[
dealing with the French[
about the cruelties of th[
had led to their downfall,[
and her manifest decline [
may be taken as reflecting[
Francesco and the House[
the following sonnet strike[

[1] " Simple, fortunate shep[
the flock without care, and th[
thou returnest to rest in thy[
 " Alas, broken up between[
in the day or in the dark nigh[
a ship that is tossed by the s[
 " Thou fearest only the wo[
thee against such war, and m[
 " And I fear Heaven and ea[
the human race; nor does a[
(Sonnet 67.)

THE POETS OF THE HERCULEAN CIRCLE

> Ne i toi campi non pose il piè sì presto
> Hannibal che combatter li convienne,
> Nè mai sì afflicta il Barbaro ti tenne
> Che al diffender non fusse il tuo cor desto.
> Et hor, Italia, onde procede questo,
> Che un piccol Gallo che l' altr' ier qui venne
> Per ogni nido tuo batte le penne,
> Senza mai ritrovarse alcuno infesto?
> Ma iusto esser mi par che 'l ciel te abassi,
> Che più non fai Camilli o Scipioni,
> Ma sol Sardanapalli e Midi e Crassi.
> Già una occha tua (se guardi a i tempi buoni)
> Scacciar lo puote de i Tarpei sassi;
> Hor aquile non pon, serpi e leoni.[1]

Another sonnet, condoling with the Marquis for the death of Rodolfo Gonzaga at Fornovo, opens finely:—

> Lassa i suspir: chè non convien tal atto
> A chi ha de l' arme Italice il governo;[2]

but hardly keeps up the strain. He has a whole series about a bust or statue of Beatrice d'Este Sforza by a certain Leone, and a single sonnet, by no means without charm in spite of its quaint conceits, on the death of Don Alfonso's first wife, Anna Sforza d'Este:—

---

[1] "No sooner did Hannibal set foot in thy fields, than he had to give battle; nor ever did the Barbarian keep thee so afflicted, but that thy heart was ready for defence.

"And, now, Italy, whence proceeds this, that a little Cock, that came here but yesterday, beats his wings over every nest of thine, without ever meeting a single foe?

"But it seems to me just that Heaven cast thee down, for thou makest no more Camilli or Scipios, but only such as Sardanapalus and Midas and Crassus.

"Of old a goose of thine (if thou lookest back to the good times) could drive him away from the Tarpeian rock; now eagles cannot, nor serpents and lions." (Sonnet 220.)

[2] "Leave thy sighs; for such things befit not him who hath the rule of the armies of Italy." (Sonnet 231.)

DUKES AND

Visto Morte dal Mc
A Carlo, che so
De che l' emp
Disse : Impunit
Nè in polve il scriss
E cum l' arco
Anna (fior de' S
Nè mai sotterra
Chè non sendo del
Morte, quanto e
Tanto sì fe in l
Lassare Italia a' Ga
Potea un dì lib
Far una altra o

Decidedly noteworthy i
analogous poems that Teb
his lyrics, they are partly ar
of the House of Gonzaga.
of Italy, the corruption of
ing peril to Christendom fr
Negroponte. It ends in a
He is the inheritor of Herc
name "; " Italy under thy
liberate the world from th
Herculean labour, and one

---

[1] " When Death saw that the N
who was arming himself again
pected much prey), she said : I

" She wrote it not in dust bu
her bow to the city of Ercole, s
the Sforzas ; nor ever under ea

" For Death, not being quite
cruel and relentless in the strife

" To leave Italy to the Gauls
free herself ; but Nature never
like this." (Sonnet 254.)

[2] Capitolo iv. *Per dar ripos*

THE POETS OF THE HERCULEAN CIRCLE

Fine too is another, in the form of a letter from the dead Rodolfo Gonzaga to the Marchese Gian Francesco; the slain hero describes his reception in Hades by the spirits of his brother Federigo and his father Lodovico (father and grandfather, respectively, of the man that he is addressing); he urges on his nephew to tread in the paths of Scipio; let him not mourn for his death, but take care of the little child that he has left.[1] Less effective is a similar piece, written in the name of Gian Francesco himself and describing his exploits at Fornovo, denying that he had entertained any negotiations with the French King.[2] These poems have value as historical documents, even apart from their literary merits, which are appreciable.

In curious contrast to the courtier Tebaldeo, is another poet, whose poems are practically contemporaneous with his and deal in part with the same cycle of events: Antonio Cammelli, called "Il Pistoia," from the Tuscan city where he was born in 1440. It is not known why or when Cammelli came to Ferrara; but, from 1487 to 1497, he filled the post of captain of the Porta di Santa Croce at Reggio. A little later he was given the same office again, at the intercession of the Marchesana Isabella; but he seems to have lost it once more, and from 1500 until his death, in 1502, he wandered about in poverty from Court to Court.

In the Lent of 1499, a tragedy by Cammelli was played

---

structed Beltrando Costabil to exhort Pope Alexander to take more effectual measures against the Turks and excite the other Powers to do the like, "considering the great danger in which the Christian Religion is placed." Archivio di Modena, *Minutario Cronologico*, February 24, 1502.

[1] Capitolo xii. *Se poi che l'alma già disciolta e scarca.*
[2] Capitolo xiii. *Chi disse esser felice chi non nasce.*

DUKES AND

before the Court of Ferrar
ment is spoken by a m
himself as the ghost of S
moral philosopher, whose
normal time, sent by Plu
case of two lovers descri
matter of fact, the play h
is taken directly, with cha
the first *novella* of the fo
story of the cruelty used
and her lover Guiscardo.
King Demetrius of Thebe
of his daughter Pamfila, ar
upon which she dies. T
species of pander, upon w
the vices of Courts. The
of some importance as bei
tragedies. It is divided
ludes. The dialogue is in *t*
ally that between the Chor
are written in lyrical meas

Cammelli's chief poetica
nary collection of caudate
part of a satirical nature.
he represents a friend as
you make sonnets. Are
even saw a hen on the road
other!" [2] In these vivid li

[1] *Tragedia de Antonio da Pis*
de Ferrara, Venice, 1508. Cf.
Tragedia di Antonio Cammelli.

[2] Sonnet 35. I refer throug
I Sonetti del Pistoia giusta l'ap

THE POETS OF THE HERCULEAN CIRCLE

and the conditions of the times, jests at his poverty and humiliation, satirises the Duke's officers and ministers. Nor does he rest there. The whole society of Italy, high and low, during the last decade of the Quattrocento and the beginning of the following century, passes before our eyes; we see the simoniacal election of Alexander VI; follow the rise and fall of Lodovico il Moro; and mark the devout, pacific bearing of Ercole, the difficulties and dangers of the minor potentates and powers. "With them," writes Professor Renier, "we can follow all the political vicissitudes of the last years of the fifteenth century, seen with the eyes of a courtier poet; enthusiastic for the Moro as long as he was potent, but not refraining from assailing him (as usually happens) after his ruinous fall."[1] Or, if we prefer, we can watch the ladies of the epoch at their toilet, and study the rival claims to supremacy in beauty of the women of all the chief cities of Italy.[2]

Nowhere, in the poetry of those days, do we find a nobler note than that struck by Il Pistoia in his sonnet on the shameful victory of Fornovo:—

> Passò il Re franco, Italia, a tuo dispetto,
> Cosa che non fe mai 'l popul romano,
> Col legno in resta e con la spada in mano,
> Con nemici a le spalle e innanti al petto.
> Cesare e Scipion, di cui ho letto,
> I nemici domôr di mano in mano;

---

[1] *Op. cit.*, p. xxxi.
[2] The Florentines (says the poet) appear beautiful, but in reality are terribly painted and made up; the women of Siena are perfectly heavenly, and the Sienese men are utterly unworthy of them; there are still some beautiful ladies among the Ferrarese, but not like what they were before the Venetian invasion, "when we saw the Slavonians bridge the Po"; the Milanese are too fat and overdressed, and behave at table like Germans. Sonnets 16, 17, 18, 19.

DUKES AND

E costui, com(
Mordendo que:
Matre vituperata d
Se Cesare acqu
Insubri, Galli,
Concubina di Mida
Ch' hai dato a
Discordia con
Chè con p
In sul transirti
Tutti i tuoi fig
Sia come
Se ben del mo
Mai non si esti

No less eloquent is the
Pope Alexander and his

Ruina de' Cristian,
Per simonia co
Da cui è fatto
Con omicidi, st
Al primo successor
Sol per pescar
E tu, d' ogn' o
Tien' de la fede
Così mal vanno le c
In man d'un si

---

[1] "The French King has
that the Roman people never
in hand, with foes at his bac
"Caesar and Scipio, of who
hand to hand; and he, like
and that, has passed clear av
"Mother disgraced by the
conquest of Insubrians, Gauls
"Concubine of Midas, foe t
the hands of Venus, discord c
"For, with little labour, as
all thy children became hens
thou didst acquire the empire
grace be wiped out." (Sonne

THE POETS OF THE HERCULEAN CIRCLE

> D' ogn' or guidare a le sue concubine.
> Tutto quel che tu fai iustizia elegge ;
> Il ciel pien d' ira ha in sen le tue ruine
> Perchè il ciel sempre un mal vivo non regge.
> Crudele a la tua legge !
> Nova pena per te la terra ordisce
> Se il gallo a l' angue mai per te se unisce.
> Scacciaranno le bisce
> Il famelico verme iniquo e tristo,
> Che divora la Croce e Jesu Cristo.[1]

While the throng listened to the words of Fra Girolamo, Il Pistoia had scoffed. Thus, just after Fornovo :—

> Ogni predicator si fa indovino :
> Hanne Firenze un sì speculativo,
> Che molti Fiorentin non bevon vino.[2]

And again, when Maximilian—"il novo Costantino"—is at Pisa, he is more emphatically contemptuous :—

> Al suon d' una campana
> Il popul fiorentin va tutto in macchia,
> Credulo al garrular d' una cornacchia.

---

[1] " Ruin of Christians, thou, false priest, with simony hast bought the divine cult ; by thee has the holy temple become perverted with murder, rapine and money.

" For the first successor sufficed the net only, to fish for a faithful throng to God ; and thou every hour with some new outrage holdest the secret keys of the Faith.

" Thus ill go things divine in the hand of a simoniac, who continually lets his concubines guide the flock.

" Justice chooses all that thou dost ; Heaven full of wrath hath thy ruin in store, because it will not suffer an evil liver for ever.

" Cruel to thy law ! The earth is preparing a new penalty for thee, if the Cock ever through thee unites with the Snake. The Vipers will hunt out the ravening worm, wicked and fell, that is devouring the Cross and Jesus Christ." (Sonnet 369. In all these sonnets, there is the obvious play upon *gallo*, " cock " or " Gaul." The Snake and Vipers are the Sforza.)

[2] " Every preacher becomes a diviner. Florence has one of them so speculative, that many Florentines drink no wine." (Sonnet 326.)

DUKES AND POE

> O Dio che nova ma
> Chè per simplicità son (
> E vendevon l'astuzia a

But, after the Friar's fall and
with reverence:—

> Pover Marzocco, come t
>
> * * *
>
> Il frate che a Cristo er:
> Ucciso hai per paura d'(

Most successful of all Can
those in the form of dialogue
dispute between the Cardinal,
the latter tries to force his (
reverend and illustrious Lords
and naturally does not find h
finer is the scene between the (
and the demon Farfarello, co(
claim his prey at the gates of

> Toc !—Chi batte ?—Amici,
> —Come ti chiami ?—Da
> —Ah ah ! io el so, il tu(
> Su su a la forca, a la
> Per te non fu fondato q
> Più giù te aspetta un
> —Lasciami venir qui (
> —No no, altro ti vuol
> —Bu bu—Chi abbaia ?—
> —Chi sei tu che mi cl

---

[1] " At the sound of a bell the peo]
credulous in the chattering of a c
By their simplicity are they almost
sell cunning to all the world." (S

[2] " Poor Marzocco, how is thy l
broker with Christ, hast thou slain
364.)

[3] Sonnet 144.

THE POETS OF THE HERCULEAN CIRCLE

—Che cosa vuoi da me ?—Questo latrone,
Che al ciel per crudeltà si fe rubello ;
Io ti dico da parte di Plutone
Che gli è per carta suo : ecco il libello.
—Io non voglio esser quello
Che a nissun patto l' altrui preda toglia ;
Piglialo, menal via, fa la tua voglia.
—Cávati fôr la spoglia,
Cammina, traditor, che ogni martire
Sarà poca vivanda al tuo fallire.[1]

Every phase in the complicated struggles and intrigues from the battle of Fornovo to the downfall of the Moro finds echo in Cammelli's later sonnets. In one of the latest, *Italia, il Turco vien*, he exhorts the princes and potentates of Italy to lay aside their private quarrels and hatreds, to unite against the common foe :—

A te serà vergogna,
Re franco, a mover contra Italia piede,
Chè a te s' aspetta mantenir la fede.

---

[1] "*Toc!* P. Who knocks ? Z. Friends, just open to me. P. What is thy name ? Z. Gregorio of Lucca. P. Ah, ah ! I know it, thy name is notorious ; hence to the gallows, to the axe, to the fire. This place was not made for thee ; another consistory awaits thee lower down. Z. Let me come hither with thy aid. P. No, no, elsewhere the cook will make it hot for thee.

"*Bow, wow!* P. Who is barking ? F. Peter, do me justice. P. Who art thou that callest me ? F. Farfarello. P. What wantest thou from me ? F. This great robber, who by his cruelty hath rebelled against Heaven. I tell thee, in the name of Pluto, that he is his by script; here is the book.

"P. I would not be the man to take away another's prey on any account. Seize him, take him away, do thy will! F. Come out of that and march, traitor; for every torment will be little recompense for thy wickedness." (Sonnet 84.)

Sonnets 83, 85, 86 are upon the same subject. An anonymous sonnet and ballata on the death of Zampante are in the *Diario Ferrarese*, col. 332. Cf. above, p. 326.

DUKES

        E s
   Un dì f
   E d' Ita

And in the French
Sforza, he discerns
dence of Italy :—

       Tu sei pr
       Tu sei ca
       E chi que

In the last sonnet
Italy, " dismembered
down and body genuf
in her history which l

      Ma perchè
      Ne aspettar
      Nella qual
        E forse,
      Prima che g
      Il nostro lun

Although but sparin
Cammelli had a fervent
On June 13, 1502, a few
she wrote to Niccolò d

[1] " Shame will it be to th Italy, for we look to thee to taken, one day this savage be France." (Sonnet 373.)

[2] " Thou art a prisoner, ar fallen and Italy is fallen; and (Sonnet 386.)

[3] " But since one season do another, bad or good, in whic perchance, for our ill luck, befc our light will be without any oil. *fatto adesso de Italia.*)

THE POETS OF THE HERCULEAN CIRCLE

lived, he offered and promised many times to put together in one work all the things composed by him, and to entitle them to us; but, since time has failed him, he has not been able to accomplish this. We understand that your Lordship has been at pains to collect them and make a codex of them, which pleases us much, and we praise you for this most pious deed. But we remind you that you must not deprive us of that right which we have in them by the disposition and bequest of the poet." Needless to say, the Count promptly reassured his illustrious correspondent: " I reply to your Ladyship," he wrote, " that not only do I desire that you should have these things of the Pistoia, but from as many excellent poets as the world possesses." [1]

This correspondence connects two of the most conspicuous Court poets of Ercole's circle together, and with Isabella. We have already frequently met with the Duke's nephew, Niccolò da Correggio, who was born, as we saw, in 1450. Courtier and soldier, he played a leading part in almost every Ferrarese festivity, and, as a condottiere of the Dukes of Milan, fought in every warlike enterprise undertaken by the House of Sforza in Italy. He had married Cassandra, one of the daughters of the great Bartolommeo Colleoni, a lady of great wit and beauty, who sumptuously entertained the French ambassador on his way from Piacenza to Ferrara to assist at the wedding of Lucrezia Borgia.[2]

---

[1] Isabella's letter and Niccolò's answer, in Renier, *op. cit.*, pp. viii, ix. Similarly, we find Jacopo Tebaldi writing to Isabella about his cousin's poems: " In his book I have found a sonnet which shows me that his intention has always been to dedicate this work to thy lofty name. I would not that my theft should deprive thee of any of thy rights; but have entitled the little book to thee." Dedicatory letter prefixed to Tebaldeo's sonnets.

[2] Cagnolo in *Lucrezia Borgia in Ferrara*, pp. 34, 35.

Although Ariosto
of the praises of B
even more pronou
who opens his mou
of my most illust
Marchioness," he v
words of the Holy
" He was certainly n
his modern biograph
ingenious and clever
composed verses and
of much more avail in
value of those poor rh
wrote for the ducal th
e di Aurora, a play
Metamorphoses, on the
very same that a conter
in line and colour at F
in the National Gallery
octaves, the choral inte
Represented in 1487, it
Italian drama after the O
in every respect to its p
1491, Niccolò wrote for Is
rima, partly derived from
with the singer's own lov

[1] Letter of August 10, 15(
Correggio, ii. p. 69.
[2] Luzio and Renier, op. cit., p
[3] The two works, Innamoran
Favola di Cefalo, are published
1507. A selection of Niccolò's l
op. cit., iv.

THE POETS OF THE HERCULEAN CIRCLE

There is, if I mistake not, a touch of genuine inspiration in one of his earlier lyrics, the sonnet written from his Venetian prison, after the disastrous battle of Argenta in 1482, urging Ferrara to submit to the inevitable :—

> Vedova, sola, ottenebrata e scura,
>   Ti veggio, alma Ferrara, in tanti affanni,
>   Che s' io contemplo a li passati danni,
>   Del tuo sterminio in tutto ho gran paura.
> Veggio il campo nemico alle tue mura,
>   Che visser già pacifiche tant' anni.
>   Temo or le forze, ora i civili inganni,
>   Se il Ciel non ha di te per pietà cura.
> Io t'amo. Tu sai ben, ch' io n' ho cagione.
>   Deh ! perchè non deponi omai l' orgoglio ?
>   Chè sai : sol l' umiltà vince il Leone.
> Più che di mia prigion di te mi doglio ;
>   Che poi che vedi in l' arme la ragione,
>   Vogli schivare il porto e dar nel scoglio.[1]

In a very limited sense, the mantle of Boiardo may be said to have fallen upon a minor poet of a different stamp: Francesco Bello, called because of his blindness Il Cieco, or Francesco Orbo da Ferrara. Recent researches have shown that he was not one of those two blind poets who, in 1477,

---

[1] " Widowed and alone, overwhelmed with darkness, do I see thee, kind Ferrara, in so great torments that, if I contemplate thy past losses, I have great fear of thy total destruction.

" I see the hostile army at thy walls, which have lived in peace so many years. Violence and civic treachery I fear alike, unless Heaven for pity takes care for thee.

" I love thee. Thou knowest well that I have cause. Ah ! why dost not henceforth lay aside thy pride ? for thou knowest humility alone conquers the Lion.

" More than for my own imprisonment I grieve for thee, who, since thou appealest to the arbitrament of arms, wilt shun the harbour and break upon the rock " (In Sanudo, *Vite dei Duchi di Venezia*, col. 1226. I have taken a slight liberty in reading *che vedi* for *ch' i' vidi* in the penultimate line).

sang at the supper-pa
brothers in the Palaz:
Mambriano, was comp
at Bozzolo, where Gia
Marchese Gian France
" I send Francesco O
former from Bozzolo
" in order that you, to
in his singing, which ge
when you shall think
back, because here I ha
to him." ² After his
settled in Mantua, whe
died a few years later.

The *Mambriano* is a
some extent after the
though conspicuously ir
We have the same min
elements, of exaggerate
enchantments, and, tho
serious than Boiardo, th
references to the authority
too, at intervals, and the:
parts of the poem.³ The

[1] G. Rua, *Postille su tre P.
Letteratura Italiana*, xi. p. 296
and Francesco da Firenze.
[2] G. Rua, *op. cit.*, p. 294.
[3] For Il Cieco, see especial
A full analysis of the poem w
Romantic Narrative Poetry of
have translated Statius. He
to a prelate of the House of
mondo ; but, in the edition p

THE POETS OF THE HERCULEAN CIRCLE

are, strictly speaking, concerned with the ostensible subject of the work. They tell us of the war waged upon Charlemagne and the Christians of France by Mambriano, King of Bithynia, who has vowed to destroy Montalbano to avenge his kinsman Mambrino, whom he supposes to have been treacherously slain by Rinaldo. Alternating with this are adventures of the paladins Orlando and Astolfo in Spain and Africa—Astolfo being again a comic character and fairly successful. The enchantress Carandina exercises her arts on both Mambriano and Rinaldo, holding the latter in amorous bondage while the invader routs Charlemagne and besieges Bradamante in Montalbano. Released by Malagigi's sorceries, Rinaldo defeats Mambriano, pursues him into Asia and conquers him, partly by force, partly by magnanimity. Mambriano marries Carandina, and the other enchantress, Fulvia, is similarly converted from the errors of her ways. It is probable that the poem originally ended with the submission of Mambriano and his alliance with the victorious Rinaldo. But, possibly after his removal from Bozzolo to Mantua and at the instance of his new patrons, the poet sings on again in nineteen cantos practically unconnected with what has gone before. He gives his hearers the exploits of Rinaldo's son Ivonetto, Orlando's pilgrimage to Compostela, fresh sorceries of Malagigi for the benefit of his cousin, and other episodes which have nothing to do with the rest of the story. And now, as in Boiardo's poem, political echoes begin to be heard—as we should expect with a Court poet of the victor of Fornovo. The blind poet is at first enthusiastic for the coming of King Charles, and proposes to celebrate his glories in song:—

that he had intended to recast the beginning of the poem and dedicate it to Ippolito d' Este.

DUKES A[...]

Perseo,
E vedi di
Che 'l non
Nè le nove
Bisogno c'
E d' altre
A voler cel
Del novo C

Costui in
Che, se 'l f
Nui lo vedr
A Cesare e
E rinfranca
Ad onta di
Già son mol
Profanament

But in the next canto
ally with the newly for
gallica nebbia, this Ga
down the Alps and tin;
with blood; and, a little
away his thoughts from
to lay down the lyre, seei
Italy."[2]   At last, in t

[1] "Perseus, mount again
a larger fountain, for the an
the nine sisters united togetl
Muses more talented and n
history the lofty memory of 1
  "He in brief while has a
corresponds to the great beg
and the vaunt from Caesar
liberate the beauteous Holy
many years has held it [insla
fanely to our disgrace" (xxxi
  [2] xxxii. 1; xxxvi. 1, 2.

THE POETS OF THE HERCULEAN CIRCLE

invasion in 1496, he breaks off at the end of Canto xlv—practically at the same point that he had reached nineteen cantos before—with the triumphal return of his paladins to Paris :—

>Nel qual tripudio con giubilo e festa
>Voglio lassarli e terminar l' historia,
>Chè 'l furor de la gallica tempesta
>Mi tra gli antichi fuor de la memoria,
>E non mi lassa far più manifesta
>Secondo il consueto la lor gloria;
>Anzi per forza mi constringe e move
>A transmutar le cose vecchie in nove.
>
>Basta ch' io v' ho condutti i paladini
>A la lor patria vittoriosi e sani,
>E soggiugati tutti i Saracini
>Che volean molestar nostri Cristiani,
>E narrato oltra i gesti peregrini
>De Renaldo e de gli altri capitani,
>In che modo il superbo Mambriano
>Fu fatto tributario a Carlo Mano.
>
>E perchè da costui ho incominciato,
>Se 'l non dispiace a vostra signoria,
>Io vo che *Mambrian* sia intitulato
>Il libro ove è fondata l' opra mia ;
>Chè simel titol da Turpin gli è dato,
>Scrittor famoso il qual non scriveria
>Per tutto l'or del mondo una menzogna,
>E chi il contrario tien vaneggia e sogna.[1]

---

[1] " In this triumph with jubilee and rejoicing am I fain to leave them and end the story, for the fury of the Gallic tempest draws the ancients out of my memory, and lets me not manifest any more their glory according to my wont; nay, by force it compels and moves me to transform old things into new.

" It is enough that I have brought you the paladins victorious and sound to their native land, and subdued all the Saracens who wished to molest our Christians, and further narrated the wondrous

DUKES AN

In the poetry, as in
the artist was already
all the rest: È nato chi l
the mighty Dantesque
of Count Niccolò and
Ariosti, both of whom
circumstances in the
Reggio in September,
the office of captain of
Count Niccolò with his
the young Lodovico, the
old, had his first sight
(then awakening to a r
horrors of the Venetian
to be associated with hi
making the boy study
vico's tastes were for lit
1493, he had been one
Ercole took with him
comedies before the Duc
The first poem of his t
written on the occasion c
in the following October
in *terza rima*, in parts in
passing away of Laura

deeds of Rinaldo and the o
Mambriano was made tribut
"And because I have be
your Lordship, I would have t
entitled *Mambriano*; for a li
writer who would not write
who holdeth the contrary ra

[1] See above, chapter vii.

THE POETS OF THE HERCULEAN CIRCLE

After this, probably gratified at his success, his father left Lodovico free to follow his own bent. Under the guidance of the humanist Gregorio da Spoleto, he plunged into the Latin poets, and began himself to compose poems in their language. He grew intimate with his fellow-pupil under Gregorio, the afterwards famous Alberto Pio of Carpi,[1] and with Ercole Strozzi; a little later, he got to know Pietro Bembo, probably through one or other of the Strozzi.

This first period of Ariosto's life was, in Carducci's much quoted phrase, *tutta latina*. All the poems that he wrote were in the language and measures of the ancients, Catullus, Horace and Tibullus being his usual models; they are partly addressed to the three friends above mentioned and to the beloved kinsman, Pandolfo di Malatesta Ariosti, who shared his tastes and studies, partly to women. One of his first poems that we can date with certainty is an ode in alcaic stanzas, *Ad Philiroem*, written in the summer of 1496, when Charles VIII was at Lyons and a new French invasion was hourly expected. In amorous dalliance with sweet Phyllis among the flowers, watching the reapers at their work, young Lodovico can jest at the rumours of Gallic fleets and armies, and the threatened downfall of his country, *turribus ausoniis ruinam*: "Me nulla tangat cura!" Thus the printed version of the ode; but in the original sketch there were four other stanzas interposed, which the poet chose to omit and which give another aspect to his indifference. They struck at the mercenary soldiers who shed their blood for gold, at the cupidity and ingratitude of the Italian despots, who robbed the children of those whose service had made

[1] In consequence of the perpetual quarrels in the Pio family, Ercole practically annexed Carpi to the Duchy of Ferrara in 1500, leaving Alberto only a nominal and partial possession.

DUKES AN

them great.[1] In a di
spirit, are the lines in a
after the French conque

> Quid nostra an Gal
> Si sit idem hinc a
> Barbaricone esse est
> Moribus ? At duci

Somewhat remarkable,
lamium which Ariosto c
Alfonso with Lucrezia B
Herculean and Romulean
the one band rejoicing in
Ferrara, the other bewaili
suffered—but both agreei
lady as *pulcherrima Virgo*

But now Ariosto, after
whole care of his family up
to appeal for aid to the
captain of the Rocca of Car
where he loved and sang in
the great work in which he
had left unfinished. In the
service of the Cardinal Ip
death of Ercole and accessio

[1] *Carm.* i. 8; Carducci, *Dell*
pp. 88–90.
[2] "What matters it to us whe
King, if there be the same hard
to be under a barbarian name th
Gods, give their deserts to these
[3] *Carm.* i. 4.

Chapter XIV
THE END OF THE HERCULEAN AGE

NO sooner had the news of the old Duke's death spread through the city than Tito Strozzi, Judge of the Twelve Sages and, therefore, nominally the representative of the people of Ferrara, solemnly came to the Castello and consigned the sceptre and sword to Alfonso, recognizing him as sovereign. Dressed in white and wearing the ducal cap, Alfonso rode in state through the city, between the Cardinal Ippolito and the Visdomino of Venice, preceded by the Cavaliere Giulio Tassoni bearing the ducal sword, followed by Don Ferrando and the other members of the reigning House, the nobles and magistrates on horseback, with mounted crossbowmen and men-at-arms, to the sound of martial music. As they rode through the vast crowd in the piazza, Alfonso turned to the Visdomino: "What think you of this people?" "A goodly folk, my lord," answered the Venetian. "I should not care to live," said the Duke, "if this people and I did not bestir ourselves in the service of the most illustrious Signoria." Before the high altar of the Duomo, Alfonso took the solemn oath of governing well and performing justice to his people, into the hands of the Cardinal. A heavy storm of snow and wind had raged, as the Duke and his train passed through the streets to the Duomo; "Verily," writes Pistofilo, "it was

an omen and a s.
have to sustain ir.

But, at first, the
which these "fur.
"To-day right ea
of Ferrara, "there
Costabili, our nota
Nobility, and, man;
countenance, he sho
write that thy fath
hath pleased God, ha
hast been declared L
nobles and people.
our soul. For, accord
grieve that the Holy
deprived of such a son
prudence and probity,
See with sincere piety.
not only by thee and his
all the right-minded; bu
sary that he should son
for; glory, but, perchan
must, nevertheless, afforc
death befitted a life spe
may hope that abundant ;
just Judge, our Saviour.
son, hast received the gove
great consent, hoping that, ;
a parent, thou wilt show
said Apostolic See and to t

[1] Sanudo, *Diarii*, vi. col. 126;
p. 493.

THE END OF THE HERCULEAN AGE

as not merely to fulfil, but to surpass by far the opinion that we have conceived of thee. We, indeed, receiving and embracing thee as our most special son (as thou art), shall do with paternal affection whatever we shall learn may tend to supporting the honour of thy Nobility and the peace of thy peoples; and all the more diligently as the newness of thy sovereignty seems the more to demand it; so that, as far as pertains to us and this Holy Apostolic See, thou shalt not feel that thou hast lost thy father Hercules."[1]

Alfonso had inherited but little of his father's popularity, and had none of his wife's culture. Brusque in manners, negligent in attire and somewhat forbidding in appearance, he left Lucrezia to her own circle of poets and humanists, while he devoted himself to his favourite mechanical pursuits, casting guns, working in metal, manufacturing majolica vessels and the like in his own private *bottega*. Rough artisans and men of low birth surrounded him, jesting freely with him, frequently admitted to his table, and even sharing in his coarser pleasures. It is clear that he disliked Lucrezia's friends. Bembo had grown more cautious and distant in his homage to the Duchess, since her husband's return, and let himself less frequently be seen in Ferrara. In this year, 1505, he published his *Asolani* at Venice, with a dedicatory letter to Lucrezia, in which he mentions "my friends, much loved by me and honoured by the world, your intimates and familiars, Messer Ercole Strozza and Messer Antonio Tebaldeo."[2] The Duke gave these two poets a severe fright at the beginning of his reign. We do not know exactly what he did or said; but, on February 3,

---

[1] Brief of January 29, 1505. *Archivio Vaticano*, xxxix. 22, ff. 252v, 253.
[2] Letter of August, 1505, in vol. viii. of the *Opere*.

DUKES ANL

Benedetto Capilupo w
that Ercole Strozzi was
all the people against hii
Duke, hinting that the
would tell her by word of
wrote to the Marquis,
benefice, because " this L
why, and it is not safe fo
the present, however, the
two remained in Ferrara ii

Firmly seated upon th
secure the friendship of Vei
dressed in black, accompan
Giulio, with a following
paid a state visit to the
the utmost cordiality. Bu
Ferrara. Throughout thi
there was great famine ai
women died of hunger in tl
the pestilence followed; sev
and thousands more left th
in July, and Tito Vespasian
fled to Reggio, where, in the
who did not long survive. Tl

[1] Luzio and Renier, *La Coltur*
d' Este, ii. 2, pp. 207, 239. In the
them both to Mantua, in Februar
autograph letters, urgently com
tection (*ibid.*, pp. 208, 239); but tl
and they were able to return to Fe

[2] Tito's son Ercole, who had beei
of Judge of the Twelve Sages, nov
April, when Antonio di Rinaldo Co

Alfonso d'Este
Third Duke of Ferrara
After Titian by Dosso Dossi

THE END OF THE HERCULEAN AGE

his quarters in Belriguardo. A copious harvest caused a general amelioration in the following year; but, in the meanwhile, an appalling tragedy had taken place which threw a dark cloud over the House of Este.

We have already seen that, before the old Duke's death, there had been some hints of a party in Ferrara prepared to put forward Don Ferrando as a pretender to the succession, and that it was rumoured that, if Alfonso had not returned from his travels in time, Ferrando would have been acclaimed Duke. There were many in the duchy that disliked Alfonso's personality and his apparent neglect of State business for his mechanical pursuits. Educated in the pompous Court of Naples, experienced in the service of France and Venice, Ferrando was intensely ambitious, and he now saw, in the discontent which was prevalent in these opening months of his brother's reign, his own way to the throne.

The origin of the affair is still shrouded in mystery. But it appears that in this same September, 1505, while Lucrezia was at Reggio, the conspirators met at Carpi—that perpetual nest of conspiracies against the House of Este—without any definite result. Besides Don Ferrando himself, the leading spirits were Count Albertino Boschetti, a man between sixty and seventy years old, and his son-in-law, Gerardo de' Roberti of Reggio, who was one of the captains of the Duke's crossbowmen. The lesser limbs of the plot were Franceschino Boccaccio of Rubiera, a creature of Ferrando's, and a priest of Gascony, called Gianni, whom Alfonso had picked up as a beggar boy during his travels, attracted by his sweet voice in singing, and admitted to his intimate circle, and who was one of the agents of his vices. Before they decided on taking definite action, the sting of revenge

was added to the cravings
Estensian brothers were dr
their parts in the impendin
 Donna Angela Borgia h
with playing the part of the
would-be Lancelot and
but had been indulging in a
account. Her extraordinar
hair which rivalled that of h
hearts of the Estensian pri
ecclesiastical profession ; the
and the bastard Giulio were b
upon the latter, allured by h
she said, in answer to a pass
" your brother's eyes are wort
person."
 Don Giulio had temporar
displeasure and been put un
having liberated from the pris
the Duke had sentenced to
September ; but he shortly ret
no danger. On November 3,
expedition in the country round
disguised, with a band of arme
assailed him ; in spite of Giuli
was overcome and dragged fron
brother stood looking on—*sta*
according to the express testimon
both his eyes with a rapier, and
was at Belriguardo when this ha

[1] Sanudo, *op. cit.*, vi.
[2] *Vita di Alfonso I d'*

THE END OF THE HERCULEAN AGE

himself hurried thither to inform him that their brother had been found horribly mutilated by unknown hands. In a passion of righteous indignation, Alfonso sprang from his seat—he was at table at the time—and ordered the most rigorous investigation to be made, himself hastening into Ferrara for the purpose.

The hideous crime had been only partially accomplished, and the physicians were able to save the sight of one eye. A few days after the event, on November 8, Ippolito—who had many good reasons for dreading the Pope—dispatched an epistle to Beltrando Costabili, which is a perfect model of hypocrisy. "Although we are certain," he bade his secretary write, "that, from the letters of the Excellence of the Lord Duke, the Holiness of our Lord will have fully understood the accident that has befallen the most illustrious lord Don Giulio, our brother; nevertheless, both because of the special duty we owe his Beatitude and because these scoundrels who have offended the said Don Giulio were once in our service, we have thought fit to tell him the same again briefly, by the means of your reverend paternity. And, therefore, from us, after kissing the feet of his Holiness, you will make him understand that, while Don Giulio was at Belriguardo and riding for pleasure in the country round after midday, he was assailed by four men, formerly our familiars, who dragged him from his horse and with repeated blows strove to extinguish the light of his eyes—albeit we still hope that, by the grace of God, the affair will pass off well. The cause of such a crime and atrocious thing, so far as we have been able to understand, has been that these men (who, we said, had been of ours) had enmity with certain of the household of Don Giulio, and it seems that his Lordship favoured these latter extremely

DUKES AND POETS IN FE

against them ; and those fellows, under:
were some differences between the said l
us (because of that priest about whom
believed that they would not be doing
offending his Lordship, and so set them
enormous an iniquity. Concerning this
the greatest sorrow that can be thought ;
that anything else could have happene
to cause us so much grief and anguish a
weighed and does weigh upon us so m
go out of our proper bounds—inasmuch
ecclesiastic, we have left nothing undo
Duke, our brother, to have these male
whom as yet we have not been able to
reverend paternity will explain to his
usual dexterity, and express to him t
we have therefrom." [1]

As a matter of fact, Ippolito had se
of the territories of the duchy, and
fallen upon himself. At the advice
Sages, Antonio Costabili, he left F
escape the first impulse of Alfonso's
wrote to Venice, requesting that the
delivered up to him, if taken. A
dezino, a Venetian subject, was arrest
having been one of the assailants of D
the Cardinal intervened vigorously
tion, the Duke bade his ambassado
Salimbeni, insist upon it, in season a
that "it is necessary for our honour
means, in our hands." The Sign

[1] Cappelli, *Lettere di Lodovico A*

THE END OF THE HERCULEAN AGE

complied; the man was at first said to have confessed, but afterwards released as innocent.[1] But already the Duke's anger had evaporated, and he could do nothing without Ippolito. Before the end of December, the Cardinal was back in Ferrara, perfectly in accord with Alfonso. Niccolò da Correggio, at the Duke's instance, attempted to bring about a reconciliation between the Cardinal and Giulio; in the presence of Alfonso, Ippolito craved pardon of Giulio, and Niccolò persuaded the two brothers to exchange the kiss of peace.[2] Needless to say that it was the kiss of Judas.

Thirsting for vengeance, Giulio made common cause with Don Ferrando, and it was decided that the Duke and the Cardinal should fall together. Machiavelli, in his famous chapter on conspiracies, observes that a plot against a single prince is a doubtful, perilous and imprudent thing; but to plot against two is utterly vain and foolish. There is another difficulty that the Florentine secretary perceives in these things, and that is what he calls "the majesty and the reverence that cling to the presence of a prince"—Shakespeare's "divinity" that "doth hedge a king." "Two of his brothers," Machiavelli says, "plotted against Duke Alfonso of Ferrara, and they used as their means the priest Gianni, the Duke's singer, who many times at their request brought the Duke among them; so that they had the opportunity of assassinating him. Nevertheless, never did one of them dare do it."[3] The delay was partly due to the difficulty of killing the two together, Ferrando being bent

[1] Sanudo, *op. cit.*, vi. coll. 255, 270, 271; Cappelli, *op. cit.*, document 5 (ducal letter of December 2, 1505).

[2] Luzio and Renier, *Niccolò da Correggio*, i. p. 244. Sanudo, *op. cit.*, vi. col. 276.

[3] *Discorsi sopra la prima deca di Tito Livio*, iii. 6.

upon taking the Duke's
should perish first. Th
the chance they needed.

Gayer than ever was
famine had abated, the
her health restored, glo
spirits, Lucrezia presided
da Correggio as her mast
played before the Court
Mercury appeared, " procl
in Heaven among the Goc
Duke in his seat," and g
announcing that there would
no more pest or famine.
with his glorious consort, f
a new Alcides.[1] The Duc
tended by her buffoons, Ba
through the streets of the
maskers, too; men secretly
federates, lurking through
crowds of disguised merrym
and the Cardinal. Gianni
Alfonso should cross their patl
arrived, none of the conspirat

The chance had been lost.
on a pilgrimage to Galicia, le
hands of Lucrezia and Ippol:
Venice. On his return, the
Ippolito's suspicions were arous
and frequently caught Gianni

[1] Letter from Bernardino de' Prosp
5, 1506. Luzio and Renier, *Niccolò*

THE END OF THE HERCULEAN AGE

physical strength, indulging in rough horse-play with the Duke,[1] which the Cardinal perceived might easily lend itself to something more serious. He warned Alfonso and had a certain Girolametto, a favourite servant of Don Giulio's, arrested.

In the meanwhile, a rumour had reached the Marquis of Mantua " of some infamous scandal, which it was our office to avert by all means in our power." Isabella, who was passionately attached to all her brothers, was wild with anxiety, and implored her husband to save Giulio from the dangers that threatened him, by inviting him to Mantua under colour of visiting their famous stables. Giulio at first seemed disposed to stand his ground; but at length, realizing the peril he was in, he fled from Ferrara and reached Mantua in safety. Here he convinced Isabella of his innocence and that he was the victim of a conspiracy. When Alfonso ordered him to return within two days, the Marquis wrote a vigorous letter on his behalf to Niccolò da Correggio, assuring him of Giulio's absolute and wholehearted fidelity to the Duke, beseeching him to obtain from his Excellence a safe-conduct for him and an extension of the two days: "and if anything else induces us to intervene in this matter, save our universal affection for all our brothers-in-law and respect for our common honour, may God never grant us anything that we want."[2] This was written on July 21; but two days later, July 23, the Count Albertino and Franceschino Boccaccio, with two of Ferrando's grooms, were arrested. Under the question,

---

[1] See Cappelli, *op. cit.*, p. cxxvi.

[2] The whole letter, which throws this completely new light upon the story, is given by Luzio and Renier, *Niccolò da Correggio*, i. pp. 245, 246.

DUKES AND POETS I[N]

they revealed everything. Gerardo
to Carpi, the priest Gianni (who
carried the plot into effect) fled to [
Ferrando either could not or [w]
summoned to his brother's presen[ce]
and craved pardon, on the groun[d]
thought only. In a paroxysm o[f]
that he would make him match
with his own hands, struck out o[f]
A solemn day of thanksgiving a[nd]
by the Commune of Ferrara, to
was some while before Alfonso
hands; Antonio Costabili and
successively sent to Mantua w[ith]
being entirely swayed by Isabell[a]
Alfonso personally met him at t[he]
to give way.² Roberti had a
Gianni arrested in Rome. On
ducal crossbowmen brought
on September 12, Boschetti,
beheaded and quartered on a
heads were fixed on the tower
where they remained many yea[rs]
For the two princes, anoth[er]
In the great central courtyard
was reared. The Court and
been summoned to attend;
were thronged with men an[d]

¹ Frizzi, iv. p. 224; Cappelli, credible?
² Sanudo, *op. cit.*, vi. col. 396.
³ Pistofilo, p. 495.

THE END OF THE HERCULEAN AGE

sight. What must have been Lucrezia's feelings, as she waited the coming as a felon of the man who had been her husband's proxy to bring her to her new home! The courtiers were in agitated suspense, the Duke himself sat in gloomy silence. At last the sound of the *Miserere* broke upon their ears, and, accompanied by brown-robed friars, the two half-blinded princes, helplessly dazed at the sunlight, were led up from the dungeons which are shown as those of Ugo and Parisina. Each attended by a masked headsman, ominously robed in red, they ascended the scaffold. Then Alfonso suddenly rose and signed to the executioners to stay their hands. He would spare his brothers' lives; the sentence was commuted to perpetual imprisonment.[1] Their goods were divided among the Duke's favourites; Niccolò da Correggio got Giulio's house in the Via degli Angeli, while Alfonso took into his own possession the splendid palace near San Francesco which their father had left to Ferrando.

It was evidently thought desirable to remove Donna Angela from the scenes, and, in December, Lucrezia married her to Count Alessandro Pio of Sassuolo.[2] We shall meet

---

[1] So, in effect, Fra Paolo da Lignago, ff. 174, 175; Cappelli, *op. cit.*, p. xxxi; Frizzi, iv. p. 225. But, in the case of Ferrando, all this must have been largely a matter of show. It was known in Venice, more than a month before, that his doom was perpetual imprisonment and that rooms were being prepared for him in the Castello (Sanudo vi. col. 388). Also, the Marquis of Mantua in surrendering Giulio had obtained a promise that his life should be spared. They were imprisoned high up in the Torre dei Leoni, and apparently not treated with any further rigour. The scope of the present volume fortunately allows me to reserve for another place the vile treatment of this tragedy by Lodovico Ariosto.

[2] "On the sixth day of December (1506), Madonna Angela Borgia went as bride to the house of the Lord Alessandro de' Pii, her bridegroom, in Ferrara, accompanied by all the Court" (Fra Paolo,

DUKES AND POETS IN

her again—not only among those
welcome the safe arrival of Ariosto's
the *Orlando Furioso*. By a strang
twenty years later, the son of this m
became the husband of Ippolito's natu

At the beginning of January, the la:
met his fate. The priest Gianni, wh
himself by entering the service of th
Riario, was brought to Ferrara fro1
difficulty saved from being torn to p
After being horribly tortured, he was
from one of the towers of the Castello,
this with much patience and apparent
than a week, he was found strangled
member of the conspiracy who deserv(
and who richly merited his fate.

Meanwhile, the papal thunderbolts h
House of Bentivoglio. Inflexible in his
back all the cities claimed by the Holy
occupied Perugia in August, 1506—Gia:
this occasion letting slip the chance o
and all his Court prisoners, and thus
through all the world, in so great a thing,
had already made his name infamous
smaller."[2] With the aid of French troop

---

f. 175v). In 1500, before coming to Ferrara, sl
to Francesco Maria della Rovere, nephew (
Giuliano and heir to the Duchy of Urbino, whc
years old; but the engagement had been bro
document 23).

[1] Sanudo, vi. coll. 532, 533. There is a hi(
treatment in Fra Paolo's Chronicle, f. 175.

[2] Guicciardini, vii.

THE END OF THE HERCULEAN AGE

the Pope was preparing to seize upon Bologna likewise. From Cesena he issued a bull ordering Giovanni Bentivoglio, instantly to leave his city, under pain of excommunication, including all who adhered to him or had any dealings with him. In October he reached Imola, where he appointed the Marquis of Mantua lieutenant-general of the enterprise —-Duke Guidobaldo of Urbino, as Gonfaloniere of the Church, being nominally the commander-in-chief of the ecclesiastical forces. "We cannot but have compassion," wrote the Gonzaga to his wife, "for this noble and to us always friendly family of the Bentivoglio, that now finds itself so in the balance; but the confidence that the Pope has placed in us compels us to do what our honour bids."[1]

Since the death of Duke Ercole, relations had grown colder between the House of Este and Giovanni Bentivoglio. There had been much bitter feeling on both sides, over questions concerning the restrictions imposed by the government of Bologna on the new Ferrarese subjects in Cento and La Pieve taking their crops out of the Bolognese territory, and the retaliatory measures adopted by the officials of the Ferrarese custom-house in levying heavy taxes and duties upon the Bolognese. "Tell them," wrote Alfonso to Ippolito, in the terms of the "new diplomacy" of the epoch, "that whatever happens is entirely their fault. We are in the right, and the Bolognese are in the wrong. Your most reverend Lordship can offer your own services as mediator; but let them know that, if they imagine that they are stronger than we, especially when they are in the wrong, and that they have more favour at Rome than we, they will be very greatly deceived, and that, when the time

[1] Letter of October 14, 1506. Luzio and Renier, *Mantova e Urbino*, p. 174.

comes, they will understand it bette[r]
misliked the new situation, seeing th[
been a kind of rampart between his
of the Church. Under compulsion,]
at-arms to swell the ecclesiastical ar[
himself to be summoned three time[
in person to pay his homage to the

On the night of November 2, the
Bologna, Giovanni and his wife Gin[e
of Milan, Annibale and Ermes to I[
governed the State during Alfon[s
them kindly; but in consequence of
which appears to have clung to the
fectious disease, he could only shelt[e
during which all the churches wer[e
services were permitted in the city.
Pope entered Bologna in triumph
demonstration of joy by the citizens,
no efforts to reconcile them to the r

It is characteristic of the rela[
the princes of Italy at this date tha[
Lucrezia found a refuge in Mantu[
led the army that had chased them
where Isabella was kindness itself t[
even there, they were not suffered
cruelty has been used against us,"
Cardinal Ippolito, "so that we can
nor on earth."[2] The new legate o[
Antonio Ferreri of Savona, pursu[

[1] Letter of October 22, 1505. Archiv[
Principi.
[2] Letter of May 1, 1507. Dallari, p. 2[

THE END OF THE HERCULEAN AGE

relentlessly with interdicts and excommunications. He compelled Annibale and his little sons to leave Mantua at the beginning of April, allowing a brief delay to Lucrezia because she was with child. The poor lady wrote piteously to Alfonso and Ippolito, her half-brothers, imploring them to let her come to find a refuge with her little girls at Ferrara, her old home, as the terms of the interdict did not include women. The Duke answered that he dared not, for fear of offending the Pope, receive her, as he would have desired, but that he had written to the legate of Bologna to beg him to allow her to come to Ferrara.[1] But in the meanwhile, urged by desperation, Annibale and his brothers collected troops and entered the Bolognese territory; their enterprise failed, and Ippolito was forced to make a show of moving against them with soldiers, to prevent their taking shelter in the Duchy of Ferrara. Alfonso wrote vigorously to him from Genoa, where he was in attendance upon the King of France who was laying siege to the revolted city, bidding him take every measure that no favour should be shown to the Bentivoglio by his subjects, so that the Pope and legate may be satisfied: " If you find any one disobeying our proclamations and orders in this matter, have him punished without any respect, in such wise that we may hear his cries even here."[2] Nevertheless, Ippolito did as little against them as he could, succeeded in gaining both their gratitude and that of the Pope, and obtained from the latter a sort of permission for Annibale to join his wife at Mantua.[3]

[1] Letters of April 3 and 8, 1507. Dallari, pp. 233, 234.
[2] Letter of May 1, 1507. Archivio di Modena, *Carteggio dei Principi*.
[3] Dallari, p. 235. Writing from Borgo San Donnino, on May 9, Annibale and Anton Galeazzo Bentivoglio thank Ippolito for not

DUKES AND POETS I[N

Cardinal Ferreri had bidden Lu(
month, or he would put Mantua u
even had one of her servants tor
State"; but Isabella, generous as
grace for her unhappy sister, who st
papal permission to take refuge
Ferrara.[1] There is a piteous letter fr(
in which she beseeches him to use
Governor of Bologna to get back ce
had been seized: "not only because
need of them, but that it may not a
utterly abandoned by your Lordshi
are to enjoy my property; the whic
I need greatly, seeing that I have te
ders and nearly forty mouths to pr(
vision on any side, since the lord my
nature that I believe your Lordsh
was in his own house, we could dr:
and that with difficulty; your Lordsl
now." And she implores him to ob
help for Annibale to maintain those
knowing to whom else to have re
fate has led me perforce to beg
Lordship may be assured that, wh(
every hour for death, and, were it
from my lady the Marchesana, wh(
I deserve, I should sometimes be h

having done what he could against the
papal brief of approval, of May 8, 1507,
23.
[1] See Dallari, p. 236.
[2] Letter dated Mantua, August 18

THE END OF THE HERCULEAN AGE

A more sinister personage than the Bentivoglio had seemed for a moment about to return to the Romagnole stage. In December, 1506, the secretary of Cesare Borgia appeared in Ferrara, to announce to the Duchess that her brother had escaped from his Spanish prison. He probably came to see if there was any chance for his master in Romagna, and Lucrezia sent him on to the Marquis of Mantua, to whom he had a letter from Cesare announcing his escape in somewhat sanctimonious terms: "I inform your Excellence that, after so many miseries, it has pleased our Lord God to deliver me and to draw me out of prison, in the way that you will learn from Federigo, my secretary, the bearer of this letter; may it please His infinite Clemency that it be for His greater service."[1] From Mantua the secretary went on to Bologna, where the Pope had him arrested. Lucrezia wrote earnestly to the Marquis, imploring him to use his influence with the Holy Father that so great a *smaccamento*—as she more forcibly than elegantly called it—should not be given to her brother, as would be the imprisonment of his servant. "I am most certain," she wrote, "that he will not be found to have done anything wrong, as he has not come to do or to say anything that can displease or cause uneasiness to his Beatitude. His Excellence would not think or dare to do such a thing towards his Holiness, and this man, if he had any commission, would first have communicated it to me, and I should not have tolerated, nor shall I tolerate that he should be the cause even of suspicion, because I am a most devout and most faithful servant of his Beatitude, as also is the most

Giovanni Bentivoglio died at Milan in the following February. Lucrezia was finally allowed to end her days at Ferrara.

[1] Letter of December 7, 1506. Gregorovius, document 53.

DUKES AND POETS IN

illustrious Lord my consort. But I
that he has come for anything else, sa
my brother's liberation." [1]

Alfonso was still with King Lou
Genoa, when the news reached Ferr
was dead. He had met a soldier's de
in the service of the King of Navarre
while assailing a rebellious vassal.
outside the city in Belriguardo whe
Raffaello, who had preached the]
Ippolito gradually broke it to her
grief," wrote the Visdomino to hi
constancy and without tears." [2] Al
by the conduct of his wife and brot

"We are beyond measure satisfie
reverend Lordship has intimated to
cation of the fate of the Duke her b
trious consort, it seeming to us tha
has proceeded according to your
experience. Likewise, we are much
ship, our consort, has borne this ca
your Lordship tells us. This we att
and virtue, and we thank you inf
supremely satisfied and gratified wi

Lucrezia came into Ferrara, not t
convent of the Corpus Domini, whe
for a few days, in continual prayer
her brother's soul. The faithful F

[1] Letter of January 15, 1507. Gregor
[2] Sanudo, *op. cit.*, vii. col. 56.
[3] Letter of April 27, 1507, to the Cardi
camp at Genoa. Archivio di Modena,

THE END OF THE HERCULEAN AGE

to her his funeral poem on Cesare's death, of which one passage will serve as an example:—

> Indulge lacrymis ; tibi, Borgia, iusta dolendi
> Causa : tuae primum gentis decus occidit, ingens
> Pace, ingens bello, frater tuus, ardua cuius
> Gloria Caesaribus par reque et nomine magnis.
> Occidit heu multo confossus vulnere ; teque
> Di vetuere pia frigentia lumina dextra
> Claudere, et exhalantem animam legere ore propinquo,
> Et lacrymis vastos plagarum abstergere hiatus,
> Condereque immensis caros ululatibus artus.
> Et iam quisque audet tanto dare frena dolori.[1]

At the end of April, Genoa had surrendered to the Most Christian King; early in May, Alfonso returned to Ferrara. For the rest, this was a gloomy year in the city. The grief of the Duchess infected the Court ; the pestilence returned, " and wrought great damage and much slaughter."

Things seemed brighter with the opening of the new year. The carnival of 1508 was rich in dramatic representations in the palace of the Estensi. On the evening of February 13, a dramatic eclogue, composed by Ercole Pio at the instance of the Cardinal Ippolito, was exhibited in the Sala Grande. The Duke and the Cardinal were there, both masked, and Lucrezia herself, surrounded by the ladies of her Court. Enamoured shepherds strove together in song, contended

---

[1] " Give way to tears ! A just cause, Borgia, hast thou for grief. The chief pride of thy race has fallen, thy brother, mighty in peace, mighty in war, whose arduous glory is equal both in deed and in name to the great Caesars. Alas! he has fallen, pierced with many wounds ; and thee the Gods have forbidden to close his dying eyes with loving hand, and to gather his passing soul upon thy lips, and with thy tears to wipe his gaping wounds and with immense lamentation bury his dear limbs. And now all dare give rein to so great a sorrow." *Caesaris Borgiae Ducis Epicedium per Herculem Strozam ad divam Lucretiam Borgiam*, pp. 30v–38v of Aldo's edition of the two Strozzi.

DUKES AND POETS I

for or against the whole race of the
the praises of the famous ladies of t
moderns, the three who now hel
upon the Eridanus, another upon
near the Metaurus"; to wit, Lu
Duchess Elisabetta of Urbino. Tl
hunters appeared, singing the prais
The time was past for mourning ar
sacrifice to the goddess Pallas fo
increase of their flocks, and to the g
might protect them and commend th
Then Ippolito's tumblers performe
singers hymned the " Diva Borgia
was thrown upon the sacrificial fire, a
in a dance. " And I went home, r
was much dancing, because it was 1
night, the time that each one has
his own house." [1]

Three more eclogues of the sam
on March 8, but appear to have b
by Antonio dall' Organo, ordered b
over-jocose and to contain things
of performance ; the second, cor
herself from Tebaldeo, presented th
into laurel, " the which, apart from
ezza of the verse and its good *senter*
mended," and apparently found

[1] Letter of February 14, 1508, from
Isabella. Luzio and Renier, *Urbino e M*
eclogue has not been preserved. Erco
famous Marco and brother of the witt
d' Este then and to every reader of the

THE END OF THE HERCULEAN AGE

third, by a poor Greek who was of the household of Ercole Strozzi, failed completely, because it lacked the moralities and intrigues of comedy. And, verily, this courtly audience had had, a few days before, some experience in the *moralità* and the *astuzie* of comedy—in the shape of the *Cassaria*, the first extant comedy of Ariosto himself.

"On Monday evening," writes Bernardino de' Prosperi to the Marchesana Isabella on March 8, after describing the failure of the three dramatic eclogues that had been represented on that day, "the Cardinal had a comedy performed, which was composed by Messer Lodovico Ariosto, his *famigliare*, and rendered in the form of a farce or merry jape, the which from beginning to end was as elegant and as delightful as any other that I have ever seen played, and it was much commended on every side." The music, and especially the wonderful scenery painted by the Duke's Court painter, Pellegrino da San Daniele, were greatly admired.[1] The *Cassaria* in this, the earlier of the two versions, is all in prose with the exception of the prologue. In its characters and plot, it is a free imitation of the classical Latin comedies; it is a rollicking piece of work, full of comical intrigue and cross-purposes, while the love-sick youths, Erofilo and Caridoro, with their sharp-witted knavish servants, contrive to rescue the two captive girls, Eulalia and Corisca, from the clutches of the vile pander Lucrano, and to involve the rich old merchant, Crisobolo, Erofilo's father, in their devices.

Although a little later the Court was again in mourning—this time for the death of Cesare's former enemy, the

[1] Cf. L zio and Renier, *La Coltura e le Relazioni Letterarie d' Isabella d' Este,* ii. 2, pp. 208, 209; Campori, *Notizie per la Vita di Lodovico Ariosto,* pp. 48, 49.

good Duke Guidobaldo, who die
was succeeded by Francesco Ma
seemed, for the rest, about to sm
this spring. Rome and Ven
Julius conferred upon Alfonso th
been some misunderstanding be
Most Serene Republic; so, on Apri
Francolino with his flotilla of
familiariter, to justify himself.
news of the birth of a son and h
was delivered of a boy to whom t
in memory of his paternal grandf
Ercole Strozzi was well to the f
cious event in his *Genethliacon*, a l
in elegiac verse, in which the glorie
Este and Borgia are all united
future hero:—

> Cresce Deûm soboles, et avi t
> Herculis, ut sacro nomen ab
> Excitet, Alphonsusque atavus
> Summus Aragoniae splendor
> Et magnis stimulet te Caesar
> Grandeque Alexander sit tibi
> Hi tibi Scipiadas referunt, refe
> Quosque tulit claros terra Pe

Hardly had the rejoicings for th

[1] "Grow up, offspring of the Gods, an(
of thy father's father, Hercules, as thou (
stream. Let thy forefathers Alfonso and
a supreme glory of the House of Arag(
stimulate thee by his mighty exploits, and
be to thee a great spur. To thee thes
bring back the Camilli, and those famo
bore." *Genethliacon*, pp. 53-56 of Aldo':

THE END OF THE HERCULEAN AGE

died away, than a mysterious horror fell upon the Court, the mystery of which has not yet been fully explained. It must, as Gregorovius notes, have reminded Lucrezia of the tragical end of her own brother, Juan of Gandia.

There lived at Ferrara a certain Barbara Torelli, daughter of Marsilio Torelli, the beautiful young widow of Ercole di Sante Bentivoglio. Her married life had been a tragedy from first to last; Ercole Bentivoglio, who had served the Republic of Florence and Cesare Borgia as condottiere, was a harsh and brutal soldier, while she was delicately nurtured and highly cultured, a poetess of no mean achievement in the vernacular. She had been wrongly accused of adultery and of attempting her husband's life by poison, while living at Urbino; and, although she had come triumphantly out of the ordeal, the latter had induced Duke Ercole to help him in taking his daughter Costanza out of her hands.[1] On the death of her husband, Barbara had retired to Ferrara, the native city of her father's family, where she took part in the life of the Court and shone in its literary society. Lovers and admirers gathered round her; it was whispered that Ercole Strozzi and a mysterious "personage of high rank" were rivals for her favours. Since she preferred the vernacular to Latin, Strozzi laid aside his wonted classical style and sang her praises in Italian sonnets. One of

[1] Cf. Letter of July 20, 1501, from Silvestro Calandra at Urbino to the Marquis of Mantua (D' Arco, *Notisie*, pp. 248, 249); letter of May 10, 1504, from Ercole Bentivoglio to the Duke of Ferrara (Dallari, p. 223). In a curious little note, apparently to the Duchess of Urbino, May 21, 1502, the Duke (Ercole) says that, to please her Ladyship, he has been content that Madonna Barbara should stay for a few days in the convent of S. Maria delle Grazie, but she has been staying too long, and, her presence being very inconvenient to the nuns, she must be taken away at once. Archivio di Modena, *Minutario Cronologico*.

these at least, the lover's longi
when absent from her presence

    O beato pensier, ch' a c
      Per aspri monti e pro*
      A Madonna, e con lei
        E godi 'l ben che di s
    Deh! perchè teco la grav
      Non può volar a que'
      E seco, come tu, star n(
      Benchè più presso a lei
    Esser questo non può : dt
      Nè perchè altrove miri,
      E ogni sua forza nel pe
    Chè oltra 'l piacer che ha
      Fansi gli spirti nel pens
      Che 'n sogno col suo be

Several other pieces in the vern
which appear to be his; they h
merit;[2] but the lame, perfumed C
sigh in vain.

[1] "Oh blessed thought, that at e"
mountains and deep waters, dost r(
and dwell with her, and enjoyest th
world's desire;

"Ah! why cannot the irksome bod
beauteous eyes, and with her, like
although nigher to her it feels more

"This cannot be. Let then my hea
elsewhere may it ever see aught else,
use in thought;

"For, beyond the delight it hath wh
in thought become so intense that in d
bliss."

[2] There are four sonnets, including t
have ventured to correct an obvious e
the seventh line), ascribed to Ercole St
Poeti Ferraresi, pp. 53-55. One of th
aurei crespi nodi," has also been
Castiglione.

THE END OF THE HERCULEAN AGE

On May 24, Ercole Strozzi and Barbara Torelli were privately married. Shortly afterwards, she gave birth to a daughter, to whom the Marquis of Mantua promised to stand as godfather. On the night of June 5, Ercole rode out, mounted on a mule, unattended, *a pigliare un poco di fresco*. He never returned alive. In the morning his body was found, covered with stabs and with the throat cut, a short way from his own house in the middle of the street near San Francesco; he was wrapped up in his cloak, his hat upon his head and his crutch lying by his side; and, as there was no blood to be seen, it was concluded that he had been brought dead to that place. "No one named the author of the assassination," says Giovio, grimly and significantly, " because the Podestà kept silence." Although justice was rigorously enforced in Ferrara, no investigation of any sort was made to find out the perpetrators of the bloody deed.

Later writers have been unanimous in recognizing that the blow came from the Castello, and that the Duke himself was at least privy to the murder. For some, the motive is found in Ercole's familiarity with the Duchess Lucrezia; for others, perhaps more plausibly, in Alfonso's own lust for Barbara Torelli. But the inscrutable despot kept his own counsels; none dared question, nor name the doer of the deed; even members of the Duke's own family seem to have been uncertain, and suspicion for a while fell—we do not know why—upon Alessandro Pio of Sassuolo, the husband of Angela Borgia.[1] Nevertheless, the silence of the Court

---

[1] On June 30, Girolamo Mugiasca, writing from Bologna to the Cardinal Ippolito, says that public report named Alessandro da Sassuolo as the cause of Ercole's death, but that suspicion had been thrown upon Masino dal Forno (Cappelli, *op. cit.*, p. lxiii. note 4).

DUKES AND P(

tells its own story. It was
and Lorenzo, the brothers (
with the widow, announced
Marquis of Mantua, hoping,
vengeance upon him who had
of his, as on their side they wo
idle words. To Barbara's ɪ
coldly answered that he was ᴠ
occurrence, " the unhappy fat‹
the consort of your Magnificeɪ
of an affectionate friend ; thaᴛ
those that Messer Ercole had leғ
had borne to Ercole himself ; an‹
Tebaldeo to represent him as ɢ
tism, according to his promise
ourselves for the services of y
love that we bore to the deᴄ‹

This Masino was one of Alfonso's faᴠ
June 6 to Isabella, telling her of w
de' Prosperi gives no hint of the m
Coltura, *etc.*, *d' Isabella d' Este*, ii
Pistofilo, the murdered man's broth
Simone Fornari of Reggio, almost
sopra l' Orlando Furioso, Florence, 15
di Filippo Strozzi (*Vite degli uomini*
77, 78), who had been present in hi
Alfonso and Lucrezia, openly accuse
of June, the Visdomino, Francesco Oɪ
so we have no hint in Sanudo's Dɪ
was regarded at Venice. On the
that, had a Dante of the Cinquecentᴏ
shores of Purgatory, he would probablʏ
as Jacopo del Cassero uttered to his
il fe' far (*Purg.* v. 77).

[1] Luzio and Renier, *op. cit.*, ii. 2, pp.
letter is dated July 10, 1508.

THE END OF THE HERCULEAN AGE

Pietro Bembo and Aldo Manuzio offered up poetic tributes at the tomb of the murdered man; Ariosto himself wrote his epitaph—eight somewhat frigid and conventional lines of elegiac verse.[1] The hapless widow alone dared to speak what was in her heart, in a sonnet which, among the lyrics of the age, stands alone in its fire and pathos:—

> Spenta è d' Amor la face, il dardo è rotto,
> E l'arco e la faretra e ogni sua possa,
> Poi ch' ha Morte crudel la pianta scossa,
> A la cui ombra cheta io dormia sotto.
> Deh! perchè non poss' io la breve fossa
> Seco entrar dove hallo il destin condotto,
> Colui che appena cinque giorni e otto
> Amor legò pria de la gran percossa?
> Vorrei col foco mio quel freddo ghiaccio
> Intepidire, e rimpastar col pianto
> La polve e ravvivarla a nuova vita;
> E vorrei poscia baldanzosa e ardita
> Mostrarlo a lui, che ruppe il caro laccio,
> E dirgli: Amor (mostro crudel!) può tanto.[2]

Shunned and neglected by all, Barbara fled from Ferrara to Venice, taking with her some of Strozzi's illegitimate children as well as her own little daughter. "One for fear,

---

[1] *Carm.* iii. 7.

[2] "Quenched is Love's torch, his arrow is broken, and his bow and quiver and all his power, since cruel Death hath shaken the tree beneath whose shadow I slept in peace.

"Ah! why cannot I enter with him into the narrow grave whither destiny has brought him, him whom scarcely thirteen days Love bound before the great stroke?

"Fain would I with my fire warm that cold ice, and remould the dust with my tears and revive it to new life;

"And then, daring and fearless, would I show it to him, who broke this dear bond, and tell him: Thou cruel monster, Love has this much power."

This sonnet, which was first published by Baruffaldi in the *Rime scelte dei Poeti Ferraresi*, p. 55, has in the second quadernario a designed echo of the sonnet, already quoted, that Strozzi had written to the poetess herself.

DUKES AND POE[TS]

another for personal interest,' [to] Mantua, "not any one has b[een in] memory nor his children, sav[e in] thought, since I kept silent [and] my horrible misfortune would [have] compassion; but I find myself m[ore] than ever."[1]

With the death of Ercole Str[ozzi the] poets and men of letters, that had [loved] and person of the late Duke Erc[ole came to an] end. Niccolò da Correggio had [died] the previous February, neglected a[nd for] Alfonso, who on his death took [back] Giulio which had been ceded to him [when] had ended his days.[2] But the loss of [one] who had been the life of so [many pageants] seems to have shed no gloom over [the court of] Ferrara, when Lodovico Ariosto made [a bigger] hit than in that of the previous y[ear] of his new comedy, the *Suppositi* or [in its] earlier prose form.

[1] Letter dated Venice, March 17, 1509. [Cf.] Renier, in the *Giornale Storico della Letterat[ura]* 249 note. Cf. Bertoni, *La Biblioteca Estense*, [who] even appealed to Duke Alfonso himself on [behalf of] Cesare.

[2] Writing to Isabella, Bernardino de' Prosp[eri said his death had] been hastened by his "grief and melancholy [at being so] great and now cast down." Luzio and Renier, [op. cit.,] ii. pp. 74, 75. In May, 1507, Alfonso had be[en asked by the] Pope to take back certain possessions from Nicc[olò and restore them] to their former owners, the Succi of Bres[cello,] concerning which are two letters of May 30 a[nd June 4] to Ippolito, in the Archivio di Modena, *Cartegg[io,* which were] perhaps the cause of Niccolò's disgrace.

THE END OF THE HERCULEAN AGE

In the prologue, which Ariosto himself recited and which, we must add, is disfigured by the obscene play on words that the corrupted taste of the age more than tolerated, the poet confesses to have followed Plautus and Terence, but only in the way of poetical imitation. Nevertheless, as Bernardino de' Prosperi noted in giving his account of the performance to the Marchesana Isabella, the play was "an entirely modern comedy."[1] Instead of a Greek town in some vague classical epoch, the scene is laid in Ferrara itself in the last decade of the fifteenth century. Instead of the sharp-witted slaves and their knavish pranks, we see the students and doctors of the Studio in their long gowns; merchants from Siena or Catania land at the quay, and pass up those very streets through which we wander to-day; there are modern japes at the expense of the corrupt ducal officials and the aggressive custom-house functionaries, though, of course, it is expressly stated that "we have, above all, a most just prince." In a word, notwithstanding a few motives and situations lifted from Terence and Plautus, we have, for the first time, a comedy of Italian life, several years before Machiavelli had composed his *Mandragola*.

With the representation upon the Ferrarese stage of the *Cassaria* and the *Suppositi*, the first regular Italian comedies upon classical models, the work of Duke Ercole in the renovation of the Italian drama may be said to have been completed. And, indeed, with this carnival of 1509 the golden age of Ferrara ended. A period of strife and disaster was about to set in. "It was a time," writes D'Ancona, "not of comedies, but of effective and real tragedies; and all Italy, especially the valley of the Po, was the scene of

---

[1] Letter of February 8, 1509. Campori, *op. cit.*, pp. 50, 51.

them."¹ In these the Duke
Ippolito, as also in his degree A
their parts. Belying the prom
the House of Este, Pope Juli
beginning of that relentless str
and the Estensi, which only e
of Clement VIII with the incorp
territories of the Church. As 1
Ercole in the Tower of the Lion
Ippolito and Alfonso, and died 1
1559, more than half a century a
half-blind man appeared in the s
the costume of a bygone age. It
released from his captivity at tl
grandson—that second Alfonso
sovereignty of the House of Este
to an end.

[1] *Origini,* ii. p.

APPENDICES

APPENDIX I

Unedited Poems of the Borsian Epoch

WHILE the courtly poetry that flourished in Ferrara during the reign of Duke Borso was mainly Latin, there was a certain amount of verse written in the vulgar tongue. The *Canzoniere* of Matteo Maria Boiardo, written, as we saw, in the last years of his reign, is the supreme example. Most of the minor poetry of this kind seems to lie still unedited on the shelves of the Italian libraries—a striking poem to a dead wanton by Andrea da Basso (in the *Rime scelte dei Poeti Ferraresi*) being one of the few exceptions. The two manuscripts of vernacular Court poetry, which I am about to describe, are both, as far as I know, unpublished.

In the library of the Vatican (*Biblioteca Vaticana, Cod. Capponiano*, 219) is an anonymous Triumph of Duke Borso, in six cantos in *terza rima*, somewhat in the spirit of the painted laudations of the Duke and Duchess of Urbino, Federigo da Montefeltro and Battista Sforza, by Pietro de' Franceschi in the Uffizi. The first canto opens :—

> Tutto il mondo non ha il più sciocho ingiegnio
> del mio nè le più ruvide parole,
> nè di trattar gran cose homo men degnio.

But his friend and gossip, Monsignor Hermolao, has suggested this great subject to the writer :—

> Il magnanimo Borso mia dolce escha,
> cibo da satiar ongni poeta,
> di sua virtù mio canto tutto invescha.
> E materia mi da sì piana e queta
> da cantare, offerendomi se stesso,
> che tutta la mia mente ne fi leta.

APPE[N]

Denanzi agli ochi me lo
tra quatro donne belle
che in compagnia van
Un ghambo d'or da quat[r]
gemme con perle grosse,
ornato pare come Dio il
Quanto egli sia glorioso e
per queste donne et altr[e]
tu, sagro Apollo, chiaro
e come summamente egli t[
cosi piacere a me fai sua
degnia dil lauro tuo verd[e]

* *

A noi non so ben dir come
giamai potesse alguno ess[o]
cosi profundo thema pred[
Vengha Virgilio e Flacco e i
e quello che Peligno tanto
e Gallo con Propertio e co
e tutti sette insieme caccian
ciò che hanno detto poeta[r]
e quel che se descrive de l
che mai non mostraranno tal
qual si farebbe di costui cl
d'esser lodato in l'alto conc
O convenente a glorioso ingie[
materia, come pati tanto to
quant' io te facio essendo d

These four ladies who ever accom[pany]
Prudence, Fortitude, Justice and Ten[
dant virtues, a canto being devo[
Prudence goes in front of him (canto ii
nobile e legiadre " under her charge-
standing, Science, Knowledge, Industr[
Experience :—

In questo modo dil suo amore [
Madonna il mio signiore inclyt[
che esser chiamato già solea M
Perciò convien che la sua fama l
e che splendor per l'universo s[
sì che se stesso in cielo se con[

On his right side goes Fortitude (cant[o

APPENDIX I

her handmaidens, Faith, Constancy, Perseverance, Courage, Loyalty and many more.

>E così acompagniato se ne viene
>a tanta perfetione de virtute
>che ongniuno divo e semideo lo tiene.
>Hor pensa quando in porto di salute
>Egli sia gionto quale fi sua fama,
>per la qual nulle lingue finno mute.
>Continuamente il cielo a se lo chiama,
>ma pur ne lo concede per molti anni
>per contentar la nostra voglia e brama.
>Foriano troppo ismesurati danni
>gli nostri se ne fosse prima tolto,
>e cason ne foria de eterni affanni.
>Non mancho danno che se'l suo bel volto
>Apollo nascondesse, ne fi alhora
>quando costui serà da noi discíolto.
>Ma la speranza ch'egli al men dimora
>tra noi cento anni come il ciel permette
>dil carcer di paura ne tien fora.

On the left side of the poet's *signior novello*, " ove se anida il core," always goes Justice (canto iv.). Temperance follows him step by step (canto v.), with her attendants: Magnificence, Liberality, Mansuetude, Modesty, Gravity and Courtesy, Continence and Purity :—

>Tra queste donne va lo amato amante
>posto nel mezo de le principesse,
>modesto, iusto, praticho, e constante.
> *   *   *   *
>Libero fi da ongni terrena peste
>più che null' altro principe non sia,
>chi voglia mie parole haver moleste.
>Io non credo ad altrui far villania
>per lodare costui che da splendore
>a tutta la terrestre monarchia.

In the sixth and last canto, the poet once more professes his unworthiness and inability adequately to express the triumph and glory of Borso's state, and humbly craves to be taken into his service:—

APPENDIX

D'altronde mai non spero esse[r]
se non indi che fi se 'l mio (
non mi è nemicho come sem[pre]
anci per dir più vero se 'l divi[no]
iudicio non mi è contra per
ma sia pietoso al ciecho per
Come si sia me par che me si
l'una e l'altra nel cor spera[n]
ben che temerità forte me i[n]
Chieggio per gratia in locho d[i]
dal mio Signior che tra soi
servi me doni piccol locho e
a ciò ch'io possa haver venti
a la debile barcha del mio
il qual convien che per lui
Forse che 'l tempo mi farà pi[ù]
che hora non son di far di
se de amarmi si scopre in
Altro ragionamento a la mia
non si farà che di sua gran[de]
la fama chui per tutto il m[ondo]
Donemi pace e vita con salu[te]
Iddio, sì ch'io mi possa pr[e]
che le mie voci non staran[no]
Il mio riposo, il mio summo
serà di haver continuament[e]
la cythra e di costui canta[re]
ricontando con verso più sop[ra]
che non fi questo, il qual
perrò che in vero è troppo
gli soi meriti degni d'alto sti[le]
e di prisco poeta laureato
e de ingiegnio mirabile e s
Vengha sì come aspetto il d[e]
tempo ch'io veggia la mia
sì ch'io me trovi stare in
che non fi algun che me sti[mi]
come forse ad altrui par c[he]
essend' io da fortuna oppr[esso]
Mi transporta a parlar la fa[ma]
de' fatti proprii più ch'io
Ma ritorniamo ne la dritta

He cannot express with words the
to which his universal popularity th[e]

APPENDIX I

testimony. Truth alone will defend his song and supplement all its deficiencies :—

> Perciò il mio canto molto non si cura
> nè cercha di haver altra compagnia
> che sola veritade integra e pura.
> Costei mi segue e vien mecho per via,
> mentr' io vo dietro al mio signior cantando
> e mostro altrui sua gloria e monarchia.
> Di lui ragiono, e lei testificando
> conferma ciò ch'io dicho e fanne fede,
> sì che da noi si sa busia haver bando.
> Al mio parere ongniuno ne lo crede,
> forse algun no, che per invidia privo
> dil lume il vero non discerne e vede.
> Ma priegho Dio che quello che hora scrivo
> mi presti un' altra volta meglior aso
> di replichar e mi mantengha vivo ;
> alhora moverò tutto Parnaso.

We have no clue to the identity of this poetic seeker for Borsian favours. At first sight, the reference to Catullus as *il mio Catullo* might lead to the hypothesis that he was a Veronese by origin, and the prayer for the *ciecho peregrino* imply that, like several other versifiers of the Quattrocento, he was physically blind. This would, however, be unduly stretching a point; the one allusion probably only means that Catullus was a special favourite with him (cf. the *il mio Tibullo* in the third sonnet by Nuvolone quoted below), and the other seems a mere metaphorical form of speech. We must, therefore, leave him for the present in his obscurity.

The case is very different with our next poet. Filippo Nuvolone was a Mantuan by origin. He was the son of that Carlo Nuvolone, whom we have already met in the circle of the Marchese Leonello among the interlocutors of Angelo Decembrio's *De Politia Litteraria*, and who was frequently employed in the service of the Estensi. Filippo studied Greek under Lodovico Carbone and Battista Guarini at the Studio of Ferrara; he seems to have divided his time between the Courts of Borso d' Este and Lodovico Gonzaga; the first Mantuan edition of the *Divina Commedia* was dedicated to him in 1472; and he died of

APPENDIX I

the pestilence at Venice in 1478.[1] I;
(*Additional MS.* 22,335) there is a man
sonnets and canzoni, dedicated by Filip
d' Este, the half-brother of Borso and E
dedicatory canzone to Alberto, in which t
professes himself to be enamoured migl
Wisdom, but in the pieces that follow ("
e de amore de Philippo Nuvoloni com
illustre et excelso signore Alberto da E:
festly to be a mortal woman. They are
and manner, copious in their parade of
no means devoid of charm. The foui
examples :—

>   Quando la donna mia nel tem
>   colui che la formò nel ciel s
>   rentuona fin la su la sua fa
>   tal dolcieza escie de i suoi l
>   El star suo grave allor ben m
>   quando devota veggio esser
>   che ogni virtute et honestà
>   racolte paian tutte insieme
>   Non miri adunque altrui se il
>   i suoi costumi e il suo gient
>   mi strigne a far de ciò men
>   chè quanto più ci penso più n
>   el dir di lei : e al ciel semp
>   sua degna alta virtù, gloria

[1] For Filippo Nuvolone, see Bertoni, *La Bi*
124 and note.

[2] Alberto d' Este was the most " difficult
frequently on bad terms with his brothers.
accidentally killing a man in the ducal palaco
He was at first high in favour with Ercole, wh
been instrumental in procuring; but in May,
for refusing to go to greet a foreign prince [a
Schifanoia was confiscated. While in exile,
the fallen Duchess of Milan, Bona, caused a d
Milanese State, and Ercole forbade him to visit
responsible for the consequences (Letter of S
di Modena, *Carteggio dei Principi*). But his
Venice procured his pardon and restoration to

APPENDIX I

Dolcie mio caro e pretioso fiore,
  non ti debio io servar fino a la morte,
  e farti un tabernaculo sì forte
  che al mondo mai nisun ti spegna fuore ?
Poi che colei che in man tiene el mio cuore
  mi ti donò per mia benigna sorte,
  e se inclinaron sue belleze acorte
  a farmi degno alhor di tanto honore.
Eschan le perle ; e spengansi i diamanti ;
  e da me lenti e fugi ogni appetito
  de haver di questo mai thesor più degno,
che par del Paradiso essere uscito.
  O me felice sopra gli altri amanti !
  O felice quel dì ! felice pegno !

Tal Dante non cantò per Beatrice,
  nè Petrarcha per Laura, nè Catullo
  per Lesbia, nè per Delia il mio Tibullo,
  nè tanto cantò Orpheo per Euridice,
nè tanto Ovidio per Chorina dice,
  e al mondo mai per donna cantò nullo,
  quanto io cantrò per debito e trastullo
  di questa una celeste alma fenice.
E sua fama saglir fin sopra el cielo
  faran mei versi ; sì che la natura
  angielicha verrà quivi a mirarla ;
  e mirata e coperta d'altro velo
  la vederemo poi su repportarla,
cantando, osanna Dio, novella e pura.

Mentre, Madonna, gli è la età fiorita,
  con tanta ligiadria, tanta belleza,
  gli sia la humanità, la gientileza,
  la clementia e humiltate insieme unita.
Perchè vi trovarete poi pentita
  haver passato el fior de gioveneza,
  e senza alchun piaciere in la vechieza
  esser venuta al fin di vostra vita.
Mentre adunque gli è el tempo e la stagione,
  aime, Madonna, a voi mi rachogliete
  nel seno vostro e ne le braza stretto.
Dolcie martiro e dolcie passione,
  dolcie mal, dolcie doglia gustarete,
  havere insieme al fin nostro diletto.

At the end of the collection, the poet addresses Duke Borso

APPENDIX

himself in an extended and highly curiou
his Excellence his amorous torments a
protection, as to one who is " vessel, ha
purity, and hostelry of all the virtues o

    Hor giunto in questa età flori
    che per el sangue calido che
    convien l'huom la persona e
    e lassar quella vita humile e
    del studio e di quelle opre le
    e in destreza e in faticha ad
    cominziommi la mente alont
    dal imparar da i libri e dal
    e venni ardito al arte milita
    E lieto e iubilante
    tolsi in man le arme presto
    e quanto studioso
    prima a i libri era, tanto a
    che foggie ogni dì nuove era
    e a ciò gran tempo io tenni
    fin che altro pensier nuovo

    Fatto el pensieri io venni a tu
    mansueta, pacificha e tranqu
    nemicha de odio, di discordi
    armata di pietate e di clem
    che goza de iracondia in se
    in cui ogni bontà se include
    dicendo enfra me stesso : No
    signor tanto clemente e tant
    chome è questa alta iradiant
    e le arme e la choraza
    offersi al tempio del bifronte
    E a te, signor soprano,
    venni dicendo: Io viverò sec
    nè più di Marte fia mio cuor
    nè de alchun caso duro ;
    ma senza noia e senza dubio

    Aime, chi fa ragion si la fa ta
    a farla senza chi gli sia prop
    a fargli obietto, e che el con
    chè giunto ch'io fui sotto el
    credendo da nemichi esser lo
    e da le insidie lor, da loro ir
    pur allor mi trovai tra guerr

APPENDIX I

tra mille spade, lanze, e mille strali,
tra mille punte penetrante al cuore,
tra tanto e gran dolore
e colpi innumerabili mortali,
che mai non tanti e tali
sentette corpo human nè sentrà mai,
chè una fiera crudel, selvaggia e pia,
co i suoi belli ochii e rai
legò secho el mio cuore e l' alma mia.

E se ella questi dua ne tirò secho
che sono i principal veri operanti
nel corpo nostro misero e terreno,
pensi qualunque qui quel che è più mecho,
poi che quelli ochii excelsi e coruschanti
traxeron questi del lor proprio seno,
perchè el bel viso angielicho e sereno
non solo ha forza ne le humane cose
far arder sassi e il fuocho uscir de giazo,
e doglia esser solazo,
ma in le celeste incognite et ascose,
che 'l fier Marte ripose,
e Saturno se alegri e Iove imbruni;
e il Sol non schaldi; e Venere non splendi;
e la lingua se infuni
Mercurio; e Cinthia a pudicitia offendi.

Costei ha forza sopra el gran Cupido,
e sopra sua pharetra, archo e saette;
e nulla gli vale arma che egli adopri;
chè ella sempre è più fiera, e ha il cuor più fido
contra i colpi de amore, e lo submette;
e lui convien che giaza e che si chopri,
e se egli advien che in nulla se dischopri,
ella lo schaza, spigne e lo domina.
Cosa inaudita et admiranda e nuova,
che amor che ha fatto prova
e in la natura humana e in la divina,
si trovi hor resupina
sua forza e suo valor contra costei,
lui che ha vinto la terra e vinto el cielo,
e vinto homini e dei;
lei porti le arme, e lui sol porti el velo!

Costei mi crucia, lania, affligie, e snerba,
e in sì fieri tormenti ognihor me involve
che più riposo e gaudio è in lo Acheronte;

APPENDIX I

e contra me sì dura e sì sup
crudele e dira e immane si d
che non mostrossi tal Iove a
nè oschura al mondo mai se
palida et ignea, tenebrosa e
se non quando costei de ira
e che dal cuor suo nascie
la crudeltà che in me spigne
E quando ella si retra
dal cruciarmi, sto sì lasso e
che meglio mi sarebbe un m
che mille essere extinto,
e uscir di tanto affanno e ta

Chè impossibile fia che huomo
tanta gran doglia quanta so
che ognihor si charcha in m
e non sol suoi pungienti e n
prova lo afflitto cuor laniato
tinti in lo impio venen che
ma più me è a noia, duolmi
che amore e lei coniurano a
e armati contra me vengono
e una cosa è straniera,
che defender da dui nulla s
e poi se amor gli inganni
voglia oprar contra questa
perde sua forza; e me crud
sì che mal si sochorre
chi sol senza arme enfra du

De che, Signor mio, excelso i
se probato è che pudicitia
triumphi del amor chome si
e tu sia vaso, porto, e vera
di pudicitia, e albergo di q
virtù che ad amore obsti,
deh, schaza aime, Signor,
fiere che induchon gli homi
nè in tuo paese sia lo albe
e inclinati, ch'io moro;
e qui benigno voglimi exau
et ultra el dolcie udire
farmi ragion de questi mei
sì ch'io possa sechuro ire i
che amor nè lei mi dichi
nè mi fazi spiaciere, iniuria

APPENDIX I

Canzon, tu trovarai quello alto Ducha
　che nel sangue da Este è un lume e un sole,
　e che triumpha al charro in pudicitia;
　e chiedigli iustitia
　con ornate et humillime parole,
　chome a signor si suole,
　di tanta noia fattami e spiaciere;
　e poi che tu harai detto, a lui te achosta
　e sta atento a vedere,
　e aspetta sua humanissima risposta.

APPENDIX I

A Selection of Unpublished

I

Pope Paul II to Borso, Duke (

DILECTE FILI SALUTEM, ETC.—Mestus
filius Jacobus Trotus orator tuus; et en
ipso sentias: quod scilicet in proseque
effitiose sese apud Nos habuerit. Certe i
data tua executus est. Et id Nos scir
monium perhibemus. Debes igitur tu il
dignus est: nec eum qui de te benemeritu
quoniam graviter peccares, si faceres.
Nobilitatem tuam tam male informavit,
et decipitur, aut unionem odit et maligna
nosti, Nos ab initio Pontificatus Nostri se
conatu quesivimus unionem omnium Chr
Italorum; ut impresentiarum enixe fa
iuvante Deo etiam cum onere Nostro i
huiusmodi Italorum cito concludendam i
plane intelligent quam recte paterne et
gredimur. Sperantes nichilominus poter
ut communem omnium patrem atque hai
ut matrem prout est habituros, observa
adiuturos, simulque abunde in commune
citum contra impiissimos hos canes Turc
trubituros, sicuti sepenumero Nobis pollic
apud S. Petrum die xx *Decembris,* 1470,
septimo.

(Archivio Segreto della S. Sede, x

APPENDIX II

II

Pope Paul II to Borso, Duke of Ferrara.

ROME,
July 10, 1471.

DILECTE FILI SALUTEM, ETC.—Nuper in urbe Roma vulgabatur de tua Nobilitate nuntium admodum triste. Quod animum Nostrum valde angebat, et propter eam paternam caritatem, qua personam tuam amplectimur, et propter statum etiam tuum et tuorum, ac alia que pro tua prudentia potes intelligere; etiam id affligebat omnes tuos benivolos, qui etsi multi tibi sunt; habes et Nos ut tibi patrem benivolentissimum. Verum postea significatum est te, Dei beneficio, periculum evasisse, ex quo plurimum letitie accepimus. Hortamur autem te in Domino ut omni studio intendas ad confirmandam valitudinem: quo et tu tibi et tuis consolationi esse possis, etiam et Nobis propter Nostram erga te paternam benivolentiam. Ceterum misisti ad Nos donum locupletissimum usque adeo, sicut ei addi nichil potuisse videretur; habemus gratias tante huiusmodi largitioni tue, sed vellemus Nobiscum egisses parcius, qui etiam dona accipere non solemus. Velit autem ipsa Nobilitas deinceps ad Nos dona non mittere, nisi cum et que petierimus; et in hunc modum animo desiderioque Nostro vehementer satisfacies. *Datum Rome apud S. Petrum die* x *Julii,* 1471, *Pontificatus Nostri anno septimo.*
(Archivio Segreto della S. Sede, xxxix. 12, f. 175v.)

III

Pope Sixtus IV to Giovanni Mocenigo, Doge of Venice.

BRACCIANO,
September 19, 1481.

DILECTE FILI SALUTEM, ETC.—Reddite Nobis sunt littere tue; ex quibus cognovimus quanta letitia tu et civitas ista affecti fueritis ob adventum dilecti filii Comitis Hieronymi nepotis Nostri eiusque consortis; quantoque honore eos exceperitis. Gratissimum fuit Nobis id audisse; tam etsi illud idem iam Nobis antea persuaseramus: novimus enim semper omni in re pre-

APPENDIX I

cipuam tuam et istius inclyti Senatus e
sinceram benivolentiam in omnes N(
recognovisse letamur summopere tue(
gratias. Nos autem versa vice animum]
Senatum ut optimum habemus ; ita eti
et parati sumus, si quando cognoveri
honestate vobis complacere. *Datum*
tembris, 1481, *Pontificatus Nostri anno u*
(Biblioteca Nazionale di Firenze, Co

IV
Pope Sixtus IV to Giovanni Moce
R

DILECTE FILI SALUTEM, ETC.—Accep
ultima octobris, quibus Nobis de reditu]
mitate gratularis. Est id Nobis gra
enim ex precipuo tuo in Nos amore
agimus tibi gratias ; et non minores pr(
egit in seditione proxima Forliviense,
Nobis fuerunt ut nihil addi posset : in qu
omnes perpetue et constantis benivoler
perta, clarissimis argumentis ostendit
Hieronymo presenti declarasti, nam pr(
per litteras suas ipse etiam sermone suo i
cutus est de summis honoribus a te ei
petuo tibi debebit. Quantum actinet a
Nostro impensum per Nos dilecto filio
apud Nos tuo, maiora ille fecit litteris
merebatur quam pro tempore et locis
potuerint ; sed pro sua modestia alite
vir singulari humanitate et preditus, qui
tia et fide procurat ut maiori non p(
satisfactione. Cui Nos et tua contem
meritis summe afficimur. *Datum Rom*
1481, *Pontificatus Nostri anno undecesi*
(Ibid., ff. 95, 95

APPENDIX II

V

Luca Pasi, detto il Faentino, to Duke Ercole of Ferrara.

ROME,
November 16, 1481.

ILLME PRINCEPS ET EX^{ME} DOMINE, ETC.—
Lo imbassatore di Vostra Excellentia inseme cum quelli di la Liga se partireno di qua a' xiv di questo per andare verso Napoli. Credo V^{ra} Illma Sig^{ria} essere stata advisata da D. Christoforo suo oratore[1] quanto la Santità del Nostro Signore habia deto et dolutese di V^{ra} Sig^{ria} per le novità di Forlì, spinto perhò dal Conte Hieronymo; il quale tuttavia insta di tyrare il nostro Signore a nove trame. Ma credo che li serà difficile, benchè Sua Santità se mostri cusì bruscho nel parlare; et tanto meno anchora quando serà venuto il Cardinale di Santo Petro ad Vincula; il quale expectamo qua di proximo. Non scio se V^{ra} Illma Sig^{ria} ha inteso a questi giorni passati di una certa rugine et diffidentia sorta tra'l S. Duca di Urbino et il Conte Hieronymo; il quale ha facto grande instantia de rimovere di qua D. Pietro Felice, imbassatore del prefato Duca; il quale perhò non l'ha voluto rimovere. Intendo anchora tramarse parentela tra'l Signore di Arimino et il Conte per la mezenità de uno suo nipote et sorella del prefato Signore. Altro al presente non c'è di novo. Bene valeat Illma D^{tio} V^{ra}, a la quale di continuo mi racommando. *Rome, xvi Novembris,* 1481.

E. V. Ill^{me} D.

Servulus Lucas Faventinus prothonotarius.

(R. Archivio di Stato in Modena, *Carteggio degli Ambasciatori—Roma.*)

VI

Pope Sixtus IV to Duke Ercole of Ferrara.

ROME,
April 18, 1482.

DILECTE FILI SALUTEM, ETC.—Scit Nobilitas tua que ad te superioribus diebus scripserimus, que oratori tuo totiens sig-

[1] i.e. Cristoforo de' Bianchi.

APPENDIX II

nificanda commisimus, ut sublata de m
pace et amicitia cum Venetis persever:
fecerunt. Id ut tibi persuaderemus, n
rationes: Italie quies, quam propter]
incommodum quod civitati isti Nostre
Nostra erga te caritas, quem nullo bello
quidem potentissimis, implicari cupieba
modo processerint, nemo est qui te n
unum certe scimus, si paternis monitis ݩ
atum, alio in loco res esset; et tamen ׀
temus etiam per presentes ad idem te ho:
suadentes, ut deposita penitus omni ׀
humaniter et benigne te cum Venetis p
initio tibi significavimus; belli consilia c
nisi perniciosa tibi et toti Italie esse, m
communem hostem Turcum magnam c
ipsam comparare, quam si inter se ď
cui dubium quin parvo negocio ea qu
Nam licet res in eo statu non sint in qu
hoc salutare opus te monuimus, tamei
longe maiora ex humanitate quam aɾ
cuturus sis; ad quos pariter quoque s
etc. die xviii *Aprilis*, 1482, *Pontificatus*

(Biblioteca Nazionale di Firenze, C

VII

Duke Ercole of Ferrara to the

ROCCA

Sul hora del disinare hozi è gionto
Mantua, et siamo stati insieme sua S
S. Duca de Urbino e questi altri conduɾ
in tale dispositione et termini che hab
victoria.

Li galioni sono anche gionti et sono

APPENDIX II

miglio, quali habiamo visti, et sono belli et bene forniti et a numero sono xi et uno gatto.

Havemo facto tribulare l'armata inimica hozi doppo disinare cum quelli cinque passavolanti che sono venuti da Ferrara; in modo che la se ne è ritirata denanti da gli ochii et è descesa gioso disotto da la Puncta un gran pezo, et non credemo che la se aproximi in qua de questi dui zorni per il gran danno se gli è facto, et stimeno che molti homini de loro siano sta guasti et cusì una galea et molte barche et fuste per assai colpi che le colseno et investiteno. Cusì pregiamo Dio succeda ogni zorno, come speremo che farà de bene in meglio, et de questa zornata sapiamo che non se ne hanno a laudare.

Domane parendo cusì ad ill^{mo} S. Duca de Urbino se trovaremo a cena a Ferrara, per che non ni è parso per hozi partirsi di qua.

Per Dio mandati victuaglia in abundantia et presto, che cusì bisogna.

Ex Rocha Potenti, xxiv Maij, 1482.[1]

(R. Archivio di Stato in Modena, *Carteggio dei Principi*.)

VIII.

Pope Sixtus IV to the Duke of Lorraine.

ROME,
November 4, 1482.

DILECTE FILI SALUTEM, ETC.—Ducale Dominium Venetorum mittet ad Nobilitatem tuam quemdam secretarium suum, qui tam Nostro quam eorum nomine nonnulla tibi exponet, honorem et utilitatem non mediocrem ipsi tue Nobilitati allatura; super quibus hortamur plenam ei fidem velis adhibere. *Datum Rome etc. die* iv *Novembris*, 1482, *Pontificatus Nostri anno duodecimo.*

(Archivio Segreto della S. Sede, xxxix. 15, f. 175.)

---

[1] On the previous day, May 23, Ercole had written to Leonora that that morning the enemy's army had come to Ficarolo, and that the fleet, *armata*, " si è presentata a la Puncta de Ficarolo " but had gone no further. Rocca Potente was near Stellata.

APPENDIX

IX

Pope Sixtus IV to Duke Er(

DILECTE FILI SALUTEM, ETC.—Fuin
servande studiosi, et si quando humani
aliena culpa ad arma deventum est, sta
cura ad illorum sedationem consilia N
nunc eo diligentius procuravimus, tuo
stanti periculo admoniti. Nam et Nob
gratia benivole prosequimur, et civitat
devastationes, ac novissimam obsidione
molesto animo perferimus ; et sicut, pac
tatibus et Nobis sancte pacis vinculo
auxiliis providere cogitavimus, ita etiar
virum Iohannem Mocenigo Ducem Ven
tras hortati sumus, ut ob Nostram et Sec
cuius loca leduntur et impugnantur, ab
ipsam Nobiscum, restitutis hinc inde a
tibi ac Sancte Romane Ecclesie de cet
desideramus eius prudentiam iustitie
Ut autem interim salubrius ac firmior
latur, dilectum filium Nostrum Franci
diaconum Cardinalem legatum Nostrur
destinandum, ut te et populos Nostro
ac spiritualibus et temporalibus favor
exegerit, promptius iuvare et reintegra
possit. Amplectere, dilecte fili, bono
Nostram, que quantum vires et auctori
patietur ut corruas. Audiet ipsum l
arcana Nostri pectoris ex eo cognosces
ac reintegrationem tuam omnibus o
salus a Domino, et non prevalebunt ir
iniquitatem. *Datum Rome etc. die* xi
ficatus Nostri anno duodecesimo.

(Ibid., ff. 246, 2

APPENDIX II

X

Pope Sixtus IV to the Citizens and People of Ferrara.

ROME,
December 13, 1482.

DILECTI FILII SALUTEM, ETC.—Excepimus gravi animi Nostri molestia que proximis diebus de civitatis et comitatus Nostri Ferrariensis incommodis et imminenti nunc obsidione renuntiata sunt; ac statim ut ingruentibus periculis occurreremus, adiunctis Nobis in vinculo sancte pacis aliis Italie potentatibus, hortati sumus etiam dilectum filium nobilem virum Iohannem Mocenigo Ducem Venetiarum, ut ab armis et impugnatione dicte civitatis Nostre desistat, et pacem hanc Nobiscum restitutis hinc inde ablatis amplectatur; in quo desideramus eius prudentiam paternis monitis Nostris et iustitie simul ac honestati acquiescere. Illud tamen in presenti rerum periculo Nos maxime consolatur ac recreat, quod et potentatum clarissime Lige Italice validissime vires continua subsidia sumministrant, et fideles animos vestros et in omne excidium paratos pro salute dilecti filii nobilis viri Herculis Ducis vestri audivimus; in quo fidem et devotionem vestram benedicimus, et in Domino plurimum commendamus. Nos quoque qui ad summittenda tam spiritualia quam temporalia auxilia, si opus fuerit, toto affectu cogitamus, et ea omnia propediem iuxta rerum exigentiam explicabimus, destinandum interim ad partes istas, et precipue ad civitatem ipsam Nostram Ferrariensem, duximus dilectum filium Nostrum Franciscum Sancte Marie Nove diaconum Cardinalem legatum Nostrum; qui Ducem, civitatem, et vos omnes Apostolice auctoritatis clipeo defendat, ac reintegrationi status dicti Ducis Ferrariensis intendat; intelligantque omnes Nos ipsum Ducem in peculiarem et amantissimum filium, et vos devotos Sedis Apostolice habere ac protectionis Nostre suffragiis adiuvandos, que omnia latius in ipsius Cardinalis adventu cognoscetis. Monemus vos, dilecti filii, et hortamur in Domino, ut bono animo sitis, et quod ad vos spectat de servanda Nobis ac Romane Ecclesie et Duci vestro civitate fidelibus et con-

APPENDIX II

stantibus animis cogitetis; in quo vos
Nobis reddetis. *Datum ut supra.*

(Ibid., ff. 245, 246.)

XI

Pope Sixtus IV to the People

Rc

DILECTI FILII SALUTEM, ETC.—Destinav
et precipue ad civitatem Nostram Ferrarie
Nostrum Franciscum Sancte Marie Nove
legatum Nostrum; ut sicut Nos, unitis hi(
sancte pacis clarissime Lige Italice potentat
tionem et stabilitatem universalem, dile
virum Iohannem Mocenigo Ducem Venet
ut ab impugnatione dicte civitatis Nostr
nobilis viri Herculis Ducis Ferrariensis se r(
pacem Nobiscum amplectatur et capta rest
pro prudentia sua pacificationi omnium in
poterit, consulat et intendat; et si hostiur
omnibus Ecclesie Romane viribus ad i]
captorum recuperationem una cum dic
studiosissime insistat. Nos enim pro off
auxilium Nostrum implorantis protection
posuimus, ut pro eius salute et status su
amantissime facturi simus. Hortamur
vestro fidem et devotionem debitas impe
vestre consuletis, et Nostram ac Sedis Ap
et gratiam maximam consequemini. *Da
Decembris, 1482, Pontificatus Nostri anno*

Simile Populo Mutinens

(Ibid., ff. 252, 253.)

APPENDIX II

XII

Pope Sixtus IV to Duke Ercole of Ferrara.

ROME,
September 17, 1483.

DILECTE FILI SALUTEM, ETC.—Vidimus que ad Nos scripsit Nobilitas tua de invasione Stellate, et quomodo cum tuis qui in promptu erant illam e manibus hostium recuperaveris, quo fit ut sicuti ex periculi magnitudine commoti fuimus, ita vehementer simus letati de virtute tua et victoria subsecuta. Rem igitur hanc non negligendam existimantes, sicuti eam semper cordi habuimus, denuo ad confederatos Nostros efficacissime scripsimus, monentes et instantes, ut gentes necessarias ad te mittantur, sicuti per Ducem Calabrie ordinatum est; idque quam primum fiat considerata periculi magnitudine, dum tempus idoneum superest. Monuimus in hoc Comitem Hieronymum, Duci Mediolani scripsimus, ut pedites illos mittat, et de stipendio tam tibi quam vicario Nostro Faventino provideat; idem Florentinis, de his que attinent ad stipendium. Prefecto mandavimus ut statim cum suis gentibus equitet. Ducem quoque Calabrie de hoc admonuimus, et Regem hortati sumus, ut hos omnes incitet ad celeriter et in tempore omnia subministrandum. Speramus Deo adiutore omnia bene successura. Tu modo ut facis studio et vigilantia tua non desis, et si aliquid faciendum videatur ulterius Nobis significes, nam nihil omittemus quod per Nos fieri poterit. *Datum Rome, etc., die* xvii *Septembris,* 1483. *Pontificatus Nostri anno decimo tertio.*

(Ibid., xxxix. 16, ff. 22v, 23.)

XIII

Pope Sixtus IV to Count Girolamo Riario.

ROME,
September 17, 1483.

DILECTE FILI SALUTEM, ETC.—Scit Nobilitas tua ordinem datum a Duce Calabrie de gentibus ad presidium Ferrarie collocandis; et quoniam in ea omne periculum vertitur, et nihil animo Nostro

APPENDIX II

magis insidet quam quomodo illius defe
intendatur, conquiescere non possimus
fuerit, ut timere amplius hostium impe
Movet Nos periculum ingens in quo pro
parum abfuit quin ab hostibus caperetur
hostes, nisi Dux Ferrarie celeri subsidic
pugnata de Ferraria actum videri potera
quamprimum curet, ut ordo ille mittenda
cutioni demandetur absque aliqua mora
efficacissime scribat, ut stipendium quoc
ipsum debetur mittat statim, sine quo
suorum uti aut eos instruere, et rebus i
et pedites quos debet propere mittat ; per:
vicario Nostro Faventino, ut cum suis ill
et necessaria auxilia prebere possit. N
ad omnes confederatos Nostros oportune s
sit res demonstramus, et nisi in tempo
postea fortasse non poterunt. Prefecto
vimus, ut statim cum gentibus suis illuc e
suas mittat. Nam vix scribere possem
Nos angat et stimulet : nec immerito,
siones fiant, in magno periculo res ille cor
supra.

(Ibid., ff. 23, 23v.

XIV

Buonfrancesco Arlotti to Duke E

ILL^mo ET EX^mo MIO SIGNORE,—

A' x de questo per el cavallaro de V^r
lettera vostra de' VII in substantia de ad
varietà, repentine et voluntarose, achadu
dì a l' altro sopra le condictione ricorc
l'oratore vostro, et demum li era la suppli
fare al Papa per riparo et adiuto più che fus

APPENDIX II

La qual lettera ben studiando et ruminando, ecco in quella medesima hora de la vostra, sopravene una comune a noi oratori da quilli Signori de campo, pur de' VII como la vostra, de adviso de la pace conclusa et stipulata como viderà V^{ra} Ex^{tia} per la inclusa copia; et subito fuo posto ordine de andare la matina a comunicarla cum la Santità de Nostro Signore, per chè quest' hora de la venuta de le prefate lettere era tarda circa le XXIV. La matina io antecipai et fuo a pallatio dal Cardinale de S^{to} Georgio comunicando la prefata lettera et repetendo de l'altre prima recevute, le quale sua S^{ria} R^{ma} volse legere et ben intendere, et ragionatoli di sopra lungamente, confessando de continuo per parere de Nostro Signore et suo la ignominia haveva questa pace, et torto vi era facto et la displicentia ne recevevano, dicendo che la verità era questa, che la Santità de Nostro Signore non potria essere meglio disposta como era anche stata per el passato a favorire le cose vostre, ma che'l se poteva dire che questa cosa gli fusse stata tolta fuora di mano, et altri havessino voluto fare al suo modo cum puoco rispecto de Sua Santità et del Conte, et dopo li era stata portata a tempo et cum modo, quando non potevano fare altro, et che ben si era cognosciuto il tutto, et che'l S. Ludovico haveva voluto cussì, et lo ill^{mo} S. Duca de Calabria consentito, li quali erano Signori del campo, et bisognava havere pacientia: Hora mo che venuta questa lettera de la conclusione de la pace, essendoli intervenuto Mess. Jacobo Trotto[1] cum el mandato, rasonevole cosa è che'l debato de quelli capituli sporti per Mess. Jacobo nel suo memoriale habia preso asexto tra loro; sì che non bisogna per hora fare altra instantia cum el Papa el quale è molto indisposto, et basterà che'l se lega la lettera comune de la pace; presto haveriti anche vui dal vostro Signore adviso como habia facto Mess. Jacobo de queste condictione che erano in debato, et sempre se puoterà scrivere per el Papa, quando se intenda meglio, che a punctamento li sia stato facto etc. Et in questo ragionamento sopragiunsino l'altri oratori, et rasonato che se fuo un pocheto cum sua R^{ma} S^{ria} de questa pace se transferissime ali pedi de la Beatitudine de Nostro Signore, admonendo-

[1] Jacopo Trotti acted as plenipotentiary for the Duke of Ferrara at the Congress of Bagnolo.

APPENDIX II

ne prima S. S^ria R^ma che se sforzassimo
dispositione del Papa, che in vero è molto s
 Presentati al conspecto di Sua Santità fu
qual como ho dicto qui inclusa serà la
senza troppo ciremonia, el Papa dixe :
como el contento ? Alhora Mess. Anne
palpitando rispose, che questo medesimo a
Maestà et che non sapeva che dire, se non
intrevenuto el Duca de Calabria, sperava f
Colligati. Similmente domandò a Mess. Z
Milano, como se contentava. Lui respose
a Sua Beatitudine la necessità era quella li
et elligere questa parte de la pace, de la
men malo. Tertio anche dimandete al Fi
che'l se remetteva, et del facto et de la
Signori, da li quali non haveva adviso alcu
verso me, dicendo : Et el Duca de Ferrar
de questa pace ? Io respose : Beatissime
dimandare de la sua contenteza, per chè Vo
ben informata, et de novo Sua Ex^tia lo
malissimo contento, et sforzatamente li
stata facta iniuria ne li modi tenuti nel p
che debba perdere el suo, abandonato da
capituli et instrumenti privati et publici
benchè la fede, constantia et pacientia su
insino qui, faciano altri come se vogliano,
et procedere unitamente in omne cosa cum
facto per el passato, et cussì quando loro vo
a lui, è forza stare paciente, et se lo è vero
consentito cum mandato et voluntate
niuno debbe però credere che quello Sig
consenti al preiudicio manifesto del h
tuttavia coacta voluntas, voluntas est, etc.
 Olduto che n'hebbe Sua Santità tutti, c
la grande prudentia de la Maestà del Re,
Fiorentini et Duca de Ferrara, la experie
Duchi de Calabria et Bari, quali sonno in fa

APPENDIX II

hano facto questa pace, consentito et iudicato essere la meglior parte; Nui, che non havemo tanta prudentia et men experientia, li volemo seguire et conformarse cum loro, et piacene quello che a loro piace, como havemo facto ne la guerra; la qual cum tanta nostra spesa havemo proseguito per salvare Ferrara et compiacere a la Maestà del Re et l'altri Colligati, et cussì eramo apti a perseverare. Ben ne dole, che non li sia più contento et satisfaction del Duca de Ferrara, ma possa che'l pare a chi ha praticato questa cosa essere cossì necessario et non potere fare altramente, Nui inseme cum quello Signore haveremo pacientia, et iudicaremo omne cosa essere per lo meglio permessa da Mess. Domenedio, a quo omnia bona et nulla mala. Et cum queste parole se levassimo da li santi pedi de Sua Beatitudine.

Signore: o fusse per la indispositione, o pur per che la materia non li fusse grata (che la indispositione ho veduto altre volte superarla) non mostrò mai Sua Santità nè in parole nè in gesti signo de piacere alcuno, anci de dispiacere, et remanendo mi drieto, me dimandò Sua Santità stessa et dixe vi confortasse per sua parte havere bona pacientia, et che considerato la deliberatione et fermeza d'altri in questa parte V^{ra} Ex^{tia} se seria trovata sola et forse mal tractata, et pur che sia salva Ferrara el tempo porta cum se novi remedii et partiti. Io rispose che per parte vostra ringratiava Sua Beatitudine et basavagli li pedi de questa sua bona voluntà et compassione vi portava, et che se hebbe mai lettere de desperatione et mala contenteza de V^{ra} Ex^{tia} erano queste ultime mandate a posta per un cavallaro, per che cum omne summissione et prostrattive ali suoi santi pedi lo raccomandava per che, havendo a lassare el Polesene ben contra sua voglia, al men li fussin acceptati alcuni capituli sporti per el suo oratore in campo, sopra de li quali senza vergogna quelli che fano per Venetiani hano variati da un dì a l'altro. Alhora Sua Beatitudine me interrumpi, dicendo: Non dire più, che per lettere del Tolentino[1] et de l'oratore de Milano ho inteso el tutto, ma doppo che Mess. Jacobo Trotto ha consentito debbeno essere stati d'accordio. Io dixe: Pater Sancte, et per la indispositione

[1] Giovanni Francesco da Tolentino, the papal plenipotentiary at the Congress.

et per il ricordo del Camerlengo sum cont
dare molestia a la Santità Vostra ; ma nor
questa lettera comune, che ben se li dica *I*
Trotto per lo ill^{mo} S. Duca de Ferrara, ho
consentendo, et un altra cosa, che ne la
Mess. Jacobo Trotto ; cosa non ho voluto
altri, ma ne resto tutto suspeso sino ha
anchela mia lettera è de' vii, como an
questo poteria acchadere per la distan
Ferrara. Et cum queste parole me le
la quale possa stavo a Roma non me par
facia. Et in gratia de V^{ra} Illma S^{ria} n
xii *Augusti*, 1484.

E. V. Ill^{me} D.D.,
Ser

(outside) Illmo P. et Exmo D^{no} D. Hercul
D^{no} meo colen^{mo}. Ferrarie.
(R. Archivio di Stato in Modena, C
tori—*Roma*.)

XV

Duke Ercole of Ferrara to the Cardi

Dux Ferrariae, etc.—Rev^{mo} et ill^{m}
simo D^{no} Hippolyto Cardinali Estensi e
Voi doveti credere che, amandovi com
Padre, stamo continuamente in desider
dì faciati maiore profecto in boni cost
che se apertengono ad uno che sia nostr
dignità del cardinalato come haveti voi, l
mente ricercha religione et doctrina, e

[1] i.e. Eiusdem Vestre Illustrissime Domi
Bonfranciscus Episcopus Regiensis.

APPENDIX II

parte non po essere reputato digno nè bono Cardinale. Unde ben che hor mai siti de tanto intellecto, che da voi medesimo ve doveresti excitare; tutavia sapendo noi, forsi meglio che non credeti, li modi vostri et come spendeti il vostro tempo : perchè da alcuni mesi in qua ne havemo havuto pur qualche noticia, che non po essere non ni habia dato displicentia; ni è parso per questa nostra paternamente racordarve et admonirve, che debiati dispensare il tempo vostro in modo che ni acquistiati reputatione et laude, et non il contrario. Et credemo che sereti molto laudato se prima, non solamente ogni die direti l'officio a le soe hore debite et attentamente, ma etiam fareti che altri sapiano et vedano, che cussì lo diceti ordinatamente. Il medesimo dicemo, che vi redundarà in gloria, se ogni die attendereti a studiare et intendere qualche bona et digna lectione, et se anche ve exercitareti et accommodareti in dire et scrivere con qualche elegantia in Lingua Latina, perchè il culto divino et la doctrina con li boni exempli di la vita sono li precipui ornamenti de uno Cardinale, et fundamenti da conseguire ciò che honestamente se desidera; et rendemosse certi che, dispartendo il tempo in queste cose, il ve ni avanzarà tanto, che anche ve potereti pigliare de li piaceri honesti, et in casa et a la campagna, che ricercha la età vostra. Ma come è dicto, quando prima se attende a le prime doe principale cose, il se ne acquista tante laude et honore, che anche le altre cose non possono essere se non commendate; et teneti mo per indubitato, che se temereti Dio, et l'havereti denanti a li ochi, tute le cose vostre ve prosperarano; et quando ve lo domenticareti, il se domenticarà de voi, et niuno vostro desiderio ve poterà succedere; nì ve vedereti mai contento. Sì che ve exhortamo et pregamo, che per vostro proprio bene et honore, et per nostra singulare consolatione, attendiati a le virtude nel modo che havemo dicto : et per ogni altra via megliore; che bene sapemo se voreti non vi mancharano boni coadiutori a dire bene l'officio, et anche preceptori de bone lettere et doctrina. Cussì fatti come speremo in voi, che sempre da Noi siati benedecto.

Noi, per Dio gratia, siamo tuti sani, et il simile de voi desideramo:

Lo è vero che lo ill.mo Don Alfonso vostro fratello a questi die,

APPENDIX II

essendo a Milano, se infirmete de alcune f(
condure qui in nave dove lo è megliorato ɛ
Ferrariae, xii Augusti, 149
N.]
(outside) Rev^{mo} et ill^{mo} D^{no}: filio nost
Hip: Sancte Lutie in Silice Car
(R. Archivio di Stato in Modena, *Car*

XVI

Isabella d'Este Gonzaga to Duke E₁

]

ILL^{MO} ET EX^{MO} SIGNOR MIO PADRE,

Li figlioli de quondam S. Messer Nico
exposto havere inteso che la Illma Sig^{ria} V
cione ha anche cassa la provisione che per
li anni passati, la quale era tutta la substaɪ
non havere altra facultà; et cum molte p
li raccommandi a V^{ra} Ex^{tia}. Io che li
miseria non ho saputo negarli questa mia
più posso ge li raccommando, supplicandol
voglia lassarli correre la provisione sua : (
magiore elimosina; et io l'haverò de si
Illma Sig^{ria} a la quale me raccommando.

Mantue, xviii Aprilis, 1497.
Ill^{me} D.V.
Filia Isabella Marchioni
(R. Archivio di Stato in Modena, Cancell
Isabella d'Este Gonzag(

XVII

Duke Ercole of Ferrara to Don (

DUX FERRARIAE, ETC.—Illmo et Rev^{do}
Julio Estensi: Salutem. Per una vostrɛ

APPENDIX II

havemo inteso le visitatione facte per voi al Illmo et Rev^{mo} Monsr Vicecancellero,[1] et al Rev^{mo} Monsr San Severino. Il tuto ni è molto piaciuto, et ve ne commendiamo grandemente, stringendovi ad governarvi cum discretione et prudentia in ogni loco et tempo, et cum ogni persona ; et al stare assiduamente a la presentia del Rev^{mo} Monsignor nostro figliolo : chè cussì facendo ni conseguireti commendatione et honore.[2] Et bene valete.

Adriani, vii Januarii, 1498.

Thebaldus

(outside) Illmo et rev^{do} filio nostro aman^{mo} D^{no} Julio Estensi, Romae.

(R. Archivio di Stato in Modena, *Carteggio dei Principi*.)

XVIII

Duke Ercole of Ferrara to Don Ferrando d' Este.

FERRARA,
April 19, 1499.

DUX FERRARIAE, ETC.—Illmo filio nostro aman^{mo} D^{no} Ferdinando Estensi.

In questa nostra andata a Venesia, havemo dato il laudo et sententia sopra le differentie de Pisa per il modo che dovereti havere veduto per la copia de epso laudo ; la quale a questa hora doveti havere havuta per la via de Messer Manfredo nostro oratore a Fiorenza. Et veramente in questa praticha de accordo et cussì nel sententiare, se siamo sforzati de fare tuto quello beneficio che havemo potuto a quella magnifica comunità de Pisa : sì per reverentia de la Illma Sig^{ria} de Venesia che l'havea in

---

[1] The Cardinal Ascanio Sforza.

[2] In the light of after events, this bidding Giulio be assiduous in attending upon the Cardinal Ippolito is invested with a sort of horror. In a letter to his father, dated January 13, 1503, Ippolito assures his Excellence that he need not remind him to keep a look out for Giulio's interests at the Papal Court, because he always cares for them as though they were his own : "Persuadasi Quella che ne le cose del S. Don Julio non vegio meno che ne le mie proprie" (R. Archivio di Stato in Modena, *Carteggio dei Principi*).

APPENDIX II

protectione, sì etiam per lo amore et be
havemo portato et portamo ad epsi Pisani
tenevemo de la pace et quiete de quella c
Italia. Et se bene epsi Pisani se sono fo
parte de epso nostro laudo: non dubita
bene il tuto, doverano restare ben satis
cognoscerano, che havemo havuto condign(
et cussì etiam per lo advenire non mar
beneficio et favore. Et se havessimo pott
et commodo, l'havessimo facto molto volt
sta necessario far talmente, che lo effecto
seguire. Et siamo in pensiero de mandai
lì a Pisa a parlare a quelli Mag^{ci} Antiani
a le cose che se hanno a fare, cum riposo
le parte; et cussì potereti far intendere qu
a sue Magnificentie. Et bene valete.

      Ferrariae, xix Aprilis, 14
       Thebaldus.
(outside) Illu. filio nostro aman^{mo} D^{no} Fer
 subito.
 (R. Archivio di Stato in Modena, *Car*

XIX

Isabella d' Este Gonzaga to Duke E

Illmo Signore, mio Padre obser^{mo},

Non posso fare, sì per lo amore che porto
ill. Messer Nicolò da Este, come per il
non piglij la protectione sua presso Vostr
mandando loro a quella Philippo Marche
farli reverentia, et farli intendere il bisogr
digni haverli raccommandati, et ad presta
epso Philippo; perchè omne beneficio, ch
ferirà in li prefati figlioli, haverò tanto acc

APPENDIX II

a contribuirlo in me propria. Et reputarollo a singular gratia da V^{ra} Ex^{tia}, a la quale sempre me raccommando.

Mantue, xiv Maij, 1499.

Illmo D.V.

Filia Isabella Marchionissa Mantue, etc.

(R. Archivio di Stato in Modena, Cancelleria Ducale, *Lettere di Isabella d' Este Gonzaga.*)

XX

Duke Ercole of Ferrara to the Cardinal Ippolito d' Este.

FERRARA,
August 19, 1499.

DUX FERRARIAE, ETC.—Illmo et Rev^{mo} d^{no} filio nostro aman^{mo} D^{no} Hyppolito Sancte Lutie in Silice Diacono Cardinali Estensi, etc. Salutem.

Havemo inteso per diverse vie, cum la maiore displicentia del mondo, che la S^{da} V^{ra} se ha facto fare le arme bianche a fine de armarse et de ingerirse in cose belliche et seve; che non facilmente haveressimo creduto, per essere alienissimo da la dignità et professione vostra, se da una persona sola il ni fosse stato significato; ma lo è tanto notorio che non lo volere credere seria grande apocagine et obstinatione. Havemo infin qui dissimulando taciuto cum la S^{da} V^{ra} molte cose, che grandemente ne offendevano, per non li vedere molto pericolo: imputando et adscrivendo tuta la colpa al aetà, et sperando che, crescendo li anni, dovesse crescere in lei il timore de Dio (da la cui clementia l'ha recevuti tanti beneficij), la gravità et modestia ecclesiastica: cio è conveniente ali pari vostri. Ma restamo assai decepti de questa nostra opinione: vedendo la S^{da} V^{ra} fare pegio et più publicamente che la non ha facto insin qui. Et perchè hora cognoscemo che la è in evidente pericolo del stato et conditione soa, non ni è parso de tacere più ultra nè di potere più dissimulare. Però considerato che lo armegiare vostro non po fare alcun bono fructo: ma bene vi po fare irregulare et digno di depositione, et privarvi de la dignità et beneficij: vi exhortamo, stringemo, et se alcuna auctorità paterna ni è restata in la S^{ria}

APPENDIX II

V^{ra}, vi commandiamo, che debiati d[
armigere, et attendere a vivere da bon
rev^{mo} Cardinale; et se forsi vi fosse persua
havesse a dare la victoria alo Illmo S. Duc
beneficio, teneti per certo che tale persua
et manco la S^{ria} V^{ra} ; perchè'l vostro arme
Signor Dio; et il provocaria ad ira et i[
contraria a la parte per la quale voi portas[
aiutare il prefato Exmo S. Duca, come tu
la S^{da} V^{ra} l'officio suo: preghi Nostro S
et victoria de Soa Ex^{tia} et de li exerciti
supplicarli per tuti li religiosi et clerici secu
intervenga lei a dicte oratione, come è [
missione. Queste serano bone arme bia
de irregularità et cum grande merito. An
mortale, et digno di excommunicatione
fosse morto qualchuno seresti irregulare
simplici chierici de venire a tale acto, s[
necessaria di la soa persona quando foss[
et non potessero altramente campare nè
licito ad uno cardinale et archiepiscopo.
che ogni picolo disfavore che havesti a
come facilmente poteria accadere, faria i
maiore, ultra la infamia et macula ind
heresti, et il pericolo de la vita vostra o de
membro. Temeti adonca Nostro Signor
li soi beneficij; et ricordativi, che se r
soi, et se non li sereti grato, vi farà cum
recognoscerè lo errore vostro. Et se li
vostro non meriti misericordia, come nor
essere pur tropo fuora de la fede et Relig
pegio. Examinati bene la conscientia vo
tione nostre, le quale sole doveriano ba[
debito di farni cosa grata, non vi movenc
Dio, del damno grande, del pericolo,
drizi a la bona via; alo Illmo S. Duca non
de aiutare Soa Ex^{tia} in le fatiche, in li [

APPENDIX II

cose sue tanto quanto se extende la auctorità et potestà vostra; perchè la S^{ria} V^{ra} ni è debitrice per li grandissimi beneficij da Soa Ex^{tia} recevuti, ultra la strectissima coniunctione, lassando l'arme ali seculari. Cussì facendo satisfareti in quella parte che potereti al debito vostro verso Soa Celsitudine, et non offendereti Nostro Signor Idio; a Nui fareti cosa gratissima et da ogni uno sereti commendato. Et bene valeat R^{ma} Do. V^{ra}.

Ferrariae, xix Augusti, 1499.

Thebaldus.

(R. Archivio di Stato in Modena, *Carteggio dei Principi*.)

XXI

Duke Ercole of Ferrara to Beltrando Costabili.

COMACCHIO,
October 5, 1500.

REVERENDE DILECTISSIME NOSTER,—

Il S. Messer Zoanne Bentivoglio per uno suo cancellero ni ha communicato havere adviso de bon loco, come il duca Valentino, il quale se prepara per venire a li danni de li Signori de Pesaro, Arimino, et Faenza, vole etiamdio venire a li danni de sua S^{ria} per insignorirse de Bologna, come de le predicte citade: cosa che non credemo gli sia per reuscire, essendo sta renovata la protectione de la Maestà Christianissima questa estate proxima passata al prefato S. Mr Zoanne et a' Bolognesi. Tutavia sua S^{ria} per havere tuta la sua speranza in la prefata Maestà et in li Sig^{ri} Locotenenti Regii, et per ricordo nostro, farà ricorso a sue M^{ta} et Sig^{rie} per essere conservato et defeso in casa sua, come è molto ben conveniente. Cognoscemo questa impresa essere di grandissimo danno ala prefata Maestà non solamente per Bologna, ma etiamdio per Faenza, Arimino, et Pesaro; perchè quando il duca Valentino on la Chiexia havesse dicte terre insieme cum Forlì, Cesena et Imola, non poteria mancho in Italia che il stato de Milano, et però li Ill^{mi} S^d Duchi de Milano non hanno mai voluto tollerare che la Chiexia desfaci tuti li Signori de dicte terre, nè che le siano date ad uno; anci hanno facto ogni opera per conservare cadiuno de dicti Signori in stato; et per valersene

meglio, gli hanno anchora dato soldo. (
che hanno facto in Italia, se sono assai
terre de Romagna per essere loco opportu
in tuti li movimenti che se fanno in Ita
experientia in la guerra mosta contra F
M.co Bartholomeo da Bergamo,[1] et poi al
Re Carlo, et ultimamente quando Vene
soccorso a Pisa per la valle de Lamone.
Chr.ma M.ta non debe tollerare che Bologn
duca Valentino, ma pur non debe perme
Romagna più de quello che'l ge ha : oltr
che quelli naturali Signori siano desfacti
senza alcuna iusta causa. Pregati adun
S.ri Locotenenti per parte nostra, che no
che'l prefato S. Messer Zoanne sia moles
data a sua S.ria in lo novo protectione, e
tianissimo Re, come anche per utile et b
la quale al presente et per lo advenire, st
termini che la è, haverà sempre tuta qu
mando, come la ha il suo ducato de Mila
valerà in tute le imprese che la farà ; cl
fusse in mane del Papa o del duca V;
etiamdio che per lo interesse de la prefa
ogni cosa ad epsi possibile perchè li Signo
et Pesaro restino in casa, et cum quest
schiavi de la Chr.ma M.ta ; non omettend
mano anchora lo interesse et preiuditio
grandissimo quando il duca Valentino ha
de quello che l'ha, et maximamente in
Sig.rie molto bene quello che lo anno p
de Nui. Svegliati per modo sue Sig.rie cl
importantia sia questa cosa per più cap
ricordare che sia per inanimare et acce
la provisione necessaria. Et certamente
M.ta et S.rie habiano una grande et vera iu
dicta impresa, cum fare intendere al Pa[

[1] i.e. The Colleonic War in 1

APPENDIX II

presente de attendere a guerre in Italia, essendo le cose del Turco inanti come sono. Et a sue Sig^{rie} ne raccomandareti, pregandole che le tengano questo nostro ricordo secreto.

La alligata sopra questa materia a Messer Zoanne Valla, voressemo che fusse mandata a salvamento et per modo che la continentia non devenisse a notitia de altri. Però pregareti quelli Signori che la vogliano mandare salvamente, facendoli intendere per che causa la sia, et vui ali cayallari regii etiam la raccomandareti.

Comachi, iv Octobris, 1500.

Post.—Se'l vi paresse che dicte lettere non havessero ad andare a salvamento per dicta via, seria da vedere se gli fusse qualche cancellero del prefato S. Messer Zoanne il quale havesse modo de mandarle. Et in effecto governati questa cosa come meglio vi parerà, aciò che le lettere non vadino in sinistro, et che la continentia sia secreta cussì a Milano come in Franza.[1]

(R. Archivio di Stato in Modena, *Minutario Cronologico*.)

XXII

Isabella d' Este Gonzaga to Duke Ercole of Ferrara.

MANTUA,
November 27, 1500.

ILL^{MO} ET EX^{MO} SIGNORE, MIO PADRE OBSER^{MO},

De bocha del Signore mio consorte et per la lettera de V^{ra} Ex^{tia} ho inteso quanto amorevolmente la me ha invitata ad venire a tuore el Jubileo; dil che gli resto molto obligata et ringratiola grandemente. Ma havendo ben considerato sopra la spesa che me accaderia a fare se volesse andare a Roma,

---

[1] The *alligata* to Giovanni Valla is in nearly the same terms. He is to appeal to the King and Monsignor de Rouen to protect Bentivoglio, with the same arguments about the importance of Bologna to the Duchy of Milan : "non pretermettendo anche de tochare lo interesse et preiuditio nostro, il quale non poteria essere magiore, come sue M^{ta} et S^{da} facilmente iudicarano, reducendosse a memoria quello che se tentava contra di Nui hora fa uno anno per mezo del Car^{le} Borgia legato del Papa : oltrache havendo o il Papa o il duca Valentino Bologna cum le altre citade de Romagna, non seria meno potente in Italia che il stato de Milano, et congiunto cum

APPENDIX II

trovo che in consciencia non spenderia
octocento ducati a limitarla più che potess
pagare el quarto, o venire a composicic
manco de docento ducati ; et ritrovandoi
dinari per le grave spese che me sono
molto indebitata, non saperia como riti
V^{ra} et Nostro Signor Dio me haverà]
rispecto alla necessità et bona disposicic
per essere graciosa de indulgentia la Sta d
confirmarà alla quaresima, passato che s
confessionale, per auctorità del quale]
de colpa et de pena, per il che venirò cu
seguire el merito. Se io fussi venuta h
per condure la venerabile Sore Osana ; ci
parlato dice che, per visitare la veneral
cosa grata a V^{ra} Ex^{tia} et a me, faria o]
mal volunteri, per havere già parechi anr
meso voto de non uscire de Mantua, p:
proprie parole, che la sii cossì trista pe
andare in torno. Non di meno quando
obedientia che la Ex^{tia} V^{ra} mi ha mand
et conducta.

 Mandarò ad essa la lectica che la mi l
gratia di quella me raccommando sempre
 Mantue, xxvii Novembris, M D.
   Ex. V.
    Filia Isabella Marchionissa]
(R. Archivio di Stato in Modena, Canc
  di Isabella d' Este Gonza[

---

altri seria anche magiore." He says nothing]
other Signori, but alludes to the Turk, and bid
Cardinal not to communicate this *ricordo* to
logico]. Similarly in an instruction to Bartolom
30, 1500, the latter is to go to the French King v
before him the Duke's opinion, according to t]
urge him to protect Bologna from the Borgia (C*c*
—*Francia*).

APPENDIX II

XXIII

Pope Julius II to the Cardinal Ippolito d' Este.

ROME,
May 8, 1507.

DILECTE FILI NOSTER salutem et apostolicam benedictionem. Littere dilecti filii nostri Antonii tituli Sancti Vitalis presbiteri Cardinalis, Bononie etc. Nostri et Apostolice Sedis Legati, magnam Circumspectioni tue laudem tribuunt. Testantur enim victoriam contra Tirannos Bentivolos nuper partam in tua singulari virtute, qui etiam armatus illis obstiteris, constituisse ; cum pro statu Nostro et Sancte Romane Ecclesie, cuius honorabile membrum et peculiaris filius es, nec discrimen nec laborem illum subterfugiendum putaveris; arcem etiam Sphilinberti magno ingenio hostibus Nostris subtraxeris. Que, et si Nobis inopinata non erant, tamen gratissima iucundissimaque fuerunt. Commendamus igitur ipsam tuam Circumspectionem in Domino, Nosque tam preclari facinoris memores gratosque pollicemur. Arcem autem Sphilinberti una cum illius oppido ut retineas te exhortamur ; et, si fieri potest, idem contra Alexandrum Pium de Soxolo, qui hostibus Nostris favit et se Sancte Romane Ecclesie hostem declaravit, efficias ut uberius a Nobis valeas commendari. *Datum Rome apud Sanctum Petrum sub annulo Piscatoris, Die viii Maj, MCCCCCVII, Pontificatus Nostri anno quarto.*

(Original Brief in the R. Archivio di Stato in Modena.)

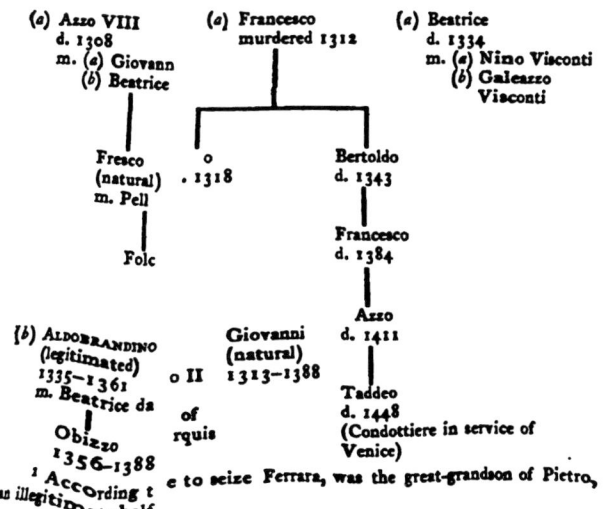

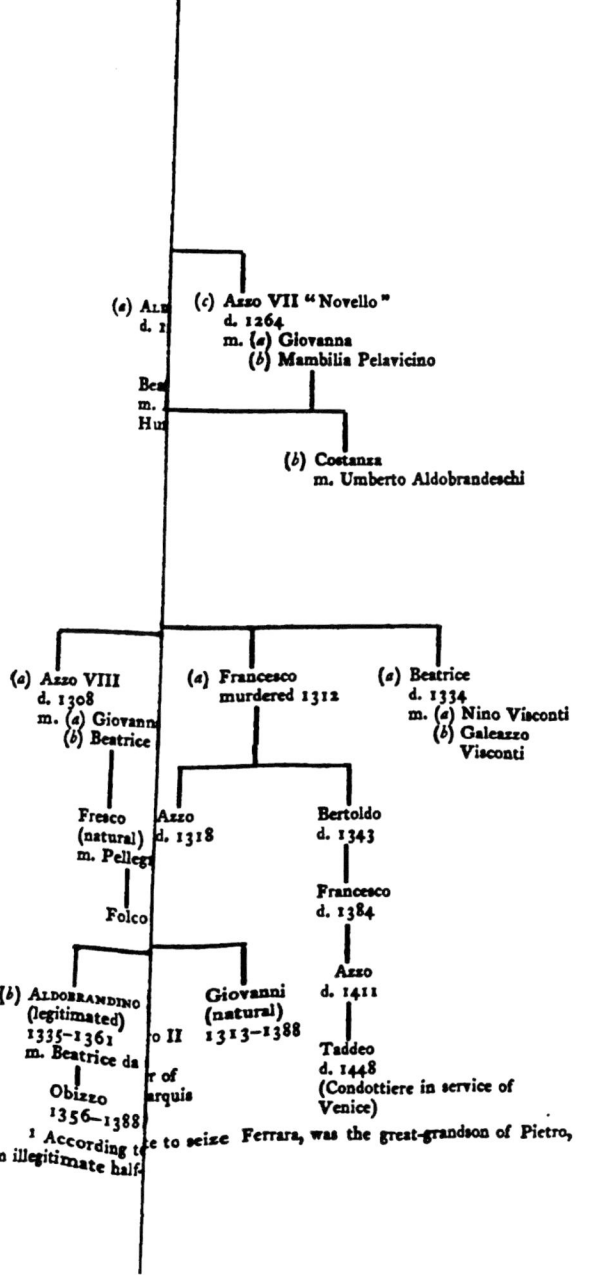

HOUSE OF ESTE (II)

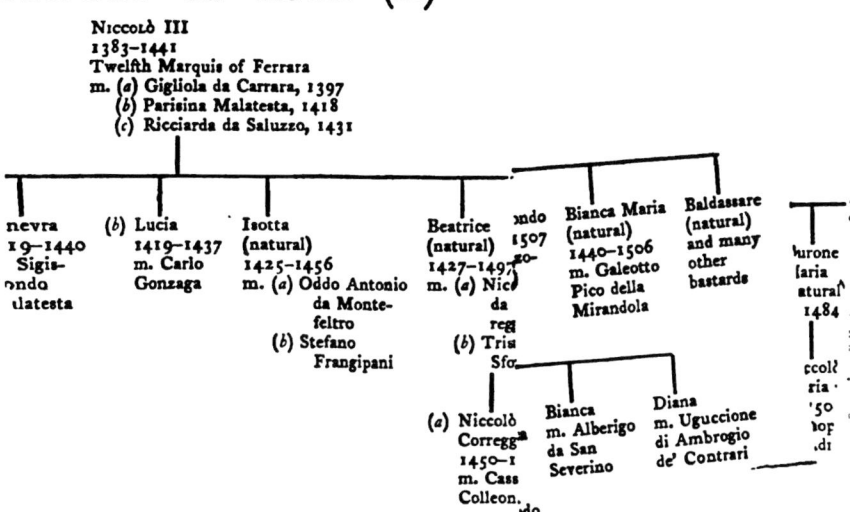

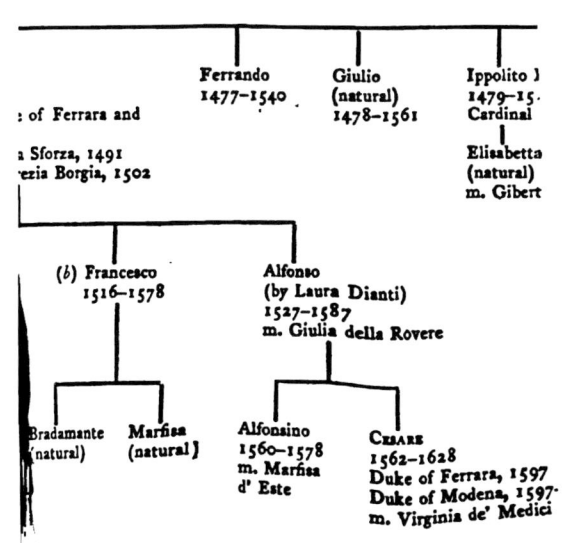

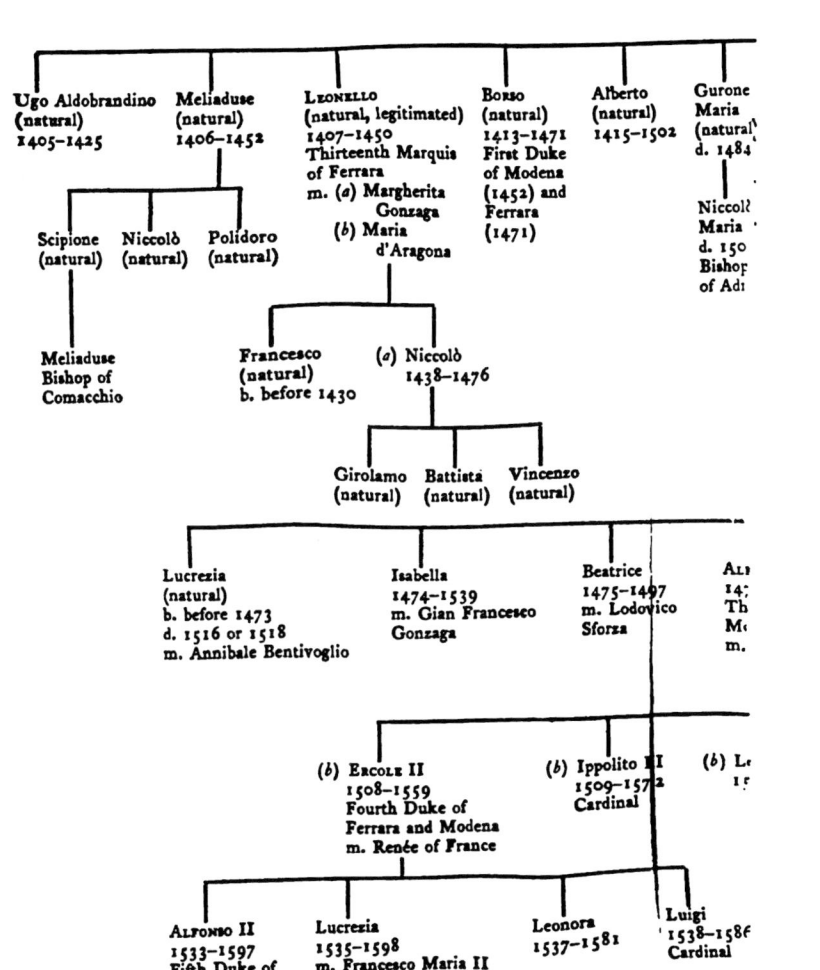

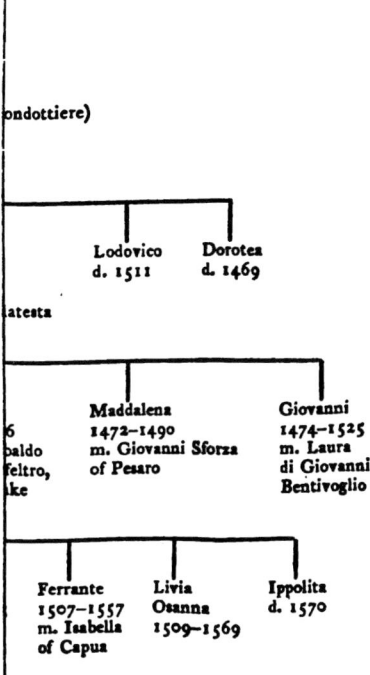

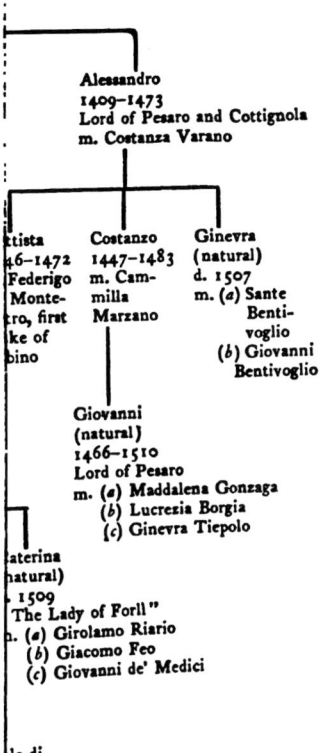

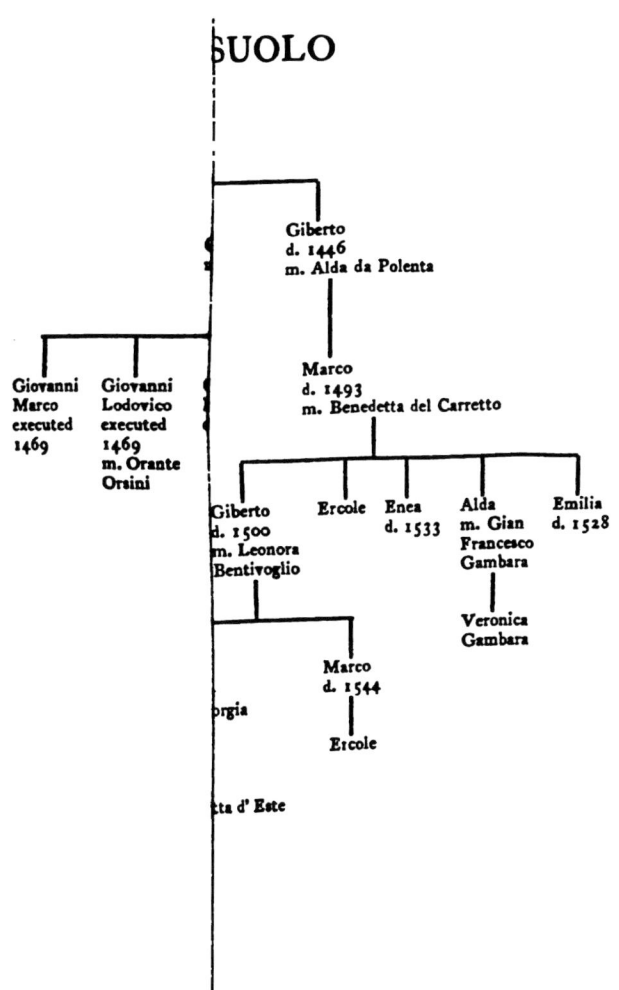

:LLA   MIRANDOLA

)
o Boiardo

| Lucrezia   Antonio
o Pio   m. Pino degli   d. 1501
 Gonzaga   Ordelaffi   m. Costanza di Sante
                                          Bentivoglio

Index of Names.

(Contemporaries only.)

A

meric de Peguilhan, 24
Ibanzani, Donato, 17, 41
Ibaresani, Caterina, 33, 34*n*
Ibaresani, Isotta, 26
lberti, Leon Battista, 50, 53, 55–57, 274
Aldobrandino di Guidone, 302, 319, 320
Aleotti, Antonio (painter), 465
Alexander VI, Pope (Rodrigo Borgia), 228–233, 235, 237, 295, 296, 300, 302, 307, 320, 328, 337–339, 349, 354, 355, 359, 360, 376, 379, 382, 384, 386–400, 402, 403, 406–412, 422–425, 432–434, 440, 444, 466, 469, 475*n*, 478, 479, 516; Appendix II, documents 21, 22
Alfonso I of Aragon, King of Naples (the "Magnanimous"), 62–64, 65, 293, 516
Alfonso II of Aragon, King of Naples (previously Duke of Calabria), 155, 156, 165, 174, 176, 181, 182, 187, 191, 192, 196, 198, 203–205, 207–209, 234, 247, 270–273, 293, 297; Appendix II, documents 12, 13, 14
Alfonso of Aragon, Duke of Bisceglie, 359, 386, 387, 398, 442
Allègre, Yves de, 355, 382, 388, 389
Alviano, Bartolommeo da, 342
Amboise, Georges de (Cardinal of Rouen), 357, 388, 391–393, 395, 437–440, 448, 461*n*, 561*n*

Andrea da Gennaro, 176, 232, 236
Andreassi, Osanna, 365, 366, 375–378; Appendix II, document 22
Angelo da Siena (painter), 55, 90
Angoulême, Madame de, 390, 391
Anna, Suora, 431, 432
Anselmo da Ferrara (poet), 25*n*
Appolonia, Suora, 403
Aragon, Beatrice of, Queen of Hungary, 237
— Isabella, of (Duchess of Milan), *see* Sforza
— Leonora of (Duchess of Ferrara), *see* Este
Arcamone, Aniello, 176, 207; Appendix II, document 14
Arduino, Isabella, 151
Arienti, Giovanni Sabadino, 195, 196, 242*n*
Ariosti, family of the, 16
— Francesco di Princivalle "Peregrinus," 59; his *Iside*, 60; correspondence with Borso, 98, 99; his account of Borso's Roman Triumph, 109–113; his history of the shrine of the Madonna, 123, 124, 139
— Francesco di Rinaldo, 59*n*, 103, 189–191, 191*n*, 490
— Galasso, 135
— Giovanna, 132
— Lippa, 16
— Malatesta, 76*n*
— Niccolò (Count), 103, 125–127, 180, 273, 326, 490–492
— Pandolfo, 491
ARIOSTO, LODOVICO, the supreme poet of the Italian Renaissance, 10; his ancestry, 16;

565

his letters, 23*n*; quoted or referred to, 67, 86, 89, 102, 127, 128, 138, 213*n*, 214, 238*n*, 274, 286, 288, 290-293, 316*n*, 344, 470, 484; his youth and Latin poems, 490-492; 505*n*, 506; his *Cassaria*, 515; his epitaph on Ercole Strozzi, 521; his *Suppositi*, 522, 523; 524

Arlotti, Buonfrancesco, 200-202, 207, 208; his account of the death-bed of Sixtus IV, Appendix II, document 14

Assassini, the, 34*n*

Assassino, Stella dello, 33, 34, 67, 77

Aurispa, Giovanni, 18, 43, 58, 59

B

Badia, Uguccione dalla, 81
Baglioni, Giampaolo, 382, 506
Bandello, 34*n*, 38*n*
Barbaro, Zaccaria, 162
Barbo, Cardinal Marco, 116
Barone (jester), 502
Basso, Andrea da (poet), 527
Bayard, 424
Beatrice, Suora, 380, 403-405, 411
Beccari, Antonio dei, 25
Becchi, Gentile, 246, 247
Belgiojoso, Carlo di, 232
Bellincioni, 225*n*
Bellini, Jacopo, 55*n*, 88
Bello, Francesco (Il Cieco da Ferrara), 485-489
Beltramino, Messere, 274, 278, 279
Bembo, Pietro, 346*n*, 425-427, 491, 495, 521
Bendedei, Battista, 157, 159-162, 171-174, 176; 356
Niccolò, 149
Bentivoglio, Annibale, 162, 217, 220, 221, 354, 405, 508, 509
Anton Galeazzo, 509*n*
Ercole, 382, 517
Ermes, 508
Ginevra Sforza, 220, 221, 508
Giovanni II, 101, 149, 162, 181, 190, 198, 199, 217, 220, 221, 354, 355, 360, 361, 382-384, 406, 507, 508, 510; Appendix II, document 21
Lucrezia d'Este, 138, 162, 193,

INDEX

432—435, 440, 441-445, 511-513; Appendix II, document 21
Girolama, 417
Guglielmo Raimondo, 431n, 432
Juan, Cardinal of Monreale, 330, 432
Juan, Duke of Gandia, 517
Lucrezia (Duchess of Bisceglie, afterwards Duchess of Ferrara), 230, 231, 354, 359, 381, 386, 387, 389-423, 424-430, 434-437, 443, 444, 469, 470, 492, 495-498, 502, 505, 511-514, 516, 517, 519
Rodrigo, see Alexander VI
Rodrigo (Duke of Bisceglie), 387, 398, 436, 437
Borgognoni, Cristoforo (architect), 460
Boschetti, Albertino, Count, 310, 497, 503, 504
Boschetti, Roberto, 150
Bourbon, Madame de (Anne of Beaujeu), 247, 248
Bresciano, Bartolommeo, 380, 381, 401-405, 411, 412, 431, 432
Brocadelli, Gentilina, 367, 369, 371, 372, 380; see also Lucia
Burchardus, 403n

C

Cagnolo, Niccolò, 417, 418n, 420n, 421, 483n
Calandra, Silvestro, 517n
Calavrese, Niccolò, 123
Calcagnino, Marietta Strozzi, 142, 258, 259n
Calcagnino, Teofilo, 80, 83, 94, 111, 115, 124, 125, 130, 135, 177
Caleffini, Ugo, 29, 34n, 40n, 54n, 66n, 78, 80, 81n, 95, 105n, 110-113, 117-121, 129n, 132n, 138, 142n, 147-149, 151n, 153n
Camino, Beatrice da, 19
Cammelli, Antonio ("Il Pistoia"), 460n, 475-483
Campo, Luchino dal, 30-32
Canale, Carlo, 230
Cantelmieri, (Condolmieri), Lodovica, 138
Cantelmo, Sigismondo, 296
Canterno, Sigismondo, 278
Capilupo, Benedetto, 244, 420, 422, 496

Cappello, Paolo, 359, 387n, 432
Capponi, Neri, 302n
Caprara, Antonia di Bartolommeo, 258, 261-263
Caraffa, Cardinal, 439
Carbone, Lodovico, 41, 121, 531
Carlo da San Giorgio, 83, 84, 84n, 103, 104, 105n
Carrara, Francesco Novello da, 27
 Gigliola da, 33
 Ubertino da, 15n
Carri, Lodovico de', 321
Carvajal, Cardinal, 328
Casa, Francesco della, 237n, 246n, 247, 248n
Casari, Niccolò, 69
Casella, Lodovico, 80, 87
Castelli, Girolamo, 80
Castello, Francesco da, 328, 333, 460
Castiglione, Baldassare, 514, 518n
Catanei, Vannozza, 230
Catherine of Siena, St., 141, 363-368, 374-376, 378, 379, 381, 401, 465, 466
Cato Senior, 69n
Cavallieri, Bartolommeo de', 390-394, 396n, 397, 398, 434, 437, 461n, 562n
Caxton, 197n
Charles V, Roman Emperor, 450
Charles VIII, King of France, 180n, 232, 236, 237, 239, 246-248, 250, 296-320, 322, 323, 327, 329, 331-335, 341, 383, 473-475, 477, 478, 487, 488, 491
Chaumont, 434, 437, 506
Cherubino da Spoleto, Frate, 194
Chrysoloras, John, 41
Cieco da Ferrara, see Bello
Ciriaco of Ancona, 55
Clement V, Pope, 13
Clement VI, Pope, 16n
Collenuccio, Pandolfo, 296, 322, 323, 385-387, 435, 445, 446
Colleoni, Bartolommeo, 100, 101, 174, 560
Colomba, Suora, 378n
Colomba of Rieti, Beata, 365, 366, 368, 371, 375, 376, 378n
Comines, Philippe de, 299, 301, 307-309, 312, 313-317, 319n, 327
Compagno, Giovanni di, 110n, 113n, 116
Contarini, Pietro, 30
Contarini, Vettor, 167, 168

Conti, Sigismondo de', 169n, 170n, 173n, 179n, 180n, 184n, 192n, 193, 196, 197n, 203n, 208n, 433n
Contrari, Ambrosio de', 189
    Ippolita de,' 216
    Niccolò de', 134, 135
    Uguccione de,' 38, 47
Corio, Bernardino, 135, 136, 199, 224n, 234, 245, 312, 314, 315n, 316
Cornaro, Cardinal, 439
Correggio, Antonio da, 265n
    Beatrice d' Este da (afterwards Sforza), 39, 55n
    Borso da, 130, 134, 281n, 341
    Cassandra Colleoni da, 483
    Galeazzo da, 318
    Gherardo da, 254
    Niccolò da (the elder), 39, 55n
    Niccolò da (the younger), 39, 73, 77, 87, 109, 130, 142, 156, 177, 186, 217, 218, 272, 405, 407, 482–485, 501–505, 522
Cortesi, Alberto, 152, 160, 168–170
Cosenza, Cardinal of, 436, 437
Cosimo, Piero di (painter), 183, 282, 289, 484
Cossa, Francesco del (Ferrarese painter), 89–94, 288
Costa, Cardinal Giorgio, 205
Costa, Lorenzo (Ferrarese painter), 464
Costabili, Alberto, 47
    Antonio, 311, 329, 332, 387, 441, 450, 496n, 500, 504
    Beltrando, 383, 384, 425n, 435, 441, 444, 445, 450n, 452, 454, 455, 456n, 474n, 494, 499, 500 ; letter from Duke Ercole to him, Appendix II, document 21
    Costanza, 18
    Rinaldo, 189, 190n
Cristofano, Giovanni di, 156
Cristoforo, Fra, da Viterbo, 372, 458
Cybo, Cardinal Lorenzo, 219

D

Dante, 11, 13, 15, 17, 42n, 52, 53n, 85, 87, 490, 520n, 533
Decembrio, Angelo Camillo, 46–49, 52, 53, 531

INDEX

Anna Sforza, 150, 222, 225-227, 237, 325, 330, 473, 474
Azzo VI (first Marquis of Ferrara), 23*n*, 24
Azzo VII "Novello" (third Marquis of Ferrara), 11, 12, 15*n*, 21, 24
Azzo VIII (fifth Marquis of Ferrara), 11, 12, 13, 24
Azzo di Francesco, 20*n*, 27
Azzo (adherent of Niccolò di Leonello), 145, 147
Baldassare (painter and medallist), 40*n*, 91, 92, 275, 463
Beata Beatrice I, 23*n*, 24, 155
Beata Beatrice II, 23*n*
Beatrice (daughter of Niccolò III), *see* Correggio
Beatrice (Duchess of Milan), *see* Sforza
Bianca Maria, *see* Pico della Mirandola
Bianca di Sigismondo, 32*n*, 38*n*
ESTE, DA, BORSO (first Duke of Ferrara), 33, 36, 40, 43, 44, 50, 52, 55*n*, 62; intrigues with King of Naples, 62, 63; 65, 67; succeeds Leonello, 68-70; made Duke of Modena and Reggio, 70-73; triumphal progress through his States, 73-76; relations with Pius II, 76-79; appearance and character, 79-82; relations with scholars and men of letters, 82-88; patronage of art, 88-92; in the frescoes of the Schifanoia, 93, 94; his relations with his nephew, 95-97; recalls Ercole and Sigismondo, 98, 99; his Italian policy, 100-102; conspiracy of the Pio against him, 103-106; letter to Lorenzo de' Medici, 107; abandons Niccolò, 108; his journey to Rome, 108-112; is made Duke of Ferrara, 113-116; desires a reform of the Church, 117; returns to Ferrara, 117; last pacific efforts, 118; death and burial, 119-121; referred to, 123-127; his corrupt officials, 131, 132; anonymous *capitoli* in his honour, Appendix I, pp. 527-531; canzone to him by Filippo Nuvolone, *ibid.*, pp. 534-537; briefs of Paul II to him, Appendix II, documents 1 and 2
Cesare (last Duke of Ferrara), 10
Costanza, 24
ERCOLE I (second Duke of Ferrara), 20*n*, 23*n*; his birth, 40; banished by Leonello, 62, 69; visits Borso, 74; probably in the Schifanoia frescoes, 94; exploits at Naples, 97, 98; returns to Ferrara and Modena, 98, 99, 100; valour at La Mulinella, 101, 102; reveals the conspiracy of the Pio, 104, 105; assists the papal army, 108; Francesco Ariosti's letters to, 110-113; crushes the Veleschi and becomes Duke, 117-121; his character, 122-124; attempts to poison his nephew, 125, 126; beginnings of his reign, 127-133; his marriage, 134-139; 142; conspiracy of Niccolò di Leonello against him, 143-150; his intrigue with Isabella Arduino, 151; relations with his wife, 152-154; aids Florence against Rome and Naples, 155; relations with Pope Sixtus, 156-162, 165, 166; quarrel with Venice, 167-170; opposes the Pope and Count Girolamo in matter of Forlì, 171-173; does not trust Sixtus, 173-175; at war with Venice and Rome, 177-188; his illness, 189, 190; besieged in Ferrara, 190-192; reconciliation with the Pope, 193-203; defeats the Venetians at Stellata, 203, 204; is forced to accept a dishonourable peace, 207-211; his pacific rule, 213, 214; patronage of the drama, 215-218; visits Pope Innocent, 219; relations with Bologna and Florence, 220, 221; makes marriages for his children, 222-227; relations with Rome, 228-231; with Lodovico Sforza, 231-239; sends Ferrando to France, 239-241; death of his wife, 241-244; letters to Ferrando, 248-249;

favours Lodovico and the French, 250, 251; letter to Alfonso, 251, 252; friendship with Boiardo, 256, 257, 261, 264, 266-269, 270-276, 277-279; disavows the latter's last action, 279, 280; his doubtful policy, 295; is angry with Ferrando, 296-299; excluded from the League, 301-304; relations with Savonarola, 304-307; receives Comines, 307, 308; tries to keep neutral, 309-315; protests against the Italian accounts of Fornovo, 317, 318; critical relations with Venice and Rome, 319-321; relies on Savonarola, 321; intervenes between France and Milan, 322-324; under Savonarola's influence, 324-328; disregards the Emperor, 328, 329; coldness with Pope and Milan, 329, 330; Savonarola's secret advice to, 330-335; yields to Venice, 335, 336; breaks with Savonarola, 337, 338, 339, 340, 341; prudent policy, 342-344; mediates between Venice and Florence, 345-349; will not aid Milan, 349-353; adheres to France, 353-359; in the year of Jubilee, 361-363; a latter-day disciple of St. Catherine, 364-369; relations with Suora Lucia and Suora Osanna, 369-381; relations with Cesare Borgia, 383-386, 389; is compelled to marry Alfonso to Lucrezia, 389-401; wants nuns from Umbria, 401-405; his distrust of the Borgias, 408; relations with Lucrezia, 411, 412, 414-419; with the French Ambassador, 421, 422; letter to the Pope, 423; relations with Cesare and France, 428, 429; his devotions, 430-432; exults at death of Alexander, 433, 434; but protects Cesare, 435; advice to Lucrezia, 436; instructions to Ippolito for the Conclave, 437-440; relations with Julius II, 441-445; quar-

INDEX

Duke Ercole to him, Appendix II, document 17
Gurone Maria, 33, 77n, 109, 111
Ippolito I (Cardinal), 151, 220, 241–243, 336, 337, 350, 351, 353, 354, 370, 386, 405–408, 412, 437–440, 446–455, 457, 470, 480, 486n, 492, 493, 498–503, 507–510, 512–515, 519n, 522n, 524; letters from Duke Ercole to him, Appendix II, documents 15 and 20; 555n; brief of Pope Julius to him, Ibid, document 23
Isabella (Marchesana of Mantua), see Gonzaga
Isotta, 55 n
Este, Da, Leonello (thirteenth Marquis of Ferrara), 33, 37, 40–43; succeeds his father, 44; relations with Guarino, 45, 46; his portrait in the *De Politia Litteraria*, 46–49; relations with his brothers, 50; his scholarship, 50–52; his sonnets, 53; patronage of artists, 54, 55; friendship with L. B. Alberti, 55–57; reorganizes the Studio, 57, 58; his Court, 59, 60; extolled by Janus Pannonius, 61; marriages and policy, 62–64; consulted by Decembrio, 64; political actions, 65; character, 65–67; death, 68; relations with Ferrarese art, 82, 88, 89
Leonora d'Aragona (first Duchess of Ferrara), 134–139, 142–148, 151–154, 156, 179, 186, 189, 190, 192, 195, 209–211, 213, 214, 220–226, 228, 230, 233, 235–244, 301, 417, 462, 490; letter from Ercole to her, Appendix II, document 7
Lucrezia, see Bentivoglio
Lucrezia, see Borgia
Margherita Gonzaga, 40, 51, 55n, 62
Maria d'Aragona, 62
Meliaduse (son of Niccolò III), 33, 36, 50, 54–56, 77n
Meliaduse (Bishop of Comacchio), 405, 416
Niccolò I (seventh Marquis of Ferrara), 15
Niccolò II "Zoppo" (tenth Marquis of Ferrara), 16, 17, 19, 21
Niccolò III (twelfth Marquis of Ferrara), 17, 20n; his accession and dominion, 26, 27; his pacific policy, 28, 29; character, 29; pilgrimages, 30–32; wives, mistresses and children, 33–40; patron of learning, 40–43; at the Council of Ferrara, 43, 44; death, 44; his vengeance on wife and son defended by Decembrio and condemned by Pius II, 49, 50n; 57, 88
Niccolò di Leonello, 62, 68, 69, 77, 95–99, 108, 109, 118, 119, 121, 123, 125, 126, 133, 143–150, 158; his children, 147n, Appendix II, documents 16 and 19
Niccolò Maria, 366, 368, 405, 416, 431
Obizzo II (fourth Marquis of Ferrara), 11, 24
Obizzo III (eighth Marquis of Ferrara), 11, 13, 15, 16, 19
Obizzo di Aldobrandino, 19
Parisina, see Malatesta
Polidoro, 77n
Ricciarda da Saluzzo, 40, 62, 123
Rinaldo (sixth Marquis of Ferrara), 11, 13, 15
Rinaldo Maria, 40, 77n, 109, 128, 130, 142, 145, 146, 148n, 333n, 431
Scipione, 77n, 147
Sigismondo (son of Niccolò III), 40, 44, 109, 128, 130, 134, 142, 144–146, 148n, 152, 156, 185, 186, 189, 222, 225, 460
Sigismondo (son of Ercole I), 162, 342, 457
Ugo di Obizzo, 17
Ugo Aldobrandino, 33, 34, 36–38, 41, 49, 505
Eugenius IV, Pope, 27, 43, 63, 79

F

Farnese, Alessandro (afterwards Paul III), 241
Giulia, see Orsini
Felice, Pietro, 173; Appendix II, document 5
Felicità, Suora, 403, 404

571

Ferdinand, King of Aragon and Castile, 182, 188, 197, 299
Ferdinand I, King of Naples, "Ferrante," 98, 101, 104, 105*n*, 134, 151, 155, 159, 161, 165, 166, 169, 170, 174, 175, 183, 188, 200, 204, 207, 208, 227, 228, 232–237, 243, 244, 246, 247, 248, 297, 432*n*, 516
Ferdinand II, King of Naples, 297, 300, 323
Ferrari, G. B., Cardinal of Modena, 378, 390, 392, 412
Ferrarino (troubadour), 24
Ferreri, Cardinal Antonio, 508–510; Appendix II, document 23
Fiorano, Alessandro da, 369, 370, 372
Fornari, Simone, 520*n*
Forno, Girolamo dal, 350
Forno, Masino dal, 519*n*
Fortuna, Scipione, 42*n*
Francesco da Ferrara, Fra (O. P), 366*n*
Francesco da Firenze (blind poet), 150, 485, 486
Frederick III, Roman Emperor (Hapsburg), 70–73, 79, 102, 103
Frederick of Aragon, Prince of Altamura, afterwards King of Naples, 233, 247, 349, 353
Franceschi, Pietro dei (painter), 89, 90, 527

G

Galasso Galassi (Ferrarese painter), 89
Garofolo (Benvenuto Tisi), 54
Gaza, Theodore, 58, 59
Geminiano di Bongiovanni (Ferrarese painter), 465
Gianni (the singer), 497, 501, 502, 504, 506
Giovanni, Frate, (O. S. F.; Johannes Ferrariensis, historian), 51, 58, 59, 73–76
Giovanni da Firenze (blind poet), 150, 485, 486
Giovanni da Tabia, Frate (O. P.), 373, 458
Giovio, 235*n*, 519
Giraldi, G. B., 66*n*, 97*n*, 105*n*, 149*n*, 227*n*

INDEX

47, 50–53, 55, 57–59, 61, 65, 86, 87
Guarini, Battista, 87, 496, 531
Guaschi, Cesare, 429
Guicciardini, *passim*

H
Henry VII of England, 450

I
Innocent VIII, Pope (G. B. Cybo), 209, 212*n*, 218, 219, 227, 228

J
Johannes Ferrariensis, *see* Giovanni
John XXII, Pope, 15
John XXIII, Pope (Baldassare Cossa), 33
Julius II, Pope (Giuliano della Rovere), 157*n*, 440–446, 452–455, 494, 495, 499, 500, 506–509, 511, 516, 522*n*, 524; Appendix II, document 23 (brief to Ippolito d' Este). *See also under* Rovere, Giuliano della

L
Ladislaus, King of Hungary, 71
Lascaris, 87
Legnago, Giovanni Antonio da, 143, 147, 148
Leonarda, Suora, 367, 381, 403, 404
Lignago, Fra Paolo da, 38*n*, 39, 340*n*, 505*n*, 506*n*
Louis of Orleans, afterwards King Louis XII of France, 247, 299, 327, 328, 341, 349, 352–359, 383, 384, 388, 390–397, 428, 429, 434, 435, 437, 438, 446, 461*n*, 481, 482; Appendix II, document 21
Lucia da Narni, Beata, 366–381, 401–404, 431, 432*n*, 465–467; Appendix II, document 22

M
Machiavelli, 101, 155*n*, 220, 384, 388, 501, 523
Maginardo, Fra, 36
Mainente, Jacomo, 151*n*.
Maineri, Francesco de' (painter), 465
Mainero, Luigi, 63
Malatesta, Isabella da Montefeltro, 184
Pandolfo, 354, 355, 382
Parisina, 34–40, 49, 505
Roberto, 104, 108, 111, 157*n*, 159*n*, 168, 176, 182–185, 187, 188; Appendix II, document 5
Sigismondo, 104
Malipiero, 175, 196*n*, 203*n*, 205, 206*n*, 211*n*, 243*n*, 312*n*, 319*n*, 336*n*, 348
Malvezzi, family, 221
Manfredi, Astorre, 220, 221, 355, 388, 413, 427
Feltrino, 348
Francesca Bentivoglio, 220
Galeotto, 157*n*, 166, 170, 181, 220
Manfredo, 228, 280, 295, 304–306, 320, 321, 323, 324, 327, 329–332, 334–338, 353, 397, 555
Marsibilia Pio, 104
Ottaviano, 221
Taddeo, 101, 104
Taddeo (of Reggio), 274
Mantegna, Andrea, 88, 90, 317
Manuzio, Aldo, 363, 364, 376, 470, 513*n*, 521
Marcello, Fra, 356
Marcello, Jacopo, 205
Marco di Galaotto, 42*n*
Maria da Parma, Suora, 466*n*
Mariano, Giovanni Antonio, 296, 298, 299, 302*n*
Marsano, Antonio da, 179
Marsuppini, Carlo, 58, 59
Martin V, Pope, 40
Martino da Tivoli, Fra (O.P.), 367, 369, 371–373, 403, 404
Marzio, Galeotto (poet), 34*n*
Masolino, Alberto, 148
Matthias, King of Hungary, 204
Maximilian, King of the Romans, 234, 236, 245, 246, 299, 300, 317, 328, 329, 349, 351, 357, 359*n*, 388, 396, 399, 400, 479
Mazzolino, Lodovico (Ferrarese painter), 464
Medici, Cosimo de', 26, 107
Giovanni, 245
Giovanni (afterwards Leo X), 449*n*
Giuliano, 137, 154
Lorenzo, 56, 107, 119, 120, 125–127, 137, 155, 158, 160, 166, 173, 188, 198, 213, 221, 227, 248*n*, 281, 449*n*
Lorenzo di Pier Francesco, 245
Piero, 100, 103, 105*n*, 107

Piero di Lorenzo, 232, 237n, 245, 246-248, 251, 309, 334, 388
 family, 22, 100, 106, 110
Mei, Antonio, 369, 371, 372
Melozzo da Forlì, 133
Montecuccolo, Baldissera da, 248, 249
Montefeltro, Elisabetta Gonzaga da, 238n, 244, 360, 376, 386, 413-417, 420-422, 427, 428, 514, 517n
 Federigo da (Count, afterwards Duke of Urbino), 101, 155, 158, 168, 169, 173, 174, 177-181, 184, 527; Appendix II, documents 5 and 7
 Guidobaldo da (second Duke of Urbino), 184, 185, 365, 372, 413, 427, 428, 435, 443, 445, 507, 515, 516
 Ottaviano, 184, 185
Monte Oliveto, Fra Girolamo da, 366n, 376, 377n, 378n
Montferrat, Cardinal of, 116
 Maria Lucrezia of, 130, 131
 Marquis of, 174
Montone, Braccio da, 37, 41, 44, 66n
Montpensier, Gilbert de Bourbon, 307, 323n
Moro, Damiano, 175, 177, 178, 180, 185
Morosini, Paolo, 149
Morton, Archbishop, 241
Mosti, Giulio, 113n, 151n
Mugiasca, Girolamo, 519n
Muhammed, 165
Mula, Alvise da, 454
 Cristoforo da, 175

N

Neroni, Diotisalvi, 100, 140
Nicholas V, Pope, 64
Nicholas of Trier, 45
Niccolò da Ferrara (O.S.B.), 14, 15, 16n, 17, 20n
Niccolò da Pisa (painter), 465
Nigrisoli, Ferrarese family, 69n
Novello, Tito di, 121
Nuvolone, Carlo, 47, 531
 Filippo, 85n; unpublished poems by, Appendix I, pp. 531-537

INDEX

Pierotto, 387n
Pietro di Benvenuto (Ferrarese architect), 92, 151n, 459
Pio, Alberto (the elder), 47, 103
  Alberto (the younger), 491
  Alessandro, 505, 519; Appendix II, document 23
  Bernardino, 105, 138n
  Emilia, 514n
  Ercole, 513, 514
  Galasso, 103
  Giberto, 103
  Giovanni (Gian) Lodovico, 103–106
  Giovanni (Gian) Marco, 105
  Giovanni (Gian) Marsilio, 105, 138n
  Giovanni (Gian) Princivalle, 105
  Leonello, 103, 105
  Manfredo, 105
  Marco, 103, 105, 109, 134, 189, 264, 265
  Tommaso, 105, 138n
Pirondoli, Cesare, 125, 126
Pisanello, Vittore, 42, 50, 51, 54, 55, 88, 89
Pistofilo, Bonaventura, 227, 493, 520n
Pistoia, Antonio da, see Cammelli
Pius II (Enea Silvio Piccolomini), 29, 30, 34n, 40, 41, 44, 46, 47, 49n, 50, 51, 66, 73, 76–80
Pius III (Francesco Piccolomini), 363, 364, 376, 438
Poggetto, Beltrando dal, 15
Poggio Bracciolini, 45, 51
Polenta, Lamberto da, 13
Polismagna, 84, 85
Poliziano, Angelo, 137n, 215–218, 484
Porcellio, 51n
Pozzi, Gian Luca, 405–408, 410, 411, 412, 434, 441
"Prete, El," 407, 410
Prisciano, Pellegrino, 128
Prosperi, Bernardino de', 310, 493n, 515, 520n, 522n, 523
Pulci, Luigi, 281

R

Ralmenz Bistors, 24
Rambaldi, Benvenuto de', 17, 88
Rangoni, Aldobrandino, 38
  Gerardo, 389
  G.F.M., 441, 445n
  Niccolò, 135

René of Lorraine, Duke, 187, 203; brief of Pope Sixtus IV to him, Appendix II, document 8
Riario, Girolamo, the Count, 133, 159, 161, 165–166, 168–173, 181, 182, 184, 187n, 188, 193, 200, 205, 207, 220; Appendix II, documents 3–5, 12–14
  Pietro, Cardinal, 133, 135, 136
  Raffaello Sansoni (Cardinal of S. Giorgio), 133, 207, 361n, 453; Appendix II, document 14
Roberti (dei), Anna, 39, 40, 91n, 129, 192n
  Ercole (Ferrarese painter), 230, 463, 464
  Gerardo, 497, 504
Rocca Berti, Filippo della (Monsignor), 415, 416, 421, 422
Romei, Laodamia, 39
Rossetti, Biagio (architect), 460–462
Rossi, the, of Parma, 174
  Pietro Maria, 185
  Pietro, 31, 32
Rouen, Cardinal of, see Amboise
Rovere, della, Felice, 455
  Francesco, see Sixtus IV
  Bartolommeo, Bishop of Ferrara, 142, 158
  Francesco Maria (afterwards third Duke of Urbino), 133, 506n, 516
  Giovanni, 133
  Giuliano, Cardinal (afterwards Pope Julius II), 133, 135, 151, 165, 173, 209, 439, 440; Appendix II, document 5. See also under Julius II
Roverella, Bartolommeo, 137
  Lorenzo, 129, 142
Rubino, Giacomo, 35, 37, 38

S

Sadoleto, Niccolò, 389
Sala, Alberto della, 31, 38; (the younger), 220
Salimbeni, Sigismondo, 500
Salinguerra, 12
Salomone, 130n, 153n
San Giorgio, Gian Antonio (Cardinal of Alessandria), 439
San Giorgio, Cardinal of (titular), see Riario, Raffaello

San Severino, Antonio Maria da, 211n
  Federigo da, 180n; Appendix II, document 17
  Francesco da, Count of Caiazzo, 226, 250, 313, 315, 317, 318, 351
  Galeazzo da, 232, 281n (not to be identified with Galeazzo Visconti), 301
  Roberto da, 155, 174–178, 185, 192, 199, 203, 206, 210
  Ugo da, 186
Sandeo, Antonio, 109, 119, 120
  Felino, 338, 370, 372
Sansoni, see Riario, Raffaello
Sanudo, Marino, *passim*
Saraceni, Gerardo, 398–400, 405, 406, 408, 410n, 413
Savonarola, Elena, 163
  Fra Girolamo, 139–142, 163, 164, 295, 302, 304–309, 312, 315, 317, 321–325, 327, 329–339, 340, 341, 363, 365, 369, 479, 480
  Marco Aurelio, 140n
  Michele, 42, 51, 52, 68, 69, 71, 72, 80, 81, 95, 140
  Niccolò, 140
Scala, Can Grande della, 15n
Scocola (buffoon), 80, 81, 93
Scrintassa, 171–173
Seregnio, Gian Giorgio, 353, 354, 433
Sforza, Alessandro, 65, 108, 111
  Angela, see Este
  Anna, see Este
  Ascanio (Cardinal), 150, 219, 229, 235, 356, 358, 438, 555
  Beatrice, see Correggio
  Beatrice d'Este, 39n, 142, 162, 213, 214, 222–225, 227, 229, 231, 233, 236–238, 245, 251, 328, 349, 463, 473, 484
  Bona, 150, 155, 203, 463, 532n
  Bianca Maria (Queen of the Romans), 245, 246
  Caterina (successively Riario and De' Medici), 159n, 166, 169, 181, 220, 355, 356, 413
  Costanzo, 112, 114, 156, 157n, 199n, 231
  Ercole Massimiliano (eighth Duke of Milan), 233, 238, 458
  Ermes, 226
  Francesco (fourth Duke of Milan), 63, 65, 461

INDEX

Stagnesio, Giovanni, 119
Steffana, Suora, 375
Stella, *see* Assassino
Strozzi, Carlo, 18
    Ercole, 469, 470, 491, 492, 495, 496, 512, 513, 515, 516–522
    Ginevra, 258
    Giovanni Francesco, 100
    Guido, 469, 520
    Laodamia, 141
    Lorenzo (the elder), 87, 140, 269
    Lorenzo (the younger), 469, 520
    Lorenzo di Filippo, 468, 469, 520n
    Lucia (Boiardo), 254
    Nanni, 18, 37
    Niccolò, 47
    Tito Vespasiano, 47, 48, 53n, 59, 60, 87, 135, 254, 255, 270, 468, 469, 493, 496

T

Tasso, 9, 25, 292
Tassoni, Giulio, 216, 240, 299, 429, 493
Tavelli, Giovanni (il Beato), 43, 54
Tavola, Cammilla dalla, 33, 132, 192n
Tebaldeo, Antonio, 218, 470–475, 495, 496, 514, 520
Tebaldi, Jacopo, 470n, 483n
Terzi, Ottobuono, 27
Tolomei, Family, 34n
Tommaso, Frate (O.P.), 325, 332
Timoteo da Modena, Frate (O.P.), 370, 372
Tolentino, Giovanni Francesco da, Appendix II., document 14
Torelli, Barbara, 517–522
Torre, Jacopo della, 53
Tortona, Tommaso da, 21
Trémoille, La, 358, 429
Tristano, Bartolommeo (architect), 460
Trivulzio, Gian Jacopo (Count of Musocco, afterwards Marshal of France), 174, 179, 186, 188, 189, 192, 206, 312, 327, 351–353
Trotti, Brandeligi, 156, 178
    Galeazzo, 156

Jacopo (successively Ferrarese Ambassador at Rome, Judge of the Twelve Sages, and Ambassador at Milan), 106, 147, 156, 178, 190, 224n, 228, 231, 232, 235, 250n, 301, 309n, 311n, 317, 318n; Appendix II, documents 1 and 14
Paolo Antonio, 156, 178
Tura, Cosimo (Ferrarese painter), 89, 90–94, 288, 462, 463
Turriani, Fra Giovacchino (General of the Dominicans), 340, 341, 367, 369, 370, 372, 373, 402, 403

U

Urbino, Dukes of, see Montefeltro and Rovere

V

Valentino, Il Duca, *see* Borgia, Cesare
Valla, Agostino, 69n
    Giovanni, 357–359, 383, 384, 395n, 461n; Appendix II, document 21
Varani, the, 211, 355
Varegnana, Andrea da, 104, 105
Venice, Doge of (Pietro Gradenigo), 13; (Francesco Foscari), 39; (Cristoforo Moro), 100; (Pietro Mocenigo), 142; (Giovanni Mocenigo), 160, 168–170, 172n, 175, 194, 196, 210, 211, Appendix II, documents 3, 4, 9, 10, 11; (Agostino Barbarigo), 237, 300, 302, 319, 320, 336, 346, 347; (Lorenzo Loredan), 441, 451, 496
Vendramin, Andrea, 111
Verdezino, Francesco, 500
Vinci, Leonardo da, 223, 461
Visconti, Filippo Maria (third Duke of Milan), 28, 44, 48, 63, 64
    Galeazzo, 222, 240, 281 (not to be identified with Galeazzo da San Severino)
Vittorino da Feltre, 62

W

Weyden, Roger Van der, 55, 88